P9-BJJ-135

新 **GRE**

数学高分 快速突破

陈向东 ➜ 编著

群言出版社
Qunyan Press

图书在版编目(CIP)数据

GRE数学高分快速突破 / 陈向东编著 .—北京 : 群言出版社，2011（2013.8重印）
　ISBN 978-7-80256-271-4

　Ⅰ. ①G… 　Ⅱ. ①陈… 　Ⅲ. ①GRE—高等数学—自学参考资料 　Ⅳ. ①O13

中国版本图书馆CIP数据核字（2011）第206613号

出 版 人　范　芳
责任编辑　孙春红
封面设计　大愚设计+赵文康
出版发行　群言出版社(Qunyan Press)

地　　址　北京东城区东厂胡同北巷1号（100006）
网　　站　www.qypublish.com
电子信箱　bj62605588@163.com　qunyancbs@126.com
总 编 办　010-65265404　65138815
发 行 部　010-62605019　62263345　65220236
经　　销　全国新华书店
读者服务　010-62418641　65265404　65263345
法律顾问　北京市国联律师事务所

印　　刷　北京四季青印刷厂
版　　次　2011年12月第1版　2013年8月第5次印刷
开　　本　880×1230　　1/16
印　　张　18.75
字　　数　360千字
书　　号　ISBN 978-7-80256-271-4
定　　价　40.00元

新东方图书策划委员会

前　　言

　　为了能真实地反映一个考生的英语能力，使 GRE 考试更具权威性或代表性，同时为了应对来自其他考试机构的竞争压力，ETS 宣布自 2011 年 8 月起，GRE 普通考试（Graduate Record Examination General Test）将在全球范围内同步改革。这次考试改革是近 60 年来史上最大的一次变革，改革后的 GRE 考试在内容和考试形式上都发生了较大的变化。整个考试由 6 个部分组成，总历时约 4 个小时，考试的时间进度表如下所示：

部分	时间(分钟)	说明	题量
1 分析性写作	60	Issue 写作	1 篇(30 分钟)
		Argument 写作	1 篇(30 分钟)
	1	休息	
2 文字推理	30	段落完形填空题	6
		同义句问题	5
		阅读理解题	9
	1	休息	
3 数量推理	35	数量比较题	8
		问题求解题	9
		数据分析题	3
	10	休息	
4 文字推理	30	段落完形填空题	6
		同义句问题	5
		阅读理解题	9
	1	休息	
5 数量推理	35	数量比较题	7
		问题求解题	10
		数据分析题	3
	1	休息	
6 实验部分	30 或 35	文字推理或数量推理	20

在上面的表格中，除了第一部分是固定的之外，其余的5个部分在考试时是随机出现的。改革之后的GRE考试形式由笔考改为机考；考试内容更加注重逻辑的考查。具体来讲，Analytical Writing的要求明确提出要言之有物，不能泛泛而论，而且以前提供两个话题选择一个写作的做法将不再实施，新的GRE作文只给出一个固定的话题。Verbal Reasoning去掉了类比反义部分，填空部分增加了段落填空题和对应填空题。

从考试形式上来看，Verbal Reasoning部分的变化最大，Analytical Writing与Quantitative Reasoning部分只是在考试时间或题量上进行了调整。根据ETS的《GRE考试官方指南》，Quantitative Reasoning部分最新的变化是：

The Quantitative Reasoning measure tests the same basic mathematical concepts，but includes more data analysis and more real-life scenarios，to better gauge your skills.

从上面这段话可以看出，Quantitative Reasoning部分仍然考查基本的数学概念，但包含了更多数据分析和更多真实生活场景，以便更好地测试考生的技能。

题型方面除了传统的单选题，还保留了2006年增加的数字填空题和多选题。多项选择题与单项选择题最大的差别仅存在于正确选项于所有选项中的比例，一些单选题好用的技巧比如代入法、排除法或猜题法都会变得不太适用。数字填空题要求自己运算出准确无误的答案，所以从整体上来看Quantitative Reasoning的难度是趋于增加的。

改革后的GRE考试更加注重真实语言环境中的逻辑思辨能力，单纯的死记硬背备考法很难再奏效。如何抓住重点，有效备考，并在传统的Quantitative Reasoning项目上继续保持优势成为每一个GRE考生热切关注的话题。本书从第一版出版以来，就成了GRE考生的必备参考书。此次修订再版，笔者研究了新GRE的考试的最新特点，整合了最新的考点，并加入了一些最新的模拟测试题。我真心希望这本书能为考生在Quantitative Reasoning方面智取高分甚至满分打下坚实的基础。

陈向东

（个人微博：http://weibo.com/cxd）

第一版前言

二十多年来,GRE 考试数学考题已有 3000 多道,有没有必要花费有限的宝贵时间把它们一一做过? GRE 数学所考查的知识点究竟是什么,有没有必要把高中数学甚至大学数学再复习一遍? GRE 数学机考之后考题有所变化,有没有必要再去做 GRE 数学笔试的试题? 许多许多的疑问以及许多许多的困惑都可以从本书中找到答案。作为一本全面系统地梳理、归纳、讲解 GRE 数学考点并对之进行分项、密集强化训练的书,其写作动因主要是基于以下几个事实:

- GRE 数学机考之后,数学考试的时间、题量及难度都有所变化,许多笔试中简单无聊的题目已不再可能成为考查的对象。而据不完全统计,80% 以上的 GRE 考生最终还是在这 3000 多道题目上辛辛苦苦地花费了大量的宝贵时间——题题必做,以求心里踏实。但大量反复地做一些考查初中甚至小学数学知识点的题目不仅仅会浪费一个人的宝贵时间(不言而喻,时间对于出国族人士而言奇缺),而且还会降低一个人的思维敏捷度与判断对错的能力(一道简单的题目做过 10 遍以上,一个人的水平会降至最初的状态)。搜集、分析二十余年的 GRE 考题,筛选、整理中国考生必做且能够真正适应机考的题目,就成了广大 GRE 考生共同的心愿。

- 由于众所周知的原因,许多考生要么因考点的遗忘,要么因数学术语的生疏,要么因方法不当,做错或根本就不会做某些题目。全面梳理考点,归纳数学术语,指点做题技巧,能使我们事半功倍——在最短的时间内突破 GRE QUANTITATIVE,从而将更多的精力用在最易提高成绩的VERBAL 和 ANALYTICAL 上,可以使我们在有限的时间内,做更多我们最应该做的事,而且把应该做的事做得更好!

- 在北京新东方学校讲授 GRE 的过程当中,很多朋友与学员都迫切希望能有一本对 GRE 数学考点进行全面讲解、剖析、归纳并提供针对性训练的书。

本书具有以下几个特点:

☞ **数学考点详尽归纳**:完全按照 ETS 的数学考试大纲,全面系统地梳理、归纳、讲解 GRE 数学考点,免去因某考点的生疏而寻读数学教科书之苦。

☞ **数学术语、解题窍门全面总结**:所有考试中遇到的或有可能遇到的数学术语均在附录中给出,并在附录中给出部分解题要诀。

☞ **分项思维密集训练**:在熟悉数学术语的基础之上,本书第二篇对各类数学考题进行分项密集强化训练。考生可通过考题进一步熟悉、掌握相关数学术语,并且熟悉相关题目的问法、句型及解题方法和技巧。

☞ **易错题、重点题与难题一览无遗**：本书挑选的所有题目全部来自于我在新东方课堂上的讲课用题、课前课后学生常问的题目以及"统计意义"上的易错题、重点题与难题，弥补了因课时限制而对数学讲解较少的缺陷。阅读本书基本上可满足90％以上考生应对GRE数学考试的要求，不用再花费时间去做历年的GRE数学考题。

☞ **最新模拟试题**：本书给出5套与GRE机考难度相当的模拟试题，考生可在考前15天左右每次用45分钟的时间进行实战模拟。

☞ **再也不用把精力、时间浪费在简单无聊的数学题上**：阅读本书必定能使你得到事半功倍的效果，从而再也不用把过多的精力、时间浪费在简单无聊的数学题上。

感谢新东方学校副校长包凡一先生对本书出版的精心策划与大力支持；真诚感谢新东方学校俞敏洪校长对本书构架的中肯意见以及对写作本书的鼓励与支持；更要感谢成千上万的学生，是他们的支持与上进精神使我能最终完成这本书；最后要感谢本书的责任编辑，他们的辛勤工作使本书更臻完美。

本书既是我多年的研究心得与教学的总结，也是考生复习经验与教训的集成，我尽力想奉献给读者一本讲解全面、结构清晰、层次分明、逻辑有序的数学参考教材，诚挚希望本书能对广大GRE考生在出国求学奋斗的道路上提供有力的帮助与支持，能够激励大家更快更好更加成功地走向世界，创造人生新的辉煌。但本人毕竟水平有限，所以我真心地希望读者及各界人士能对本书的不足之处不吝赐教。

祝大家成功！

陈向东

目　录

第 一 篇

GRE Quantitative 总论

虽然 Quantitative Reasoning 的难度增加了,但考查考生的能力基本不变,主要集中在以下三个方面:

(1) 基本数学技能

(2) 基本数学概念的理解

(3) 定量推理、建模及利用数量方法解决问题的能力

测试中的一些问题以现实生活为背景提出,其他问题则为纯数学背景。测试包括对 Arithmetic(算术)、Algebra(代数)、Geometry(几何)以及 Data analysis(数据分析,包括概率统计与图表)四个方面的技能、概念和能力的检测。本书接下来的章节将从以上四个主要方面帮助考生夯实基础,提升实战能力,智取 Quantitative Reasoning 高分。

第 一 章

GRE 数学考试的目的、出题原则及核心考点

一、GRE 数学的考试目的

GRE 数学考试,其主要目的是测试考生是否具备以下能力:

1. 精通算术运算(Proficiency in arithmetical operations)

2. 精通代数方程的求解(Proficiency in solving algebraic equations)

3. 具有把文字信息转变成数学术语的能力(Ability to convert verbal information to mathematical terms)

4. 具有构想几何图形以及数之间的相互关系的能力(Ability to visualize geometric shapes and numerical relationships)

5. 具有用直觉的和非常规的方法去解决一般数学问题的能力(Ability to devise intuitive and unconventional solutions to conventional mathematics problems)

6. 具有在真实生活场景中运用数学的能力(Ability to apply basic mathematical concepts to real-life scenarios)

二、GRE 数学的出题原则

在 GRE 数学考试中，一般都假定以下信息为真：

- All numbers used are real numbers.
- All figures lie on a plane unless otherwise indicated.
- All angle measures are positive.
- All lines shown as straight are straight. On the computer-based test, lines that appear "jagged" can also be assumed to be straight (lines can look somewhat jagged on the computer screen).
- Figures are intended to provide useful information for answering the questions. However, except where a figure is accompanied by a "Note" stating that the figure is *drawn to scale*, solve the problem using your knowledge of mathematics, not by visual measurement or estimation.

细心的读者会发现，上述假设实际上就是 ETS 出题的原则。即：

- 所有的数都是实数
- 除非题目中专门指出，假设所有图形都在同一个平面内
- 所有的角的测量值都是正数
- 所有显示为直线的线均可当作直线来处理（在机试中，因为电脑显示器的原因，直线可能会看起来呈"锯齿状"）
- 伴随问题的图形将为解题提供有用的信息。但是，只有在问题中指出本图形是**按比例画出（drawn to scale）**时，才可以用目测或估计而得到的信息去解题。否则，只能运用你的数学知识去回答问题。这一解题原则可以简称为**"只能读图，不能度量"**的原则。

三、GRE 数学的核心考点

GRE 的数学考试，主要包括以下内容：

1. Arithmetic（算术）

divisibility	可约性
factorization	因式分解
prime numbers	质数
remainders	余数
odd and even integers	奇偶数
arithmetic operations	算术运算
exponents	指数
radicals	根式
estimation	估算
percent	百分比
ratio	比率
rate	比例
absolute value	绝对值
the number line	数轴
decimal representation	十进制
sequences of numbers	数列

2. Algebra(代数)

operations with exponents	指数运算
factoring and simplifying algebraic expressions	因式分解和代数式的化简
relations	(代数)关系
functions	函数
equation	方程
inequalities	不等式
solving linear and quadratic equations and inequalities	解一次与二次方程及不等式
simultaneous equations and inequalities	解联立方程和不等式
setting up equations to solve word problems	列方程解数学题
coordinate geometry including graphs of functions, equations, and inequalities, intercepts, and slopes of lines.	坐标几何,也叫解析几何 包括函数的图像、方程、不等式以及截距和斜率。

3. Geometry(几何)

parallel lines	平行线
perpendicular lines	垂线
circles	圆
triangles	三角形
isosceles	等腰
equilateral	等边
30^0—60^0—90^0 triangles	30^0—60^0—90^0 三角形
quadrilaterals	四边形
other polygons	其他多边形
congruent and similar figures	全等和相似图形
three-dimensional figures	三维图形
area	面积
perimeter	周长
volume	体积
the Pythagorean theorem	勾股定理
angle measurement in degrees	角度计算
the ability to construct proofs is not tested	不考几何证明

4. Probability and Statistics(概率与统计)

basic descriptive statistics	基本的描述统计学
mean	平均值
median	中位数
mode	众数
range	极差
standard deviation	标准差
interquartile range	四分位数间距
quartiles	四分位数
percentiles	百分位数
elementary probability	初等概率
probabilities of compound events and independent events	复合事件和独立事件的概率
combinations	组合
permutations	排列
Venn diagrams	维恩图

5. Tables and Graphs(表格和图形)

line graphs	线图
segmented bar graph	堆积柱形图
bar graphs	柱形图
circle graphs	饼图
boxplots	箱形图
scatterplots	散点图

上述 5 大部分的内容,在考试时所占的大致比例如下图所示。

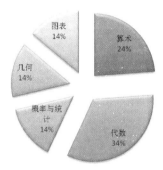

虽然变革后的 GRE 数学试题的难度增加了,但其考查的内容基本上是小学或初中教科书中的内容,考生需要懂算术、具备一些初等代数知识并知道一点几何知识就可以了。概率与统计部分只考一些很基础的知识,试题不会涉及 inferential statistics(推断统计学)的内容,更不会涉及包括 trigonometry(三角学)、calculus(微积分)和其他更高水平的数学内容,higher-level mathematics(高等数学)的内容基本上也不会涉及。GRE 数学旨在考查考生是否具备初等数学的基本知识,以及是否具有进行清晰推理的能力。考生只要掌握了本书中所讲述的内容,就可以从容地应对 GRE 数量推理考试。

第 二 章
GRE 数学考试经典题型及其解题策略

GRE 数学在机考中包括两个部分,每一部分都是 20 道小题。大多数的小题都是各自独立的,我们把它们叫做离散数量题;还有少量几道题是基于同一图表或数据的,我们把它们称作数据分析题。两个部分 40 道题分布如下:

- 15 道数量比较题:每个部分平均 7 至 8 道
- 19 道离散数量题:大约 11 道单选题,4 道多选题,以及 4 道数字填空题,这些题在两个部分之间大致平均分布
- 6 道数据分析题:每一部分平均 3 道——均为离散数量题,多为单选题

从选项或答案的表现形式上,这 40 道题又可分为以下 4 大类:

- Quantitative Comparison questions(数量比较题)
- Multiple-choice questions—Select One Answer Choice(单项选择题)
- Multiple-choice questions—Select One or More Answer Choices(多项选择题)
- Numeric Entry questions(数字填空题)

接下来,我们将分别讲解每一类题的特点及解题技巧。

一、Quantitative Comparison Questions(数量比较题)

Quantitative Comparison 主要测试考生是否具有快速准确的推测两个数的大小或感知有没有足够的信息来判断两个数大小的能力。数量比较题通常会给出两个数值,分别为 Quantity A 和 Quantity B,而考生的任务是比较它们的大小。这类题目通常只有四个备选项,分别是:

(A) Quantity A 中的数值较大

(B) Quantity B 中的数值较大

(C) 两者相等

(D) 无法判断出哪个数量较大

在有些题目中,这些数量的相关信息会集中在其上方。在这种情况下,考生进行比较时必须考虑这些信息。

下面是这类题型的"Direction":

> **Compare Quantity A and Quantity B, using additional information centered above the two quantities if such information is given, and select one of the following four answer choices:**
>
> **(A) Quantity A is greater.**
>
> **(B) Quantity B is greater.**

（C）The two quantities are equal.

（D）The relationship cannot be determined from the information given.

A symbol that appears more than once in a question has the same meaning throughout the question. *

对"Direction"进行解读，我们可以得到下表：

你应该选择	当
（A）Quantity A is greater.	Quantity A is greater all the time, no matter what.
（B）Quantity B is greater.	Quantity B is greater all the time, no matter what.
（C）The two quantities are equal.	The two quantities are equal all the time, no matter what.
（D）It is impossible to determine which quantity is greater.	The answer is not one of the first three choices.

1. 数量比较题的解题步骤

① Size up the question;

② Check both quantities for possible shortcuts and for clues as to how to proceed;

③ Deal with each quantity;

④ Consider all possibilities for any "unknown" (variables);

⑤ Compare the two quantities (Columns A and B);

⑥ Check your answer if you have time.

下面我们将通过一个例子来透析解答数量比较题时的基本步骤：

例 1：

Column A	Column B
$xy \neq 0$	
$x^2 + y^2$	$(x+y)^2$

（A）if the quantity in Column A is greater

（B）if the quantity in Column B is greater

（C）if the quantities are equal

（D）if the relationship cannot be determined from the information given

解：本题的正确答案是（D），具有一定的难度。请读者仔细体会如何运用上面所讲的数量比较题的六步解题策略来攻破此类题目。

深度剖析：

① 从整体上看，一方面本题中既包含有二次代数表达式，又包含有因式。另一方面，题目中有两个变量（x 和 y），却没有方程组，因此不能通过计算来确定任何一个变量的精确数值。

② 从表面上看，做比较的两个数好像并没有共同的项可以通过数值运算而约去。但是两个代数式的外形很相似，因此考生很容易想到通过对这两个数或其中的某一个代数式的变换而使这两个代数式具有可比性；

---

* 由于在真实考试中，凡涉及比较关系的题目选项体现如上说法，故全书练习部分对凡涉及此题型的选项均略。

从目前看，A 栏中的数 (x^2+y^2) 是不可分解的，而 B 栏中的数却可分解为

$$(x+y)^2 = x^2+y^2+2xy$$

③ 注意到 B 栏中的代数式分解后的前两项与 A 栏中的数完全一致，因此可以约去两栏中相同的部分，这样本题就转化为 A 栏中的 0 与 B 栏中的 2xy 做比较。

④ x 和 y 都是可正可负的变量，因此考生在做这类题时一定要考虑到所有的可能性。在本题中若 x 和 y 的符号一致，即 x 和 y 同为正数或同为负数时，B 栏中的数将比 A 栏中的数大；但是若 x 和 y 的符号不一致，即 x 和 y 为一正一负时，B 栏中的数将比 A 栏中的数小。

⑤ 此时考生已获得了解答本题所需的足够信息，即（D）为正确答案。因为 A 栏与 B 栏中的数的大小依赖于两个变量的符号，因此此时就没有必要再把分数或其他的数代入两个代数式中进行验证。从题目中所提供的信息不能确定两栏中数的大小。

⑥ 检查第三步的计算，确认符号正确。如果你对你的分析过程表示满意，就 Confirm 答案（D）。

2. 数量比较题的应试策略

1）熟悉四个选项所代表的意思。因为所有数量比较题的选项都是一样的，熟悉选项有助于快速解题。

2）避免不必要的计算。为了比较两个量的大小，有时并不需要算出具体的数值，只要根据题目中给出的条件进行化简，变换或估算就可以得到答案。请考生牢记：计算并非是数量比较题所着重考查的内容，因此不要做一些没完没了的计算。

3）谨记几何图形不一定都按比例画出。如果图中没有明确给出某一个点的位置，某一个角的大小或某一条线的长短，就不能主观地按照题目中所给出的比例进行比较。看起来像是中点，或者是一个锐角，或者是一条较短的线段，其实都是不确定的。总之，不要依赖于图形的形状去做比较。

4）用数字来代替变量。有些数量比较题里面含有比较复杂的代数表达式，要比较它们的大小，费力耗时，但如果我们用具体的数来代入的话，就能很快地排错误答案。代入法常选的数是 0，1 和 -1。请注意一点，用代入法时，不是从代入的数中去选正确的答案，而是优先去排除错误的答案。代入任意一个数，基本上就可以排除掉两个答案，再代入一个数，就可以把正确的答案给选出来。

5）先化简来再比较。如果比较的两栏都包含有比较复杂的代数或算术表达式时，最好先化简，设法使比较的两个数的形式更接近，然后再进行比较。

6）善用排除法。如果考生能够找到任何一个可以让 Quantity A 大于 Quantity B 的情况，那么就可以立即排除两个选项：答案不可能是"Quantity B 更大"或者"两个数量相等"。如果要选"Quantity B 更大"这项，那么 Quantity B 就必须在任何情况下都比 Quantity A 大，但考生已经知道一种相反的情况了，所以这个选项不正确。同样，既然两个数量并不能在任何情况下都相等，那么答案就不可能是"两个数量相等"。正确答案要么是"Quantity A 更大"或"无法确定哪个数量更大"。如果最终确定 Quantity A 在任何情况下都大于 Quantity B，那么这项就是正确答案；然而，如果可以知道任何一个 Quantity A 小于 Quantity B 的情况，那么答案就是"无法确定哪个数量更大"。然而，如果在排除了两个选项后，考生依然不能确定哪是正确答案，那么就在剩下的两个选项中快速猜一个，然后进入下一题。

7）知道何时不能选 D。当 A 栏和 B 栏都是确定的数字是，答案不可能是 D。

考生在做数量比较题时，除了要灵活掌握上述 7 个关键技巧之外，还要注意以下两点：

1）在两栏之间进行乘除运算时，要确保所使用的数都是正数。

2）在两栏中出现的同一符号在两栏所代表的意思相同。

二、Multiple-choice questions—Select One Answer Choice(单项选择题)

1. 单项选择题的解题步骤

单选题是考生熟悉的标准题型。每道题有五个选项,其中只有一个为正确答案。其解题步骤如下:

① Size up the question

② Size up the answer choices

③ Look for a shortcut to the answer

④ Set up the problem and solve it

⑤ Verify your response before moving on

下面,我们将通过一个例子来说明怎样用这五个步骤来解答单项选择题。

例2: The average of 6 numbers is 19. When one of those numbers is taken away, the average of the remaining 5 number is 21. What number was taken away?

(A) 2   (B) 8   (C) 9

(D) 11   (E) 20

解: 本题的正确答案是(C),这是一道中等难度的题目。60%以上的考生都能对这类题目做出正确的解答。

深度剖析:

① 这个题目涉及算术平均数的概念。要解答这个题目,考生需要对计算算术平均数的公式相当熟悉。但是应当注意的是本题并没有让求算术平均数,而是让求一系列数中的某一个数。

② 快速扫描一下选项以便能发现一些解题的线索。注意到在五个选项中中间的三个选项的数都相当接近,因此要先仔细观察这两个数值偏差较大的选项。选项(A)有可能是正确的答案,因为19和21的差就是2。但是本题不是问两个算术平均数的差,所以可以排除掉(A)这个迷惑选项;(E)也有可能是一个迷惑选项,因为20刚好等于19与21的和的一半。但是大多数考生都会认为这个问题不会这么简单,所以本题的正确答案应在(B)、(C)和(D)三个选项中找。

③ 如果考生的直觉很好,一般都会意识到解这个题目的小窍门。考生可以通过比较两组数的和而得到题目的答案。在第六个数被取走之前,六个数的和是114(即19×6);在第六个数取走之后,剩余五个数的和是105(即21×5)。前后两个和的差是9,并且9就是取走的那个数的值。

④ 如果考生一时想不起上面那个比较简便的方法,也可用常规的方法来解这个题,设这六个数为 a, b, c, d, e, f,则由题意可得:

$$\left. \begin{array}{l} \dfrac{a+b+c+d+e+f}{6}=19 \\ \Rightarrow a+b+c+d+e+f=114 \\ \dfrac{a+b+c+d+e}{5}=21 \\ \Rightarrow a+b+c+d+e=105 \end{array} \right\} \Rightarrow f=9$$

⑤ 如有时间,请检查公式是否正确,计算是否有误,并且确信没有把19和21的位置弄错了(注:考生在慌乱之中很容易犯这类错误)。

2．解答单项选择题的的应试策略

1）从选项中寻找解题线索。

有些题，看起来很复杂，但其实题目的要求很简单，如果先看了选项，你就很容易知道该道题的求解方向在什么地方，从而能节省大量的时间。比如有些题不要求过于精确的计算，从选项中可以了解到只要求保留一位小数，那你在解题的过程中就没有必要过于精确；再比如有些题，从选项中你可以了解到只让你求运算结果的个位数，你就没有必要把准确的结果给完整地算出来；还有些题选项本身的离散性就很大，不同选项之间的数值差别比较大，你仅需要简单的估算就能找到正确的答案。这些都能大大地节约你的宝贵时间。

2）用代入法，请从 C 项开始代入。

当一道单项选择题的 5 个选项都是具体的数字时，可以考虑用代入法。把 5 个选项逐一代入，肯定能找到正确的答案，但耗时较长，在考试时间有限的情况下，这种方面的实用性较差。但在 GRE 数学测试中，如果 5 个选项都是具体的数值，那这些数值一定能从小到大排列，即 A 项的值最小，E 项的最大。这时如果我们先把 C 项的值代入，如果发现刚好就选 C，如果发现数值较小，正确答案肯定不是 D 就是 E；如果发现数值较大，正确答案不是 A 就是 B。通过这种方法可以大大缩短代入法的时间成本。

3）正确答案一定在 5 个选项当中。

请不要怀疑选项的正确性，如果你算出的结果与 5 个选项都不一致，那一定是你算错了，这是你要重新读题，看看是否漏掉了哪些重要的信息；或者检查你的运算过程，看是不是有些地方算错了；或者检查一下你的计算方面是否合适。

4）在猜题时，优先排除明显错误的答案。

当有些题确实不知道怎么解，或者没有时间求解时，可以猜题。为了提高准确率，先把明显错误的选项排除掉。哪些是我们应该优先排除的选项呢？答案肯定是正数，而选项的数是负数；答案必须是奇数，而选项的数是偶数；答案必须小于 100，而选项的数大于 100；比率必定小于 1，而选项的数大于 1。这一类的选项都是应该被直接排除的。

5）基于题目给出的条件去做题。

一定从题目给出的条件出发去做题，而不添加自己的常识，或人为地添加一些假设去做题。

6）根据题目的要求去做题。

题目要求什么，我们就去求解什么。不要把 GRE 的数学题当成我们小学或初中的数学作业来做。比如对一些涉及方程求解类的问题，有两个未知数，一个是 x，另一个是 y。题目中要你求 y 的值，你就不要根据惯例，先求 x，再求 y，这样会浪费大量的时间。

三、Multiple-choice questions—Select One or More Answer Choices
（多项选择题）

多项选题其实是单项选择题的一种变体。这种类型的问题可能有 3～12 个选项，正确答案数则不定，可能只有一个，也可能全部都是。在此提醒诸位考生，通常来说，多选题的正确选项不止一个。下面是 ETS 官方给出的相关说明：

多选题的解题步骤和策略与单选题基本相同,最主要的区别是,多选题要得分,考生必须把所有正确的选项都给找出来。

例3: The integer m is greater than 1. If m is the square of an integer, which of the following numbers must also be the square of an integer?

Indicate all such numbers.

(A) $81m$

(B) $25m + 10\sqrt{m} + 1$

(C) $4m^2 + 4\sqrt{m} + 1$

例3: m 是一个大于 1 的整数。如果 m 是某一个整数的平方,那么下面哪一个数也必定是某个整数的平方?

解: 本题只要对每一个选项求平方根,且能断定平方要是一个整数就可以了。

(A) 选项: $\sqrt{81m} = 9\sqrt{m}$,因为 m 是一个平方数,所以 $81m$ 也是一个平方数。

(B) 选项: $\sqrt{25m + 10\sqrt{m} + 1} = \sqrt{(5\sqrt{m} + 1)^2} = 5\sqrt{m} + 1$,$\sqrt{m}$ 是一个整数,所以 $25m + 10\sqrt{m} + 1$ 是一个平方数。

(C) 选项:不太容易直接判断 $4m^2 + 4\sqrt{m} + 1$ 是一个平方数,我们不防用假设代入法。假设 m 是等于 4(当然 9、25 或其他的数也可以,不过 4 的计算量小一点),则 $4m^2 + 4\sqrt{m} + 1 = 73$,73 显然不是一个完全平方数,所以(C)选项被排除掉。

综上所述,本题的正确答案是(A)和(B)。

例4: Which two of the following numbers have a product that is greater than 70?

(A) - 9   (B) - 8

(C) 7   (D) 6

例4: 下面哪两个数的积大于 70?

解: 根据题意,这一道多选题的答案是两个,并且是两个选项的乘积。选项与选项之间有关联:两个数的积要大于一个正数,这两个数只能都是正数,或都是负数。因此正确答案不是(A)和(B),就是(C)和(D),显然 7 与 6 的乘积小于 70,因此正确的答案是(A)和(B)。

例 5: In triangle ABC, the measure of angle A is $25°$ and the measure of angle B is greater than $90°$. Which of the following could be the measure of angle C? Indicate all possible values.

A. $12°$ B. $15°$ C. $45°$

D. $50°$ E. $70°$

例 5: 在△ABC 中，∠A 等于 $25°$，∠B 大于 $90°$。∠C 可能是多少度？

选出所有可能正确的值。

解： 三角形的内角和是 $180°$，根据题意可得：

$$\left.\begin{array}{l}\angle A+\angle B+\angle C=180° \\ \angle A=25°\end{array}\right\} \Rightarrow \angle B+\angle C=155°$$

$$\angle B>90° \Rightarrow \angle C<155°-90°$$

$$\angle C<65°$$

所以本题的正确答案是（A）、（B）、（C）和（D）。

例 6: Each employee of a certain company is in either Department X or Department Y, and there are more than twice as many employees in Department X as in Department Y. The average (arithmetic mean) salary is $\$35,000$ for the employees in Department X and is $\$45,000$ for the employees in Department Y. Which of the following amounts could be the average salary for all of the employees in the company?

Indicate all such amounts.

(A) $\$36,000$ (B) $\$38,000$

(C) $\$39,000$ (D) $\$40,000$

(E) $\$41,000$ (F) $\$42,000$

(G) $\$44,000$

例 6: 某公司的员工不是 X 部门的就是 Y 部门的，X 部门的员工人数是 Y 部门的 2 倍以上。X 部门员工的平均薪水是 $\$35,000$，Y 部门员工的平均薪水是 $\$45,000$。下面哪一选项有可能是该公司所有员工的平均工资？

选出所有满足条件的选项。

解： 求解这类问题的关键是先找出最大和最小的可能值。因为题目中告诉我们低薪水的人数较多，所以平均工资的最大可能值肯定不会超过 $\$40,000$（$\frac{35000+45000}{2}$），最小可能值肯定大于 $\$45,000$。由此，我们可以锁定正确答案在（A）、（B）和（C）三个选项中间。再根据低薪水人数是高薪水人数的 2 倍以上，我们可以确定出所有员工平均薪水的最大可能值是：

$$\frac{2×35000+1×45000}{2+1}=38333（美元）$$

所以，本题的正确答案是（A）和（B）。

例 7: Which of the following could be the units digit of 57^n, where n is a positive integer? Indicate all such digits.

(A) 0   (B) 1   (C) 2

(D) 3   (E) 4   (F) 5

(G) 6   (H) 7   (I) 8

(J) 9

例 7: 下面哪一项有可能是 57^n 的个位数字，其中 n 是一个正整数？选出所有满足条件的选项。

解： 当 $n=1,2,3,4,5\cdots\cdots$ 时，57^n 的个位数分别是 $7,9,3,1,7,9,3,1\cdots\cdots$，即当 n 连续变化时，57^n 的个位数按 $7,9,3,1$ 的规律循环，因此本题的正确答案是（B）、（D）、（H）和（J）。

小结：多项选择题的出题方式比较灵活，选项不再局限于 5 个，而是在 3 个到 12 个之间；答案通常在 2 个以上，有时可能全部选项都是符合题意的答案；但也有少部分所谓的多选题，其实正确答案只有 1 个，此时你一定要相信自己选择的正确性，千万不能强迫自己再选出一个错误的答案出来，如下面这道题所示：

例 8：The total amount that Mary paid for a book was equal to the price of the book plus a sales tax that was 4 percent of the price of the book. Mary paid for the book with a ＄10 bill and received the correct change, which was less than ＄3.00. Which of the following statements must be true?

Indicate all such statements.

(A) The price of the book was less than ＄9.50.

(B) The price of the book was greater than ＄6.90.

(C) The sales tax was less than ＄0.45.

例 8：Mary 买一本书所付的钱等于书的定价外加定价 4％ 的税金。Mary 用 1 张 10 美元的钞票买了一本书，收到的零钱是正确的，且不多于 3 美元。下面哪一句话一定正确？

选出所有满足条件的选项。

解：假设书的定价是 x 美元，则根据题意，Mary 付的钱应该是 $(1+0.04)x$，再根据零钱不多于 3 美元这一条件，我们可以得到下面的不等式：

$7<(1+0.04)x<10$

$\Rightarrow 6.73<x<9.62$

由此可见（A）和（B）这两个选项都是错误的。因此，保有（C）选项是正确的。用 10 美元去买书，还有找零，税金不可能超过 0.4 美元。

注意：本题是让选择"must be true"的选项，所以只能先（C），如果题目中的最后一句话改为"Which of the following statements could be true"，则（A）、（B）和（C）都是该题的正确答案。

四、Numeric Entry questions（数字填空题）

数字填空题是唯一不提供备选答案的题型。该类型题的答案可能是或正或负的整数、小数或分数。数字填空题要得分，考生须使用键盘，在问题正下方的空格中输入答案。下面是 ETS 官方给出的相关说明：

> **Enter your answer as an integer or a decimal if there is a single answer box OR as a fraction if there are two separate boxes — one for the numerator and one for the denominator.**
>
> **To enter an integer or a decimal, either type the number in the answer box using the keyboard or use the Transfer Display button on the calculator.**
>
> - **First, click on the answer box — a cursor will appear in the box — and then type the number.**
> - **To erase a number, use the Backspace key.**
> - **For a negative sign, type a hyphen.**
> - **For a decimal point, type a period.**

- To remove a negative sign，type the hyphen again and it will disappear；the number will remain.
- The Transfer Display button on the calculator will transfer the calculator display to the answer box.
- Equivalent forms of the correct answer，such as 2.5 and 2.50，are all correct.
- Enter the exact answer unless the question asks you to round your answer.

To enter a fraction，type the numerator and the denominator in the respective boxes using the keyboard.

- For a negative sign，type a hyphen. A decimal point cannot be used in the fraction.
- The Transfer Display button on the calculator cannot be used for a fraction.
- Fractions do not need to be reduced to lowest terms，though you may need to reduce your fraction to fit in the boxes.

1. 数字填空题的应试策略

1）确保你的答案与题目的要求相一致

因为填空题没有选项来指引答案的形式，所以考生一定要认真地读题，明确题目中要求的答案形式。有些题的答题框前后会有相关的标识，这些标识通常都表明了本题对答案的具体要求，考生一定要特别留意这些标识，看清答案要求是英尺单位还是英里单位，是用百分数表示还是用小数表示，数量级是用百万表示，还是用十亿表示，这些都相当重要。

2）按题目要求进行四舍五入

如果题目要求对答案进行四舍五入，一定要近似到题目要求的精度。比如对 59.7 这个答案，题目要求四舍五入到最近的整数，考生最后在答题框中输入的数只能是 60。如果某道题的计算过程比较复杂，包括很多步，为了得到准确的答案，每一步的计算都要非常精确，只是在最后填写答案时，根据题目的要求进行四舍五入。如果题目没有要求对答案进行四舍五入，直接键入精确的计算结果。

3）检查结果是否合理

根据题目给出的信息进行估算或判断自己算出的结果是否合理。比如，是否存在数量级的问题，人数或苹果数是否算出了小数等。

4）合理使用计算器

如果回答问题时，考生使用屏幕计算器，计算结果正是考生要输入的数字，考生可以点击计算器上的 TRANSFER DISPLAY 长条键，读数就会自动显示到空格中。

5）等同于正确答案的其他答案也可得分

比如，一道题的正确答案应为 2.5，那么 2.50 也是可以的，除非题目要求答案精确到小数点后一位。另外，分数不需要化简：假设正确答案是 $\frac{1}{3}$，考生的答案如果是 $\frac{2}{6}$，或者其他等于 $\frac{1}{3}$ 的分数也都可以得分。如果某道填空题的答案应为分数，会有两个空格。考生应将分子输入上面一格，将分母输入下面一格。

13

2. 典型例题解析

例 9： The average (arithmetic mean) of the 11 numbers in a list is 14. If the average of 9 of the numbers in the list is 9，what is the average of the other 2 numbers?

□

Click on the answer box, then type in a number. Backspace to erase.

例 9： 11 个数的平均值（算术平均值）是 14。如果该列数中有 9 个数的平均值是 9，那么剩下的两个数的平均值是多少？

| 36.5 |

解： 根据题意可知，剩下的两个数的值等于 11 个数的和减去 9 个数的和，由算术平均值的定义可得，剩下的两个数的平均值为：

$$\frac{11\times14-9\times9}{2}=36.5$$

例 10： The total amount of Judy's water bill for the last quarter of the year was ＄40.50. The bill consisted of a fixed charge of ＄13.50 plus a charge of ＄0.0075 per gallon for the water used in the quarter. For how many gallons of water was Judy charged for the quarter?

□ gallons

Click on the answer box, then type in a number. Backspace to erase.

例 10： Judy 去年最后一季度总的水费是 ＄40.50。该费用包括 ＄13.50 的固定收费和水费，该季度所使用的水按每加仑 ＄0.0075 标准收取。问 Judy 应该交多少加仑水的水费？

| 3600 | 加仑

解： 设 Judy 应该交 x 加仑水的水费，根据题意我们可以写出方程：

$$13.50+0.0075x=40.5$$

解方程可得 $x=3600$ 加仑。

例 11： A merchant made a profit of ＄5 on the sale of a sweater that cost the merchant ＄15. What is the profit expressed as a percent of the merchant's cost?

Give your answer to the <u>nearest whole percent</u>.

□ ％

例 11： 一商人卖一件成本为 15 美元的羊毛衫可获利 5 美元。该商人的利润是成本的百分之多少？

把百分比四舍五入到整数 | 33 | ％

解： 根据题意利润百分比是 $\left(\dfrac{5}{15}\right)\times100\%$，整数百分比是 33％。

注意： 如果考生用计算器来算该题时，直接转移计算结果时，答题框中得到的数是 33.333333，这个数是错误的，因为它不符合题目的要求，所以考生必须把答题框中小数后的 3 都删去。尽管 33％，等同于 0.33，但如果在答题框中输入 0.33，同样是错误的，因为答题框的后面已经有一个百分号了，再填入 0.33，就相当于把题目的答案缩小了 100 倍。

考生一定要根据题目的要求去填空，千万不能在答题框中填入 33.3，更不能填入 0.333。

例 12： Judy plans to visit the National Gallery once each month in 2012 except in July and August when she plans to go three

例 12： Judy 计划在 2012 年每月参观国家美术馆 1 次，但在 7 月和 8 月，每月要参观 3 次。单次门票价格是 3.5 美元；3 个月内

times each. A single admission costs $3.50, a pass valid for unlimited visits in any 3-month period can be purchased for $18, and an annual pass costs $60.00. What is the least amount, in dollars, that Judy can spend for her intended number of visits?

[ ] dollars

例 13: On a certain French-American committee, $\frac{2}{3}$ of the members are men, and $\frac{3}{8}$ of the men are Americans. If $\frac{3}{5}$ of the committee members are French, what fraction of the members are American women?

可以无限次参观的季票价格是 18 美元；年票的价格是 60 美元。Judy 最少要花多少美元来完成她的参观计划？

49.5 dollars

解：Judy 计划在 2012 年参观 16 次美术馆，买次票的价格是，小于年票的价格。如果她 7、8 和 9 这三个月买季票，其他的九个月份买 9 张次票，则所花的钱是：

$$18+9\times\$3.5=\$49.5$$

所以，Judy 至少要花 49.5 美元才能完成她 2012 年参观美术馆的计划。

例 13: 在某一个法美委员会里，$\frac{2}{3}$ 的成员是男性，且 $\frac{3}{8}$ 的男性是美国人。如果委员会中有 $\frac{3}{5}$ 的人是法国人，那么委员会中美国女性成员的占比是多少？

$$\frac{3}{20}$$

解：根据题意，美国人占比是 $1-\frac{3}{5}=\frac{2}{5}$；美国男性成员的占比是 $\frac{2}{3}\times\frac{3}{8}=\frac{1}{4}$；所以美国女性成员的占比是 $\frac{2}{5}-\frac{1}{4}=\frac{3}{20}$。

技巧点睛：可以用假定法，用简单易用的数来代替题目中不太确定的量。在本题中，我们可以假定委员会的总人数是 3、8 和 5 的最小公倍数（这样便于计算），即 120 人。代入题目中我们可以得到：

总人数＝120 人

男性人数＝$120\times\frac{2}{3}$＝80 人

美国男性＝$80\times\frac{3}{8}$＝30 人

法国人数＝$120\times\frac{3}{5}$＝72 人

美国人数＝120－72＝48 人

美国女性＝48－30＝18 人

例 14: Working alone at its constant rate, machine A produces k car parts in 10 minutes. Working alone at its constant rate, machine B produces k car parts in 15 minutes. How many minutes does it take machines A and B, working simultaneously at their respective constant rates, to produce k car parts?

minutes

例 15:

Distribution by Rank of the 800 Faculty Members at Central State University (CSU) in 1990

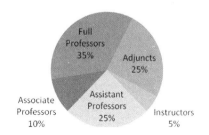

所以,女性占总人数的比例 $=\dfrac{18}{120}=\dfrac{3}{20}$

注意: 在本题中,如果在答题框中直接键入,其结果也是正确的。

例 14: A 机床单独工作时,10 分钟可生产 k 个汽车零件,B 机床单独工作时,15 分钟可生产 k 个汽车零件。请问 A 机床和 B 机床共同加工 k 个汽车零件需要多少分钟?假定整个过程中 A 和 B 的工作效率不变。

6

minutes

解: 根据题意 A 机床每分钟生产 $\dfrac{k}{10}$ 个零件,B 机床每分钟生产 $\dfrac{k}{15}$ 个零件。A 和 B 共同工作时每分钟加工的零件数是 $\dfrac{k}{10}+\dfrac{k}{15}=k\left(\dfrac{1}{10}+\dfrac{1}{15}\right)=k\left(\dfrac{25}{150}\right)=\dfrac{k}{6}$。

所以 A 和 B 共同生产 k 个零件要耗时 $k\div\dfrac{k}{6}=6$ 分钟。

技巧点晴: 为了保证结果的正确性,我们还可以对计算的结果进行估算。工作速度较快的两个 A 同时生产 k 个零件需要 5 分钟;工作速度较慢的两个 B 同时生产 k 个零件需要 7.5 分钟;所以 A 和 B 共同加工 k 个零件所用的时间应该是,由此可以得到前面计算的结果 6 分钟基本上合理的。

例 15: 从 1990 年到 2000 年,中央州立大学的教职工人数增加了 20%。如果助理教授、副教授、正教授的总人数保持不变,讲师的人数增加了 50%,那么该校在 2000 年时有多少名助教?

340

解: 由于 2000 年时,教职工人数增加了 20%,所以教职工的总数 $=800\times(1+20\%)=960$ 人;在 1990 年,教职工中各种教授的总人数

From 1990 to 2000 the number of faculty members at CSU increased by 20%. If the total number of assistant, associate, and full professors remained the same, and the number of instructors increased by 50%, how many adjunct faculty were there in 2000?

$$\boxed{}$$

$=800\times(35\%+10\%+25\%)=560$ 人；在 2000 年，讲师的人数增加了 50%，所以此时讲师的人数 $=800\times5\%(1+50\%)=60$ 人；所以教职工中助教的人数是：$960-560-60=340$ 人。

例 16：

House Prices	Number of Houses
$100,000 — $133,000	12
$134,000 — $166,000	25
$167,000 — $199,000	8

The table shows the distribution of prices of 45 houses for sale in a certain region.

Select two of the following choices and place them in the blanks below so that the resulting statement is true.

$175,000 $185,000 $190,000

at most $42,000   at least $57,000

If the highest price of the 45 houses is _____ , then the range of the prices of the 45 houses is _____ .

Click on a choice, then click on a blank.

例 16： 表中给出了某一地区 45 座房子销售价格的分布情况。从下面的选项中选取一个填入接下来的空格中使该陈述成立。

如果这 45 座房子的最高售价是 **$190,000**，那么这 45 座房子的售价的变化范围是 at least **$57,000**。

解： 由表中数据可知，房子的最低售价是 $100,000，最高售价是 $199,000，所以最高差价是 $99,000。由此可以推知，第一个空要在前三数中选取，第二个空要在后两个数中选择。对前三个数分别进行考察，发现当房子的最高售价定在 $190,000，最低售价取最大值 $133,000 时，房子售价的最小浮动范围是 $57,000。

例 17： The symbol $\triangle$ represents one of the four operations of addition, subtraction, multiplication, and division, and $3 \triangle 1 = 3$.

For each of the following equations, indicate whether the equation must be true, must be false, or could be either true or false.

例 17： 附号 $\triangle$ 代表加、减、乘和除四种运算中的某一种，并且 $3 \triangle 1 = 3$。

请指出下面的方程是"一定正确"，还是"一定错误"，或是"可能正确，也可能错误"。

解： $3 \triangle 1 = 3$，而 $\triangle$ 又可代表"加、减、乘和除"四种运算，经过观察我们发现：

$$3 \times 1 = 3$$
$$3 \div 1 = 3$$

所以我们可以推出 $\triangle$ 在该题中既可以表示

Equation	Must Be True	Must Be False	Could Be True or False
6 △ 2 = 3			
6 △ 2 = 4			
6 △ 2 = 12			

Click on your choices.

"乘号",又可以表示"除号"。我们把"乘号"和"除号"分别代入到题目中的几个式子中,如果一个式子能同时满足"乘"和"除"两种运算,那么该方程就一定正确;如果"乘"和"除"这两种运算都不能满足,那么该方程就一定错误;如果只能满足"乘"和"除"这两种运算中的一种,那么该方程就既可能正确又可能错误。

五、应对 GRE 数学考试的基本解题技巧

1. 先略读题目再作解答,答题时应适可而止。 有些考生喜欢一边看题目,一边就开始列方程计算。这是很不明智的,因为有时题目的要求可能与自己做的结果并不一致。正确的方法是把整个题目略读一遍,在答题之前先浏览一下五个选项,这对我们正确选择答题方式有很大的帮助。通常答案会以不同的形式给出,如小数形式、分数形式等,或以不同的单位给出,如分、秒等,演算时要留心以正确的形式给出答案,抓住问题的关键所在之后再作解答,以免把时间花费在不必要的计算上。有一部分内容不要求考生进行复杂的算术运算,通常进行概念性的比较即可得出答案。即使需要一定的运算,进行到能够比较大小时就应停止,不一定要算出最后的结果,请看下面的这道题。

例 18：

Column A	Column B
$32^3 \times 2$	$32^2 \times 65$

解：将 Column A 与 Column B 中的量相除有

$$\frac{32^3 \times 2}{32^3 \times 65} = \frac{32 \times 2}{65} = \frac{64}{65} < 1$$

$$\Rightarrow 32^3 \times 2 < 32^2 \times 65$$

所以本题的(B)是正确答案。本题不能将 $32^3 \times 2$ 与 $32^2 \times 65$ 具体算出后再进行大小比较,否则既浪费了时间又容易把题做错。

2. 如果所给出的供比较大小的两个量都不是变量,也不涉及几何图形,则其关系一定是确定的,不能选择(D)选项。另外,几何图形不一定是按比例画出的,因此进行大小判断时,不能从图上观察,而是应使用数学概念。例如比较 A 与 B 的大小,按试卷上所绘图形可能明显地 $A < B$,而实际上则可能是 $B < A$ 或是两个角的大小不能确定。考生碰到这种情况时,重新画一个图对正确解题常常是很有帮助的,如果考生自己画出的图在满足题目的已知条件下是可以变化的,那么(D)就是正确答案。

例 19：

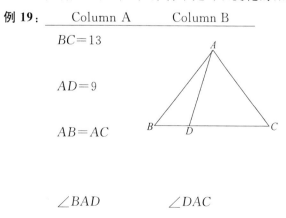

Column A	Column B
BC = 13	
AD = 9	
AB = AC	
∠BAD	∠DAC

解：从已知图形看,∠BAD < ∠DAC,而实际上存在∠BAD > ∠DAC 的可能性,因为根据题中所给的条件,AD 的位置有两种情况,如右图所示：当 AD 在高 AE 的左边时,∠BAD < ∠DAC;而当 AD 在高 AE 的右边时,则 ∠BAD > ∠DAC。因此根

据本题所给出的信息，$\angle BAD$ 和 $\angle DAC$ 的大小关系不能确定，即正确答案是(D)。

3. 对于较复杂的量的大小比较问题，一般情况下可先将两个量相减或相除，然后根据相减后的量与 **0** 的关系(大于、小于或等于)，及相除后的量与 **1** 的关系(大于、小于或等于)，去确定相比较量的大小。

例 20：

	Column A	Column B
	$x \neq -1$	
(1)	$x^2 + 6x$	$+8x - 1$
	$a > 2$	
(2)	$a^6 - 2a^4$	a^2

解：(1) 本题中的两个代数式的大小不能直接得出，将两式相减则有：

$$(x^2 + 6x) - (+8x - 1) = x^2 - 2x + 1$$
$$= (x-1)^2 > 0$$

所以$(x^2 + 6x) > (-8x - 1)$，本题的正确答案选(A)。

(2) 这个题可通过将两代数式相除的办法得到答案：

$$\frac{a^6 - 2a^4}{a^2} = a^4 - 2a^2 = a^2(a^2 - 2)$$
$$> 1 \Rightarrow a^6 - 2a^4 > a^2$$

所以本题的正确答案是(A)。

4. 巧妙使用代入法，有时可用排除法。

(1) 以简单的数值取代变量，可以省去运算。对于有些难于直接判定大小的代数式的比较题目，可代入不同的数，再观察其相对关系。可选择一些特定的数，如正数、负数、0、大于 1 或小于 1 的数等，其结果发生变化，则选择(D)选项。试用心体会下面这个例子：

例 21：

Column A	Column B
$a > 0$, $b > 0$	
$\dfrac{a}{b}$	$\dfrac{a+2}{b+2}$

解：设 $a=1$，$b=2$，则 $\dfrac{a}{b} = \dfrac{1}{2} < \dfrac{1+2}{2+2} = \dfrac{3}{4}$，若设 $a=2$，$b=1$，则 $\dfrac{a}{b} = 2 > \dfrac{2+2}{1+2} = \dfrac{4}{3}$

因此无法比较两栏数的大小，所以答案为(D)。

(2) 挑选可能的答案代入进行验算。把选项中的数值或变量代入验算，可以快速求解，避免冗长的计算过程。

例 22：A haberdasher（男子服饰经销商）sells neckties for \$7 each and shirts for \$12 each. If he sells \$95 worth of ties and shorts, what is the least amount of ties he could have sold?

(A) 3   (B) 4   (C) 5
(D) 6   (E) 7

解：领带与衬衫的数目必为整数。如果男子服饰经销商（haberdasher）卖了 3 条领带（\$21），则剩下 \$74，无法被 12 整除。如果他卖了 4 条领带（\$28），则剩下 \$67，亦不能被 12 整除。如果他卖了 5 条领带（\$35），剩下 \$60，可被 12 整除。所以(C)为正确选项。

(3) 有时使用排除法。有些选项一看就知不正确，做题时可先将这些选项排除掉，再从其他的几个选项中选一个，在时间紧迫的情况下，即使用猜的方法也比较容易猜中。

5. 比较大小要特别提防陷阱，必要时采用近似计算；对于变量一定要注意其符号的可变性。比较大小要掌握正确的思维路线，在最短的时间内求得正确的答案，适当地运用"近似值"的概念，可以大大地节省考试时的宝贵时间；对复杂的数学运算，如果能采用近似计算，既能得到正确答案，又可节省大量的时间。但是否能采用近似计算，取决于五个选项的值是否相差较大。但是比较简单的题可能会因为粗心大意而做错。请考生体会下面这个例子：

例 23：

Column A	Column B
$x^2=64$	
x	8

解：本题的正确答案是（D）。因为 $x^2=64$，$x=\pm 8$，所以无法比较大小。

再请看一个例子，体会对于变量一定要注意其符号的可变性的重要意义：

例 24：

Column A	Column B
$\dfrac{p}{q}=5$	
p	q

解：若 $p=5$，$q=1$，则有 $p>q$；但是若 $p=-5$，$q=-1$，则显然 $p<q$。所以 p 与 q 的大小关系不能确定，也即（D）是正确答案。

6. 冗长的题目不可轻易放过，沉着应付定义运算考题。

有些应用题比较冗长，看起来好像很烦，但事实上这类题多半也仅仅是烦在看题上，并不需要太多的计算。有些题甚至是一旦题目看明白，答案就出来了。因此遇到这类题目一定不要无所适从，而要沉着应战。

试题中有时会出现 ETS 自创的定义或符号，考生不要因为自己从未见过就以为自己不会而轻易放过去。对这类题目只要根据题目的定义或公式把数据代入，通常都比较容易得分。

例 25：A sequence of operations $\{A_1, A_2, \ldots A_n\}$ is defined as follows $A_1(x)=x$, $A_2(x)=2x^2\ldots A_n(x)=nx^n$. If A_2 is performed on x, and then A_4 is performed on the result, what is the final result?

(A) $4x^4$ (B) $8x^4$ (C) $64x^4$

(D) $64x^8$ (E) $4x^8$

解：不能正确解答本题的考生大多数都是不能正确理解"If A_2 is performed on x"这句话。这句话的主要意思是把 A_2 的值当 x 来运算，即以 $2x^2$ 来替代 $A_1(x)=x$ 中的 x，因此有：

$$A_n(x)=nx^n \Rightarrow A_n(A_2(x))=n(A_2(x))^n$$
$$=n(2x^2)^n=2^n n x^{2n}$$
$$A_4(A_2(x))=2^4\times 4\times x^{2\times 4}=64x^8。$$

7. 对题目要仔细阅读，弄清提供的信息及要回答的问题，特别注意答非所问。 例如题目中以分钟为单位，而答案中却要求以秒为单位。

8. 答题时要注意借助图形。 未给出图形时，有时为了做题需要，应自己画一个。图表题是中国考生的弱项，本书将在后面分出一章给以详尽的讲解。

总而言之，GRE 数学部分还是有技巧可言的。但技巧归技巧，扎实的基本功和一定的练习却更是必不可少的。本书接下来的篇章中已把 GRE 的考试要点，以及全真试题中的易错题、重点题及难题全部列出，并附以参考译文和透彻的讲解，希望能对期望在 GRE 数学方面节省时间并取得高分的考生有所帮助。

第 三 章

中国考生在 GRE 数学考试中的常见错误

GRE 数学考题的内容大体上不超出中国的高中生所学的内容,因此 GRE 的数学考试对大多数过五关、斩六将、历经高考磨难的中国大学生构不成太大的挑战,但这并不是说大多数的中国考生都能在考试中取得优异的成绩。因为 GRE 考试毕竟不能等同于我国的小学和中学数学考试,其中充满了大量的数学专业词汇,以及少量的某些中国大学生相对较生疏的统计和概率方面的内容。要想在 GRE 数学方面拿高分甚至满分,就必须克服这些障碍。下面把中国考生在 GRE 数学考试中易犯的错误总结一下,希望能对考生有所帮助。

1. 英文理解能力较差。对英语句型(尤其是两个事物相比较时)理解不清。由于题目本身是用英文叙述,若阅读能力欠佳,则无法掌握问题的核心所在,即使数学能力很强,也无法创造佳绩。例如在数学题中经常出现的 the ratio of A to B 表示 $A:B$,但若考生理解成 $B:A$,那就肯定不能把题解对;There is twice as much A as B 的意思与 A is twice as much as B 的意思完全一样,即都是 $A=2B$ 而不是 $B=2A$;又如 more (less) than..., as twice as...,或者 decrease to, decrease by 等词语都是比较容易理解错的。再如,Seven less than $5x$ 究竟意思为 $7<5x$ 还是 $5x<7$ 呢?(见本书第 74 页第 6 题)。对于这些题,一定要分清句子的结构,弄清比较的两个主体或是变化前后的数量。在平时做题时要多留心。对于这种题应认真地多研读几遍。

2. 对数学术语不熟悉。一些比较生僻的数学术语是考生做题的巨大障碍,例如 progression, binomial, denominator, complementary angle 等,若考生对这些词语的意思把握不到位,会导致对整个题目的理解出现偏差。对于这种情况,一方面要在平时尽可能地多熟悉数学术语,另一方面要在做题时多回忆以前的数学知识,结合词根来猜出该数学术语的意思。例如书中有一道考题,让考生比较 The value of the units' digit in 6^{47} 与 The value of the units' digit in 5^{77} 的大小。许多考生由于不知道 the units' digit 的意思为个位数字,从而使用对数或开方来进行运算,白白浪费了好多时间。(解题思路:本题的正确答案为(A)。本题让考生比较 6^{47} 的个位数字的值 与 5^{77} 的个位数字的值的大小。解题时用到了本书第二篇中所讲到的整数 n 次幂后所得的数的个位数的循环特点。6 的任意次幂的个位数都是 6,而 5 的任意次幂的个位数也都为 5)。

换句话说,知道每一个词表达的数学含意是正确解答数学问题的关键所在。首先要熟悉的就是四则运算——"加减乘除"的表示方法。

Operation	Symbol	Result	Example
addition	$+$	Sum	18 is the sum of 15 and 3 $18 = 15 + 3$
subtraction	$-$	Difference	9 is the difference of 16 and 7 $9 = 16 - 7$
multiplication	$\times$	Product	39 is the product of 13 and 3 $39 = 13 \times 3$
division	$\div$	Quotient	4 is the quotient of 24 and 6 $4 = 24 \div 6$

在 GRE 的数学考试中有许多不同的单词却表达相同的数学含意(如下表),这些词通常给出了数量与运算之间的关系,所以熟悉这些词所表达的数学含意是至关重要的。在此,笔者强烈建议考生熟记本书附录内容。

Equality	is	
	is equal to	
	is the same as	
	the result is	
	yields	
	gives	
Inequalities	A is greater than B	$A>B$
	A is greater than or equal to B	$A\geqslant B$
	A is less than B	$A<B$
	A is less than or equal to B	$A\leqslant B$
Addition ($A+B$)	the sum of A and B	
	the total of A and B	
	A added to B	
	A increased by B	
	A more than B	
	A greater than B	
Subtraction ($A-B$)	A minus B	
	A less B	
	the difference of A and B	
	from A subtract B	
	A take away B	
	A decreased by B	
	A diminished by B	
	B is subtracted from A	
	B less than A	
Multiplication ($A\times B$)	A multiplied by B	
	the product of A and B	
Division ($A\div B$)	A divided by B	
	the quotient of A and B	
Factors and Divisors ($A\times B=C$)	A and B are factors of C	
	A and B are divisors of C	
	C is divisible by A and by B	
	C is a multiple of A and of B	

这些内容掌握好以后,可以试着自己出几道数学题看一看,是否存在障碍。如果有,就要重新认真学习上面两个表格中的内容,直到非常熟练为止。

3. 缺乏技巧,反应太慢。要在 45 分钟之内答完 28 道,每题停留的时间平均也就一分钟多一点儿,但图表题一般至少得花 1 分多钟甚至两分钟才能把题目看清楚,而且有些题目很耗时,演算过程很冗长,所以做题速度必须得快,还要讲究解题技巧,才能在短短的时间内做完。

4. 考点的遗忘。 由于一些数学知识点学过得早,可能已经遗忘。只要考生在考前把本书所列举的考点加以复习,并把所附难题做一遍,就不会有问题。

5. 读题的遗漏。 在匆忙中易把数量的单位或其他重要的信息丢掉,常见的有百分数(percent)与小数,米与厘米等。

6. 计算失误。 常见的计算失误是一些同学把简单问题复杂化,结果既浪费了时间又做错了题。这类错误在 Quantitative Comparison 中容易发生。例如有一道考题比较 $\frac{1}{3}+\frac{1}{5}+\frac{1}{7}$ 与 1 的大小,不用计算一下子就可以判断出它的值小于 1,因为 3 个 $\frac{1}{3}$ 加起来才等于 1,而 $\frac{1}{5}$ 和 $\frac{1}{7}$ 都很明显地小于 $\frac{1}{3}$。还有一些比较题,可以通过约去同类项的方法加以简化。绝大多数的 GRE 数学题不需要繁杂的计算,因此可以说 ETS 考的就是一种思维方式。

7. 忽略数量换算。 注意一些题所给的数量的单位和最后所问的数量的单位不同,一定要注意答题前将其进行转换,有时需要多留心题后给的括号,因为在某些情况下,括号内的内容在选择时会用得上。

8. 图形题的读图方法不妥当。 有些考生觉得看图很麻烦,因此很讨厌图形题。其实图形题也仅是麻烦一点儿,一旦熟悉了图形题的套路,考生就会感觉图形题也仅是"a piece of cake"。首要的是掌握正确的看图方法,读图方法可能因人而异,比较有效的方法是先略读。所谓略读就是对于一个图先看其大概,抓其比较重要的信息,如题目的主要名词,分清图中曲线的意义或表中每行(或每列)的意义,弄清时间或地域的差别,对这些内容只要有简单的印象即可。因为考生很难通过一次读题就建立不同的量之间的关系,即使把说明的小字都读下来,也未必都能看懂,未必能对做题有较大的用处。因此我们只要知道每个题与图表中的哪一部分对应,然后回到图中去找,一般效率和准确率都会较高。

第 二 篇

GRE 数学分类思维训练

第 一 章

算术（Arithmetic）

第一节 整 数（Integers）

一、The Concept of Integers（整数的概念）

1. Natural Numbers（自然数）：大于零的正整数。如：1，2，3，……其中 1 为最小的自然数。

2. Odd Numbers（奇数）：不能被 2 所整除的整数。如：1，−1，3，−3……

3. Even Numbers（偶数）：能够被 2 所整除的整数。如：0，2，−2，4，−4……

4. Prime Numbers（质数）：除了 1 和它本身之外，不能被其他正整数所整除的自然数，如：2，3，5，7，11……其中 2 是最小的质数。

5. Composite Numbers（合数）：除了 1 和它本身之外，还有其他因子的自然数，如：4，6，8，9，10……其中 4 是最小的合数。（注：质数和合数都不能为负数，0 和 1 既不是质数也不是合数。）

6. Mutual Prime Numbers（互质数）：如果两个数的最大公约数为 1，那么这两个数叫做互质数。例如：13 和 15，19 和 23 等。

7. Multiple and Divisible（倍数和约数）：当整数 a 能被另一个整数 b 所整除时，a 称为 b 的倍数，b 称为 a 的约数或因数。例如：10 是 5 的倍数，5 是 10 的约数。

8. Common Multiple（公倍数）：如果一个数同时是几个数的倍数，则称这个数为它们的公倍数；公倍数中最小的称为最小公倍数（least 或 lowest common multiple）。例如：12，24，36 等都是 2，4，6，12 的公倍数，其中 12 是它们的最小公倍数。

9. Common Factor or Divisor（公约数或公因数）：如果一个数同时是几个数的约数，则称这个数为它们的公约数或公因数；公约数中最大的被称为最大公约数（公因数）（greatest common factor or divisor）。例如：2，7，14 都是 28，42，70 的公约数，14 是它们的最大公约数。

10. Perfect Square（完全平方数）：若一个整数开平方后还是整数，则这个数被称之为完全平方数。例如：4，9，16，25……完全平方数均为自然数。

11. Perfect Cube（完全立方数）：若一个整数开三次方后还是整数,则这数称之为完全立方数。例如:$-27,-8,0,8,27……$

12. Quotients and Remainders（商和余数）：当一个正整数除以另一个正整数其商不为整数时就存在商和余数问题。余数和商为大于或等于零的整数,余数总小于除数。例如15除以7时,其商为2,余数为1。

13. Consecutive Integers（连续整数）：按从小到大的顺序相连的几个整数称为连续整数。例如:$-2,-1,0,1,2$是五个连续的整数。连续正整数的算术平均值是首项和末项的算术平均值。

二、The Properties of Integers（整数的性质）

1. Odd and Even（奇偶性）

(1) n 是整数,则 $2n$ 为偶数,$2n+1$ 为奇数。

(2) 奇数个奇数相加减其结果必为奇数。

(3) 偶数个奇数相加减其结果必为偶数。

(4) 奇数和偶数相加减,其结果必为奇数。

(5) 任意多个偶数相加减,其结果必为偶数。

(6) 若 n（n 为大于1的自然数）个整数连乘其结果为奇数,则这 n 个整数必然都是奇数。

(7) 若 n（n 为大于1的自然数）个整数连乘其结果为偶数,则这 n 个整数中至少有一个为偶数。

(8) 若 n（n 为大于1的自然数）个连续整数相加等于零,则 n 必为奇数。

(9) 若 n（n 为大于1的自然数）个连续奇数相加等于零,则 n 必为偶数。

(10) 若 n（n 为大于1的自然数）个连续偶数相加等于零,则 n 必为奇数。

(11) 自然数间相加或相乘必然还是自然数。

(12) 自然数间相减必然为整数(可正可负)。

(13) 奇数个连续整数的算术平均值等于这奇数个数中中间大小那个数的值。

(14) 偶数个连续整数的算术平均值等于这偶数个数中中间两个数的算术平均值。

(15) 任何一个大于2的偶数都可以表示为两个质数的和。

例1：下面哪个数不能表达为两个质数的和?

　　(A) 21　　　(B) 14　　　(C) 18

　　(D) 28　　　(E) 23

解：这五个选项中,(B),(C),(D)都是大于2的偶数,因此由以上定理可知都不是正确答案;而(A)和(E)都是奇数,若两个数相加为奇数,则这两个数必定是一个为奇数,另一个为偶数。在所有的质数中2是惟一的一个偶数,因此若(A)和(E)可表达为两个质数的和,则必有一个2,所以只需将(A)和(E)分别减2,看所得差是否为质数,即可得出答案。$21-2=19$ 为质数,$23-2=21$ 不为质数,因而正确答案为(E)。

(16) 2个连续的自然数相乘必然为2的倍数,3个连续的自然数相乘必为6的倍数。

(17) 若3个连续自然数的算术平均值为奇数,则这三个自然数的乘积必为8的倍数(也即两个连续的偶数相乘为8的倍数)。

例如: $\dfrac{4+5+6}{3}=5$,则 $4\times5\times6=120$ 可被8整除。

2. Factor and Multiple（约数和倍数）

（1）如果整数 a 能被整数 b 整除，则 a 能被 b 的因数（或约数）所整除。

（2）如果 a 为质数，n 为**非负整数（non-negative integers or whole numbers）**，则 a^n 的因数为 $n+1$ 个（包括 1 和 a^n）。

（3）0 为任何一个非 0 整数的倍数，1 为任何一个整数的约数，任何一个质数有且只有 1 和它本身两个约数。

（4）最小公倍数的求解步骤：

① 所有的数分别表示为各自的质因数的乘积；

② 如果所有的乘积中有公因数，则将式子中相同的质因子都提出来，且只保留指数较大的一个因子作为公因数，除去其他乘积中指数较小的公因数；

③ 将剩下的乘积中的所有因数乘起来，就得到最小公倍数。

（5）最大公约数的求解步骤：

① 将所有的数表示成自己的质因数乘积的形式；

② 将式子中相同的质因子都提出来，并取幂指数较小的一个作为其相应的公因数；

③ 将取出的公因数相乘，就得到了最大公约数。

例 2：求 84 和 90 的最小公倍数和最大公约数。

解：$\because 84=2^2\times3\times7$，$90=2\times3^2\times5$

$\therefore$ 它们的最小公倍数 $=2^2\times3^2\times5\times7=1260$

它们的最大公约数 $=3\times2=6$。

（6）最大公约数和最小公倍数的性质：

① 设 (a,b) 表示 a 和 b 的最大公约数，$[a,b]$ 表示 a 和 b 的最小公倍数，则有如下的公式：$\dfrac{a\times b}{(a,b)}=[a,b]$（注：此式仅适用于两数的情况）；

② 若 m 为自然数，则 ma 和 mb 的最大公约数为 a 和 b 的最大公约数的 m 倍；

③ 若 m 为自然数，则 ma 和 mb 的最小公倍数为 a 和 b 的最小公倍数的 m 倍；

④ 若 a 和 c 的最大公约数为 1，则 $a\times b$ 和 c 的最大公约数等于 b 和 c 的最大公约数；

⑤ 若 a 和 c 的最大公约数为 1，且有 c 是 $a\times b$ 的一个因子，则必有 c 是 b 的一个因子；

⑥ 若 a 和 b 互质，且 c 可被 a 整除，c 也可以被 b 整除，则 c 可被 $a\times b$ 整除（注：必须在互质这一条件的限制下，该结论才成立）；

⑦ 两个自然数分别除以它们的最大公约数，所得的商互质；

⑧ 两个数的最小公倍数与最大公约数的乘积等于这两个数的乘积。

3. The Divisibility of Integers（整数的整除特性）

（1）Here are some shortcuts to determining divisibility by common numbers：

If the integer has this feature	Then it is divisible by
It ends in 0，2，4，6 or 8	2
The sum of the digits is divisible by 3	3
The number formed by the last 2 digits is divisible by4	4
The number ends in 5 or 0	5
The number meets the tests for divisibility by 2 and3	6
The number formed by the last 3 digits is divisible by 8	8
The sum of the digits is divisible by 9	9
奇数位的和减去偶数位的和所得的差可被 11 整除	11

（2）当一整数被 3，4，5，8，9 除，不能被除尽时的余数特征

① 整数的各位的和被 3 除余几，则这个整数被 3 除余几；

② 整数的后两位被 4 除余几，则这个整数被 4 除余几；

③ 整数的最后一位被 5 除余几，则这个整数被 5 除余几；

④ 整数的最后 3 位被 8 除余几，则这个整数被 8 除余几；

⑤ 整数各位的和被 9 除余几，则这个整数被 9 除余几。

（3）若 a 可被 b 整除，b 可被 c 整除，则 a 可被 c 整除

（4）若一个等式 $b+c+\ldots+l=m+n+\ldots+s$ 中仅除一项之外其余各项均可被 a 整除，那么此项也被 a 整除

例 3：$3a^2+8b^3+16c+d=4e+24f+48g$

解：这个等式共有 7 项，若除 d 以外的 6 项都能被 4 整除，则 d 也能被 4 整除。

（5）若 a 和 b 仅为 2 位自然数，且 a，b 有如下的性质：a 的个位等于 b 的十位，a 的十位等于 b 的个位，也即 a 和 b 仅数位倒置，则这样的数必有：$(a+b)$ 是 11 的倍数，$(a-b)$ 为 9 的倍数。且将个位和十位相加为几就是 $(a+b)$ 为 11 的几倍，个位和十位差的绝对值为几就是 $(a-b)$ 为 9 的几倍。

例 4：19 和 91

解：$(91-19)=72$ 因 $9-1=8$，所以 $(91-19)$ 为 9 的 8 倍

$(91+19)=110$ 因 $9+1=10$，所以 $(91+19)$ 为 11 的 10 倍

（6）若数 n 为自然数，且 n 不被 3 整除，则 n^2 被 3 除余 1

（7）若 n 为奇数，则 n^2 被 4 除余 1

（8）若自然数 a 被自然数 m 除，余数为自然数 c；若 a 被 n 除其余数也为自然数 c，则 a 被 m，n 的最小公倍数除，余数仍为自然数 c。

（9）一个数要想被另一个数整除，该数需含有对方所具有的所有质数因子

（10）计算整除常用的方法（字母表达法）

大多数的考生在考试时遇到整除问题都往往采用代入数的方法，但这种方法不一定保险，下面将举例介绍一种较为保险的方法——字母表达法。

例 5：若自然数 n 被 3 除余 2，被 4 除余 1，问 n 被 12 除余几？

解：既然 n 被 3 除余 2，则 n 可写为 $n=3A+2$，A 为某一自然数

既然 n 被 4 除余 1，则 n 可写为 $n=4B+1$，B 为某一自然数

$\Rightarrow 3A+2=4B+1 \Rightarrow 3A+2 = 4(B'+1)+1 \Rightarrow$

$3A+2=4B'+5 \Rightarrow 3A-3=4B'$，其中 B' 为一自然数

由最后一个式子可知，$3A-3$ 为 3 的倍数，根据上面讲述的性质可知 $4B'$ 也为 3 的倍数，而 4 和 3 互质，依最大公约数、最小公倍数中讲述的性质可知 $4B'$ 必为 12 的倍数，而原数 n 就是 $4B'+5$，所以 n 被 12 除余 5。

4. The Concept and Properties of Common Mode(同余的概念和性质)

(1)同余定义：若两个整数 a，b 被自然数 m 除有相同的余数，那么称 a，b 对于模 m 同余，用式子可表示为：

$$a \equiv b \pmod m，此式可读为 a 同余 b，模为 m$$

(2)同余的性质

① 反身性：$a \equiv a \pmod m$

② 对称性：若 $a \equiv b \pmod m$，那么 $b \equiv a \pmod m$

③ 传递性：若 $a \equiv b \pmod m$，$b \equiv c \pmod m$，那么 $a \equiv c \pmod m$

④ 加减性：若 $a \equiv b \pmod m$，$c \equiv d \pmod m$，那么 $a \pm b \equiv c \pm d \pmod m$

⑤ 可乘性：若 $a \equiv b \pmod m$，$c \equiv d \pmod m$，那么 $a \times c \equiv b \times d \pmod m$

⑥ 若 $a \equiv b \pmod m$，那么 $a^n \equiv b^n \pmod m$，其中 n 为自然数

⑦ 若 $a \times c \equiv b \times c \pmod m$，$c$ 和 m 的最大公约数为 1，则 $a \equiv b \pmod m$

例 6：2001 年的元旦是星期六，问 2002 年的元旦是星期几？

解：2001 年有 365 天，根据同余的概念及性质，我们可以得出下式：

$$365 = 52 \times 7 + 1 \equiv 8 \pmod 7$$

由上式可知 2002 年元旦是星期日。

5. The Properties of Consecutive Integers(连续整数的性质)

(1)任何两个连续整数中，一定是一奇一偶

(2)任何三个连续整数中，恰有一个数是 3 的倍数，而且这三个连续整数之积能被 6 整除

(3)任何两个连续整数之间除了 1 之外，没有别的公因数，即任何两个连续整数是互质的

(4)$k + 1$ 个连续整数 n，$n+1$，$n+2$，……，$n+k$ 的和是 $\left(n + \dfrac{k}{2}\right) \times (k+1)$

三、The Basic Properties of Square(平方数的基本性质)

1. 平方数的个位是 0,1,4,5,6,9 之一

2. 偶平方数能被 4 整除

3. 奇平方数能被 8 整除余一，即它可写为 $8k + 1$，k 为整数

4. 在相邻的两个自然数的平方之间不存在其他的完全平方数

5. 任何两个相邻自然数之积不是完全平方数

6. 两个奇数的平方之和不是完全平方数

四、自然数 n 次幂的尾数特征

1. 尾数为 2 的数的幂的个位数一定以 2,4,8,6 循环

2. 尾数为 3 的数的幂的个位数一定以 3,9,7,1 循环

3. 尾数为 4 的数的幂的个位数一定以 4,6 循环

4. 尾数为 6 的数的幂的个位数一定以 6 循环

5. 尾数为 7 的数的幂的个位数一定以 7,9,3,1 循环

6. 尾数为 8 的数的幂的个位数一定以 8,4,2,6 循环

7. 尾数为 9 的数的幂的个位数一定以 9,1 循环

例 7：3^{321} 和 7^{123} 的个位哪个大？

解：由以上整数的 n 次幂的特征可知，3 和 7 的 n 次幂的个位数都是每 4 次就循环一次，又由 $321 \div 4$ 余 1，$123 \div 4$ 余 3 可知 3^{321} 的个位数为 3，7^{123} 的个位数与 7^3 的个位数是一样的，即 7^{123} 的个位数为 3，因而 3^{321} 和 7^{123} 的个位相同。

五、The Properties of Factors（与因子有关的特性）

1. 因子数的求法：将数 n 分解为质因子相乘的形式，然后将每个质因子的幂指数分别加 1 之后连乘所得的结果就是 n 的因子的个数，即：

$$n = a^x \cdot b^y \cdot c^z (a, b, c \text{ 为质数})$$
$$\text{因子数} = (x+1)(y+1)(z+1)$$

例 8：求 252 的因子个数。

解：$252 = 2^2 \cdot 7 \cdot 3^2$
所以因子数为 $(2+1)(1+1)(2+1) = 18$

2. 若自然数 n 不是完全平方数，则 n 的因子中小于的占一半，大于的也占一半

3. 若自然数 n 是完全平方数，则 $\sqrt{n}$ 也为 n 的一个因子，在 n 的所有因子中除去 $\sqrt{n}$ 之外，小于 $\sqrt{n}$ 的因子占一半，大于 $\sqrt{n}$ 的因子也占一半

例 9：若 k 和 s 都是自然数，且满足 $k > s$，$k \times s = 42$，问 k 有多少个可能的值？

(A) 4 　　(B) 6 　　(C) 7

(D) 8 　　(E) 10

解：因为 $k \times s = 42$，又 $k > s$，所以可以推得必然有 $k > \sqrt{42}$ 成立，否则将会使 $k < s$，又因为 $k \times s = 42$，即 k 为 42 的一个因子，因而原题转化为问：42 有多少个大于 $\sqrt{42}$ 的因子。由上述性质可知有如下计算：$42 = 2 \times 3 \times 7$，则 42 有 $(1+1)(1+1)(1+1) = 8$ 个因子，即 42 有 $\frac{8}{2} = 4$ 个大于 $\sqrt{42}$ 的因子，因而 k 有 4 个可能的值，答案为 (A)。

4. 推论：任何一个自然数若有奇数个因子，则此自然数必为完全平方数，若它有偶数个因子，则此数必不为完全平方数

5. 若自然数 n 有 m 个因子，且 m 为大于 2 的质数，则 n 必为某一质数的 $m-1$ 次方

例 10：若某一自然数除了 1 之外只有 2 个因子，则这个自然数必为：

(A) 奇数　　(B) 偶数　　(C) 4 的倍数

(D) 某一质数的平方　　(E) 质数

解：既然这个数除了 1 之外只有 2 个因子，则这个数应有 3 个因子（因把 1 加上）；因为 3 是一个大于 2 的质数，所以它必然是某一质数的 $(3-1)$ 次方，答案为 (D)。

6. 只有 1 个因子的自然数只有 1 个，它是 1

7. 只有 2 个因子的自然数都是质数

8. 有两个以上（不包括两个）因子的数都是合数

第二节　分数、小数和百分比
（Fractions, Decimals and Percent）

一、Fractions and Decimals（分数和小数）

In a fraction $\frac{a}{b}$, ($b \neq 0$) a is the numerator（分子）and b is the denominator（分母）. The denominator of a fraction can never be 0, because division by 0 is not defined.

1. The Concept of Fractions（分数的概念）

（1）**Proper Fractions（真分数）**

值小于 1 的分数。例如：$\frac{2}{3}$，$\frac{3}{4}$

（2）**Improper Fractions（假分数）**

值大于或等于 1 的分数。例如：$\frac{4}{4}$，$\frac{9}{4}$

（3）**Simple Fraction（既约分数）**

亦称为"最简分数"。当一分数的分子和分母没有大于 1 的公约数时，称为"既约分数"。例如：$\frac{3}{4}$

（4）**Mixed Number（带分数）**

带分数是指一个数由一个整数和一个分数构成。例如：$1\frac{2}{5}$

2. The Properties of Fractions（分数的性质）

（1）**Addition and Subtraction of Fractions（分数的加法和减法）：**

两个不同分母的分数相加减时，首先把它们变成相同分母的分数（Equivalent Fractions），然后分母不变把分子相加减，在两个分数通分时，取两分数的分母的最小公倍数（least common multiple）。

（2）**Multiplication and Division of Fractions（分数的乘法和除法）：**

两个分数相乘时，把分子分母分别相乘，然后再约分，也可先约分再把分子分母相乘；

两个分数相除时，把除数的分子分母交换位置，然后再与被除数相乘。

Time Saver：Just as in multiplication, when you divide fractions, always combine and factor terms within each fraction, where possible, before you actually do the division.

3. The Properties of Decimals（小数的性质）

In the decimal system, the position of the period or decimal point determines the place value of the digits. For example, the digits in the number **8,796.435** have the following place values：

　　　　8——**thousands' digit**（千位数字）

　　　　7——**hundreds' digit**（百位数字）

　　　　9——**tens' digit**（十位数字）

　　　　6——**ones or units' digit**（个位数字）

　　　　4——**tenths' digit**（十分位数字）

3——**hundredths' digit**（百分位数字）

5——**thousandths' digit**（千分位数字）

注意：**digit** 是"数字"，即 **0,1,2,3,4,5,6,7,8,9** 这十个阿拉伯数字；**number** 是"数"，如 **898** 是一个数，由 **3** 个 **digit** 组成。

4. Scientific Notation（科学计数法）

Decimals are expressed as the product of a number with only one digit to the left of the decimal point and a power of 10.

例如：0.0000486 可用科学计数法表示为：4.86×10^{-5}

$8,245,000$ 可用科学计数法表示为：8.245×10^{6}

GRE problems involving decimal numbers sometimes require you to combine these numbers by either multiplying or dividing.

（1）**Multiplying decimal numbers**（小数相乘）. The number of decimal place (digits to the right of the decimal point) in a product should be the same as the total number of decimal places in the numbers you multiply. So to multiply decimal numbers quickly：

Multiply，but ignore the decimal points

Count the total number of decimal places among the numbers you multiplied

Include that number of decimal places in your product

例 11：$0.01 \times 0.02 \times 0.03$ 6 decimal places altogether

$1 \times 2 \times 3 = 6$ Decimals temporarily ignored

$0.01 \times 0.02 \times 0.03 = 0.000006$ Decimal point inserted

（2）**Dividing decimal numbers**（小数相除）. When you divide (or compute a fraction)，you can move the decimal point in both numbers by the same number of places either to the left of right without altering the quotient (value of the fraction). Here is a related examples：

$$228 \div 0.03 \left(\text{or } \frac{228}{0.03} \right) = \frac{22800}{3} = 7200$$

二、Percent，Fraction and Decimal Conversions（百分数、分数及小数的转换）

Many GRE questions will require you to convert percents, fractions, and decimals back and forth from one form to another. Percents are usually less than 100，but they can be 100 or greater as well. Percents greater than one hundred convert to numbers greater than 1.

例 12：How many fifths are in 280%

(A) 1.4   (B) 2.8   (C) 14

(D) 28   (E) 56

解：Convert 280% to a fraction，then reduce to lowest terms（化为最简分式）

$$280\% = \frac{280}{100} = \frac{28}{10} = \frac{14}{5}$$

So，the correct answer is (C).

例 13：A clerk's salary is \$320.00 after a 25% raise. Before the clerk's raise，the

解：320\$是办事员以前工资的 125%，所以我们可用代数法列方程求解：

31

supervisor's salary was 50% greater than the clerk's salary. If the supervisor also receives a raise in the same amount as the clerk's raise, what is the supervisor's salary after the raise?

(A) $370   (B) $424   (C) $448

(D) $480   (E) $576

设以前的工资为 x,则由题意可得出:$1.25x = 320 \Rightarrow x = \$256$

所以管理员的工资 $= \$256 \times 150\% + (\$320 - \$256) = \$448$

三、Problems Involving Ratio and Proportion (比率和比例问题)

GRE ratio problems sometimes involve a whole divided into two or more parts，where your task is to determine either (1) the size of one of the parts (2) the size of the whole. You can solve these problems by setting up algebraic equations.

一个**比率(ratio)**可以表示成许多方式,例如:the ratio of 3 to 4 可被表达为 3 to 4，3:4 或 $\frac{3}{4}$。注意比率中项的顺序是重要的,即 3 to 4 和 4 to 3 不同。

A proportion is simply a statement that two ratios are equal. Since you can express ratios as fractions，you can express a proportion as an equation—for example，$\frac{18}{27} = \frac{2}{3}$. If one of the four terms is missing from the proportion，you can solve for the missing term using algebra.

例 14: Among registered voters in a certain district, the ratio of men to women is 3:5. Of the district currently includes 24,000 registered voters, how many additional men must register to make the ratio 4:5?

(A) 2000   (B) 3000   (C) 4000

(D) 5000   (E) 6000

解: 本题的正确答案为(B),求解可分为三步:

(1) Set up a proportion to determine the current number of registered male voters and female voters:

$$\frac{3}{8} = \frac{x}{24,000} \Rightarrow 8x = 72,000 \Rightarrow x = 9,000$$

Of the 24,000 voters，9,000 are men，and 15,000 are women.

(2) Determine the number of male voters needed altogether for a 4:5 men/women ratio，given that the number of female voters remains unchanged (15,000):

$$\frac{4}{5} = \frac{x}{15,000} \Rightarrow 5x = 60,000 \Rightarrow x = 12,000$$

(3) Since the district currently includes 9,000 male voters，3,000 more are needed to make the ratio 4:5.

第三节　重点试题精练及解析

(A) if the quantity in Column A is greater;

(B) if the quantity in Column B is greater;

(C) if the two quantities are equal;

(D) if the relationship cannot be determined from the information given.

1. How many positive whole numbers less than 81 are NOT equal squares of whole numbers?

　　(A) 9

　　(B) 70

　　(C) 71

　　(D) 72

　　(E) 73

1. 小于81且不等于整数的平方(square)的正整数(positive whole numbers)有多少个?

解：本题的正确答案是(D)。该题也就是问小于81的非完全平方数有多少个。小于81的完全平方数有1,4,9,16,25,36,49,64共8个,而小于81的正整数有80个,所以小于81的非完全平方数有80－8＝72个。

2. 23(784)　　　　24(783)

2. **解**：本题的正确答案为(B)。解答该题时要注意解题技巧。通过对比,我们不难发现两者乘积之间的相互联系,把它们转化为(23×783)的形式:

$$23×784＝23×783＋23;$$
$$24×783＝23×783＋783$$

显然前者小于后者。

3. A printer numbered consecutively the pages of a book, beginning with 1 on the first page. In numbering the pages, he printed a total of 189 digits.

The number of pages in the book　　　100

3. 一个打印员为某本书的页码编号,第一页从1开始。在计算页码时,他共打印了189个数字(digit)。

解：本题的正确答案是(B)。"digit"是"数字"的意思,诸如1,2,3等。10和1000分别是两位数(two-digit number)和三位数(three-digit number),每个数中分别有两个和三个"digit"(数字)。该打印员在打印标号时共打印了189个数字,除去9个仅有个位的数字,还可打印90个两位数字,一共是99页,与100比较,99＜100。

4. m, p, and x are positive integers and $mp = x$

$$m \qquad\qquad x$$

4. m、p 和 x 都是正整数，且 $mp = x$。

解：本题的正确答案为（D）。由于题目中并没有说明 m、p 和 x 是互不相同的正整数，所以当 $p = 1$ 时可解得 $m = x$；当 $p \neq 1$ 时可解得 $x > p$。综上所述 m 和 x 的大小无法判断。

5. $n = 7 \cdot 19^3$

The number of distinct positive factors of n 10

5. 解：本题的正确答案为（B）。该题也就是让考生求 n 的正因子（positive factor）的个数。本章中介绍的因子求解法则是：
$$n = a^x \cdot b^y \cdot c^z \, (a, b, c \text{ 为质数})$$
因子数 $= (x+1)(y+1)(z+1)$
根据此法则可得 n 的因子个数为
$$(1+1) \times (3+1) = 8$$

6. Seven is equal to how many thirds of seven?

(A) $\dfrac{1}{3}$

(B) 1

(C) 3

(D) 7

(E) 21

6. 7 等于多少个 $\dfrac{7}{3}$ （thirds of seven）？

解：本题的正确答案为（C）。$7 \div \dfrac{7}{3} = 3$

考生在解答该题时要注意英语中分数的表示形式：

几分之一为 one ＋ 序数词

三分之一：one third

四分之一：one forth or a quarter

7. How many positive integers less than 20 are equal to the sum of a positive multiple of 3 and a positive multiple of 4?

(A) Two

(B) Five

(C) Seven

(D) Ten

(E) Nineteen

7. 小于 20 且等于 3 的正倍数（positive multiple）与 4 的正倍数的和的正整数有多少个？

解：本题的正确答案是（D）。满足题中要求的正整数可表示为：
$$n = 3a + 4b \, (a, b \geqslant 1)$$

a	1	1	1	1	2	2	2	3	3	4
b	1	2	3	4	1	2	3	1	2	1
n	7	11	15	19	10	14	18	13	17	16

所以满足题目要求的数共有 10 个。本题不一定非数出 10 个不可，当数出 7 个以上时，就可猜出 10 就是正确答案，因为不可能是 19 个。

8. $2\frac{1}{2}$ percent of 1,120 $2^2 \cdot 7$

9.

7	8	9	10	11
16	15	14	13	12
17	18	19	20	21
26	25	24	23	22
27	28	29	30	31

The figure above consists of 25 squares. If the figure were folded along the dotted diagonal to form a flat triangle, then 26 minus the number in the square that would coincide with the square containing 26 would be

(A) 13   (B) 14   (C) 15

(D) 16   (E) 17

10. What is the remainder when 6^3 is divided by 8?

(A) 5   (B) 3   (C) 2

(D) 1   (E) 0

11. $4-n \ \Box \ 6$

$4-n \ \Box \ 5$

Which of the following symbols should be substituted for $\Box$ to make both of the statements above true for all integers n such that $-2 < n \leqslant 3$?

(A) $\leqslant$ (B) $<$ (C) $=$

(D) $>$ (E) $\geqslant$

8. 解：本题的正确答案为(C)。GER考题中带百分比的题很多,计算时不要忽略%号。另一方面,考生在做该题时,要注意因式的分解及合并,简化计算过程,节省宝贵的时间。

$1,120 \times 2.5\% = 7 \times 4 \times 40 \times 2.5\% = 28$

9. 左边的图形由25个正方形(square)组成。如果这个图形沿对角线(diagonal)(虚线)对折形成一个平的三角形,那么26减去与含26的正方形相对应的正方形内的数字应该是:

解：本题的正确答案是(D)。根据图形可知,对折后与含26的正方形相对应的正方形所含的数字是10,26－10＝16。

10. 6^3 被8除的余数(remainder)是多少?

解：本题的正确答案为(E)。考生在做该题时,可不必先急于算出6^3,然后再除以8,可以这样计算:$6^3 = (2 \times 3)^3 = 2^3 \times 3^3 = 8 \times 3^3$,由此可知$6^3$被8除的余数为0。

11. 下面哪一个符号应当代替"$\Box$",使上面两个式子对所有的满足$-2 < n \leqslant 3$的整数都成立?

解：本题的正确答案是(A)。该题实际上也就是找一个符号填入两个式子中,使得当n取$-2 < n \leqslant 3$之间的所有整数时,下边的两个式子都成立。

$4-n \ \Box \ 6 \Rightarrow -2 \ \Box \ n$

$4-n \ \Box \ 5 \Rightarrow -1 \ \Box \ n$

在上面两式中等号是不可能成立的,因为根据题意可知n的所有可能取值是$-1,0,1,2$

12. Of the following, which is most nearly equal to $\frac{2}{3}$?

(A) $\frac{3}{4}$ (B) $\frac{5}{6}$ (C) $\frac{7}{9}$

(D) $\frac{11}{15}$ (E) $\frac{15}{21}$

12. 下面哪一个数最接近 $\frac{2}{3}$？

解：本题的正确答案为（E）。该题中五个选项的数值均可表示为 $\frac{2}{3}+$ 余项，余项分别为 $\frac{1}{12}$，$\frac{1}{6}$，$\frac{1}{9}$，$\frac{1}{15}$，$\frac{1}{21}$ 而分母值越大，余项值就越小，就越接近 $\frac{2}{3}$，所以最接近 $\frac{2}{3}$ 的数是 $\frac{15}{21}$。

13. One month Mary used $\frac{1}{6}$ of her monthly salary for a car payment and $\frac{1}{4}$ more than the car payment for rent. What fraction of her monthly salary did Mary use that month for the car payment and rent combined?

(A) $\frac{5}{24}$ (B) $\frac{3}{8}$ (C) $\frac{5}{12}$

(D) $\frac{1}{2}$ (E) $\frac{7}{12}$

13. 某月 Mary 用月薪的 $\frac{1}{6}$ 来支付车款，房租比车款多 $\frac{1}{4}$。Mary 这个月用于支付车款和房租的钱占其月薪的比例为多少？

解：本题的正确答案为（B）。考生在解此题要注意对比较级的正确理解。More than 前后两事物才是比较体，more 前的分数"1/4"是后者（payment for the car）的 1/4，而不是总体（salary）的 $\frac{1}{4}$，因此车款和房租两者占月薪的比例为：

$$\frac{1}{6}+\frac{1}{6}\left(1+\frac{1}{4}\right)=\frac{3}{8}$$

14. For which of the following pairs of integers is the least common multiple of the integers minus their greatest common divisor the greatest?

(A) 3, 12

(B) 5, 6

(C) 10, 20

14. 下列哪一对数的最小公倍数与最大公约数的差最大？

解：本题的正确答案是（D）。"the least common multiple"是最小公倍数；"the greatest common divisor"是最大公约数

(A) $12-3=8$

(B) $30-1=29$

(C) $20-10=10$

(D) 11，12

(E) 15，30

15. x percent of 24 is 12

x	50

16. When $x+2$ is divided by 5 the remainder is 3

The remainder when x is divided by 5	2

17. $$n=7 \cdot 19^3$$

The number of distinct positive factors of n	10

18. $$1<n<5$$

n is an integer

The sum of the first n odd integers that are greater than zero	n^2-1

19.

$$754 \overline{) 4\,5\,3\,\square}$$
$$\underline{4\,5\,2\,\triangle}$$
$$6$$
$$8$$

In the correctly worked division problem above, each of the symbols $\square$ and $\triangle$ represents a digit.

$\square$	$\triangle$

(D) $132-1=131$

(E) $30-15=15$

15. 解：本题的正确答案为(C)。做此题时，考生一定不要粗心大意，把百分数当小数来处理：

$$24x=12 \Rightarrow x=0.5 < 50$$

要注意 x 后面的 percent，由此可得

$$24 \times x\% =12 \Rightarrow x=50$$

16. 当 $x+2$ 被 5 除时，余数(remainder)是 3。

解：本题的正确答案是(B)。设 n 为整数，$\dfrac{x+2}{5}$ 的余数为 3，则有：

$$x+2=5n+3$$
$$x=5n+1$$

所以 x 被 5 除时余数是 1。

17. 解：本题的正确答案为(B)。任一个正整数 n 都可以分解为质因子(positive factor)幂(exponent)乘积的形式。对于本题中的 7 和 19 都是质数，所以 7×19^3 有 $(1+1) \times (3+1)=8$ 个因子，具体为：

$$1,7,19,19^2,19^3,7 \times 19,7 \times 19^2,7 \times 19^3。$$

18. 解：本题的正确答案为(A)。左项为大于 0 的前 n 个奇数的和，注意前 n 个大于 0 的奇数的和为 n^2，n 为个数，例如 $1+3=2^2$，$1+3+5=3^2$，$1+3+5+7=4^2$ 等。

19. 在上面正确的除法(division)计算中，$\square$ 和 $\triangle$ 分别代表一个数字。

解：本题的正确答案为(B)。考生经仔细观察就可发现，此题其实根本就不需要计算：在上面的除法中，两个带有符号的数的十位上的数分别为 3 和 2，而余数只是一个 1 位数，显然在减法过程中需向被除数的十位借 1，因而 $\square < \triangle$。

20. In a list of numbers, the first number is 3, the second is 4, and each subsequent number is the sum of all the preceding numbers in the list. If the 20th number in the list is x, what is the 25th number in the list?

(A) $7x$ (B) $16x$ (C) $32x$

(D) $35x$ (E) $161x$

21. Which of the following numbers is both a factor of 48 and a multiple of 6?

(A) 2   (B) 8   (C) 12

(D) 16   (E) 18

22. The least common denominator of

$\frac{1}{2}, \frac{1}{3}$, and $\frac{1}{4}$ 15

23. 3×10^4 is greater than 4×10^3 by what percent?

(A) 25% (B) 75%

(C) $133 \frac{1}{3}\%$ (D) 650%

(E) 750%

24. If r and s are positive integers, each greater than 1, and if $11(s-1)=13(r-1)$, what is the least possible value of $r+s$?

(A) 2

(B) 11

(C) 2

(D) 24

(E) 26

---

20. 在一个数列中,首项为 3,第二项为 4,并且下一项是前面所有项的和。若该数列中第 20 项是 x,问第 25 项是多少?

解:本题的正确答案为(C)。第 20 项为 x,则前 19 项的和也是 x,第 21 项为 $2x$,22 项为 $4x$,由此可推出第 25 项是 $32x$。

21. 下面哪一个数既是 48 的因子(facor)又是 6 的倍数(multiple)?

解:本题的正确答案为(C)。几个数中显然只有 12 满足题目的要求。

22. 解:本题的正确答案为(B)。"the least common denominator"是最小公分母,也就是分母的最小公倍数,2,3 和 4 的最小公倍数是 12,所以 $\frac{1}{2}$,$\frac{1}{3}$ 和 $\frac{1}{4}$ 的最小公分母为 12。

23. 3×10^4 比 4×10^3 大百分之几?

解:本题的正确答案为(D)。在解答此题时,考生一定不要认为大百分之几一定是小于 100%,如本题:

$$(3 \times 10^3 - 4 \times 10^3) / 4 \times 10^3 = 6.5$$
$$= 650\%。$$

24. 若 r 和 s 都是大于 1 的正整数(positive integer),且有 $11(s-1)=13(r-1)$,问 $r+s$ 的最小值是多少?

解:本题的正确答案是(E)。"the least possible value"是"最小值"的意思。

一个数要想被另一个数整除,必须含有对方所含有的质数因子。由题中的已知条件可得:$s-1=\dfrac{13(r-1)}{11}$,$s-1$ 必为一个大于零的整数,所以等式右项中的 $13(r-1)$ 必能被 11 整除,而 13 很明显不能被 11 整除,因此 $r-1$ 必须能被 11 整除,而 r 最小值为 12,

25. $\dfrac{1}{\dfrac{1}{3}+\dfrac{1}{5}+\dfrac{1}{7}}$ $\dfrac{1}{3}+\dfrac{1}{5}+\dfrac{1}{7}$

25. 解：本题的正确答案为（A）。解答此题要注意技巧，考生只要稍加观察，就会发现：

$\dfrac{1}{3}+\dfrac{1}{5}+\dfrac{1}{7}<\dfrac{1}{3}+\dfrac{1}{3}+\dfrac{1}{3}=1$，由此式可以

得到：$\dfrac{1}{\dfrac{1}{3}+\dfrac{1}{5}+\dfrac{1}{7}}>1>\dfrac{1}{3}+\dfrac{1}{5}+\dfrac{1}{7}$

26. $d=5.03894$ and $\boxed{d}$ is the decimal expression for d rounded to the nearest thousandth.

　　The number of decimal
　　places where d and $\boxed{d}$ differ　　4

26. $d=5.03894$ 且 $\boxed{d}$ 是 d 四舍五入到千分位的小数表达（decimal expression）。

解：本题的正确答案是（B）。"to the nearest"是汉语中"四舍五入"最常见的表达方式。所以 $\boxed{d}=5.039$。解答该题的关键在于精确理解比较左项的意义，注意：Where 引导的定语从句修饰的是 places，即左项意义为 d 和 $\boxed{d}$ 的小数位置上的数不相同的数目。d 和 $\boxed{d}$ 在千分位，万分位，十万分位 3 个位置上的数都不同。

27. When integer n is divided by 9, the remainder is 2.

　　The remainder when
　　n is divided by 3　　　　　　2

27. 整数 n 被 9 除时，余数（remainder）为 2。
　　n 被 3 除的余数 2。

解：本题的正确答案为（C）。根据题意整数 n 可以表示为：$n=9m+2$，其中 m 是整数，显然 $9m$ 可以被 3 整除，所以 n 被 3 除时余数仍为 2。

28. The sum of n different positive integers is less than 100. What is the greatest possible value of n?

(A) 10
(B) 11
(C) 12
(D) 13
(E) 14

28. n 个不同正整数的和小于 100，问 n 的最大值（the greatest possible value）是多少？

解：本题的正确答案是（D）。要求 n 的最大值，就要使每个加数都尽可能的小。而题中已限制加数为不同的正整数，所以要使加数的个数最多，只能从最小正整数开始，依次从小到大取值，即 $1+2+3\cdots\cdots<100$。任取 $n=13$，则 1 加至 13 的和为 91，小于 100 而不可能再加上 14，否则将不能满足小于 100 的条件。

29. If p is a prime number greater than 11, and p is the sum of the two prime numbers x and y, then x could be which of the following?

(A) 2
(B) 5
(C) 7
(D) 9
(E) 13

30. Of the positive integers that are multiples of 30 and are less than or equal to 360, what fraction are multiples of 12 ?

(A) $\dfrac{1}{6}$

(B) $\dfrac{1}{5}$

(C) $\dfrac{1}{3}$

(D) $\dfrac{2}{5}$

(E) $\dfrac{1}{2}$

31. If x, y and z are consecutive integers and $x<y<z$, which of the following must be true?

Ⅰ xyz is even.

Ⅱ $x+y+z$ is even.

Ⅲ $(x+y)(y+z)$ is odd.

(A) None   (B) Ⅰ only

(C) Ⅱ only   (D) Ⅰ and Ⅲ only

(E) Ⅰ, Ⅱ, and Ⅲ

29. 若 p 是比 11 大的质数（prime number），且 p 等于两个质数 x，y 的和，则 x 可能是下面的哪一个？

解： 本题的正确答案为(A)。考生在解答此题时，应比较熟悉质数、奇数与偶数之间的相互关系。p 是比 11 大的质数，所以 p 必是奇数。而 p 同时又是两质数的和，由于一个奇数只可能是一个奇数与一个偶数之和，故 x、y 中必有一个是 2（因为除 2 以外，其他质数均为奇数）。若 y 取 2 时，则 x 无论取五个选项中的哪一个都不能满足题意，所以必有 $x=2$。

30. 在小于等于 360 的 30 的正倍数中，12 的倍数占了几分之几？

解： 本题的正确答案是(E)。该题也就是求 30 和 12 的最小公倍数占了小于等于 360 的 30 的正倍数的几分之几。解答该题的关键在于理解"of"这个介词的作用。意为"…中"，而 that 引导的定语从句修饰这些正整数，fraction 译为分数，what fraction 译为几分之几？30 与 12 的最小公倍数是 60，是 30 的倍数并且小于等于 360 的正整数共有 12 个，很显然是 60 的倍数并且小于等于 360 的正整数共有 6 个，所以 $\dfrac{1}{2}$ 是正确答案。

31. 若 x，y，z 是连续整数（consecutive integers），且 $x<y<z$，则下面哪一个一定正确？

Ⅰ xyz 是偶数。

Ⅱ $x+y+z$ 是偶数。

Ⅲ $(x+y)(y+z)$ 是奇数。

解： 本题的正确答案为(D)。由 x,y,z 是连续整数可知，则这一个数存在两种形式：奇偶奇或偶奇偶。因为有一个数是偶数，则其乘积就一定为偶数，所以无论是哪种情况，xyz 总是偶数；$x+y+z$ 只在奇偶奇情形是偶数；$(x+y)$ 和 $(y+z)$ 都是奇数，故乘积必为奇数，因此一定正确的是Ⅰ和Ⅲ。

32. The product of two consecutive positive integers CANNOT be

(A) a prime number

(B) divisible by 11

(C) a multiple of 13

(D) an even number less than 10

(E) a number having 4 as its units digit

32. 两个连续正整数的积不能是：

解：本题的正确答案是(E)。解决这类数字规律题一般情况下应采用排除法，通过找反例的途径来排除错误选项。(A) 不对，因为惟一的例外是 $1 \times 2 = 2$；(B) 显然不对，如 10 与 11,11 与 12 等；(C) 同理也不对；(D) 两个连续整数的积是一个偶数是肯定的，但完全可以大于 10，所以不对。(E) 找不到反例，两个连续正整数的积的个位数不可能为 4。两个连续整数的积的个位数是由它们的个位数的积所决定的，考生很容易发现在 0 到 9 这 10 个数中任意两个连续整数的积的个位数都不等于 4，即两个连续整数的积的个位数不可能是 4。

33. When a certain number is divided by 7, the remainder is 0. If the remainder is not 0 when the number is divided by 14, then the remainder must be

(A) 1

(B) 2

(C) 4

(D) 6

(E) 7

33. 某数被 7 除时余数为 0,若被 14 除时余数不为 0,那么余数一定是

解：本题的正确答案为(E)。该数是 7 的倍数，可分两种情况：

(1) 该数是 7 的奇数倍,可写成：
$$7n = 7 \cdot (2k+1) = 14k+7,$$
其中 $n = 2k+1$

(2) 该数是 7 的偶数倍,可写成：
$$7n = 7 \cdot 2k = 14k, \text{其中 } n = 2k$$

由以上可知，当该数不能被 14 整除时，其余数一定是 7。

34. How many of the positive integers less than 25 are 2 less than an integer multiple of 4?

(A) Two   (B) Three   (C) Four
(D) Five   (E) Six

34. 在比 25 小的正整数中,有多少个数比 4 的倍数小 2?

解：本题的正确答案为(E)。考生仔细考虑一下就会发现，该题其实就是找小于 $(25+2)$ 的正整数中有多少是 4 的倍数，因为 $(25+2) \div 4 = 6$ 余 1,所以有 6 个数比 4 的倍数小 2。

35. If y is the average (arithmetic mean) of n consecutive positive integers, $n>1$, what is the sum of the greatest and least of these integers?

(A) $2y$　　(B) ny　　(C) $\dfrac{y}{2}$

(D) $\dfrac{y}{n}$　　(E) $\dfrac{2n}{y}$

36. The product of two integers is 6.

The sum of the two integers　　　3

37. A positive integer with exactly two different divisors greater than 1 must be

(A) a prime

(B) an even integer

(C) a multiple of 3

(D) the square of a prime

(E) the square of an odd integer

38. What is the least prime number greater than 83?

35. 若 y 是 n 个连续正整数(consecutive positive integers)的算术平均数,且 $n>1$,这些数的最大值和最小值的和是多少?

解:本题的正确答案是(A)。连续正整数具有一个特殊的性质,即 n 个连续正整数的算术平均值为这 n 个数中最大数与最小数的算术平均值。由此可知,在本题中最小值和最大值的和为这 n 个数的算术平均值的两倍,即为 $2y$。

36. **解:**本题的正确答案为(D)。两整数乘积为 6,则这两个整数可同时取正值,也可同时取负值。当这两个数同时取正值时,它们的和大于 3,而当它们同时取负值时,则它们的和将显然小于 3,所以本题为无法判断。

37. 仅有两个不同的大于 1 的因子的正整数一定是:

解:本题的正确答案是(D)。大多数考生在做本题时都用了排除法,虽然用排除法也可把本题做对,但是这种方法却是不对的。考生在解答本题时一定要正确理解题意,该题问的是具有两个大于 1 的不同因子的数一定是什么样的数,并不一定这样的数都具有两个大于 1 的不同因子。因此解答本题时不应当用找反例的排除法,而是找这个选项是否包含了所有的具有这个性质的数。这样就排除了诸如(E)这类的选项,因为 4 也具有这个性质,而它不是奇数的平方。具有两个不同的大于 1 的因子的数,共有 3 个因子而因子数求解公式中只有质数的平方才具有 3 个因子。所以(D)是正确答案。请注意问题中的"must be"。

38. 比 83 大的最小质数(prime number)是多少?

解:本题的正确答案为(D)。因为质数是只有 1

(A) 85   (B) 87   (C) 88

(D) 89   (E) 91

和它本身而不再有其他因子的数，而(A)、(B)、(C)和(E)均有其他因子，所以此题的正确答案为(D)。

39.

| The number of different prime factors of 48 | The number of different prime factors of 72 |

39. 解：本题的正确答案为(C)。对于求质因子个数的题，一般都要先把它们写成质因子相乘的形式：

$$48 = 2^4 \times 3$$
$$72 = 2^3 \times 3^2$$

可以发现两者各有两相同质因子2,3。注意不要把题目问的质因子数与因子数相混，否则就会错误地得到48的因子数$(4+1) \times (1+1) = 10$ 比72的因子数 $(3+1) \times (2+1) = 12$ 少。

40.

| The number of different positive divisors of 12 | The number of different positive divisors of 50 |

40. 12的不同*正因子*(positive divisor)个数

50的不同正因子个数

解：本题的正确答案为(C)。先把12,50分解成质因子乘积形式

$$12 = 2^2 \times 3^1$$
$$50 = 2^1 \times 5^2$$

因此，它们的因子数均为 $(1+1) \times (2+1) = 6$ 个。

41. The number that is as much greater than 63 as it is less than 101   84

41. 解：本题的正确答案是(B)。左项为比63大的量与比101小的量相同的数，注意题中that引导的定语从句修饰前面的"the number"，而"as much as"是指什么和什么一样多，因此可设该数为x，由题意可得：

$$x - 63 = 101 - x \Rightarrow x = 82$$

42. A K-number is a positive integer with the special property that 3 times its units' digit is equal to 2 times its tens' digit.

The number of K-numbers between 10 and 99   3

42. K是一个具有特殊性质的正整数：其个位数(units)的3倍等于十位数(tens)的2倍。

解：本题的正确答案为(C)。该题中的K-number为题中定义的一个函数，其个位数与十位数的关系为：$3m = 2n$（m为个位数,n为十位数）。题目中的左项为10到99之间的

43. Of the following, which is greatest?

(A) $\dfrac{1}{2}$ (B) $\dfrac{7}{15}$ (C) $\dfrac{49}{100}$

(D) $\dfrac{126}{250}$ (E) $\dfrac{1,999}{4,000}$

43. 下列数中,哪一个最大?

解:本题的正确答案为(D)。五个数中显然只有 $\dfrac{126}{250}$ 大于 $\dfrac{1}{2}$,其余均小于或等于 $\dfrac{1}{2}$。

44. $n=2^4 \cdot 5^6$

K is an integer.

10^k is a factor of n.

The greatest possible

value of 10^k 10,000

44. 解:本题的正确答案是(C)。10^k 是 n 的一个因子,因此有:$10^k \leqslant 2^4 \cdot 5^6 = 2^4 \cdot 5^6 = 2^4 \cdot 5^4 \cdot 5^2 = 10^4 \cdot 5^2$,所以 10^k 的最大可能值为

$$10^4 = 10000。$$

45. $3+\sqrt{49}$ $8+\sqrt{9}$

45. 解:本题的正确答案为(B)。

$$3+\sqrt{49}=3+7=10, \quad 8+\sqrt{9}=8+3=11 > 10$$

46. If $n=pqr$, where p, q, and r are three different positive prime numbers, how many different positive divisors does n have, including 1 and n?

(A) 3   (B) 5   (C) 6

(D) 7   (E) 8

46. 若 $n=pqr$,其中 p, q, r 是 3 个不同的正质数(positive prime numbers),n 有多少个不同的因子,包括 1 和 n?

解:本题的正确答案为(E)。由因子数求解公式可得 $n=p \cdot q \cdot r$,当 p,q,r 为质数时 n 的因子数为 $(1+1)(1+1)(1+1)=8$ 个。

47. In a certain two-digit number, the units' digit is twice the tens' digit.

     The tens' digit   5

47. 在某个两位数(two-digit number)中,个位数字是十位数字的 2 倍。

解:本题的正确答案是(B)。units' digit 指个位的数字;tens' digit 指十位的数字。个位数字是十位数字的 2 倍,那么个位数字只可能是:$2,4,6,8$;十位数字只可能是:$1,2,3,4$,否则将无法满足上面关系。

48. $11 \times 13 \times 17 \times 19 \times 23$

A decrease of 1 in which of the factors above would result in the greatest decrease in the product?

48. 上式中哪一个因子(factor)的值减小 1 将导致该式的乘积减少最大?

解:本题的正确答案为(A)。设 n 为上式中的

(A) 11   (B) 13   (C) 17
(D) 19   (E) 23

49. Each of the following numbers has two digits blotted out. Which of the numbers could be the number of hours in x days, where x is an integer?

(A) 25■,■06

(B) 50■,■26

(C) 56■,■02

(D) 62■,■50

(E) 65■,■20

50. Of the following, which is closest to $\dfrac{0.26 \times 397}{9.9}$?

(A) 1   (B) 10   (C) 70

(D) 100   (E) 700

51. Which of the following numbers is NOT the sum of three consecutive odd integers?

(A) 15   (B) 75   (C) 123

(D) 297   (E) 313

任一个因子,则当 n 减少 1 时,其乘积将减少 $\dfrac{1}{n}$,所以 n 越小时减少的越多。

49. 下面的每个数都被涂掉了两个数字。问下列哪一个是 x(x 是一个整数)天的小时数?

解: 本题的正确答案是(E)。考生在解答该题时要注意应用整除的原则:一个数要想被另一个数整除,必须具有该数所具有的所有的质数因子。因为满足答案的数必须是 x 天的小时数,即 24 的倍数,$24 = 2^3 \cdot 3$。

如果一个数能被 24 整除,那么这个数必须满足三次被 2 整除和一次被 3 整除。能够被 3 整除的数的特性是各个数位上的数字的和能够被 3 整除,由于五个选项的百位、千位数未知,所以不能够用 3 来判定;同时由于这五个选项的千位数未知,所以也不可能用 8 来判定,退而求其次只能够用 4 来判定。而从本章的讲解部分可知,判定一个数能否被 4 整除,主要看这个数的后两位数能否被 4 整除。很显然,(E)为正确答案。请体会本题中的"could be"。

50. 下列选项中,哪一项最接近 $\dfrac{0.26 \times 397}{9.9}$?

解: 本题的正确答案为(B)。因为题目只是要求求近似值,且五个选项的数相差较大,因此考生可以按照下面的方法取各数的近似值进行计算:

$$\frac{0.26 \times 397}{9.9} \approx \frac{0.25 \times 400}{10} = 10$$

51. 下列哪一个不是 3 个连续奇整数(consecutive odd integer)的和?

解: 本题的正确答案是(E)。设 3 个连续奇整数分别为 $2n+1$,$2n+3$,$2n+5$,其中 n 为正数,则 3 个连续奇整数的和 $= (2n+1) + (2n+3) + (2n+5) = 3(2n+3)$,因此 3 个连续奇整数的和必为 3 的倍数。本题中只有(E)不是 3 的倍数。

52.

The number of positive divisors of 24	The number of positive divisors of 50

52. 解：本题的正确答案是（A）。比较的左右项分别为 24 和 50 正因子（positive divisor）的数目，根据因子数求解公式可得：$24 = 2^3 \cdot 3$，所以 24 的因子数为 $(3+1)(1+1) = 8$；$50 = 5^2 \cdot 2$，所以 50 的因子数 $(2+1)(1+1) = 6$。

53. $\dfrac{1}{5}$ $\qquad$ $\dfrac{1}{5} - \dfrac{1}{6} + \dfrac{1}{7} - \dfrac{1}{8} + \dfrac{1}{9}$

53. 解：本题的正确答案为（A）。细心的考生会发现该题实际上不需要计算，只需比较几个数的大小即可：

$$\frac{1}{6} > \frac{1}{7}, \frac{1}{8} > \frac{1}{9}$$

$$\Rightarrow -\frac{1}{6} + \frac{1}{7} - \frac{1}{8} + \frac{1}{9} < 0$$

$$\Rightarrow \frac{1}{5} > \frac{1}{5} - \frac{1}{6} + \frac{1}{7} - \frac{1}{8} + \frac{1}{9}$$

54. $\dfrac{2 \times 2 \times 2 \times 2 \times 2}{2 + 2 + 2 + 2} =$

(A) 1 $\qquad$ (B) 2 $\qquad$ (C) 4

(D) 8 $\qquad$ (E) 16

54. 解：本题的正确答案为（C）。

$$原式 = \frac{2^5}{2 \times 4} = 4$$

55. $\qquad$ n is an even integer.

The number of different prime factors of n	The number of different prime factors of $2n$

55. 解：本题的正确答案为（C）。比较的左项为 n 的不同质因子（prime factor）数，比较的右项为 $2n$ 的不同质因子数。对于 2 来说，只有 1 个质因子，即 2 本身；而 n 为偶数，所以 2 本来就是 n 的质因子，因此 n 与 $2n$ 的质因子数相同。

56. A dresser drawer contains 15 garments. If 40 percent of those garments are blouses, how many are not blouses?

(A) 6 $\qquad$ (B) 8 $\qquad$ (C) 9

(D) 10 $\qquad$ (E) 12

56. 一梳妆台的抽屉中有 15 件衣服，若那些衣服的 40% 是上衣，那么有多少件不是上衣？

解：本题的正确答案为（C）。根据题意可得：

$$15 \times (1 - 40\%) = 9 \text{ 件}$$

57. If k is an integer and $5^k < 20000$, what is the greatest possible value of k?

(A) 6 $\qquad$ (B) 7 $\qquad$ (C) 8

(D) 9 $\qquad$ (E) 10

57. 若 k 是整数，且 $5^k < 20000$，那么 k 的最大值（greatest possible value）是多少？

解：本题的正确答案为（A）。先把 20000 化成乘积的形式：

$$20000 = 2 \times 10^4 = 2 \times (2 \times 5)^4 = 2^5 \times 5^4$$

因为 $5^2 < 2^5 < 5^3$，所以 k 最大能取 $2+4 = 6$。

58. 8^6 　　　　　　　　　4^9

58. 解：本题的正确答案为(C)。对两数的幂比较大小时，一般要将它们化成同底或同指数的形式，具体化成哪种形式，要因题而易。对于本题可化成同底的形式：
$$8^6=(2^3)^6=2^{18}$$
$$4^9=(2^2)^9=2^{18}$$

59. A bonus of $450 plus a 9 percent increase in annual salary　　　A bonus of $500 plus an 8.5 percent increase in annual salary

59. 解：本题的正确答案为(D)。比较的左项为 $450 的奖金加上年薪增加 9%；比较的右项为 $500 的奖金加上年薪增加 8.5%。因为不知道年薪为多少，所以无法判断两者孰大孰小。

60. Richard's salary, which is greater than $10,000, is 75 percent of Sandra's salary. Ted's salary is 80 percent of Richard's salary.

Sandra's salary　　　Ted's salary

60. Richard 的薪水是 Sandra 薪水的 75%，且多于 $10,000，Ted 的薪水是 Richard 薪水的 80%。

Sandra 的薪水　　　Ted 的薪水

解：本题的正确答案为（A）。该题中出现的 $10,000 是考生做题的干扰信息，因为考生只需根据 Ted＝ 80% Richard，Richard＝ 75% Sandra 就可得出他三人的薪水关系如下：

Ted's＜ Rrichard's＜Sandra

61. On a trip, Marie drove 200 miles in 5 hours using gasoline that cost her $1.49 per gallon.

Marie's average speed for the trip in miles per hour　　　Marie's gas mileage for the trip in miles per gallon

61. 某旅程中，Marie 5 小时开出了 200 英里，汽车使用的汽油价格是每加仑 1.49 美元。

解：本题的正确答案为(D)。比较的左项为以英里每小时为单位，Marie 旅程的平均速度；比较的右项为以英里每加仑为单位，Marie 旅程的汽车里程。根据题目中所提供的信息可以求出 Marie 旅程的平均速度＝200/5 ＝ 40mile/h；但是题目中未给出汽车所消耗的汽油数，因此无法计算每加仑汽油能行驶的英里数，从而也就无法判断两数的大小。

62. The number 10^{30} is divisible by all of the following EXCEPT

(A) 250　　　　(B) 125

62. 10^{30} 能被下面除_____之外的所有的数整除 (divisible)。

解：本题的正确答案为(E)。把 10^{30} 分解可得：
$$10^{30}=(2\times5)^{30}=2^{30}\cdot5^{30}$$

(C) 32 (D) 16

(E) 6

显然 10^{30} 没有质因子 3,而(E)选项 6 含质因子 3,所以 10^{30} 不能被 6 整除。

63. The greatest The greatest

  prime factor prime factor

  of 15   of 14

63. 15 的最大质因子 14 的最大质因子

解:本题的正确答案为(B)。该题是个考生比较 15 和 14 的最大质因子(greatest prime factor)的大小。由 $15=3\times5$ 可得 15 的最大质因子是 5;由 $14=2\times7$ 可得 14 的最大质因子是 7,所以前者小于后者。

64. What is the greatest positive integer n so that 2^n is a factor of 12^{10}?

(A) 10 (B) 12 (C) 16

(D) 20 (E) 60

64. 正整数 n 最大能取多少使得 2^n 是 12^{10} 的因子?

解:本题的正确答案为(D)。将 12^{10} 分解成质因子幂乘积的形式:
$$12^{10}=(2^2\times3)^{10}=2^{20}\times3^{10}$$
因此 n 最大可取 20。

65. If a certain company purchased its computer terminals for a total of \$540,400 and each of the terminals was purchased for \$350, how many terminals did the company purchase?

(A) 1,624   (B) 1,544

(C) 1,434   (D) 1,384

(E) 1,264

65. 若某公司购买计算机终端总计花费 \$540,400,且每一台计算机终端花费 \$350,那么公司购买了多少台终端?

解:本题的正确答案为(B)。根据计算机终端的总额和单价可得终端数量为:
$$\$540,400/\$350=1544。$$

66. At College C there are from 2 to 4 introductory philosophy classes each semester, and each of these classes has from 20 to 30 students enrolled. If one semester 10 percent of the students enrolled in introductory philosophy failed, what is the greatest possible number who failed?

(A) 12 (B) 10 (C) 8

(D) 6 (E) 3

66. 学院 C 每学期开 2 到 4 个班的哲学导论,每个班的在册学生为 20~30 人。若某一学期有 10% 的选哲学导论课的学生不及格,问最多有多少人不及格?

解:本题的正确答案为(A)。因为不及格的比例已经给出,所以不及格最多的情况是有尽可能多的学生选哲学导论课,也即学院 C 每学期开设四个哲学导论班,每个班有 30 人选修,这样不及格人数为 $4\times30\times10\%=12$ 人。

67. 3^4 4^3

67. 解： 本题的正确答案为（A）。该题中作比较的两项的数值都比较小，因此可以直接计算：

$$(3^4 = 81) > (4^3 = 64)。$$

68. Of the following, which is the closest approximation to

$$\sqrt{\frac{(97.942)(0.261)}{(0.51)^2}}?$$

(A) 1   (B) 5   (C) 10

(D) 20   (E) 100

68. 下列哪一项的值最接近于

$$\sqrt{\frac{(97.942)(0.261)}{(0.51)^2}}?$$

解： 本题的正确答案为（C）。五个选项中的数值之间差距较大，因此可以在一定的范围内做近似计算，并且可以保证结果的可靠性。观察后发现 0.51^2 的值与 0.261 相近，而 97.942 的值又与 100 相近，所以根据题意可得：

$$\sqrt{\frac{(97.942)(0.261)}{(0.51)^2}} \approx \sqrt{\frac{(100)(0.25)}{0.25}}$$
$$= \sqrt{100} = 10$$

69. In each of the years 1983 and 1984, the total number of automobiles sold in the United States was 1.2 million more than in the previous year.

Percent increase in the number of automobiles sold in 1983 over 1982	Percent increase in the number of automobiles sold in 1984 over 1983

69. 在 1983 年和 1984 年这两年的每一年中美国汽车的总销售量均比前一年增加 120 万辆。

解： 本题的正确答案为（A）。比较的左项为 1983 年比 1982 年汽车销售数量增长的百分数，比较的右项为 1984 年比 1983 年汽车销售数量增长的百分数。因为题目中未给出 1982 年的汽车销售量，所以某些考生认为该题无法进行比较。其实不然，考生经仔细分析都会发现，两个百分数的大小虽然不能确定，但是他们的相对大小还是可以确定的：

设 1982 年销售汽车 x 万辆，则 1983 年比 1982 年销售增长的百分比 $= 120/x$，1984 年比 1983 年增长的百分比 $= 120/(x+120)$，两个百分比的分子相同，但分母不同，显然 $x < x+120$，因此前者增长的百分比大于后者。

70. A school district has 1,989 computers, which is approximately one computer for every 68.6 students. Of the following, which is the closest approximation, in

70. 一校区有 1989 台计算机，大约为 68.6 名学生一台，以千为单位，下面哪一项最接近校区的学生数？

解： 本题的正确答案为（C）。此题比较简单，大

thousands, of the number of students in the school district?

(A) 30

(B) 120

(C) 140

(D) 160

(E) 200

多数的考生都会这样来解这道题：由平均68.6 人一台电脑可得该校区共有 1989×68.6≈136,445≈140,000 名学生。但是考生要注意的一点是，本题只是让求近似解，因此可以通过取近似值的办法来大大简化计算过程，1989≈2000，68.6≈70，由此可以口算出该校区学生人数为 140 千。

71. A certain spiral staircase is designed so that each step after the first one is turned 20° counterclockwise from the one immediately below it, how many of the steps make up $2\frac{1}{2}$ complete revolutions?

(A) 18　　(B) 36　　(C) 38

(D) 45　　(E) 50

71. 某一螺旋梯按照高一级台阶相对于低一级台阶逆时针旋转 20° 来设计，问 $2\frac{1}{2}$ 圈的旋梯共有多少级台阶组成？

解：本题的正确答案为（D）。"revolution"意为旋转一周，由题意可得台阶数为：

$$360° \times 2\frac{1}{2} \div 20° = 45$$

72. If n is an odd integer, then $n^2 - 1$ must be

(A) a prime number

(B) an odd integer

(C) divisible by 8

(D) a multiple of 2^n

(E) a positive integer

72. 若 n 是奇数，则 $n^2 - 1$：

（A）质数

（B）奇数

（C）能被 8 整除

（D）2^n 的倍数

（E）正整数

解：本题的正确答案为（C）。因为 n 是奇数，所以 n 可以表达成 $n = 2k + 1$，k 是整数。由此可得：

$n^2 - 1 = (n+1)(n-1) = (2k+2)2k = 4k(k+1)$，显然 $k(k+1)$ 是两个连续整数的乘积，必然为一偶数，所以 $(n^2 - 1)$ 能被 8 整除。

73. x is the sum of the first 25 positive even integers. y is the sum of the first 25 positive odd integers.

$$x \qquad\qquad y + 25$$

73. x 是前 25 个**正偶数**（positive even integer）之和，y 是前 25 个**正奇数**（positive odd integer）之和。

解：本题的正确答案为（C）。由第 n 个偶数总比第 n 个奇数多 1（n 为正整数），可知前 25 个正偶数之和比前 25 个正奇数之和大 25。

74. In a new housing development，one house sold for \$140,000，and all the rest sold for \$100,000 each.

| The average (arithmetic mean) selling price of all the houses sold in the new development | \$102,000 |

74. 在一个房地产的开发项目中，一幢房卖了 \$140,000，剩下的每幢房都卖了 \$100,000。

| 在这个项目中平均每间房屋的售价 | \$102,000 |

解：本题的正确答案为(D)。比较的左项为该开发项目中所有房子的平均售价，但是题目中并未给出房子的总数，所以我们只知道其平均价格在 \$100,000 与 \$140,000 之间，而无法判断这些房子的平均价格与 \$102,000 谁大谁小。

75. k is an integer greater than 1.

| The number of positive divisors of 3^k | $k+1$ |

75. k 是比 1 大的整数。

| 3^k 的正因子 (positive divisor) 个数 | $k+1$ |

解：本题的正确答案为(C)。根据因子数的求解法则可知，3^k 的不同正因子个数为 $k+1$ 个。

76. When the even integer n is divided by 7, the remainder is 3.

| The remainder when n is divided by 14 | 10 |

76. 当一个偶数 n 被 7 除时，余数是 3。

解：本题的正确答案为(C)。比较的左项为 n 被 14 除时的余数。由 n 被 7 除余 3 可知 n 可表示为 $n=7k+3$，其中 k 是整数。又因为 n 是偶数，所以 k 必为奇数，因此 n 又可表示为：

$n = 7(2m+1)+3 = 14m+10$，m 是整数，所以 n 被 14 除余数是 10。

77. If the sum of five consecutive even integers is 70，what is the value of the greatest of the five integers.

(A) 12   (B) 14   (C) 18
(D) 20   (E) 22

77. 若 5 个连续偶数(consecutive even integer) 的和为 70，则 5 个数中数值最大的数是多少？

解：本题的正确答案为(C)。5 个连续偶数构成了一个公差等于 2 的等差数列。对于等差数列有如下性质：$a_{n-m}+a_{m+n}=2a_n$。对这 5 个连续偶数应用此公式可得：$a_1+a_5=a_2+a_4=2a_3$，因此这 5 个数的和 $=5a_3=70$，所以 $a_3=14$，最大数 $= a_5=(14+4)=18$。

78. n is a positive integer.

$$n^{100} \qquad 100^n$$

79. 10 percent of 25 percent of $\$69.97$

35 percent of $\$69.97$

80. $\sqrt{26}+\sqrt{10}$ \qquad 8

81. The sum of the first 50 positive integers is 1,275. What is the sum of the integers from 51 to 100, inclusive?

(A) 2,525 \quad (B) 2,550 \quad (C) 3,25
(D) 3,775 \quad (E) 5,050

82. $d=561.165$

The tenths digit of $10^2 d$

The tenths digit of $\dfrac{d}{10^2}$

83. $\dfrac{4^6-4^4}{4^5-4^3}$ \qquad 1

78. 解： 本题的正确答案为(D)。因为 n 是可变的正整数，所以 n^{100} 和 100^n 的大小关系比较复杂，考生在做此类题时，可以把比较简单的特殊值代入来检验：

令 $n=1$，则 $(n^{100}=1)<(100^n=100)$；

令 $n=100$，则 $n^{100}=100^n=100^{100}$；

令 $n=10$，则 $(n^{100}=10^{100})>(100^n=10^{20})$。

79. 解： 本题的正确答案为(B)。比较的左项为 $\$69.79$ 的百分之二十五的百分之十，即为 $\$69.79$ 的 2.5%，显然小于比较右项的 $\$69.79$ 的 35%。

80. 解： 本题的正确答案为(A)。由 $\sqrt{26}>5$，$\sqrt{10}>3$ 可推出 $\sqrt{26}+\sqrt{10}>8$。

81. 前 50 个正整数的和是 1275，问从 51 至 100 的整数(包括 51 和 100)的和是多少？

解： 本题的正确答案为(D)。为简化计算，考生可把从 51 到 100 之间的整数拆开来计算：

$51=50+1, 52=50+2, \cdots 100=50+50$，由此可得：

$$51+52+\cdots100 = 50\times50$$
$$+(1+2+\cdots+50)$$
$$=3775$$

82. 解： 本题的正确答案为(B)。比较的左项为 $10^2 d$ 十分位上的数字；比较的右项为 $\dfrac{d}{10^2}$ 十分位上的数字。$10^2 d=56116.5$，$\dfrac{d}{10^2}=5.61165$，因此其十分位上的数分别为 5,6。

83. 解： 本题的正确答案为(A)。

$$\frac{4^6-4^4}{4^5-4^3}=\frac{4^4(4^2-1)}{4^3(4^2-1)}=4$$

84. The average
(arithmetic mean)   1
of $\frac{10}{11}$ and $\frac{11}{10}$

84. **解**：本题的正确答案为（A）。解此题时要注意使用较为简便的方法，由题可得：

$$\frac{1}{2}\left(\frac{10}{11}+\frac{11}{10}\right)=\frac{1}{2}\left(2-\frac{1}{11}+\frac{1}{10}\right)$$

$$=1+\frac{1}{2}\left(\frac{1}{10}-\frac{1}{11}\right)>1$$

85. The numbers in a table are arranged in 10 rows and 4 columns such that one number is placed at the intersection of each row and column. How many numbers are contained in the table?

(A) 14　　　(B) 40　　　(C) 400

(D) 10^4　　　(E) 4^{10}

85. 一表格中的数字排成 10 行和 4 列以使每个数字被排在行和列的交点处，问表格中包含有多少个数字？

解：本题的正确答案是（B）。4 行和 10 列中共有 40 个交点，所以表格中共包含 40 个数字。

86. In how many of the integers between 1 and 100 does the digit 5 occur exactly once?

(A) 10　　　(B) 18　　　(C) 19

(D) 20　　　(E) 21

86. 在 1 至 100 之间的数字中，5 仅在它们中出现 1 次的整数有多少？

解：本题的正确答案是（B）。解答本题的关键是考生一定要记住 5 只能在这些数字中出现 1 次，5 在其中出现两次的数字应排除掉，即 5 要么在个位，要么在十位，个位与十位都出现 5 的数字(55)应排除掉。个位上有 5 的数字是：5，15，25，35，45，65，75，85 和 95；十位上有 5 的数字是：50，51，52，53，54，56，57，58 和 59，一共是 18 个。

87.

$$\begin{array}{r} YX7 \\ +6Y \\ \hline Y7X \end{array}$$

In the sum above, if X and Y each denote one of the digits from 0 to 9, inclusive, then $X=$

(A) 9　　　(B) 5　　　(C) 3

(D) 1　　　(E) 0

87. 在上述求和中，若 X 和 Y 表示 0～9 中的一个数字(包括 0 和 9)，则 $X=$

解：本题的正确答案为（E）。由上面的加式可知，十位没有向百位上进位，由此可以推出 $X=0$，或 $X=1$。若 $X=1$，则表明个位没有向十位进位，显然无论 Y 等于几都不会有 $7+Y=1$ 成立；因而 X 只能是 0，则 $Y=3$。正确选项为（E）。

88. If n is any prime number greater than 2, which of the following CANNOT be a prime number?

88. 若 n 是任一个大于 2 的质数，下面哪一项不能是质数？

解：本题的正确答案是（E）。考生在解这类数字

(A) $n-4$ (B) $n-3$ (C) $n-1$

(D) $n+2$ (E) $n+5$

规律题时应采用排除法,把选项代入逐个排除。(A) $9-4=5$;(B) $14-3=11$,(C) $3-1=2$,(D) $3+2=5$,(E) 无论如何也得不到质数,因为大于 2 的质数都是奇数,奇数加 5 必为大于 2 的偶数,所以 $n+5$ 不可能是质数。

89. A 12-inch ruler is marked off in sixteenths of an inch. What is the distance, in inches, from the zero mark to the 111th mark after the zero mark?

(A) $6\dfrac{1}{4}$ (B) $6\dfrac{15}{16}$

(C) $7\dfrac{3}{7}$ (D) $9\dfrac{1}{4}$

(E) $11\dfrac{1}{16}$

89. 一把 12 英寸的尺子以每英寸的 $\dfrac{1}{16}$ 划分。从 0 刻度到 111 刻度之间的距离为多长?

解:本题的正确答案是(B)。"sixteenth of an inch"指把一英寸 16 等分,每个刻度为 $\dfrac{1}{16}$ 英寸。从 0 刻度到 111 刻度之间共有 111 个 $\dfrac{1}{16}$ 英寸,所以其距离为 $111\times\dfrac{1}{16}=6\dfrac{15}{16}$。

90. If the range of the six measurements 140, 125, 180, 110, 165, and x is 80, which of the following could be the value of x?

(A) 60

(B) 85

(C) 190

(D) 220

(E) 245

90. 若 6 个数 140,125,180,110,165 和 x 的范围是 80,那么 x 可能是下面的哪一个数值?

解:本题的正确答案为(C)。6 个数的范围实际上就是这六个数中最大数与最小数的差。题目中已知的 5 个数的取值范围显然小于 80,所以 x 值可以是 6 个数中最大数或最小数:

若 x 是最大数,则 $x=110+80=190$

若 x 是最小数,则 $x=180-80=100$

91. Saplings are to be planted 30 feet apart along one side of a straight lane 455 feet long. If the first sapling is to be planted at one end of the lane, how many saplings are needed?

(A) 18   (B) 16

(C) $15\dfrac{1}{6}$ (D) 15

(E) 14

91. 在一条 455 英尺长的直道上,每隔 30 英尺种植一棵小树苗。若第一棵小树苗种植在直道的一端,问共需要多少棵小树苗?

解:本题的正确答案是(B)。$455\div30=15$ 余数为 5,因此共需种 16 棵小树苗。

92. The 10 households on a certain street have household incomes that range from $34,000 to $150,000 and an average (arithmetic mean) household income of $60,000. If the household with the highest income and the one with the lowest income are excluded. What is the average household income for the remaining 8 households?

(A) $41,600

(B) $47,000

(C) $52,000

(D) $61,000

(E) $75,000

93. If a and b are integers and $a-b=6$, then $a+b$ CANNOT be

(A) 0

(B) less than 6

(C) greater than 6

(D) an even integer

(E) an odd integer

94. If p and r are prime numbers, which of the following must also be prime?

(A) pr (B) $p+r$

(C) $pr+1$ (D) p^2+r^2

(E) None of the above

---

92. 某一街道上 10 个家庭的家庭收入在 34,000 美元至 150,000 美元之间,平均(算术平均)家庭收入为 60,000 美元。若把收入最高的家庭和收入最低的家庭排除在外,那么剩余 8 个家庭的平均收入是多少?

解:本题的正确答案是(C)。由题意可得:

$$\frac{60000\times10-34000-150000}{8}=52{,}000\text{ 美元}$$

93. 若 a 和 b 是整数,且 $a-b=6$,那么 $a+b$ 不能是:

解:本题的正确答案为(E)。由题可得:

$$a=b+6\Rightarrow a+b=2b+6$$

所以 $a+b$ 必然是偶数。

94. 若 p 和 r 是质数(prime number),则下面哪一个也一定是质数?

解:本题的正确答案为(E)。此题可用排除法。质数就是除了 1 和它本身之外,没有其他因子的数,因此(A)选项是显然不正确的;由 $5+7=12$ 可以断定(B)也是错误的,实际上两个质数的和为偶数;$5\times7+1=36$ 可否定(C)是错误的;$3^2+5^2=34$ 可断定(D)也是错误的。

第 二 章
代数(Algebra)

代数题对大多数的中国考生并不陌生,GRE考试中所出现的考题大都是我国初中课本中的内容,主要包括数的乘方及开方,变量和代数表达式以及方程和不等式等方面的内容。

第一节 数的乘方及开方
(Powers and Roots of Numbers)

一、基本概念

1. Powers of Numbers（乘方）：这种求 n 个相同因数的积的运算,叫做乘方,乘方的结果叫做幂。在 a^n 中,a 叫做底数,n 叫做指数,a^n 读作 a 的 n 次方。a^n 看作是 a 的 n 次方的结果时,也可读作 a 的 n 次幂。二次方也叫平方,三次方也叫立方。

正数的任何次幂都是正数;负数的奇次幂是负数,负数的偶次幂是正数。

2. Roots of Numbers（开方）：一般地,如果一个数的平方等于 a,这个数就叫做 a 的平方根(也叫做二次方根),换句话说,如果 $x^2 = a$,则 x 就叫做 a 的平方根。

一般来说,一个正数有两个平方根,这两个平方根互为相反数,零的平方根为零。在式子 $\pm\sqrt[2]{a}$ 中,a 叫做被开方数,2 叫做根指数。

正数 a 的正的平方根,也叫做 a 的算术平方根;零的平方根也叫做零的算术平方根,因此零的算术平方根仍旧为零。

二、幂的基本性质

1. $a^m \cdot a^n = a^{m+n}$

2. $a^m \div a^n = a^{m-n}$

3. $(a^m)^n = a^{mn}$

4. $a^{-m} = \dfrac{1}{a^m} (m > 0, a \neq 0)$

5. $a^{\frac{m}{n}} = \sqrt[n]{a^m}$（$\dfrac{m}{n}$ 为最简分数,当 n 为正偶数时,a^m 必为非负数）

6. $(a \cdot b)^m = a^m \cdot b^m$

7. $\dfrac{a^x}{b^x} = \left(\dfrac{a}{b}\right)^x$

8. $a^0 = 1 (a \neq 0)$

9. Powers and Corresponding Value（指数及其相应的幂）

For the GRE, memorize the exponential values in the following table, you'll be glad your did, since these are the ones that you're most likely to see on the exam.

Base	Power and Corresponding Value						
	2	3	4	5	6	7	8
2	4	8	16	32	64	128	256
3	9	27	81	243			
4	16	64	256				
5	25	125	625				
6	36	216					
7	49	343					

三、Exponents，Roots and Real Number Line(幂、方根与实数轴)

1. Exponents and the Real Number Line(幂和实数轴)

Raising numbers to powers can have surprising effects on the size and/or sign (negative vs. positive) of the base number. This is one of the test-makers' favorite areas! The impact of raising a number to an exponent (power) depends on the region on the number line where the number and exponent fall. Here are the four regions you need to consider：

(1) Less than -1 (to the left of -1 on the number line)

(2) Between -1 and 0

(3) Between 0 and 1

(4) Greater than 1 (to the right of 1 on the number line)

例 1：If $-1<x<0$, which of the following expressions is smallest in value?

(A) x^2　　(B) x^3　　(C) x^0

(D) $-x$　　(E) $\dfrac{1}{x^3}$

解：本题的正确答案为(E)。五个选项从小到大的顺序依次是：(E)，(B)，(A)，(D)，(C)。其分析如下所示：

(C) equals 1 （any non-zero term raised to the power of zero equals 1）

(D) is a positive number between 0 and 1

(A) is a positive number between 0 and $|x|$, which is the value of (D)

(B) is a negative non-integer between 0 and x

(E) is a negative number less than (to the left of) -1

2. Roots and the Real Number Line (平方根及实数轴)

As with exponents，the root of a number can bear a surprising relationship to the size and/or sign (negative vs. positive) of the number (another favorite area of the test-makers). Here are our observations you should remember.

(1) If $n>1$, then $1<\sqrt[3]{n}<\sqrt{n}<n$(the higher the roots, the lower the value). However, if n lies between 0 and 1, then $n<\sqrt{n}<\sqrt[3]{n}<1$ (the higher the root, the higher the value).

(2) The square root of any negative number is an imaginary number(虚数)，not a real number. Remem-

ber：you won't encounter imaginary numbers on the GRE.

（3）Every positive number has two square roots：a negative number and a positive number（with the same absolute value）. The same holds true for all other even-numbered roots of positive numbers.

（4）Every negative number has exactly one cube root, and that root is a negative number. The same holds true for all other odd-numbered roots of negative numbers.

（5）Every positive number has only one cube root, and that root is always a positive number. The same holds true for all other odd-numbered roots of positive numbers.

四、The Operation Rule of Radicals(根式的运算法则)

1. Combining Radicals（根式的合并）

（1）Addition and Subtraction(加法与减法)：If a term under a **radical** is being added to or subtracted from a term under a different radical，you cannot combine the two terms under the same radical.（注：根式相加减时,不能把不同根式下的数直接相加减。）

如：$\sqrt{x}+\sqrt{y}\neq\sqrt{x+y}$

$\sqrt{x}-\sqrt{y}\neq\sqrt{x-y}$

$\sqrt{x}+\sqrt{x}=2\sqrt{x}(\neq\sqrt{2x})$

（2）Multiplication and Division(乘法与除法)：Terms under different radicals can be combined under a common radical if one term is multiplied or divided by the other，but only if the root is the same.（注：仅当两根式的幂指数相同时,才能把它们的根式的下面的数相乘除。）

如：
$\sqrt{x}\times\sqrt{x}=x$ $\qquad$ $\sqrt{42.8}\times\sqrt{42.8}=42.8$

$\sqrt{x}\sqrt{y}=\sqrt{xy}$ $\qquad$ $\sqrt{10}\sqrt{5}=\sqrt{50}=5\sqrt{2}$

$\dfrac{\sqrt{x}}{\sqrt{y}}=\sqrt{\dfrac{x}{y}}$ $\qquad$ $\dfrac{\sqrt[3]{125}}{\sqrt[3]{8}}=\sqrt[3]{\dfrac{125}{8}}=\dfrac{5}{2}$

2. Simplifying Radicals（化简根式）：

On the GRE, always look for the possibility of simplifying radicals by moving part of what's inside the radical to the outside. Check inside your square-root radicals for factors that are squares of nice tidy numbers（especially integers）.

注：在 GRE 考试中,如根式下面有可提取到根式外面去的因子,一定要把该因子提到根式的外面去,若分母上有根式时,一般要先把分母上的根式约去,这样可以使运算的步骤大为简化。

下面表中的的平方根和立方根都是 GRE 考试中经常用到的,若考生能熟记下表中的内容,将会使考试时做题的速度大为提高。

Common square roots	Common cube roots
$\sqrt{121}=11$	$\sqrt[3]{8}=2$
$\sqrt{124}=12$	$\sqrt[3]{27}=3$
$\sqrt{169}=13$	$\sqrt[3]{64}=4$
$\sqrt{196}=14$	$\sqrt[3]{125}=5$
$\sqrt{225}=15$	$\sqrt[3]{216}=6$
$\sqrt{625}=25$	$\sqrt[3]{343}=7$
	$\sqrt[3]{512}=8$
	$\sqrt[3]{729}=9$
	$\sqrt[3]{1000}=10$

第二节　实数 (Real Number)

一、基本概念

(1) Number Line(数轴)：

规定了原点、方向和单位长度的直线。数轴上的点和实数一一对应。从原点出发朝正方向的射线上的点对应正数，相反方向的射线上的点对应负数，原点对应数为零。

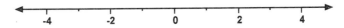

(2) Absolute Value (绝对值)：

某数在数轴上与零点之间的距离称为该数的绝对值。例如：$|-3|=3$

(3) Rational Numbers (有理数)：

正整数、负整数、正分数、负分数以及零统称为有理数。有理数可以写成 $\frac{m}{n}$ 的形式，其中 m 和 n 都是整数，且 n 不等于零。

(4) Irrational Numbers(无理数)：

不循环的无限小数。例如用正方形的一边去度量它的对角线时，所得的比值 $\sqrt{2}$ 就是一个无理数，写成小数 1.414…… 时是无限不循环的。又如，圆周率 $\pi=3.141592653……$，也是一个无理数。

(5) Positive and Negative Numbers(正数和负数)：

All real numbers except zero are either positive or negative.

注：零既不是正数也不是负数。

(6) Real Number(实数)：

有理数和无理数统称为实数。与实数相对的为虚数(imaginary numbers)。虚数的内容在 GRE 考试中不做要求。

All real numbers correspond to points on the number line(数轴) and all points on the number line correspond to real number.

二、实数的分类

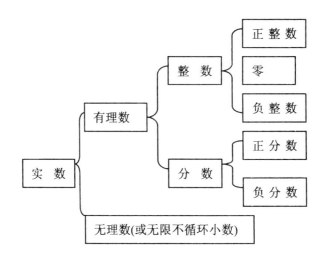

三、实数的性质

(1) 有理数集对四则运算是封闭的(零不能作除数),而两个无理数的和、差、积和商却不一定是无理数。

(2) 有理数和无理数之间的运算有以下的规律:

有理数±无理数＝无理数

非零有理数×无理数＝无理数

$\dfrac{\text{非零有理数}}{\text{无理数}}=\text{无理数}$

$\dfrac{\text{无理数}}{\text{非零有理数}}=\text{无理数}$

(3) 有理数与无理数集无公共元素,即有理数≠无理数。

(4) 有理数与无理数集都具有稠密性(即实数集和数轴上所有点组成的集合是一一对应的)和有序性(即可以比较大小)。

(5) 如果 x,y 和 z 都是实数,则关于 x,y 和 z 有下列性质成立:

① $x+y=y+x$,和 $xy=yx$

② $(x+y)+z=x+(y+z)$,和 $(xy)z=x(yz)$

③ $x(y+z)=xy+yz$

④ 如果 x 和 y 都是正数,那么 $x+y$ 和 xy 都是正数

⑤ 如果 x 和 y 都是负数,那么 $x+y$ 是负数,xy 是正数

⑥ 如果 x 是正数,y 是负数,那么 xy 是负数

⑦ 如果 $xy=0$,那么 $x=0$ 或 $y=0$

⑧ $|x+y|\leqslant|x|+|y|$

⑨ 在实数中互为相反数的两个数的和为零;反之,若两数的和为零,那么这两个数必为互为相反数。

第三节 变量和表达式 (Variable and Expression)

Variable and Algebraic Expression (变量和代数表达式)

Algebra is based on the operations of arithmetic and on the concept of an unknown quantity, or variable. Letters such as x or y are used to represent unknown quantities. For example, suppose Tom has 6 more books than Jack has. If G represents the number of books that Jack has, then the number of books that Tom has is $G+6$. As another example, if Robby's present salary S is increased by 10%, his new salary is 1.1S. A combination of letters and arithmetic operations, such as

$$G+5, \ 7x^2-5x+3 \quad \text{and} \quad \frac{4x}{3x^2-6}$$

is called an algebraic expression.

The expression $7x^2-5x+3$ consists of the terms $7x^2$, $-5x$, and 3, where 7 is the coefficient of x^2, -5 is the coefficient of x^1, and 3 is a constant term (or coefficient of $x^0=1$). Such an expression is called a second degree (or quadratic) polynomial in x since the highest power of x is 2. The expression $G+6$ is a first degree (or linear) polynomial in G since the highest power of G is 1. The expression $\frac{4x}{3x^2-6}$ is not a polynomial because it is not a sum of terms that are each powers of x multiplied by coefficients.

第四节 因式分解 (Factorable Expression)

因式分解在解方程、不等式以及在代数式的运算中具有举足轻重的地位,灵活运用因式分解的技巧是准确快速解答许多数学题的关键。常见的因式分解方法主要有以下四种。

一、提取公因式法

如果一个多项式的各项含有公因式,可以把公因式作为多项式的一个因式提出来,用这个因式去除这个多项式,把所得的商作为另一个因式,这种因式分解的方法叫做提取公因式法。此法是分解因式最常用的方法,也是在因式分解时,首先考虑的方法。

提取公因式的基本思维方式是"求同",为了"求同",常要对给定的多项式进行适当的恒等变形,创造提取公因式的条件。

二、运用公式法

在因式分解中,有时需要运用乘法分式(甚至反复应用公式),因式分解常用的公式有:

(1) $a^2-b^2=(a+b)(a-b)$

(2) $a^3-b^3=(a-b)(a^2+ab+b^2)$

(3) $a^3+b^3=(a+b)(a^2-ab+b^2)$

(4) $a^2+2ab+b^2=(a+b)^2$

(5) $a^2-2ab+b^2=(a-b)^2$

(6) $a^3+3a^2b+3ab^2+b^3=(a+b)^3$

(7) $a^3-3a^2b+3ab^2-b^3=(a-b)^3$

(8) $a^2+b^2+c^2+2ab+2bc+2ca=(a+b+c)^2$

三、分组分解法

把多项式的项通过适当分组来分解因式的方法,叫做分组分解法。

运用分组分解法分解因式时,对多项式恰当分组的要求是:分组后各组能分解因式,并且在各组分解因式的基础上,能完成对整个多项式的因式分解,分组是为进行因式分解创造条件,是搭桥,所以在考虑如何适当分组时,通常要进行尝试和估算,分组的基本方向是"求同",也即把各项联系起来。

四、十字相乘法

由多项式乘法得到:

$$(a_1x+c_1)(a_2x+c_2)=a_1a_2x^2+(a_1c_2+a_2c_1)x+c_1c_2$$

反过来可以得到:

$$a_1a_2x^2+(a_1c_2+a_2c_1)+c_1c_2=(a_1x+c_1)+(a_2x+c_2)$$

利用这个公式,我们可以用下面的写法,尝试把某个二次三项式如 ax^2+bx+c 分解因式,先把 a 分解成 $a=a_1a_2$,把 c 分解成 $c=c_1c_2$,并把 a_1,a_2,c_1,c_2 排列如下:

这里斜线交叉相乘之积的和是 $a_1c_2+a_2c_1$,如果它等于二次三项式中一次项系数 b,那么 a_1x^2+bx+c 就可以分解为:

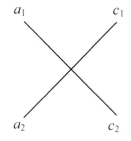

$$(a_1x+c_1)(a_2x+c_2)。$$

这种经过画十字交叉线的帮助把二次三项式分解因式的方法叫做十字相乘法。

对于二次项系数为 1 的二次三项式 x^2+px+q,通过观察可以发现,如果能找到 a,b,使得 $1\times b+1\times a=a+b=p$, $a\times b=q$,那么就有 $x^2+px+q=(x+a)(x+b)$。

以上四种方法是因式分解的常用方法,一般而言,把一个多项式分解因式,可按下列步骤进行:

(1) 多项式各项有公因式时,应先提取公因式;

(2) 各项没有公因式时,看能否用公式法分解;

(3) 对于二次三项式可考虑用完全平方公式或十字相乘法求解;

(4) 如果运用上述方法不能分解时,再看能否用分组分解法分解。

例 2:分解因式 $27x^2(3x-y)^2-9x(y-3x)$

解:原式$=27x^2(3x-y)^2-9x(y-3x)=9x(3x-y)[3x(3x-y)+1]$
$$=9x(3x-y)(9x^2-3xy+1)$$

例 3:分解因式 $x^2-21xy+98y^2+x-7y$

分析:如果把 $98y^2$ 看作常数项,那么原式的前三项是关于 x 的二次三项式,用十字相乘法分解得到的一个因式,恰好是 $x-7y$,用提取公因式法可再行分解。

解：原式 $= (x-7y)(x-14y)+x-7y=(x-7y)(x-14y+1)$

第五节　方程（Equations）

一、Linear Equations with One Variable（一元线性方程）

Algebraic expressions are usually used to form equations, which set two expressions equal to each other. Most equations you'll see on the GRE are linear equations, in which the variables don't come with exponents. To solve any linear equation containing one variable, you goal is always the same: isolate the unknown (variable) on one side of the equation. To accomplish this, you may need to perform one or more of the following operations on both sides, depending on the equation:

(1) 在方程的两边同加上或同减去某个数或某个代数表达式；

(2) 在方程的两边同乘上或同除以某个不为零的数或代数表达式；

(3) 通过交叉相乘法约去两边的分母；

(4) 把方程的两边同时平方或 n 次方去掉方程中的根号。

Performing any of these operations on both sides does not change the equality; it merely restates the equation in a different form.

1. Add or subtract the same term from both sides of the equation（在方程的两边同时加上或减去相同的项）

在求解 x 的过程中，需要在方程的两边同时加上或减去同一个数或表达式。

例 4：假设 $2x-8=x-10$，求 x 的值。

解：首先在方程的两边同减去 x，接着合并同类项：

$$2x-8-x=x-10-x$$
$$x-8=-10$$
$$x=-2$$

2. Multiply or divide both sides of the equation by the same non-zero term（在方程的两边同乘以或同除以一个非零项）

在求解 x 时，需要在方程的两边同乘以或同除以一个不为零的数。

例 5：假设 $\dfrac{11}{x}-\dfrac{3}{x}=12$，求 x 的值。

解：首先合并含有 x 的项，$\dfrac{11-3}{x}=12$

接下来在方程的两边同乘以 x，以消去方程左边分母中的 x：$12x=8$

最后在方程的两边同除以 12，可得 $x=\dfrac{2}{3}$

3. If each side of the equation is a fraction, your best bet is to cross-multiply（若方程的两边都是分式，则最好先交叉相乘约去分母）

当原方程的两边是两个分式时,用交叉相乘法消去分式,即用方程左边的分子乘以方程右边的分母,用方程右边的分子乘以方程左边的分母,并用这两个乘积组成新的方程。因为新方程和原方程很明显是等价方程,所以求解原方程的解的问题就转化为求新方程的解的问题。

例 6：假设 $\dfrac{9}{6x+2}=\dfrac{8}{3-x}$,求 x 的值。

解：首先按上述方法将方程两边交叉相乘得到 $9(3-x)=8(6x+2)$

然后把方程展开,合并同类项可得 $57x=11$

最后把方程的两边同除以 57 可得 $x=\dfrac{11}{57}$

4. Square both sides of the equation to eliminate radical signs(把方程的两边同时平方以消去根号)

当方程中的未知数在根号的下面时,首先要通过把方程的两边平方的方法消去根号,然后求解方程的解(在求解开立方的或更高次方的根号下的未知数时也用与此类似的方法)。

例 7：假设 $2\sqrt{3x-5}=3$,求 x 的值。

解：把方程的两边平方可得 $4(3x-5)=9$

把括号展开,并合并同类项可得 $12x=29$

两边同除以 12 可得 $x=\dfrac{29}{12}$

二、Linear Equations with Two Variables(二元线性方程)

对于如同 $x+2=y+3$ 形式的方程,我们称之为二元线性方程。在解这类方程时,我们无法得到这个方程的数值解,因为未知数 x 的数值由未知数 y 所决定,而未知数 y 的值反过来又被 x 所决定。但是我们可以用 y 来表达 x,或用 x 来表达 y,即

$$x=y+1,\quad y=x-1$$

要确定二元线性方程的数值解,需要两个独立的具有相同未知数的线性方程,这两个方程联立构成二元线性方程组。在求解这类方程组通常有两种方法,即：

(1) The substitution method(代入法)

(2) the addition-subtraction method(加减消元法)

下面将分别讲解这两类方法。

1. The Substitution Method

用代入法求解二元线性方程组的解时,可按下列步骤进行：

Ⅰ　In either equation isolate one variable (x) on one side

Ⅱ　Substitute the expression that equals x in place of x in the other equation

Ⅲ　Solve that equation for y

Ⅳ　Now that you know the value of y, plug it into either equation to find the value of x

例 8：假如 $\dfrac{3}{5}p+q=3q-1$,且 $5q=10-p$,求 $\dfrac{p}{q}$ 的值。

解：把已知的两式联立成方程组可得：

$$\begin{cases} \dfrac{3}{5}p+q=3q-1 & ① \\ 5q=10-p & ② \end{cases}$$

由②式可得 $q=2-\dfrac{1}{5}p$　　　　③

把③式代入①式可得 $\dfrac{3}{5}p+2-\dfrac{1}{5}p=$

$$3\left(2-\frac{1}{5}p\right)-1$$

合并同类项并化简可得 $p=3$

把 $p=3$ 代入③式可得 $q=\frac{7}{5}$

所以 $\frac{p}{q}=3\div\frac{7}{5}=3\times\frac{5}{7}=\frac{15}{7}$

2. The Addition-Subtraction Method(加减消元法)

用加减消元法解二元线性方程组时,可按下列步骤进行:

Ⅰ Make the coefficient of either variable the same in both equations (you can disregard the sign).

Ⅱ Make sure the equations list the same variables in the same order.

Ⅲ Place one equation above the other.

Ⅳ Add the two equations (work down to a sum for each term), or subtract one equation from the other, to eliminate one variable.

Ⅴ Repeat steps Ⅲ～Ⅴ to solve for the other variable.

例9: 假设 $5x+3y=-7$,且 $2x-5y=4$,求 x 的值。

解: 本题是只要求 x 的值,因此用加减消元法除去 y 即可:

$$5x+3y=-7 \qquad ①$$
$$2x-5y=4 \qquad ②$$

把①式两边同乘以 5,把②式两边同乘以 3 可得:

$$25x+15y=-35 \qquad ③$$
$$6x-15y=12 \qquad ④$$

把③式和④式相加可得 $31x=-23$,即 $x=\dfrac{-23}{31}$。

综上所述,二元线性方程组一般具有如下的形式:

$$\begin{cases} a_1x+b_1y=c_1 \qquad ① \\ a_2x+b_2y=c_2 \qquad ② \end{cases}$$

在解这类方程时一般用代入法或加减消元法,但是在用这两种方法解题时应注意以下几点:

Ⅰ 若 $\dfrac{a_1}{a_2}=\dfrac{b_1}{b_2}=\dfrac{c_1}{c_2}$,则此时方程为等价方程,方程组有无数个解;

Ⅱ 若 $\dfrac{a_1}{a_2}=\dfrac{b_1}{b_2}\neq\dfrac{c_1}{c_2}$,则此时方程为矛盾方程,方程组没有解;

Ⅲ 若 $\dfrac{a_1}{a_2}\neq\dfrac{b_1}{b_2}$,则方程组有惟一解。

三、Quadratic Equation with One Variables(一元二次方程)

An equation is quadratic if you can express it in this general form:

$$ax^2+bx+c=0$$

In this general form, x is the variable, a, b and c are constants (numbers), $a\neq0$, b and c can equal 0.

Every quadratic equation has exactly two solutions. (These two solutions are called roots.) All quadratic equations on the GRE can be solved by factoring.

1. Factorable Quadratic Equations(可分解因式的一元二次方程)

To solve any factorable quadratic equation, follow these three steps:

① Put the equation into the standard form: $ax^2+bx+c=0$.

② Factor the terms on the left side of the equation into two linear expression (with no exponents).

③ Set each linear expression (root) equal to zero and solve for the variable in each one.

因式分解时用得最多的,且最有用的是十字相乘法,其具体操作步骤如下所示:

把 m_1,m_2,m_3 和 m_4 排成如右图所示的方式:

若 m_1,m_2,m_3 和 m_4 满足 $m_1\times m_2=a$,$m_3\times m_4=c$ 和 $m_1\times m_4+m_2\times m_3=b$,则一元二次方程恒等于$(m_1x+m_3)(m_2x+m_4)=0$。因此,方程的根 $x_1=-\dfrac{m_3}{m_1}$,$x_2=-\dfrac{m_4}{m_2}$。

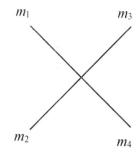

通常情况下,将方程变为 $x^2+\dfrac{b}{a}x+\dfrac{c}{a}=0$,这时 $m_1=m_2=1$,$m_3\times m_4=\dfrac{c}{a}$,$m_3+m_4=\dfrac{b}{a}$,方程恒等于$(x+m_3)(x+m_4)=0$。因此,方程的根 $x_1=-m_3$,$x_2=-m_4$。

例 10:$2x^2-7x-15=0$

解:注意到 x^2 的系数是 2,而 2 是个质数,因此只能分解成 1×2,所以本方程可写成如下的形式:

$$(2x\quad)(x\quad)=0$$

接下来比较关键的一步就是找括号中缺少的常数,也即把-15分解,-15的所有因子的可能组合有以下四种:

$(1,-15)$,$(-1,15)$,$(3,-5)$,$(-3,5)$

把这四组数分别代入上面括号中的 $2x$ 和 x 的后面,发现 $(3,-5)$ 是惟一的一组合适的数据,也即原方程可写成:

$$(2x+3)(x-5)=0$$

即 $2x+3=0$ 或 $x-5=0$,也即 $x=-\dfrac{3}{2}$,或 $x=5$。

四、Quadratic Equations that Can't be Factored(不能分解因式的二次方程)

并不是所有的二次方程都可用分解因式的方法给予解决,当二次方程不能用分解因式法解时就要运用二次方程的求根公式来解。对于 $ax^2+bx+c=0$ 形式的一元二次方程,其解可用求根公式表示如下:

$$x_1=\frac{-b+\sqrt{b^2-4ac}}{2a},\quad x_2=\frac{-b-\sqrt{b^2-4ac}}{2a}$$

当 $b^2-4ac=0$ 时,方程有两个相等的根;当 $b^2-4ac>0$ 时方程有两个不相等的根;当 $b^2-4ac<0$ 时,方程在实数的范围内没有根。

二次方程的两个根具有两个非常重要的性质,即:

$$① \ x_1+x_2=-\frac{b}{a}, \quad ② \ x_1 \cdot x_2=-\frac{c}{a}$$

例 11:求 $x^2-8x+9=0$ 的根。

解:把 $a=1$,$b=-8$,$c=9$ 代入求根公式可得:

$$x=\frac{-(-8)\pm\sqrt{8^2-4\times1\times9}}{2\times1}$$

$$=\frac{8\pm2\sqrt{7}}{2}=4\pm\sqrt{7}$$

五、Non-Linear Equations with Two Variables(二元非线性方程)

在数学中,求二元非线性方程的解是非常复杂的,但在 GRE 考试中所遇到的有关二元非线性方程的题都相当简单,一般说来他们都遵循一定的原则。要正确解答这一方面的题目,你只要记住以下三条普遍原则即可:

Sum of two variables, squared：$(x+y)^2=x^2+2xy+y^2$

Difference of two variables, squared：$(x-y)^2=x^2-2xy+y^2$

Difference of two squares：$x^2-y^2=(x+y)(x-y)$

例 12:若 $x^2-y^2=100$,且 $x+y=2$,那么 $x-y$ 的值是多少?

解:由已知可得：$x^2-y^2=(x+y)(x-y)=100$

把 $x+y=2$ 代入可得 $x-y=50$

六、Equations that Can't be Solved(不可求解的方程)

不是所有的一元方程都是可求解的,同理不是所有的二元线性方程组都是可求解的。在 GRE 考试中通常涉及到三种不可求解的方程:

(1) Identities

(2) Quadratic Equations in Disguise

(3) Equivalent Equations

1. Identities(等同)

在考试中一定要当心那些可化简为 $0=0$ 的形式的方程,要知道这样的方程是不可解的。

例 13:

Column A	Column B
$3x-3-5x=x-7-3x+4$	
x	0

解:本题正确的答案是(D),把方程的两边化简后,我们可以得到下式

$$-2x-3=-2x-3$$

$$0=0$$

所以 x 可以是任意的实数。

2. Quadratic Equations in Disguise(伪装的二次方程)

有一些方程看起来像似线性方程(不包含指数项的未知数),实际上是二次方程。用求解线性方程的方法是不能求得此类方程的解的,这类方程的解只能化为二次方程后用解二次方程的方法来解决。对 GRE

考试来说有两种情况需要注意：

① The same variable inside a radical also appears outside：

$$\sqrt{x} = 5x \Rightarrow (\sqrt{x})^2 = (5x)^2 \Rightarrow x = 25x^2$$
$$\Rightarrow 25x^2 - x = 0$$

② The same variable that appears in the denominator of a fraction also appears elsewhere in the equation：

$$\frac{6}{x} = 5 - x \Rightarrow 6 = x(5 - x) \Rightarrow x^2 - 5x + 6 = 0$$

例 14：

Column A	Column B
$4x = \sqrt{2x}$	
x	$\dfrac{1}{8}$

解：本题的正确答案是（D）。$4x = \sqrt{2x}$ 是伪装的二次方程，所以它一定有两个解：

$$16x^2 = 2x \Rightarrow x(8x - 1) = 0$$
$$\Rightarrow x = 0 \text{ 或 } x = \frac{1}{8}$$

因为 $\dfrac{1}{8}$ 只是方程 $4x = \sqrt{2x}$ 的一个解，所以这个数量比较题的正确答案是（D）。

3. Equivalent Equations（同等方程）

在某些情况下两个方程看起来像是一个二元一次线性方程组，而实际上它们只是同一个方程的不同表达方式。

例 15：

Column A	Column B
$a + b = 30$	
$2b = 60 - 2a$	
a	b

解：第二个方程经过化简后变为 $a + b = 30$。由此可知，两个方程实际上是同一个方程，因此 a 和 b 的大小不能确定，即本题的正确答案也是（D）。

TIME SAVER：When you encounter any Quantitative Comparison question that calls for solving one or more equations，stop in your tracks before taking pencil to paper. Size up the equation to see whether it's one of the three unsolvable animals you learned about here. If so，then unless you're given more information the correct answer must be（D）。

第六节　代数不等式（Algebraic Inequalities）

不等式是表示两个量或两个表达式不等关系的式子。关系式 $A \neq B$，$A < B$，$A > B$，$A \geq B$ 和 $A \leq B$ 分别表示 A 不等于 B、A 小于 B、A 大于 B、A 大于或等于 B（或 A 不小于 B）和 A 小于或等于 B（或 A 不大于 B）。不等式可以分为条件不等式（condition inequalities）和绝对不等式（absolute inequalities）。例如 $x^2 + 2 \leq 3x$ 是条件不等式（因为它只当 $1 \leq x \leq 2$ 时才成立）；以如 $x^2 + 1 > 0$ 是绝对不等式（因为它对任何实数都成

立）。单独一个不等式不可能确定变量值,只能定出变量范围,但一个不等式组或绝对值不等式很有可能使变量值固定。

1. 不等式的性质

① 若 $a>b$, $b>c$, 则 $a>c$

② 若 $a>b$, 则 $a+c>b+c$

③ 若 $a>b$, $c>d$, 则 $a+c>b+d$(即两个或几个同向不等式两边分别相加,所得不等式与原不等式同向)

④ 若 $a>b$, $c>0$, 则 $ac>bc$

⑤ 若 $a>b$, $c<0$, 则 $ac<bc$

⑥ 若 $a>b>0$, $c>d>0$, 则 $ac>bd$(即两个或几个两边都是正数的同向不等式两边分别相乘,所得的不等式与原不等式同向)

⑦ 若 $a>b>0$, 且 n 为大于 1 的整数, 则 $a^n>b^n$

⑧ 若 $a>b>0$, 且 n 为大于 1 的整数, 则 $\sqrt[n]{a}>\sqrt[n]{b}$

⑨ 若 $0<a<b$, 且 m 为大于零的数, 则 $\dfrac{a+m}{b+m}>\dfrac{a}{b}$

⑩ 若有 $\dfrac{a_1+a_2}{b_1+b_2}>\dfrac{a_1}{b_1}\Rightarrow\dfrac{a_2}{b_2}>\dfrac{a_1}{b_1}$

$\qquad\dfrac{a_1+a_2}{b_1+b_2}=\dfrac{a_1}{b_1}\Rightarrow\dfrac{a_2}{b_2}=\dfrac{a_1}{b_1}$

$\qquad\dfrac{a_1+a_2}{b_1+b_2}<\dfrac{a_1}{b_1}\Rightarrow\dfrac{a_2}{b_2}<\dfrac{a_1}{b_1}$

2. 绝对值不等式的基本性质

① $|ab|=|a|\cdot|b|$

② $\left|\dfrac{a}{b}\right|=\dfrac{|a|}{|b|}$

③ $|x|\leqslant a\Leftrightarrow -a\leqslant x\leqslant a$, $a>0$

④ $|x|\geqslant a\Leftrightarrow x\geqslant a$ 或 $x\leqslant -a$, $a>0$

⑤ $a\leqslant |x|\leqslant b\Leftrightarrow a\leqslant x\leqslant b$ 或 $-b\leqslant x\leqslant -a$, 其中 $0<a<b$

⑥ $||a|-|b||\leqslant|a+b|\leqslant|a|+|b|$

⑦ $||a|-|b||\leqslant|a-b|\leqslant|a|+|b|$

3. 不等式的解法

You can solve algebraic inequalities in the same manner as equations. Isolate the variable on one side of the equation, factoring and canceling wherever possible. As in solving an equation, the same number can be added to or subtracted from both sides of the inequality, or both sides of an inequality can be multiplied or divided by a positive number without changing the truth of the inequality. However, multiplying or dividing an inequality by a negative number reverses the order of the inequality.

像解方程一样,一元一次不等式总可以通过去括号、去分母、移项、合并同类项,化为 $ax>b$ 形式的不等式,其解的情况是:

当 $a>0$ 时, $x>\dfrac{a}{b}$, 当 $a<0$ 时, $x<\dfrac{a}{b}$

当 $a=0$ 时,若 $b<0$,则解为一切实数;若 $b\geqslant0$ 时不等式无解。

例 16: $\dfrac{4x-2}{-5}>2$

解: $\dfrac{4x-2}{-5}>2\Rightarrow 4x-2<-10$

$\Rightarrow 4x<-8\Rightarrow x<-2$

4. 不等式求解时的注意事项

① 若不等式两边同乘以负号,不等号要改变方向;

② 对于绝对值不等式,当把绝对值符号展开时,要写清不等式的范围;

例 17: $|x-4|<3$, $\quad|x-4|>3$

解: $|x-4|<3\Rightarrow-3<x-4<3\Rightarrow1<x<7$

$|x-4|>3\Rightarrow x-4>3$ 或 $x-4<-3\Rightarrow x>7$

或 $x<1$

③ 对于一元一次不等式组(其实绝对值不等式可看为一元一次不等式组)可在数轴上标出区间范围。

第七节 数 学 归 纳 法

用数学归纳法证明一个与自然数有关的命题的步骤是:

(1) 证明当 n 取第一个值 n_0 时结论正确;

(2) 假设当 $n=k$ $(k\geqslant n_0)$ 时结论正确,证明当 $n=k+1$ 时结论也正确。

以上是用数学归纳法的步骤,在考试中虽然并不要求用数学归纳法去解题,但是却会考到对数学归纳法的概念的理解。

例 18: 若一个集合中含有自然数 3,则以下哪个选项可以帮助判断是否所有是 3 的倍数的自然数都在这一集合中

（Ⅰ） 如果自然数 n 在这个集合中,则 $n+3$ 也在这个集合中

（Ⅱ） 如果自然数 n 在这个集合中,则 $n-3$ 也在这个集合中

(A) Ⅰ only　　　　(B) Ⅱ only

(C) Ⅰ and Ⅱ　　　(D) none

解: 因 3 已在这一集合中了,而 3 是 3 的 1 倍,实际上完成了上述数学归纳法中的第(1)步,这时Ⅰ中指出当 n 在集合中,$n+3$ 也在集合中,由此完成了上述数学归纳法的第(2)步,因从 $3\to6$ 在,从 $6\to9$ 在……,所有是 3 的倍数的自然数就都在集合中了,而Ⅱ中与数学归纳法中第(2)步指出的正好相反了,应往大走 $(k\geqslant n_0)$,而不应往小,因而答案为(A)。

第八节 极 限

在 GRE 考试中,一般说来是不会涉及求极限方面的问题,但笔者认为极限这一概念考生还是应该了解的,下面将通过举例来讲解一下极限问题。

例 19: 问 $a_n=1+\cfrac{1}{1+\cfrac{1}{1+\cfrac{1}{1+\cdots}}}$,问当 $n=1{,}000$ 时,a_n 的值约等于多少?

解: 很多考生在做这道题时想通过尝试几个值而猜一个答案,这是不对的。实际上原题问 $n=1{,}000$ 时,a_n 的值,这时 n 的值非常大,因此可以认为:

$a_{n=1000}=a_{n=1000-1}$,而 $a_{n=1000}$

$$=1+\cfrac{1}{1+\cfrac{1}{1+\cfrac{1}{1+\cdots}}}\text{(1000 个)}\qquad ①$$

$$a_{n=1000-1}=1+\cfrac{1}{1+\cfrac{1}{1+\cfrac{1}{1+\cdots}}}\text{(1000−1 个)}②$$

从上面的两个式子中，可以看出①式中的分式的分母部分就是 $a_{n=1000-1}$，因而有 $a_{n=1000}=1+\cfrac{1}{a_{n=1000-1}}$，前已述及 $a_{n=1000}=a_{n=1000-1}$，从而有 $a_{n=1000}=1+\cfrac{1}{a_{n=1000}}$，转化为解一个类似于 $x=1+\cfrac{1}{x}$ 的方程。

第九节　函数(Functions)

1. 定义

设在某变化过程中的两个变量(**variable**)x 和 y，y 随 x 而变化，而且依赖于 x。如果变量 x 取某个特定的值，y 依确定的关系取相应的值，则称 y 是 x 的函数。记作 $y=f(x)$，其中 x 称为自变量(**independent variable**)，y 称为因变量(**dependent variable**)。x 的变化范围称为函数的"定义域"，与 x 对应的 y 的取值称为"函数值"，其全体称为函数的"值域"。GRE 数学考试中会出现诸如括号、圆圈和方框等各种形式的函数表达式。

An algebraic expression(代数式) in one variable can be define a function of that variable. A function is denoted by a letter such as f or g along with the variable in the expression. For example, the expression x^3+3x^2-4 defines a function f that can be denoted by

$$f(x)=x^3+3x^2-4$$

The expression $\dfrac{\sqrt[3]{5z-2}}{3z+8}$ defines a function g that can be denoted by

$$g(z)=\dfrac{\sqrt[3]{5z-2}}{3z+8}$$

Once a function $f(x)$ is defined, it is useful to think of the variable x as an input and as the output. A given expression defines a function if there is no more than one output for a given input. However, more than one input can give the same output; For example, if $f(x)=|2x-4|$, then $f(3)=f(1)=2$

2. Function Notation(函数的表示方法)

The symbols "$f(x)$" or "$g(x)$" do not represent products; each is merely the symbol for an expression, and is read "f of x" or "g of z". Function notation provides a short way of writing the result of substituting a value for a variable. If $x=1$ is substituted in $f(x)=x^3+3x^2-4$, the result can be written $f(1)$

$=0$, and $f(1)$ is read the "value of f at $x=1$". Similarly, if $z=0$ is substituted in the second expression, the value of g at $z=0$ is $g(0)=\dfrac{\sqrt[3]{2}}{8}$.

"$f(x)$"和"$g(x)$"仅是函数表达的符号,函数还可以有其他的方式来表达。在GRE数学考试中会出现诸如括号、圆圈和方框等各种形式的函数表达式。考题中经常给出一些特殊符号来定义各种函数,例如:x□$y=x^2-y^2$,那么□表达了x与y之间的运算关系,$3□2=3^2-2^2=9-4=5$;再如 $x^*=\dfrac{1}{x}$,则 $\left(\left(\left(\dfrac{1}{2}\right)^*\right)^*\right)^*=2$。

3. Domain of a Function(函数的定义域)

函数的定义域是指函数中自变量所允许的取值范围。例如函数 $f(x)=x^3+3x^2-4$ 的定义域是全体实数;函数 $g(z)=\dfrac{\sqrt[3]{5z-2}}{3z+8}$ 的定义域是 $z\neq-\dfrac{8}{3}$;函数 $f(x)=\sqrt{1-x^2}$ 的定义域是 $-1\leqslant x\leqslant1$,也可表示为$[-1,1]$。另外我们还可设定函数 $f(x)=x^3+3x^2-4$ 的定义域,例如我们可以设定函数的定义域是 $-2\leqslant x\leqslant3$。

第十节　重点试题精练及解析

1.
$$y^2=x^2-1 \text{ and } x\neq0$$

$$y^4 \qquad\qquad x^4+1$$

1. 解:本题的正确答案为(B)。
$$y^4=(x^2-1)^2=x^4+1-2x^2$$
由 $x\neq0$ 可知 $x^2>0$
$$\Rightarrow y^2<x^4+1$$

2. Let $\boxed{x}=3$, if x is an odd integer;

Let $\boxed{x}=6$, if x is an even integer.

r and s are integers, $3r$ is odd, and $5+s$ is odd.

$$\boxed{r} \qquad\qquad \boxed{s}$$

2. 如果 x 是奇数,令 $\boxed{x}=3$;

如果 x 是偶数,令 $\boxed{x}=6$。

r 和 s 是整数,$3r$ 是奇数,$5+s$ 是奇数

解:本题的正确答案为(B)。要解答此题,首要的是判断 r、s 的奇偶性。根据本章中所讲的奇数和偶数的性质可知若 $3r$ 是奇数,则 r 也是奇数;$5+s$ 是奇数,可推出 s 是偶数。再根据题目所给出的运算规则,可推知:
$$\boxed{r}=3,\quad \boxed{s}=6。$$

3. On a certain number line, if -7 is a distance 4 from n and 7 is a distance of 18 from n then $n=$

(A) 25

(B) 11

(C) 3

3. 在某一数轴(number line)上,假如 -7 与 n 的距离是4,且7与 n 的距离是18,问 n 等于多少?

解:本题的正确答案是(E)。涉及数轴上的两个数距离问题,要用到绝对值的概念。

由题义可得:

(D) -3

(E) -11

$|-7-n|=4 \quad n=-11, n=-3$

$|7-n|=18 \quad n=-11, n=25$

n 的值要同时满足以上两个等式，所以 $n=$ -11。

考生在解答此类题目时，一定要注意下面这句话的确切含义：

(1) 7 is a distance of 4 from n.

(2) 7 is the distance of 4 from n.

上面第一句话用了不定冠词，应理解为 7 与 n 之间的距离是 4；第二句话用了定冠词，应理解为 7 是 4 和 n 之间的距离。

4. If $y=\dfrac{a}{a+b}$ and $x=\dfrac{a}{b}$, what is y in terms of x?

(A) $-\dfrac{1}{x}$　　(B) $1+x$　　(C) $1+\dfrac{1}{x}$

(D) $\dfrac{1}{1+x}$　　(E) $\dfrac{x}{1+x}$

4. 若 $y=\dfrac{a}{a+b}$，$x=\dfrac{a}{b}$，求 y 用 x 来表示的表达式？

解： 本题的正确答案是(E)。考生在解这类题时不必求出 a 或 b，只需将 y 化成具有 x 的形式即可：

$$y=\frac{a}{a+b} \Rightarrow y=\frac{1}{1+\dfrac{b}{a}}$$

$$=\frac{1}{1+\dfrac{1}{x}}=\frac{x}{x+1}$$

5.

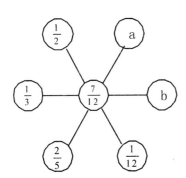

The sum of each pair of numbers in diametrically opposite positions is equal to the number in the center.

　　　　a　　　　　　　b

5. 处于完全相反位置上的一组数的和等于中心位置上的数。（注：diametrically opposite 在题目中是"正相反地，完全相反地"的意思。）

解： 本题的正确答案为(B)。由题意可得：

$$a+\frac{2}{5}=b+\frac{1}{3}, \frac{2}{5}>\frac{1}{3} \Rightarrow a<b$$

6. Which of the following equations can be used to find the value of x if 7 less than $5x$ is 5 more than the product of 3 and x?

(A) $5x - 7 = 5 + 3x$

(B) $5x - 7 = 5 + (3 + x)$

(C) $7 - 5x = 5 + 3x$

(D) $7 - 5x = (5 + 3)x$

(E) $7 - 5x + 5 = 3x$

7. x and y are positive numbers.

$$\left(\frac{x+y}{2}\right)^2 - \left(\frac{x-y}{2}\right)^2 \qquad 0$$

8. The number of connections C that can be made through a switchboard to which T telephones are connected is given by the formula $C = \frac{T(T-1)}{2}$. How many more connections are possible with 30 telephones than with 20 telephones?

(A) 435   (B) 245   (C) 190

(D) 45   (E) 10

9.

$$\frac{a + \dfrac{b}{c}}{\dfrac{d}{e}}$$

If the value of the expression above is to be halved by doubling exactly one of the five numbers a, b, c, d, or e, which should be doubled?

(A) a (B) b (C) c

(D) d (E) e

10. $\qquad y = 5x^4 - 3x^5 + 8x^6$

---

6. 若 $5x$ 减 7 比 3 与 x 的积大 5，下列哪一个方程（equation）可以用于得到 x 的值？

解：本题的正确答案是（A）。7 less than $5x$ 可表示为 $5x - 7$，5 more than the product of 3 and x 可表示 $3x + 5$ 由题意可得出方程：$5x - 7 = 3x + 5$

7. 解：本题的正确答案为（A）。

$$\left(\frac{x+y}{2}\right)^2 - \left(\frac{x-y}{2}\right)^2 = xy$$

$$x > 0, \ y > 0 \Rightarrow xy > 0$$

8. 连接有 T 门电话的交换机所能形成的连络数目 C 由公式 $C = \frac{T(T-1)}{2}$ 给定。30 门电话能比 20 门电话多出多少连络？

解：本题的正确答案是（B）。30 门电话的连络数目：$C_{30} = \frac{30(30-1)}{2} = 435$

20 门电话的连络数目：$C_{20} = \frac{20(20-1)}{2} = 190$

$$C_{30} - C_{20} = 435 - 190 = 245$$

9. 若要通过加倍 a, b, c, d 和 e 这五个数中某一个数而使上面表达式的值减半，问应当加倍哪一个数？

解：本题的正确答案是（D）。这道题中的表达式是个繁分式，要使分式的值减半，要么使分母的值加倍，要么使分子的值减半。而本题的要求是通过加倍某个数的方法使整个分式的值减半，所以就要从分式的分母 $\frac{d}{e}$ 入手。要使 $\frac{d}{e}$ 的值加倍，只有使 d 的值加倍。

10. 解：本题的正确答案为（A）。考生在解答此题时，可以用 $x = 2$ 和 $x = -2$ 直接代入题干中给出的函数式，求出函数值，再进行判断大

The value of y if $x=-2$	The value of y if $x=2$

小;但更为简单的方法只需判断 x 的正负号即可,因为 y 的第一、三项均为 x 的偶数次幂,所以 $x=\pm2$ 代入均相等,第二项 $(-3x^5)$ 是奇次幂,其结果与 x 的符号相反, $x=-2$ 代入第二项时,其值为正, $x=2$ 代入第二项时,其值为负,因此 $x=-2$ 时 y 的取值大于 $x=2$ 时 y 的取值。

11.

$$m+2=8,\quad r-2=7$$

$4[(m+2)+(r-2)]$	$(m+2)(r-2)$

11. **解**:本题的正确答案为(A)。解答此题时,考生不必将 m 和 r 的具体值算后再代入比较的左项和右项求解,而是将 $(m+2)$ 与 $(r-2)$ 直接代入比较的左项和右项即可:

$$4[(m+2)+(r-2)]=4\times(8+7)=60$$
$$(m+2)(r-2)=8\times7=56$$

12.

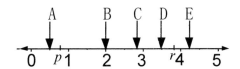

According to the number line above, which of the following points has a coordinate most nearly equal to $p\times r$?

(A) A   (B) B   (C) C
(D) D   (E) E

12. 根据左面的数轴(number line),下面哪一个点的坐标最近似于 $p\times r$?

解:本题的正确答案是(C)。因为本题只是要求求近似值,所以应根据题目中的"Figure drawn to scale"进行估值计算:

$$p\approx0.7,r\approx3.8\Rightarrow p\times r=2.66$$

最接近于 C 点的坐标。

13.

$$10^{20}=\frac{10^{100}}{10^n}$$

n	5

13. **解**:本题的正确答案为(A)。此题主要考查考生是否掌握了幂的运算法则

$$10^{20}=\frac{10^{100}}{10^n}=10^{100-n}$$
$$\Rightarrow 20=100-n\Rightarrow n=80$$

14.

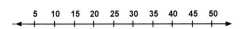

On the number line above, what number corresponds to a point that is $\frac{2}{5}$ of the distance from 10 to 40?

14. 在左面的数轴上,哪一个数字所对应的点是 10 与 40 之间距离的 $\frac{2}{5}$?

解:本题的正确答案是(E)。大多数的考生容易误选(C)选项,但该题是问哪一点的坐标把 10 与 40 之间的距离分成 $\frac{2}{5}$ 和 $\frac{3}{5}$ 两段,所以

(A) 6   (B) 8   (C) 12

(D) 15   (E) 22

计算未知点的坐标应当从 10 开始，即为

$$10+30\times\frac{2}{5}=22。$$

15. On a number line, the distance between the two points with coordinates -5 and 1 is how much less than the distance between the two points with coordinates 2 and 14?

(A) 6   (B) 8   (C) 10

(D) 12   (E) 16

15. 在数轴上，坐标为 -5 和 1 的两点之间的距离比坐标为 2 和 14 两点之间的距离少多少？

解：本题的正确答案为（A）。

-5 和 1 之间距离 $=|1-(-5)|=6$

2 和 14 之间的距离 $=|14-2|=12$

两者之差等于 6。

16.

p	24	1	8	15
23	5	7	14	16
4	6	r	20	22
10	12	19	21	3
11	18	25	2	9

In the figure above, if the sum of each column, row, and five-element diagonal is equal to x, what is the value of $p+r$?

(A) 13   (B) 17   (C) 20

(D) 23   (E) 30

16. 在左面图形中，若每行（row）、每列（column)以及对角线（diagonal）上的 5 个元素的和都为 x，问 $p+r$ 的值是多少？

解：本题的正确答案是（E）。根据每行每列及对角线上的数字和都相等可得：

$$p+5+r+21+9$$
$$=10+12+19+21+3$$
$$\Rightarrow p+r=30$$

17. If $x^2=68$, which of the following could be true?

(A) $-9<x<-8$

(B) $-8<x<-7$

(C) $-8<x<8$

(D) $7<x<8$

(E) $9<x<10$

17. 若 $x^2=68$，下列哪项可能正确？

解：本题的正确答案为（A）。考生在解答此题时，一定要注意本题只是问可能性。$x^2=68$ $\Rightarrow x=\pm\sqrt{68}$，$8<|x|=\sqrt{68}<9$，所以我们如果能在选项中找到 $8<x<9$ 或 $-9<x<-8$ 即可。

18. For all real numbers p and r,

$$p\diamondsuit r=pr-p+r.$$

$$(-4)\diamondsuit 5 \qquad\qquad 5\diamondsuit(-4)$$

18. 对于所有的实数（real number）p 和 r，有 $p\diamondsuit r=pr-p+r$ 成立。

解：本题的正确答案为（A）。$\diamondsuit$ 表示一种函数运算法则，解答该题只要将数据代入表达式进行计算就可以了：

$$(-4)\diamondsuit 5=-4\times 5-(-4)+5=-11$$
$$5\diamondsuit(-4)=5\times(-4)-5+(-4)=-29$$

19.

$$x > z$$

$$y > z$$

$$x + y \qquad z$$

19. 解：本题的正确答案是(D)。考生在做该题时一定要注意思维的严密性。也就是说考生不但要注意到正数是越加越大，而且要注意到负数是越加越小。只要考生能想到这一点，就不会把本题做错。当 x 和 y 都是正数时，显然有 $x+y > z$；但是当 x 和 y 都是负数时，则不能判定 $x+y$ 与 z 孰大孰小。例如：$-1 > -2$，$-1.1 > -2$，那么 $x+y = -2.1$ 就小于 -2 了，所以本题应为无法判断。

20. The expression $(x+4)(2x-3)$ is equivalent to which of the following?

I $\ 2x(x+4)-3(x+4)$

II $\ (x-4)(2x+3)$

III $\ 2x^2 - 12$

(A) I only   (B) II only

(C) III only   (D) II and III only

(E) I, II, and III

20. 表达式 $(x+4)(2x-3)$ 与下面哪一个等价？

解：本题的正确答案为(A)。把 I 式提取公因式 $(x+4)$ 可以得到 $(2x-3)(x+4)$，故与 I 式等价。把其余两项的多项式展开，发现它们与 $(x+4)(2x-3)$ 不存在等价关系。

21.

$$x > y \ \text{and} \ xy \neq 0$$

$$\frac{x+y}{x} \qquad \frac{x+y}{y}$$

21. 解：本题的正确答案是(D)。这是一个易犯错误的考题，考生在解此类考题时一定要注意考虑到正负数的问题。x,y 同取正数，同取负数和 x 为正 y 为负时所得到的结果是不同的，因此本题无法判断。

22.

$$3x + 4 = 13$$

$$11 - y = 6$$

$$6x \qquad 4y$$

22. 解：本题的正确答案为(B)。由题目中的两个等式可以得到：

$$3x = 9, \ y = 5 \Rightarrow 6x = 18 < 4y = 20$$

23. $\dfrac{n}{4} + \dfrac{r}{8} = \dfrac{s}{3} + \dfrac{t}{6}$

$n, r, s,$ and t are positive integers.

$$2n + r \qquad 2s + t$$

23. 解：本题的正确答案是(A)。考生在解这道题时一定要小心题目中的陷阱。n, r, s, t 都是正数，所以题目中等式的两边也都是正数。考生稍加观察就可注意到 $2n+r$ 等于等式的左边乘以 8，而 $2s+t$ 则等于等式的右边乘以 6。两个本来相同的数一个乘以

8,而另一个则乘以6,当然是乘以8所得的那个数大于乘以6的那个数,也即$2n+r>2s+t$。

24. x copies of sports magazine X cost a total of \$12.

The total cost, in dollars, of m copies of fashion magazine M	$\dfrac{12m}{x}$

24. **解**：本题的正确答案为(D)。比较的左项为以美元为单位，m 份时装杂志 M 的总成本。由题目中所给出的已知条件，只能算出杂志 X 的单价；因为题目中并未给出杂志 M 与杂志 X 的成本之间的关系，所以无法判断二者的大小。

25.

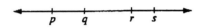

p, q, r, and s are the coordinates of the points indicated on the number line.

$p+q$	$r+s$

25. p, q, r 和 s 是左面数轴上所指示的点的坐标。

解：本题的正确答案是(B)。美国数学中所有的数轴都画成双箭头，但不管是单箭头还是双箭头，所有的数轴都是由左至右递增的，所以本题显然有 $r+s>p+q$。

26. On the number line, 1.4 is halfway between which of the following pairs of numbers?
(A) -1.4 and 2.4
(B) -1 and 2
(C) -0.3 and 3.1
(D) 0.15 and 1.55
(E) 0.4 and 1

26. 在数轴上，1.4 是下面哪一对数的中点？

解：本题的正确答案为(C)。在数轴上，若一点是另外两点的中点，则该点的坐标应是另外两点坐标的和的一半。根据这条定理，可以推出 1.4 是 -0.3 和 3.1 两点的中点。

27. $7x^2=21$

x	2

27. **解**：本题的正确答案是(B)。大多数做错该题的考生一发现 x 有两个值，$+\sqrt{3}$ 和 $-\sqrt{3}$，就认为该题无法判断大小，犯了惯性思维的毛病。考生需要注意的是在本题中不管 x 等于 $+\sqrt{3}$ 还是 $-\sqrt{3}$，其值均小于 2。

28. t is an integer.

$\dfrac{1}{1+2^t}$	$\dfrac{1}{1+3^t}$

28. **解**：本题的正确答案为(D)。比较二者大小，实际是比较 2^t 和 3^t 大小，而 2^t 和 3^t 大小又依赖于 t 的取值：

29. Among the 900 spectators at a football game, there was a total of x students from College C and a total of y students who were not from College C.

| The number of spectators at the game who were not students | $900-x-y$ |

29. 在一足球赛的 900 名观众中，总共有 x 名学生来自学院 C，不是来自生学院 C 的学生总数为 y。

解： 本题的正确答案为（C）。比较的左项是观看足球赛的非学生人数。根据题目考生可以这样理解，900 名观众由学生和非学生组成，而学生又由学院 C 的和非学院 C 的学生组成，由此很容易得到非学生观众人数为 $900-x-y$。

30.
$$2x+5y=24$$
$$1\leqslant x\leqslant 3$$

| x | | y |

30. **解：** 本题的正确答案为（B）。因为 $2x+5y=24$ 是一条直线方程，因此考生可以用边界条件法进行求解，所谓边界条件法，就是只取 x 区间的两端判断 y 的区间：

$x=1$ 时，$y=5.4$；$x=3$ 时，$y=3.6$，由此可以得出：$3.6\leqslant y\leqslant 5.4$

31.

x	t	u
t	a	b
u	b	c

If y is a two-digit number with tens digit t and units digit u and the table above is a multiplication table for t and u (for example, $t\times u=b$), then $y^2=$

(A) $a+2b+10c$

(B) $10a+20b+c$

(C) $10(a+2b+c)$

(D) $100(a+2b+c)$

(E) $100a+20b+c$

31. 若 y 是一个两位数（two-digit number），其十位数字（tens digit）为 t，个位数字（units digit）为 u，且上面表格是 t 和 u 的乘法表（例如：$t\times u=b$），那么 y^2 等于多少？

解： 本题的正确答案是（E）。由题意可得：

$$y=10t+u\Rightarrow y^2=(10t+u)^2$$
$$=100t^2+20tu+u^2$$

由 t 和 u 的乘法表可得 $t^2=a$，$tu=b$，$u^2=c$，则 $y^2=100t^2+20tu+u^2=100a+20b+c$。

32. $x>0$

32. **解：** 本题的正确答案为（D）。对于这种比较题，一般要分区间进行讨论：

$$x+1 \qquad\qquad x^2$$

$$0 < x < \frac{1+\sqrt{5}}{2} \text{ 时}, x+1 > x^2$$

$$x = \frac{1+\sqrt{5}}{2} \text{ 时}, x+1 = x^2$$

$$x > \frac{1+\sqrt{5}}{2} \text{ 时}, x+1 < x^2$$

33. For all real numbers v, the operation v^* is defined by the equation $v^* = v - \dfrac{v}{3}$. If $(v^*)^* = 8$, then $v =$

(A) 15   (B) 18   (C) 21

(D) 24   (E) 27

33. 对于所有的实数（real number）v，运算（operation）v^* 被定义为方程 $v^* = v - \dfrac{v}{3}$，若 $(v^*)^* = 8$，那么 v 等于多少？

解：本题的正确答案是（B）。由题意可得：

$$v^* = v - \frac{v}{3} = \frac{2}{3}v \Rightarrow (v^*)^*$$

$$= \frac{2}{3} \cdot \frac{2}{3} \cdot v = \frac{4}{9}v = 8 \Rightarrow v = 18$$

34.
$$y = x^2 - 16x + 64$$

The least value of y 0

34. y 的最小值   0

解：本题的正确答案为（C）。可以把 y 的表达式化成一个数的平方的形式：$y = (x-8)^2 \geqslant 0$

35. If x is an integer and $x^2 < 37$, what is the greatest possible value of x minus the least possible value of x ?

(A) 5   (B) 6   (C) 10

(D) 12   (E) 36

35. 若 x 是整数且 $x^2 < 37$，则 x 的最大可能值与其最小可能值的差是多少？

解：本题的正确答案为（D）。由不等式 $x^2 < 37$ 可以得到 x 的取值范围是：$-\sqrt{37} < x < \sqrt{37}$；再根据 x 只能取整数，可得 x 的最大可能值与最小可能值的差为 $6 - (-6) = 12$。

36.
$$x > 1$$

$$\frac{x^3}{3} \qquad\qquad \frac{x^2}{2}$$

36. 解：本题的正确答案为（D）。考生在解比较的前后两项有相同多项式的题时，一般要消去该项或具有共同系数的某项，然后再进行比较。如本题可以提出系数：提出 x^2 或 $\dfrac{x^2}{2}$ 即变成比较 $\dfrac{x}{3}$ 与 $\dfrac{1}{2}$ 或 x 与 $\dfrac{3}{2}$ 的大小，再根据 $x > 1$ 的取值范围，可知无法判断比较两项的大小。

37. Pencils have the same unit cost regardless of the number sold. x pencils cost a total of 0.5, and n pencils cost a total of y dollar.

$$n \qquad\qquad 2xy$$

38. If $\sqrt{x^2y}=3$ and $xy=18$, what is the value of y?

(A) $\dfrac{1}{2}$ (B) $\dfrac{1}{\sqrt{2}}$ (C) 3

(D) 6   (E) 36

39. $$x+y=10,\ 3x>15$$
$$y \qquad\qquad 5$$

40. From an estate, x dollars was distributed such that each of two children received $\dfrac{x}{5}$ dollars and the widow received the remaining $90,000$.

$$x \qquad\qquad 126,000$$

41. $F_n=2^{(2^n)}+1$ for any nonnegative integer n.

$$F_0 \qquad\qquad 3$$

42. $$x=1$$

---

37. 铅笔的单价（unit cost）与其销售量无关，x 支铅笔卖 0.5，n 支铅笔卖 y 美元。

解：本题的正确答案为（C）。单价不变，即
$$\frac{0.5}{x}=\frac{y}{n}\Rightarrow n=2xy$$

38. 若 $\sqrt{x^2y}=3$ 且 $xy=18$，y 值是多少？

解：本题的正确答案为（E）。把题目中给出的两个等式分别平方可得：
$$x^2y=9,\ x^2y^2=18^2,$$
$$\Rightarrow \frac{x^2y^2}{x^2y}=\frac{18^2}{9}\Rightarrow y=\frac{18^2}{9}=36$$

39. 解：本题的正确答案为（B）。$3x>15\Rightarrow x>5$，而 $x=10-y$，综合两者可以得到 $10-y>5$，从而可以推出 $y<5$。

40. 从一遗产中，分发 x 美元，两个孩子各自得到 $\dfrac{x}{5}$ 美元，遗孀得到剩下的 $90,000$。

解：本题的正确答案为（A）。因为两个孩子各得 $\dfrac{x}{5}$ 美元，所以遗孀得到的 $\dfrac{3}{5}x$ 美元即为 $90,000$，由此可求出 $x=150,000>126,000$。

41. $F_n=2^{(2^n)}+1$，n 是任意非负整数（nonnegative integer）。

解：本题的正确答案为（C）。某些考生在做该题时，会做如下的化简：
$$F_n=2^{(2^n)}+1=4^n+1$$
实际上这样的做法是不对的，对于本题正确的解法如下：
$$F_0=2^{(2^0)}+1=2^1+1=3$$

42. 解：本题的正确答案为（C）。把 $x=1$ 代入比较的左项可得：

$$\frac{\left(x+\frac{1}{2}\right)^2}{\left(x-\frac{1}{2}\right)^2} \qquad\qquad 9$$

$$\frac{\left(x+\frac{1}{2}\right)^2}{\left(x-\frac{1}{2}\right)^2} = \frac{\frac{9}{4}}{\frac{1}{4}} = 9$$

43.
$$y=1+(-x)^3$$

$$y \qquad\qquad 1+x^3$$

43. 解：本题的正确答案为(D)。因为当 x 取正值，取负值或取零时，两者大小是变化的。

44. If the sum $r+s$ is 2 less than the difference $r-s$, then $s=$

(A) -2 (B) -1 (C) 0

(D) 1 (E) 2

44. 若 $r+s$ 的值比 $r-s$ 的值小 2，则 $s=$

解：本题的正确答案为(B)。由题意可得：
$$r+s=r-s-2 \Rightarrow s=-1$$

45.
$$x>1$$

$$(x^3)^2 \cdot (x^3) \qquad\qquad x^{11}$$

45. 解：本题的正确答案为(B)。考生在做此类题时要注意正确使用幂的运算法则，特别是要注意区分下列两种形式：
$(x^a)^b=x^{ab}$，$x^a \cdot x^b=x^{a+b}$，切勿将二者混淆。此题中有 $(x^3)^2(x^3)=x^6 \cdot x^3=x^9$，因为 $x>1$，所以 $(x^3)^2 \cdot (x^3)<x^{11}$。

46. In 1988, Mr. Smith's annual income was greater than Mrs. smith's annual income. In 1989, Mr. Smith's annual income decreased by p percent, where as Mrs. Smiths annual income increased by p percent ($p>0$)

Mr. and Mrs. Smith's combined annual income in 1988	Mr. and Mrs. Smith's combined annual income in 1989

46. 在 1988 年 Mr. Smith 比 Mrs. Smith 的年收入多。在 1989 年，Mr. Smith 的收入减少百分之 p，而 Mrs. Smith 的收入增加了百分之 p（$p>0$）。

解：本题的正确答案为（A）。比较的左项为 1988 年 Mr. 和 Mrs. Smith 的年收入和；比较的右项为 1989 年 Mr. 和 Mrs. Smith 的年收入和。设 Mr. 和 Mrs. Smith 1988 年的收入分别为 x 和 y，且 $x>y$，则 1989 年两人的收入分别为 $x(1-p\%)$ 和 $y(1+p\%)$，他们的总收入为 $x(1-p\%)+y(1+p\%)=x+y+(y-x)p\% < x+y$。

47.
$$x>0$$
$$(\sqrt{x}+1)^2 \qquad\qquad x^2+1$$

47. 解：本题的正确答案为(D)。本题可用特殊数值法进行求解，若把 $x=1$ 和 $x=100$ 代入比较的左右两项会发现两数的大小随 x 取值的不同而不同。

48. The value of y will decrease as the value of x increases in which of the following equations?

(A) $y=x$　　　　　(B) $y=x-2$

(C) $2-y=3-x$　　(D) $2x-y=4$

(E) $x+2y=1$

48. 下面哪个等式中的 y 值随 x 值的增加而减小？

解： 本题的正确答案为(E)。此题也就是让考生找 y 是 x 的减函数的选项。而题目中的五个选项都是一次线性方程，我们知道对于一次方程 $y=kx+b$ 来说，当 k 大于零时，y 是 x 的减函数；当 k 小于零时，y 是 x 的增函数。在本题的五个选项中只有(E)选项的 k 值等于 $-\dfrac{1}{2}$ 小于零。

49.
$$a=-219$$

$$a^7+a^{15} \qquad a^8+a^{14}$$

49. 解： 本题的正确答案为(B)。根据负数的奇次幂为负，偶次幂为正可得：

$$a^7+a^{15}<0, a^8+a^{14}>0$$

50.
$$x^2+2x+1 \qquad x^2$$

50. 解： 本题的正确答案为(D)。把比较的左右两项同时减去 x^2 后，发现此题实际上就是让比较 $2x+1$ 与 0 的大小。因为 x 可以取任意实数，所以本题为无法判断。

51.
$$2^x+2^x=$$

(A) 2^{x+1}　　(B) 2^{x+2}　　(C) 2^{2x}

(D) 4^x　　(E) 4^{2x}

51. 解： 本题的正确答案为(A)。

$$2^x+2^x=2\times2^x=2^{x+1}$$

52. What is the cost, in cents, of using a certain fax machine to send n pages of a report if the total cost for sending the first k pages is r cents and the cost for sending each additional page is s cents? (Assume that $n>k$.)

(A) $r+s(n-k)$　　(B) $r+s(n+k)$

(C) $rs(n+k)$　　(D) $kr+s(n-k)$

(E) $kr+ns$

52. 用某台传真机发送 n 页的报告，若最初 k 页总计费用为 r 美分，每额外多一张加收 s 美分，则以美分为单位使用该传真机发送 n 页报告需多少钱？（假设 $n>k$）

解： 本题的正确答案为(A)。最初 k 页总共花 r 美分，其余 $(n-k)$ 张共花 $s(n-k)$ 美分，因此发 n 页共需 $r+s(n-k)$ 美分。

53. $f(t)=kt$ for all t, where k is a constant, and $f(3)=\dfrac{1}{2}$

$k \qquad\qquad f(1)$

53. 对所有 t 有 $f(t)=kt$，其中 k 是常数，且 $f(3)=\dfrac{1}{2}$

解： 本题的正确答案为(C)。此题只须将 $t=1$ 代入 $f(t)$ 表达式：

$$f(1) = k \times 1 = k$$

54.

$$-4 \leqslant x \leqslant 4$$
$$-8 \leqslant y \leqslant -4$$

The greatest possible value of $25x - 12.5y$

200

54. 解：本题的正确答案为（C）。此题实际上是让求 $25x - 12.5y$ 的最大值，考生只须取 x 的最大值（$x=4$），而取 y 的最小值（$y=-8$）即可，然后把 x 和 y 的值代入 $25x - 12.5y$ 可得其最大可能值为 200。

55. If x is $11\frac{1}{9}$ percent more than y, then y is what percent less than x?

(A) 9%　　　(B) 10%　　　(C) 11%

(D) 12%　　　(E) 15%

55. 若 x 比 y 大百分之 $11\frac{1}{9}$，则 y 比 x 小百分之几？

解：本题的正确答案为（B）。由题意可得：

$x = \left(1 + 11\frac{1}{9}\%\right)y = \frac{10}{9}y$，因此 y 用 x 来表示为 $y = \frac{9}{10}x$，所以 y 比 x 小 10%。对于这种题，千万不要认为 x 比 y 多 $11\frac{1}{9}\%$，就认为 y 比 x 少 $11\frac{1}{9}\%$。做题时一定要按题干给出的关系写出 x 与 y 的关系式，找出两者之间相互的比例关系，得到正确答案。

56.

$$x > 0$$

$\frac{1}{x} + 1$　　　　$\frac{1}{x+1}$

56. 解：本题的正确答案为（A）。

$$\Rightarrow \frac{1}{x+1} < 1 < \frac{1}{x} + 1$$

57.

$$n = \frac{k + \frac{r}{s}}{\frac{t}{v}}$$

In the equation above, k, r, s, t, and v represent positive numbers. Multiplying which one of these numbers by 2 will reduce the value of n to $\frac{1}{2}$ of its present value?

(A) k　　　　　(B) r (C) s

(D) t　　　　　(E) v

57. 在左面方程中，k，r，s，t 和 v 都是正数（positive number），其中哪个数乘以 2 将使 n 值减少到某前值的 $\frac{1}{2}$？

解：本题的正确答案为（D）。n 是一个分式，要使一个分式的值减小一半，要么使分式的分子的值减小一半，要么使分式的分母的值增加一倍。本题所给出的繁分式的分母为 $\frac{t}{v}$，因此只有把 t 的值增加一倍，才能使 n 的值减小一半。

58. $x = y^2$, $1 = cy$

xc y

59. $x > 1$

2^x x^2

58. 解：本题的正确答案为（C）。因为 $1 = cy$，所以 $c = \dfrac{1}{y}$，由此可推出 $xc = \dfrac{x}{y} = \dfrac{y^2}{y} = y$

59. 解：本题的正确答案为（D）。对于这种类型的比较题，可以把题中的未知数赋几个特殊值来确定。一般情况下这种题有近一多半是不能确定结果的，对于本题：

$x = 2$ 时，$2^x = x^2$

$x = 3$ 时，$2^3 = 8 < x^2 = 9$

第 三 章

文字题（Word Problems）

从严格意义上来讲，文字题并不能算是一种单独的题型，它更像是一种综合性比较强的题型。它不仅会涉及算术、代数、几何等方面的知识，还会涉及经济学、统计学以及物理学上的一些基本概念。因此，要突破这种题型，除了有一定的数学知识，并对经济学、统计学以及物理学的一些基本概念有一定的了解之外，还要求考生有比较强的阅读理解能力以及抽象推理能力。换句话说，就是要求考生具备把冗长复杂的文字变成简单明晰的数学表达式的能力。

如何把复杂晦涩的文字转变成简单明了的数学表达式呢？下面表格汇总了 GRE 数学考试中最常用的转换规则，希望考生能够全面透彻地掌握，并达到融会贯通、举一反三的水平。

English Words	Mathematical Moaning	Symbol
is, was, will be, had, has, will have, is equal to, is the same as	Equals	$=$
plus, more than, sum, increased by, added to, exceeds, received, got, older than, farther than, greater than	Addition	$+$
minus, fewer, less than, difference, decreased by, subtracted from, younger than, gave, lost	Subtraction	$-$
times, of, product, multiplied by	Multiplication	$\times$
divided by, quotient, per, for	Division	$\div$
more than, greater than	Inequality	$>$
at least	Inequality	$\geqslant$
fewer than, less than	Inequality	$<$
at most	Inequality	$\leqslant$
what, how many, etc.	Unknown quantity	x (or some other variable)

解文字题的关键是把文字变成数学表达式，因为很多数学表达式是以代数表达式的方式呈现的，所以很多书上又把文字题称为代数文字题。上面表格中的内容学完了，测试一下，看自己能否把下面左列的文字变成右侧的数学表达式。

English Words	Algebraic Expressions
The sum of 5 and some number is 13.	$5+x=13$
John was 2 years younger than Sam.	$J=S-2$
Bill has at most $100.	$B\leqslant100$

English Words	Algebraic Expressions
The product of 2 and a number exceeds that number by 5 (is 5 more than).	2N＝N＋5
In 7 years Erin will be twice as old as she was 8 years ago.	x＋7＝2(x−8)

通过系统研究,GRE 数学考试中的代数文字题基本上可以分为11大类:

- 加权平均问题
- 货币问题
- 投资问题
- 运动问题
- 流水行船问题
- 工作问题
- "牛吃草"问题
- 混和物问题
- 鸽巢原理(抽屉原则)
- 年龄问题
- 集合问题

本章接下来的部分将分类举例讲解这11大类问题。

第一节　加权平均问题(Weighted Average Problems)

The formula for determining the average (A) of a series of terms (numbers) is：

$$A=\frac{a+b+c+\cdots}{n}$$

where **n** equals the number of terms (numbers in the series). When some numbers among the terms to be averaged are given greater "weight" than others, however, you have to make some adjustments to the basic formula to find the average.

例 1: Tom's average monthly salary for the first four months that he worked was $ 4000. What must his average monthly salary be for each of the next eight months, so that his average monthly salary for the year is $ 4,800?

解: The $ 3,000 salary receives a weight of 4, while the unknown salary receives a weight of 8, if x represents the unknown salary, then we can approach this problem in strict algebraic fashion：

$$\frac{4(4000)+8x}{12}=4800\Rightarrow x=5200$$

Tom's salary for each of the next eight months must be $ 5200 for Tom to earn an average of $ 4,800 a month during the entire 12 months.

第二节　货币问题(Currency (Coin and Bill) Problems)

Currency problems are really **quasi-weighted-average(准加权平均)** problems, because each item (bill or coin) in a problem is weighted according to its monetary value. Unlike weighted average problems, however, the "average value" of all the bills or coins is not at issue. In solving currency problems, remember the following:

1. You must formulate algebraic expressions involving both number of items (bills or coins) and value of items.

2. You should covert the value of all moneys to a common unit (that is, cents or dollars) before formulating an equation. If converting to cents, for example, you must multiply the number of nickels by 5, dimes by 10, and so forth.

例 2: Mike has $ 2.05 in dimes and quarters. If he has four fewer dimes than quarters, how much money does he have in dimes?

解: Letting x equal the number of dimes, $x+4$ represents the number of quarters. The total value of the dimes (in cents) is $10x$, and the total value of the quarters (in cents) is $25(x+4)$, or $25x+100$. Given that Mike has $ 2.05, the following equation emerges:
$$10x+25x+100=205 \Rightarrow x=3$$
Mike has three dimes, so he has 30 cents in dimes.

第三节　投资问题(Investment Problems)

GRE investment problems usually involve interest and require more than simply calculating interest earned on a given principal amount at a given rate. They usually call for you to set up and solve an algebraic equation, although sometimes you can solve these problems intuitively.

一、基本概念

① **Discount(折扣)**：商品按原定价格扣除百分之几出售。If a price is discounted by n percent, the price becomes $(100-n)$ percent of the original price.

② **Interest(利息)**：借款人支付给贷款人的报酬。利息可分单利(simple interest)和复利(compound interest)两种计算方法。

③ **Simple Interest(单利)**：计算利息的一种方法。不管期限长短,仅按本金(principal)计算利息,其所生利息不再加入本金重复计算利息。

④ **Compound Interest(复利)**：单利的对称。经过一定的期限,将所生利息加入本金再计利息,逐期滚算,俗称"利上滚利"。

⑤ **Rate or Percent of Interest(利率)**：亦称"利息率",指一定时期内利息额同贷出金额的比率,有年利率、月利率和日利率。

⑥ **Profit(利润)**：Gross profit is equal to revenues minus expenses, or selling price minus cost.

例 3: A certain appliance costs a merchant $40. At what price should the merchant sell the appliance in order to make a gross profit of 30 percent of the cost of the appliance?

解: 设 x 为销售价,则由题意可列出方程 $x-40=40\times30\%$,解这个方程可得 $x=\$52$。

二、基本性质

(1) **Selling Price(销售价)**＝Cost(原价或价值)±Gain 或 Loss(盈或亏)

$$=\frac{c \pm cr}{100}=\frac{c(1 \pm r)}{100}$$

(2) **Discount(折扣)**＝Cost(原价)×Discount Rate(折扣率)

Discount Price(折扣价)＝原价－折扣

(3) **Interest(利息)**

① **Simple Interest (单利)**＝Principal(本金)×Interest Rate(利率)×Time(时间)，式中时间单位与利率的时间单位应一致。以单利计算的本金利息和＝$p(1+n \cdot r)$，其中，p 为本金，n 为时间，r 为利率。

② **Compound Interest(复利)**：$A=P(1+r)^n$，式中：A 为本利和(principal＋interest)，P 为本金(principal)，r 为利率(rate or percent of interest)，n 为期数。

注意： 单利与复利计算时，一定要注意单位换算，如是以半年为单位计算复利，还是以三个月为单位计算复利

例 4： Mrs. Jones sold two house for $80,000 each. One house was sold at a 20 percent loss and the other at a 20 percent gain.

The gain minus the loss　　　　0

解： 一个房子盈20％和另一个房子亏20％的销售价相同，都是$80,000，因而盈的房子的原价比亏的房子的原价低，从而盈与亏的差数为负数，所以本题的正确答案为（B）。

例 5： Mr. Richard plans to invest $20,000 in an account paying 6％ interest annually. How much more must he invest at the same time at 3％ so that his total annual income during the first year is 4％ of his total initial investment?

(A) $32,000　　(B) $36,000

(C) $40,000　　(D) $47,000

(E) $49,000

解： **Letting x equal the amount invested at 3％, then Mr. Richard's total investment is $20,000＋x$. The interest on $20,000 plus the interest on the additional investment equals the total interest from both investments. You can state this algebraically as follows：**

$20,000 \times 0.06 + 0.03x$

$=(20,000+x) \times 0.04 \Rightarrow x=40,000$

Richard must invest $40,000 at 3％ for his total annual income to be 4％ of her total investment ($60,000).

第四节　运动问题(Motion Problems)

Motion problems involve the linear movement of persons or objects over time. Fundamental to all GRE motion problems is the following simple and familiar foumula：

Distance(距离)＝Rate(速度)×Time(时间)

Nearly every GRE motion problem falls into one of four categories：

（1）**Two objects moving in opposite directions(反向运动)**：反向运动有两种，一是两个物体同时同地向相反的方向运动，二是两个物体同时但相隔一定距离向相反的方向运动。在上述任何一种情况下，$d_1 + d_2 = d$，这里 d_1 和 d_2 分别表示第一和第二个物体在一定的时间里移动的距离，d 表示两个物体移动的距离之和。

（2）**Two objects moving in the same direction(同向运动)**：亦称"追赶运动"，两个物体同时同地以不同的速度向相同的方向运动，被称为"同向运动"。

（3）**One object making a round trip(往返运动)**：表示从某地出发再回到某地的运动。

（4）**Perpendicular or Right-angle(垂直运动)**：指两个物体运动的方向相互垂直。For example，where one object moves in a northerly direction while another moves in an easterly direction. However，this type is really just as much a geometry as an algebra problem，because you determine the distance between the two objects by applying the Pythagorean Theorem to determine the length of a triangle's hypotenuse.

例 6：How far can Scott drive into the country if he drives out at 40 mph，returns over the same road at 30 mph，and spends eight hours away from home including a one-hour stop for lunch?

解：Scott 实际的开车时间是 7 小时，这 7 小时由两部分时间组成，一部分是他从家开车到乡村所用的时间，另一部分是他从乡村返回所用的时间。设他开车外出所用的时间为 x，则他返回所用的时间为 $7-x$，把这两个代数表达式代入运动公式可得：

Formula：Rate $\times$ Time $=$ Distance

Going：$(40)x = 40x$

Returning：$(30)(7-x) = 210-30x$

因为 Scott 所做的是往返运动，所以来回距离相等，于是我们可得出下列方程：

$$40x = 210-30x \Rightarrow x = 3$$

即 Scott 在外出时，以 40 mph 的速度运行了 3 小时，也即根据题中条件他可以开车到 120 英里远的郊外。

注意：Regardless of which types of motion problem you're dealing with，you should always start with the same task：set up two distinct equations patterned after the simple motion formula $(r \cdot t = d)$.

第五节　流水行船问题

船在江河里航行时，除了本身的前进外，还受到流水的推动或顶流，在这种情况下计算船只的航行速度、时间和所行的路程，叫做流水行船问题。流水行船问题是行程问题的一种，因此行程问题中的三个量（速度、时间和路程）的关系在这里将反复用到。此外流水行船问题还有以下两个基本公式：

顺水速度＝船速＋水速

逆水速度＝船速－水速

这里，船速是指船本身的速度，也就是在静水中单位时间里所走过的路程；水速是指水在单位时间里流过的路程。顺水速度和逆水速度分别是指顺水航行和逆水航行时船在单位时间里所行的路程。

例 7： 某船在静水中的速度是每小时 15 千米，它从上游甲地开往下游乙地共花去了 8 小时，水速每小时 3 千米，问从乙地返回甲地需要多少时间？

分析： 要想求从乙地返回甲地需要多少时间，只要分别求出甲、乙两地之间的路程和逆水速度。

解： 从甲地到乙地，顺水速度：$15 + 3 = 18$（千米/小时）

甲乙两地路程：$18 \times 8 = 144$（千米）

从乙地到甲地的逆水速度：$15 - 3 = 12$（千米/小时）

返回时逆行所需的时间：$144 \div 12 = 12$（小时）

注：鸟或飞机在风中飞行问题与流水行船问题相类似，在解决这类问题时，只要把流水行船问题中的水速换成风速即可。

第六节　工作问题（**Work Problems**）

Work problems involve one or more "workers"(people or machines) accomplishing a task or job. 在工作问题中完成某项工作所用的时间与参加该项工作的人数成反比，也就是说，劳动者越多，工作就完成得越快。下面是解决工作问题的通用公式：

$$\frac{A}{x} + \frac{A}{y} = 1$$

In this formula：x and y represent the time needed for each of two workers to complete the job alone; A represents the time it takes for both x and y to complete the job working in the aggregate (together).

So each fraction represents the portion of the job completed by a worker. The sum of the two fractions must be 1, if the job is completed.

在工作问题中一般要出现三个量：工作总量、工作时间（完成工作总量所需的时间）和工作效率（单位时间内完成的工作量）。这三个量之间有下述一些关系：

工作效率×工作时间＝工作总量

工作总量÷工作时间＝工作效率

工作总量÷工作效率＝工作时间

例 8： Worker W produces n units in 5 hours. Workers V and W, working independently but at the same time, produce n units in 2 hours. How long would it take V alone to produce n units?

解： W 在 5 小时里制造了 n 个，则 W 每小时制造 $\frac{n}{5}$ 个，而 V 和 W 同时独立地工作时在 2 小时内制造了 n 个，则 V 和 W 每小时制造 $\frac{n}{2}$ 个，因而 V 每小时制造 $\left(\frac{n}{2} - \frac{n}{5}\right)$ 个。从而 V 制造 n 个需要的时间为 $n \div \left(\frac{n}{2} - \frac{n}{5}\right) = 3\frac{1}{3}$（小时）。

第七节 "牛吃草"问题

"牛吃草"问题与工作问题有些相似,在实际解题时可以把此类问题看作是工作问题来解决,"草的总量"可以看作是工作总量,"牛吃草"可看作是工人做工。这类问题区别于工作问题的地方是:在工作问题中总的工作量是一定的,而在"牛吃草"类的问题中,"草"的总量却是在不断变化的,这就是"牛吃草"问题的困难所在。下面将通过举例来讲解一下有关"牛吃草"的问题。

例9: 牧场上有一片匀速生长的草地,可供27头牛吃6周,或供23头牛吃9周,那么它可供21头牛吃几周? 这类问题称为"牛吃草"问题。

分析与解答: 做这类问题困难在于草的总量有变,它每天,每周都在均匀地生长,时间越长,草的总量就越多,草的总量是由两部分组成的:(1)某个时间期限前草场上原有的草量;(2)这个时间期限后草场每天(周)由于生长而新增的草量;因此,必须设法找出两个量来。

下面就用这个题目为例对"牛吃草"类的问题进行分析。

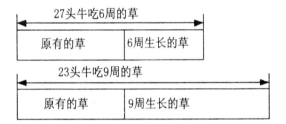

从右面的线段可以看出 23 头牛吃 9 周的总草量比 27 头牛吃 6 周的总草量要多。多出部分相当于 3 周新生长的草量。为了求出一周新生长的草量,就要将问题进行转化。27 头牛 6 周吃草量相当于 $27 \times 6 = 162$ 头牛一周吃草量(或一头牛吃 162 周);23 头牛 9 周吃草量相当于 $23 \times 9 = 207$ 头牛一周吃草量(或一头牛吃 207 周)。这们一来我们可以认为每周新生长的草量相当于 $(207 - 162) \div (9 - 6) = 15$ 头牛一周的吃草量。

需要解决的第二个问题是牧场上原有的草量是多少? 用 27 头牛 6 周的总吃草量减去 6 周新生长的草量(即 $15 \times 6 = 90$ 头牛吃一周的草量)即为牧场原有的草量。所以牧场上原有草量为 $27 \times 6 - 15 \times 6 = 72$ 头牛一周的吃草量(或者为 $23 \times 9 - 15 \times 9 = 72$)。

牧场上的草 21 头牛几周才能吃完呢? 解决这个问题相当于把 21 头牛分成两部分。一部分看成专吃牧场上原有的草，另一部分看成专吃新生长的草。但是新生长的草只能维持 15 头牛的吃草量，且始终可保持平衡（前面已分析过每周新生的草恰好够 15 头牛吃一周）。故分出 15 头牛吃新生长的草，另一部分 21－15 ＝6（头）牛去吃原有的草，所以牧场上的草够吃 72÷6 ＝ 12（周），也就是这个牧场上的草够 21 头牛吃 12 周。

第八节　混和物问题（Mixture Problems）

In mixture problems, you combine substances with different characteristics, resulting in a particular mixture or proportion. Here are some typical scenarios:

Wet Mixtures involving liquids, gases, or granules, which are measured and mixed by volume or weight, not by number (quantity).

Dry Mixtures involving a number of discreet objects, such as coins, coolies, or marbles, that are measured and mixed by number (quantity) as well as by relative weight, size, value, and so on.

　　溶液混和问题通常要涉及浓度和百分比，而固态物质相混和的问题则通常涉及到原始数目和数量。但是不管是溶液混和还是固态物质混和，解决它们的思路都是一样的，即要牢牢抓住混和前后的不变量。

例 10： How many quarts of pure alcohol must you add to 15 quarts of solution that is 40％ alcohol to strengthen it to a solution that is 50％ alcohol?

解：The original amount of alcohol is 40% of 15. Letting x equal the number of quarts of alcohol that you must add to achieve a 50% alcohol solution, $0.4 \times 15 + x$ equals the amount of alcohol in the solution after adding more alcohol. You can express this amount as 50% of $(15+x)$. Thus, you can express the mixture algebraically as follows:

$$0.4 \times 15 + x = 0.5(15+x) \Rightarrow x = 3$$

You must add three quarts of alcohol to achieve a 50% alcohol solution.

Caution： *Mixture problems often involve units of measurement-such as weight, price, and distance. This feature gives the test-makers a great opportunity to trap you by commingling ounces and pounds, cents and dollars, inches and feet, an so forth. Don't fall for this ploy! Once you set up your equation, always convert terms to the same unit of measurement. You'll be glad you did.*

第九节 鸽巢原理(抽屉原则)

若有 m 只鸽子,飞往 n 个巢穴($m > n$),则至少有一个巢中的鸽子数大于等于 2 只,这即为鸽巢原理。(若用抽屉原则表达即为:有 m 个球,放入 n 个抽屉中〔$m > n$〕,则至少有一个抽屉球的数目大于或等于 2)。这一简单的原理在 GRE 考试中经常遇到。

例 11: 有 0—9 这十个数字分别写在 10 张纸片上,随机从这十张小纸片中抓,问至少抓几个小纸片才能保证所抓小纸片上必有两个小纸片上所写数字相加等于 10?

解: 在 0—9 这十个数字中可以相加等于 10 的仅有(1,9),(2,8),(3,7),(4,6),除此之外还有 0 和 5 这两个数,因此就组成了 6 个巢穴分别是(前四个):(1,9),(2,8),(3,7),(4,6),0,5,则原题转化为取几个纸片能保证有两个属于前 4 个"巢穴"中的任一个巢穴。根据鸽巢原理所取纸片至少应比"巢穴"多,因而至少应取 6+1=7 个纸片。

第十节 年龄问题(Age Problems)

Age problems ask you to compare ages of two or more people at different points in time. In solving age problems, you might have to represent a person's age at the present time, several years from now, or several years ago. Any age problem allows you to set up an equation to relate the ages of two or more people, as in the following examples:

(1) If A is 5 years younger than B at the present time, you can express the relationship between A's age and B's age as $A = B - 5$ (or $A + 5 = B$)

(2) Ten years ago, if X was twice as old as Y, you can express the relationship between their ages as $2(Y - 10) = X - 10$, where X and Y are the present ages of X and Y.

例 12: Fred, Geri, and Holly were each born on May 15, but in different years. Fred is twice as old as Geri was 4 years ago, and Holly is five years older than Geri will be one year from now. If the total age of Fred, Geri, and Holly is 78, how old is Fred?

解: 设 Fred,Geri 和 Holly 现在的年龄分别为 F,G 和 H,根据题意 Fred 现在的年龄是 Geri 四年前年龄的 2 倍可得:F=2(G−4);又根据题意 Holly 现在的年龄比 Geri 一年后的年龄大 5 岁可得:H=G+6;再由三人目前的年龄之和等于 78 可得:

$$F + G + H = 78 \Rightarrow 2(G - 4) + G + (G + 6)$$
$$= 78$$
$$\Rightarrow G = 20$$
$$\Rightarrow F = 2(G - 4) = 32$$

第十一节　集合问题(Problems Involving Overlapping Sets)

Overlapping set problems involve distinct sets that share some number of members. GRE overlapping problems come in one of two varieties:

1. Single overlap (easier)
2. Double overlap (tougher)

例 13： The inventory at a certain men's clothing store includes 480 neckties (领带), each of which is either 100% silk or 100% polyester(多元酯),40% of the ties are striped, and 130 of the ties are silk, 52 of the silk ties are striped. How many of the ties are polyester but are not striped?

解： This double overlap problem involves four distinct sets: striped silk ties, striped polyester ties, non-striped silk ties, and non-striped polyesters ties. Set up a table representing the four sets.

Neckties	Silk	Polyester	Total
Striped	**52**	140	**480×40% =192**
Non-striped	78	? = 210	288
Total	**130**	350	**480**

Given that 130 ties are silk (see the left column), 350 ties must be polyester (see the right column). Also, given that 40% of the 480 ties (192 ties) are striped (see the top row), 140 of the polyester ties (192－52) must be striped. Accordingly, 350－140, or 210, of the ties are polyester and non-striped.

在上面的表格中,根据题意可直接得出的已知条件都已用黑体字标出,根据这些已知数据很容易求出不带条纹的领带是210条。

注：GRE 考试中出现的代数文字题的类型很多,限于篇幅,本书不能一一列举。但是"万变不离其宗",其他类型的文字题大都可转化为上面讲解的几种方法给予解决。

第十二节　重点试题精练及解析

1. Brand R coffee costs $3.25 per pound and brand T coffee costs $2.50 per pound.

   The number of pounds of brand R in a

1. R 牌咖啡每磅$3.25,T 牌咖啡每磅$2.50。

解：本题的正确答案为(D)。比较的左项为 R 与 T 混合后每磅值$3.00 的咖啡中 R 牌咖

mixture of brands
R and T that costs
$3.00 per pound

1.2

啡的磅数。设 R 和 T 各有 x 和 y 磅,根据题意列出方程:

$$3.25x + 2.50y = 3.00(x+y) \Rightarrow x = 2y$$

显然,我们只能得到 R 和 T 两种牌子的咖啡在混和咖啡中所占的比例,若要求出 R 牌咖啡的确切重量,还必须给出混和咖啡的总重量或者 T 牌咖啡的重量。

2. A manufacture packages soap powder in containers of three different sizes. The amount of soap powder in a full large container could fill exactly 3 of the medium containers or exactly 5 of the small containers. If an equal number of small and large containers are to be filled with the amount of soap powder that would fill 90 medium containers，how many small containers will be filled?

(A) 25   (B) 27   (C) 30
(D) 45   (E) 55

2. 一名制造商把洗衣粉装入三种不同尺寸的容器中。装满的大容器中的洗衣粉的量可以装满 3 个中型容器或 5 个小容器中,若相同数目的小容器和大容器所盛的洗衣粉能装满 90 个中型容器,问小容器的数目是多少?

解: 本题的正确答案是（A）。设装满的大容器中的洗衣粉量为 a,则中型容器中可以盛洗衣粉量为 $\frac{1}{3}a$,而小容器中可以盛 $\frac{1}{5}a$,设可以装入 90 个中型容器中的洗衣粉可以放入 n 个大容器和 n 个小容器中,则由题义可得到下面的等式:

$$n \times (a + \frac{1}{5}a) = 90 \times \frac{1}{3}a \Rightarrow n = 25$$

3. A rectangular floor 18 feet by 10 feet is to be completely covered with carpeting that costs x dollars per square yard. In terms of x, how many dollars will the carpeting cost?
(1 yard＝3 feet)

(A) 20x (B) 28x (C) 60x
(D) 180x (E) 540x

3. 一长为 18 英尺,宽为 10 英尺的长方形地板要全部铺上每平方码 x 美元的地毯。以 x 为单位,地毯总共需花多少钱?（1 码＝3 英尺）

解: 本题的正确答案为（A）。解答该题时,考生一定要注意前后单位的变化,一时疏忽很易选(D)。考虑单位变化,$\frac{18}{3} \times \frac{10}{3} \times x = 20x$。

4. In a certain country，a person is born every 3 seconds and a person dies every 10 seconds. Therefore，the birth and death rates account for a population growth rate of one person every

(A) $3\frac{1}{3}$ sec   (B) $4\frac{2}{7}$ sec   (C) 7 sec

4. 在某一个国家,每 3 秒钟有一个人出生,每 10 秒钟有一个人死亡。这一出生率和死亡率从而说明该国的人口增长率是多少秒一个人?

解: 本题的正确答案为（B）。每 3 秒出生 1 个人,那么 30 秒钟将出生 10 人,每 10 秒 1 个人死亡,那么 30 秒钟将死亡 3 个人,30 秒钟

(D) $11\frac{2}{3}$ sec   (E) 13sec

净出生 7 人，$\frac{30}{7}=4\frac{2}{7}$ 秒，所以人口增长率为

$4\frac{2}{7}$ 秒每人。

5. Ms. Rogers bought an electric range on the installment plan. The cash price of the range was \$400. The amount she paid was \$120 down and 12 monthly payments of \$28 each.

The amount she paid for the electric range in excess of the cash price	\$56

5. Rogers 太太用分期付款的方法购买了一个电气灶，这个灶的现金价格为 400 美元，她首期付 120 美元，以后每月付 28 美元，分 12 个月付完。

解： 本题的正确答案是(C)。设她超出现金价格的付款为 x，则有

$$400+x=120+28\times12\Rightarrow x=56$$

注：down=down payment 首期付款

6. The price of an article of clothing was reduced from \$25 to \$20. The reduced price of the article was then increased by x percent to return it to \$25.

x	20

6. 一件衣服的价格从 \$25 降到 \$20，减价后衣服的价钱又涨了 $x\%$，该衣服的价格升至原价 \$25。

解： 本题的正确答案为（A）。由题意可列出下面的方程：

$$\$20(1+x\%)=\$25\Rightarrow x=25$$

7. A widow received $\frac{1}{3}$ of her husband's estate，and each of her three sons received $\frac{1}{3}$ of the balance. If the widow and one of her sons received a total of \$60,000 from the estate, what was the amount of the estate?

(A) \$90,000   (B) \$96,000
(C) \$108,000   (D) \$135,000
(E) \$180,000

7. 一个寡妇继承了她丈夫 1/3 的产业，她的 3 个儿子每人继承了剩余部分的 1/3。如果这个寡妇和她其中的一个儿子共从该产业中得到 60000 美元，问该产业共值多少钱？

解： 本题的正确答案为（C）。"the balance"是指产业的剩余部分，每个儿子继承了剩余部分的 $\frac{1}{3}$，则每个儿子继承了产业的 $\frac{2}{3}\times\frac{1}{3}=\frac{2}{9}$，设该产业值 x 美元，则有：

$$(\frac{2}{9}+\frac{1}{3})x=60000\Rightarrow x=108000 \text{ 美元}$$

8. At 9:00 a. m. train T left the train station and two hours later train S left the same station on a parallel track. If train T averaged 60 kilometers per hour and train S averaged 75 kilometers per hour until S

8. 火车 T 于上午 9:00 离开车站，两小时后，火车 S 离开同一车站，且运行在平行的轨道上。若火车 T 的平均速度为 60Km/h，火车 S 在超过火车 T 之前的平均速度为 75Km/h，在几点钟 S 超过 T？

passed T, at what time did S pass T?

(A) 2:00 p.m.　　(B) 5:00 p.m.

(C) 6:00 p.m.　　(D) 7:00 p.m.

(E) 9:00 p.m.

解：本题的正确答案为（D）。设 x 小时后 S 追上 T，此时两火车运行的距离相等，即：

$$(x+2) \cdot 60 = x \cdot 75 \Rightarrow x = 8,$$

S 在 T 出发 10 小时后，即 7:00 p.m. 追上 T。

9. The charge for a telephone call made at 10:00 a. m. from City Y to City X is $0.50 for the first minute and $0.34 for each additional minute. At these rates, what is the difference between the total cost of three 5-minute calls and the cost of one 15-minute call?

(A) $0.00

(B) $0.16

(C) $0.32

(D) $0.48

(E) $1.00

9. 上午 10 点时从 Y 城向 X 城打电话，第一分钟收费 0.5 美元，此后每附加一分钟收 0.34 美元。以这个标准计费，打 3 个 5 分钟的电话与打一个 15 分钟的电话之间的差价是多少？

解：本题的正确答案是（C）。

3 个 5 分钟的电话费为：$3 \times (0.5 + 0.34 \times 4) = 5.58$

15 分钟的电话费：$0.5 + 0.34 \times 14 = 5.26$

差价为：$5.58 - 5.26 = 0.32$

本题还有一个较为简便的算法，3 个 5 分钟的电话与一个 15 分钟的电话的时间相同，它们惟一的区别是 3 个 5 分钟的电话比一个 15 分钟的电话多了两个"第一分钟"，考生只要找出这两个"第一分钟"与两个"非第一分钟"的差价就可以了，即为 $2 \times (0.5 - 0.34) = 0.32$。

10. If the cost of a long-distance phone call is c cents for the first minute and $\frac{2}{3}c$ cents for each additional minute, what is the cost, in cents, of a 10-minute call of this type?

(A) $\frac{5}{3}c$　(B) $6c$　(C) $\frac{20}{3}c$

(D) $7c$　(E) $\frac{23}{3}c$

10. 若长途电话费为第一分钟收 c 美分，以后每增加一分钟，加收 $\frac{2}{3}c$ 美分，那么按这种计费方式打 10 分钟的电话需付多少钱（以美分为单位）？

解：本题的正确答案为（D）。由题意可得：

$$c + (10-1) \cdot \frac{2}{3}c = 7c。$$

11. A consumer insulates a house with material bought at 20 percent off the listprice of $370. If the consumer also receives a rebate of $25 from the manufacturer of the material, how much does the material cost the consumer?

11. 一名装修房子的消费者以 20% 的折扣买了标价为 370 美元的材料，若该消费者同时还从材料制造商那里获得 $25 回扣，问这个消费者买材料花了多少钱？

解：本题的正确答案是（D）。"20% off the listing price"指打了 20% 的折，等同于 at a discount of 20%，由题意可得该消费者买材

(A) $238　(B) $240　(C) $263

(D) $271　(E) $325

12. On July 1st the ratio of men to women in Club X was 9 to 20. During the month, 2 additional men and 2 additional women joined the club, and no members dropped out.

| The ratio of men to women in Club X at the end of July | $\dfrac{1}{2}$ |

13. When $\dfrac{2}{5}$ of a certain number is added to the number and this sum is subtracted from 108, the result is the original number. What is the original number?

(A) 35　　(B) 45　　(C) 54

(D) $\dfrac{135}{2}$　　(E) 270

14. What was the original price of an item if a discount of 20 percent reduced the price to $100?

(A) $80　　(B) $120　　(C) $125

(D) $150　　(E) $250

15. A purchase plan for a stereo receiver requires 20 percent of the total cost as a down payment and monthly payments of $30.

| The total cost of the stereo receiver | $450 |

料花的钱为：

$$370×（1-20\%）-25=271$$

12. 7月1日 X 俱乐部的男女比例是9：20。这个月中又有2名男子和2名妇女加入该俱乐部，且无会员退出。

解：本题的正确答案为（D）。比较的左项是在7月底 X 俱乐部的男女比。考生在做此题时，最易犯的错误是把9：20当成是男女的人数，从而进行计算时得到$(9+2):(20+2)=\dfrac{1}{2}$，认真思考，考生就能发现9：20是比例，而2是数字，两者不能相加。

13. 108减去某数与其$\dfrac{2}{5}$的和等于该数，问这个数是多少？

解：本题的正确答案为（B）。设该数为 x，则由题意可得：

$$108-(1+\dfrac{2}{5})x=x\Rightarrow x=45$$

14. 若一商品打折（discount）20%后价钱降到$100，那么它原来的价钱是多少？

解：本题的正确答案为（C）。"a discount of 20 percent"表示打折20%，设该商品原价为 x，则有：

$$x(1-20\%)=\$100\Rightarrow x=\$125$$

15. 一个购买立体声接收机的方案要求将总值的20%作为首期付款，同时需要每月付30美元的分期付款。

解：本题的正确答案是（D）。"down payment"是指分期付款中的首期付款。因为该题并没有说明分期付款的期限，所以无法判断该立体声接收机的价格是多少。

16. Jill has $6x$ red marbles and $4y$ green marbles. Bill has half as many red marbles as Jill, but he has twice as many red marbles and green marbles combined as Jill.

       The number of green marbles that Bill has $9x+8y$

16. Jill 有 $6x$ 颗红色弹珠和 $4y$ 颗绿色弹珠。Bill 的红色弹珠数是 Jill 的一半,但是他的红色弹珠和绿色弹珠数之和是 Jill 的两倍。Bill 拥有的绿弹珠数 $9x+8y$

解: 本题的正确答案为(C)。Bill 的红弹珠数应为 $3x$;由题意中得他的绿色弹珠应为:
$$(6x+4y)\times 2-3x=9x+8y。$$

17. Of the 400 cadets in a graduating class, 30 percent were women and, of these, $\frac{1}{5}$ became instructors. If the number of men who became instructors was twice the number of women who became instructors, how many of the men became instructors?

(A)120　(B) 48　(C) 40　(D) 24　(E) 20

17. 在一个拥有 400 名警察的毕业班中,30％是女生,并且在这些女生中,有 $\frac{1}{5}$ 的人当教师。假如男生中当教师的人数是女生中当教师的人数的两倍,问有多少男生当教师?

解: 本题的正确答案是(B)。根据题意可得:
男生当教师的人数 $=400\times 30\%\times \frac{1}{5}\times 2=48$。

18. A company paid \$500,000 in merit raises to employees whose performances were rated A, B, or C. Each employee rated A received twice the amount of the raise that was paid to each employee rated C; each employee rated B received $1\frac{1}{2}$ times the amount of the raise that was paid to each employee rated C. If 50 workers were rated A, 100 were rated B, and 150 were rated C, how much was the raise paid to each employee rated A?

(A) \$370　　(B) \$625　　(C) \$740
(D) \$1,250　(E) \$2,500

18. 某公司给业绩为 A,B,C 级的员工发放 \$500,000 的奖金。每一个 A 级员工所拿奖金等于每一个 C 级员工的两倍;每一个 B 级员工所拿的奖金是每一个 C 级员工的 $1\frac{1}{2}$ 倍。若 50 个员工被评为 A 级,100 个员工被评为 B 级,150 个员工被评为 C 级,那么每个 A 级的员工得到的奖金是多少?

解: 本题的正确答案为(E)。设 C 级雇员的奖金为 x,由题意可得:
$$50\times 2x+100\times 1\frac{1}{2}x+150x=500,000$$
解方程可得 $x=\$1,250$,所以 A 级员工的奖金为 \$2,500。

19. Mrs. Jones sold two houses for \$80,000 each. One house was sold at a 20 percent loss and the other at a 20 percent gain.

       The gain minus the loss   0

19. 琼斯太太以每幢\$80,000 的价格卖了两幢房屋。一座房子以亏损 20％售出,另一座房子以赢利 20％售出。

解: 本题的正确答案是(B)。两幢房子一幢亏损,一幢赢利,但最后的售价相同,这说明它们的原价一定不同,设亏损房屋价为 x,获

利房屋价为 y，则由题意可得：

$$x(1-20\%)=80{,}000 \Rightarrow x=\frac{80{,}000}{(1-20\%)}$$

$$y(1+20\%)=80{,}000 \Rightarrow y=\frac{80{,}000}{(1+20\%)}$$

$$\Rightarrow x>y \Rightarrow y-x<0$$

20. Mechanical toy cars A，B，and C，each traveling at its own uniform rate, started from the same point at the same time and raced a 400-meter course.

When A crossed the finish line. B was 40 meters behind A，and C was 58 meters behind A.

When B crossed the finish line, how many meters was C from the finish line?

(A) 16

(B) 18

(C) 19

(D) 20

(E) 22

20. 机械玩具车 A、B 和 C 在同一时间、同一地点出发,各自以均匀的速度参加 400 米比赛。当 A 越过终点线时,B 车落后 A 车 40 米,C 车落后 A 车 58 米,问当 B 车越过终点线时,C 车离终点线还有多远?

解: 本题的正确答案为(D)。此题是一道极易被考生做错的题。大多数考生都这样认为:当 A 到终点时,B 和 C 相差(58-40)=18 米,由于 B 和 C 都是匀速行驶的,所以 B 车到终点时,两者的距离保持不变,仍为 18 米。而实际上,因为 B 和 C 两车的运动速度不同,所以在最后的 40 米,B 和 C 两车之间的距离会加大。B 和 C 匀速运动,在前 360 米相差了 18 米,设在最后的 40 米 B 和 C 相差的距离将增大 x,则根据题意可列出下面的方程:

$$\frac{18}{360}=\frac{x}{40} \Rightarrow x=2$$

所以 B 车越过终点时,C 车距中点还有 18+2=20 米。

21. Ms. Smith got an 8 percent cost of living raise of $20 per week.

Ms. Smith's new weekly salary	$260

21. 史密斯太太的工资每周增加 20 美元——相当于她的薪水的 8%。

解: 本题的正确答案为(A)。"cost of living"生活费用,即薪水或工资(salary)的意思,由 8% cost of living raise 等于 \$20 可得,史密斯太太新的周薪为:

$$20 \div 8\% + 20 = 270$$

22. A speed of 30 miles per hour is equivalent to a speed of 44 feet per second. A speed of 33 feet per second is equivalent to a speed

22. 每小时 30 英里的速度与每秒 44 英尺的速度相等,每秒 33 英尺的速度与每小时 x 英里速度相等。

$$x \qquad\qquad 22.5$$

解：本题的正确答案为(C)。根据题干中给出的速度的不同单位之间的等价关系,考生可以直接列出下面的方程：

$$\frac{30}{44} = \frac{x}{33} \Rightarrow x = 22.5$$

23. A school bus has 10 double seats in each of 2 rows. Two students can sit in each double seat. If an empty bus starts out and makes two stops, picking up three times the number of students at the second stop as at the first stop, and if the bus is then filled to seating capacity, how many students got on the bus at the second stop?

   (A) 5   (B) 10   (C) 15

   (D) 20   (E) 30

23. 某辆校车有两排座椅,每一排有 10 个双人座,每个双人座上可坐两个学生。若一辆空汽车开出并在途中停了两次,第二次停车时上车的学生人数是第一次停车时上车的学生人数的 3 倍,并且汽车在第二次停车后满载,问第二次停车时有多少个学生上车？

解：本题的正确答案是(E)。设第二次停车时有 x 人上车,则

$$x + \frac{x}{3} = 10 \times 2 \times 2 \Rightarrow x = 30。$$

24. The daily rate for a hotel room that sleeps 4 people is \$39 for one person and x dollars for each additional person. If 3 people take the room for one day and each pays \$21 for the room, what is the value of x?

   (A) 6   (B) 8   (C) 12

   (D) 13   (E) 24

24. 某旅馆的 4 人间的每天收费是住 1 个人 39 美元,并且每多 1 人加收 x 美元。若 3 个人住该屋 1 天,并且每人付 21 美元,问 x 的值是多少？

解：本题的正确答案是(C)。解答本题的关键是对" and x dollars for each additional person"的理解。若考生能把这句话理解到位,那么就很容易把这道题做对。住一个人收 39 美元,住两个人收 $39+x$ 美元,住 3 个人收 $39+2x$ 美元,由题意可得：

$$39 + 2x = 21 \times 3 \Rightarrow x = 12。$$

25. A buzzer sounds every 15 minutes. If the buzzer sounded at 12:40, which of the following could be a time at which the buzzer sounded?

   (A) 4:05   (B) 5:30   (C) 6:45

   (D) 7:15   (E) 8:10

25. 一蜂鸣器每 15 分钟响一次,若该蜂鸣器在 12:40 响了,问下面哪一个可以是蜂鸣器响的时间？

解：本题的正确答案是(E)。蜂鸣器12:40响后,根据题意可知该蜂鸣器只有在12:40 + 15n 时才会再响,其中 n 为整数,也即蜂鸣器可能响的时间可能是一个小时中的 55 分、10 分、25 分和 40 分,由此可知五个选项中只有(E)满足这一条件。

26. A certain company has found that the number of labor hours required to produce x items is directly proportional to the square root of x. If 3 labor hours are required to produce 20 items, how many labor hours are required to produce 40 items?

(A) $3\sqrt{2}$　　(B) 6　　(C) $\dfrac{20}{\sqrt{3}}$

(D) 12　　(E) $3\sqrt{20}$

26. 某公司发现,生产 x 件产品所需工作时间与 x 的平方根(square root)直接成正比,生产 20 件产品需要 3 个工作时间,问生产 40 件产品需多少工作时间?

解:本题的正确答案为(A)。根据题中给出的工作时间与生产产品的数量的平方根成正比关系可以列出等式:$\dfrac{x}{3}=\sqrt{\dfrac{40}{20}}\Rightarrow x=3\sqrt{2}$

27. The cost, in dollars, for an appliance repair at a certain company is $1.2p+20h$, where p is the wholesale price of the parts, in dollars, and h is the number of hours it takes to repair the appliance. What is the cost of repairing an appliance if the wholesale price of the parts is \$15 and it takes 2 hours to repair it?

(A) \$12　(B) \$18　(C) \$20

(D) \$40　(E) \$58

27. 某公司一设备的修理成本,以美元计,为 $1.2p+20h$,其中 p 是零件的批发价格(以美元计),h 是修理设备所用的小时数。如果零件的批发价是 15 美元,并且花了 2 小时修理,那么修理这个设备的成本是多少?

解:本题的正确答案为(E)。解答该题时,只要把数据代入题中所给的公式即可:
$$1.2\times15+2\times20=58$$

28. Three salespeople are paid commissions in proportion to the amount of their sales, which total \$25,000, \$40,000, and \$60,000, respectively. If a total of \$20,000 is allocated for these three commission, what is the amount of the largest commission paid?

(A) \$8,000　　(B) \$8,400

(C) \$9,600　　(D) \$10,000

(E) \$12,000

28. 付给 3 名推销员的佣金与他们的销售额成正比,他们各自总的销售额分别为 25000 美元,40000 美元和 60000 美元,若共拨出 20000 美元作为 3 人的佣金,问最大的佣金额是多少钱?

解:本题的正确答案是(C)。设最大佣金额为 x 美元,由题意可以得到下面的比例式:
$$\frac{60000}{25000+40000+60000}=\frac{x}{20000}\Rightarrow x=9600 \text{ 美元}$$

29.

PAIRS OF SHOES SOLD BY COMPANY S

Note: Drawn to scale.

29. 8750 双鞋以左面的图样表示,每只鞋的图样代表多少双鞋?

解:本题的正确答案为(B)。本题的图形下面注有"Drawn to scale",所以图形中的鞋样都成比例,图中靠下的位置,鞋样只有半只,所

If 8,750 pairs of shoes are represented in the pictograph above, how many pairs of shoes does each 👞 represent?

(A) 350　　(B) 700　　(C) 730

(D) 830　　(E) 1,400

以图中共有 $12\frac{1}{2}$ 个鞋样,共代表 8750 双鞋,设每只鞋样代表 x 双鞋,则有:

$$12\frac{1}{2}x = 8750 \Rightarrow x = 700$$

30. A basket contains a total of 30 apples and pears. If it contains $1\frac{1}{2}$ times as many apples as pears, how many pears does it contain?

(A) 9　　(B) 10　　(C)12

(D) 18　　(E) 20

30. 一篮子中苹果和梨的数量一共是 30 个,若苹果的个数是梨的 $1\frac{1}{2}$ 倍,那么篮子有多少个梨?

解:本题的正确答案为(C)。设篮中有 x 个梨,则苹果为 $1\frac{1}{2}x$ 个,由题意可得:

$$1\frac{1}{2}x + x = 30 \Rightarrow x = 12$$

31. The decorating committee for a dance plans to fringe the 3-inch-wide end of a streamer by making small cuts every $\frac{1}{16}$ inch. How many cuts must be made to fringe the end?

(A) 45　　(B) 46　　(C) 47

(D) 48　　(E) 49

31. 一舞蹈的装潢委员会计划在一条幅的 3 英寸终端做边穗,若每 $\frac{1}{16}$ 英寸剪一下,需要剪多少次来给终端做边穗?

解:本题的正确答案是(C)。3 英寸是 $\frac{1}{16}$ 英寸的 48 倍,每 $\frac{1}{16}$ 英寸剪一下,共剪 47 下即可。

32. If two trains are 120 miles apart and are traveling toward each other at a constant rate of 30 mph and 40 mph, respectively, how far apart will they be exactly 1 hour before they meet?

(A) 10 miles　(B) 30 miles

(C) 40 miles　(D) 50 miles

(E) 70 miles

32. 若两辆火车相距 120 英里远,且分别以每小时 30 英里和每小时 40 英里的速度对开,问它们相遇前 1 小时相距多远?

解:本题的正确答案是(E)。考生略加思考就知,本题根本就不需要计算。相遇前 1 小时,也就是两辆火车还要开 1 小时才能相遇,而两辆火车的速度分别是 30 英里/小时和 40 英里/小时,在 1 小时中两辆火车各行驶 30 英里和 40 英里,也就是相遇前 1 小时相距 70 英里。

33. The scores reported for a certain multiple-choice test were derived by subtracting $\frac{1}{3}$ of the number of wrong answers from the

33. 某一多项选择考试的分数的计算是用答对的题数减去答错题数的 $\frac{1}{3}$。在一个由 40 道题组成的测验中,若无题遗漏,且考试分数

number of right answers. On a 40-question test, if none of the questions was omitted and the score reported was 20, how many <u>wrong</u> answers were there?

(A) 5 (B) 10 (C) 15 (D) 25 (E) 30

34. A grocer buys apples at the regular price of 38 cents per pound.

| The amount saved by the grocer on a purchase of 100 pounds of apples if the price per pound is x cents less than the regular price | The additional amount paid by the grocer on a purchase of 100 pounds of apples if the price per pound is x cents more than the regular price |

35. On a highway there is an electric pole every 96 feet. If the poles are numbered consecutively, what is the number of the pole 2 miles past pole number 56?
(1 mile＝5，280 feet)

(A) 109 (B) 110 (C) 152
(D) 165 (E) 166

36. In a certain room, all except 18 of the people are over 50 years of age. If 15 of the people in the room are under 50 years of age, how many people are in the room?
(A) 27 (B) 30 (C) 33 (D) 36
(E) It cannot be determined from the information given.

37. Sixty-eight people are sitting in 20 cars and each car contains at most 4 people.
What is the maximum possible number of

为 20,问答错的题数有多少个?

解：本题的正确答案为(C)。设答错题数为 x 个,则由题意可得：
$$(40-x)-\frac{1}{3}x=20\Rightarrow x=15$$

34. 一个杂货商以每磅38美分的通常价格购买苹果。

解：本题的正确答案为(C)。比较的左项为若杂货商以每磅比通常价格少 x 美分的价格购买 100 磅苹果可以省下的钱。比较的右项为若杂货商以每磅比通常价格多 x 美分的价格购买 100 磅苹果所多付的钱。左项为等于 $100x$,右项也等于 $100x$。

35. 在一条高速公路上每隔 96 英尺有一根电线杆。若电线杆连续计数,问超过 56 号电线杆 2 英里远的电线杆的标号是多少?

解：本题的正确答案是(E)。由 1 mile＝5280 feet 可知,2 英里的长的公路中共有(5280×2)/96＝110 根电线杆,所以题目中所求的电线杆的标号是 110＋56＝166。

36. 在某一房间中,除了 18 个人外其余人的年龄都超过 50 岁。若房间里小于 50 岁的人数为 15,那么该房间里总共有多少人?

解：本题的正确答案为(E)。该题根本未涉及 50 岁以上的人数,故不能确定。

37. 68 个人坐在 20 辆汽车中,每辆汽车最多可坐 4 个人,仅坐 1 个人的车的最大可能数目是多少?

cars that could contain exactly 1 of the 68 people?

(A) 2   (B) 3   (C) 4

(D) 8   (E) 12

38. Art，Bob，and Carmen share a prize of $400. If Art receives twice as much as Bob，and if Bob receives $\frac{1}{2}$ as much as Carmen，how much does Carmen receive?

(A) $20   (B) $40   (C) $80

(D) $140   (E) $160

39. A time-study specialist has set the production rate for each worker on a certain job at 22 units every 3 hours. At this rate what is the minimum number of workers that should be put on the job if at least 90 units are to be produced per hour?

(A) 5   (B) 8   (C) 12

(D) 13   (E) 30

40. A certain money market account that had a balance of $48,000 during all of last month earned $360 in interest for the month. At what simple annual interest rate did the account earn interest last month?

(A) 7%   (B) 7.5%   (C) 8%

(D) 8.5%   (E) 9%

解：本题的正确答案是(C)。要想使仅坐1人的车的数目最多,其他车就应尽可能地多坐人,即其他的车应都坐4个人。设仅坐1人的车的数目为 x,则

$$\frac{68-x}{20-x}=4 \Rightarrow x=4$$

38. Art,Bob,Carmen 分享 400 美元的奖金,若 Art 接受的奖金数是 Bob 的两倍,并且 Bob 接受的奖金数是 Carmen 的 1/2,问 Carmen 的奖金是多少?

解：本题的正确答案是(E)。设 Carmen 的奖金为 x,Bob 的为 $\frac{1}{2}x$,则 Art 是 Bob 的两倍也为 x,由题意可得：

$$x+\frac{1}{2}x+x=400 \Rightarrow x=160$$

39. 一位时间研究专家确定某项工作的生产速度是每人每 3 小时生产 22 件。在这个速度下,若每小时最少生产 90 件,问需要多少工人参加工作?

解：本题的正确答案为(D)。生产的速度为每人每小时 $\frac{22}{3}$ 件,故每小时生产 90 件需要：

$$90 \div \frac{22}{3} \approx 12.2 \approx 13 人,$$

显然 12 个人是无法完成每小时至少 90 件的工作,所以共需要 13 个工人参加工作。

40. 某一账目在最后整整一个月的时间里有余款(balance)48000 美元,且该账目在这个月获得 360 美元的利息,问其最后一个月以多少年单利率获得利息?

解：本题的正确答案是(E)。该题指 48000 美元的余款在最后整整一月中不变,并获得 360 美元利息,这 360 美元一定不包含于 48000 美元中,因为利息当然是这个月结束后挣得的,并且题目中已提及 simple annual interest，即本题以单利计利，利息不参予计利。则年利率为：

$$\frac{360}{48000}\times12=9\%$$

41. To obtain an FHA mortgage for ＄50,000 or more，the home buyer must have a down payment equal to 4 percent of the first ＄25,000 of the mortgage amount and 5 percent of the portion in excess of ＄25,000. At settlement the buyer pays a mortgage insurance premium equal to 3 percent of the mortgage amount. What is the maximum FHA mortgage，if any，a buyer can obtain if the buyer has only ＄6,000 available for the down payment and insurance premium?

(A) ＄62,500   (B) ＄71,875

(C) ＄78,125   (D) ＄125,000

(E) The home buyer cannot obtain an
    FHA mortgage.

41. 为了获得 50000 美元或更多的 FHA 的住房抵押贷款，购房者的首期付款必须相当于第一期住房抵押贷款 25000 美元的 4％和超过 25000 美元以上部分的 5％。在入住时，购房者付一个相当于住房抵押贷款量 3％的住房贷款保险费。若一个购房者仅有 6000 美元付首期付款和保险费，问该购房者能从 FHA 获得的最大的住房贷款额是多少？

解：本题的正确答案是(C)。题目中出现了许多金融业的词语，例如 mortgage 指住房抵押贷款，down payment 指首期付款，insurance premium 指保险费，另外 Settlement 指入住或安家，住房抵押贷款指付了首期的 down payment 后就可以搬入新房了。

设最大住房抵押贷款额为 x，则由题意可得：
$25000\times4\%+(x-25000)\times5\%+x\times3\%=6000\Rightarrow x=78125$

42. Working alone, a small pump takes twice as long as a large pump takes to fill an empty tank. Working together at their respective constant rates, the pumps can fill the tank in 6 hours. How many hours would it take the small pump to fill the tank working alone?

(A) 8   (B) 9   (C) 12

(D) 15   (E) 18

42. 单独工作时，一个小水泵充满一个空水箱所花的时间是大水泵的两倍。两个水泵保持其各自通常的速度共同工作时，共需花 6 个小时灌满水箱。若小水泵单独工作时，需花多长时间才能灌满水箱？

解：本题的正确答案是(E)。设小水泵需花 x 小时灌满水箱，则大小泵需花 $\frac{x}{2}$ 小时灌满小箱，由题意可得：

$$(\frac{1}{x}+\frac{2}{x})\times6=1\Rightarrow x=18$$

43. $d>0$

43. **解**：本题的正确答案是（B）。"simple annual interest" 指年单利。根据本章中介绍的单利计算公式可得 d 美元以 11％的单

The total interest earned on d dollars invested for 3 months at 11 percent simple annual interest

$\frac{11}{3}(\frac{d}{100})$ dollars

利投资 3 个月所挣得的利息为：

$$d \times \frac{11}{100} \times \frac{3}{12} = \frac{d \times 11}{100 \times 4} < \frac{11}{3}(\frac{d}{100})$$

44. In a history class that consisted of 30 students, the number of seniors was 3 more than twice the number of juniors, and $\frac{3}{10}$ of the students were neither juniors nor seniors.

The number of juniors in the class

6

44. 一历史班由 30 名学生组成,高年级学生人数等于低年级学生人数的二倍加 3,且有 $\frac{3}{10}$ 的人既不是低年级学生也不是高年级学生。

解：本题的正确答案为(C)。设该班中低年级学生人数为 x,由题意可得到下面的方程：

$$x + (2x+3) + \frac{3}{10} \times 30 = 30 \Rightarrow x = 6$$

45. A candy assortment consists of seven flavors of chocolate-covered creams packed in two-layered boxes with 27 creams in each layer. The flavors are always packed in rows so that the flavor varies with each piece in the following order: vanilla, orange, cherry, vanilla raspberry, lime, pecan, cherry, lemon. How many chocolate-covered vanilla creams are needed to pack 200 boxes of the assortment?

(A) 600　　(B) 1,200　　(C) 1,800
(D) 2,400　　(E) 3,600

45. 一份包括 7 种口味的巧克力奶糖被装在双层盒子中,每层装 27 块奶糖。每行放置的奶糖块块口味不同且以如下口味顺序放置：vanilla,orange,cherry,vanilla,raspberry,lime,pecan,cherry,lemon。问 200 个糖果盒中需要装多少块 vanilla 口味的巧克力奶糖？

解：本题的正确答案是(D)。糖果盒的每行 9 块糖中有 2 块是 vanilla 口味,每层有 $27 \div 9 = 3$ 行,每个盒子中有 2 层糖,那么每个盒子中 vanilla 口味的奶糖有 $2 \times 3 \times 2 = 12$ 块,所以两个盒子有共有 vanilla 口味的奶糖 $12 \times 200 = 2400$ 块。

46. After a store had sold k television sets for p dollars each, it reduced the price p of each set by 5 percent and then sold twice as many sets at this reduced price.

The total revenue from the sale of all of these television sets

$2.95pk$

46. 一家商店以每台 p 美元售出 k 台电视后,把每台电视机的价格(p 美元)降低了 5%,然后以降低后价格卖出了 2 倍量的电视机。

解：本题的正确答案为(B)。比较的左项为卖出这些台电视机的总销售额：

$$pk + 2kp(1-5\%) = 2.9pk$$

47. A research scientist wants to study a certain attribute of dogs. It is estimatedthat approximately 5 percent of all dogshave this attribute. If the scientist wants to study a sample of N dogs having the attribute, approximately how many dogs should be screened in order to abtain the desired sample size?

(A) $\frac{N}{5}$ (B) $5N$ (C) $20N$

(D) $105N$ (E) $120N$

48. Water is to be poured at a rate of 2.5 gallons per minute into a 500-gallon tank that initially contains 50 gallons of water.

The percent of the tank's capacity that will be filled 1 hour   60 percent after water begins to be poured in

49. The illumination E, in footcandles, provided by a light source of intensity I, in candles, at a distance D, in feet, is given by $E = \frac{I}{D^2}$. For an illumination of 50 footcandles at a distance of 4 feet from a source, the intensity of the source must be

(A) 50 candles

(B) 200 candles

(C) 800 candles

(D) 1,600 candles

(E) 2,500 candles

47. 一科学家想研究狗的某种特性。据估计约有5%的狗具有这种特性。若这位科学家想把N只具有这种特性的狗作为一个样本来研究,那么为了得到期望的样本大小,大约需要筛选多少条狗?

解: 本题的正确答案为(C)。设需筛选 x 条狗,则由题意可得:
$$x \times 5\% = N \Rightarrow x = 20N$$

48. 水以每分钟2.5加仑的速度注入一个容量为500加仑的水箱中,且该水箱在注入水之前已装有50加仑的水。

解: 本题的正确答案是(B)。比较的左项为水开始注入1小时后,水箱中的水将占水箱的容量的百分比:
$$\frac{50 + 2.5 \times 60}{500} = 40\%$$

注: 未能做对该题的考生一般对都认为 will be filled 指1小时后水箱中有百分之几的容量还有待水的注入,这种理解是不对的。这里的 will be filled 一般将来时的使用是针对从句 after water begins to be poured in 中的 begins 这个一般现在时而言的,指开始注入水后的1小时,水箱中的水所占的水箱容量的比例。

49. 一强度为I(以烛光为单位)的光源,在距离D(以英尺为单位)处的光的亮度E(以英尺烛光为单位)被定义为 $E = \frac{I}{D^2}$。若在离某光源4英尺的地方,光的强度为50英尺烛光,那么该光源的强度一定是

解: 本题的正确答案是(C)。解答本题的关键是对题目中所描述的对物理概念的理解。根据 $E = \frac{I}{D^2}$ 可得:$I = E \cdot D^2 = 50 \times 4^2 = 800$

注: Intensity *n.* 强度

Illumination *n.* 亮度(物理学概念)

Footcandle *n.* 英尺烛光(亮度单位)

第 四 章

集合、排列、组合与概率
(Sets, Permutation, Combination and Probability)

在 GRE 的数学考试中,有相当比例的考题会涉及数据的统计描述:比如元素与集合、级数与数列、排列与组合、统计与概率等。这些问题虽然并不十分困难,但因我国考生在这方面所受到的训练普遍较少,并且这类题在新 GRE 数学考试中出现的频率越来越高,难度也逐渐加大,所以要想在数学方面取得高分乃至满分,考生必须加强这一部分的学习。考虑到我国考生在这一方面容易丢分,本书将此部分单独列为一章进行讲解。

第一节　与集合有关的问题 (Problems Involving Sets)

一、集合的分类及定义

A set is simply a group of two or more numbers or other terms.

具有某种属性的事物的全体称为集合,它一般由一组数或其他符号构成。组成集合的每个事物称为该集合的元素(element)。如果 S 是一个有限数量的集合,那么 $|S|$ 被定义为元素的数目。例如:$S=\{2,7,17,25\}$,则 $|S|=4$。

Relationship between Sets(集合之间的关系)

1. Union(并集): the union of set A and set B 是指两个或多个集合中的所有元素,对两个集合 A, B 可表示为:$A\bigcup B$。

2. Intersection(交集): the intersection of set A and set B 是指两个或多个集合中的所有共同元素,对两个集合 A, B 可表示为:$A\bigcap B$。

3. Disjoint or Mutually Exclusive:指两个集合中没有共同元素。

4. 全集:将各个子集中所有元素非重复地都加起来就是全集,用 I 表示。

5. 非集:非某集合元素组成的集合,称为这集合的非,对单集合 A 可记为 $\overline{A}$。

二、集合的一般公式

1. $\overline{A\bigcap B}=\overline{A}\bigcup\overline{B}$,即 A 交 B 的非等于 A 非并上 B 非

2. $\overline{A\bigcup B}=\overline{A}\bigcap\overline{B}$,即 A 并 B 的非等于 A 非交上 B 非

3. $|A\bigcup B|=|A|+|B|-|A\bigcap B|$(对于两个集合而言)

4. $|A\bigcup B\bigcup C|=|A|+|B|+|C|-|A\bigcap B|-|A\bigcap C|-|B\bigcap C|+|A\bigcap B\bigcap C|$(对于三个集合而言)

例 1:某班上学生选修三门课,数学、语文、英语,选修数学的有 35 人,选修语文的有 30 人,

解:我们可以设选修数学的人数为 A,选修语文的人数为 B,选修英语的人数为 C,则由题

选修英语的有 32 人,既选修数学又选修语文的有 20 人,既选修语文又选修英语的有 15 人,既选修数学又选修英语的有 22 人,而三门课都选修的有 8 人,且知道所有的人至少选修一门课,问这个班上共有多少人?

意可知:

$$A\cap B=20 \qquad A\cap C=22$$
$$B\cap C=15 \qquad A\cap B\cap C=8$$

求这个班共有多少人,就是求 A, B, C 的全集,依据上述三个集合的公式,$|A\cup B\cup C|=|A|+|B|+|C|-|A\cap B|-|A\cap C|-|B\cap C|+|A\cap B\cap C|$,则有全班共应有 $I=35+30+32-20-22-15+8=48$ 人。

三、Venn diagram(韦恩图)

用封闭曲线(内部区域)表示集合及其关系的图形称为韦恩图(Venn Diagram),也叫文氏图。韦恩图用两个或三个相交的圆来表示,这些圆通常会被放到一个矩形之中。由于图形简明、直观,因此很多与集合相关的问题可以借助韦恩图来快速求解。

如下图所示,A、B 和 C 三个集合用圆表示,矩形 I 代表全集。

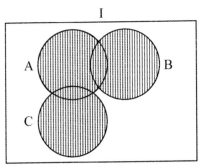

从图中我们可以得出 $|A\cup B|=|A|+|B|-|A\cap B|$,$|B\cup C|=|B|+|C|$

例 2: Of the 410 students at Xinhua High School,240 study Spanish and 180 study French. If 25 students study neither language,how many study both?

解: 根据题意画韦恩图如下:

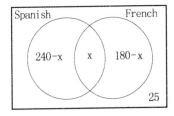

设两种语言都学习的人数为 x,把 x 填在两圆的交叉处,仅学习西班牙语的人是 $240-x$,仅学习法语的人是 $180-x$。至少学习一门语言的人数是 $410-25=385$ 人,所以:

$$385=(240-x)+x+(180-x)$$
$$\Rightarrow x=420-385=35$$

第二节 描述统计问题(Problems Involving Descriptive Statistics)

数据可以用统计学的方法进行描述。统计度量通常可以分三类:集中趋势的度量(measures of central tendency),位置的度量(measures of position)以及离散性的度量(measures of dispersion)。

一、集中趋势的度量(measures of central tendency)

集中趋势的度量表明数据的集中情况,通常用三种方法来表示:the arithmetic mean(算术平均数),median(中数)以及 mode(众数)。

1. Arithmetic mean or Average(算术平均数): in a set of n measurements, the sum of the measurements divided by n. 比如 4,10,14,20,5 这五个数的算术平均数是:

$$\frac{4+10+14+20+5}{5}=10.6$$

2. Weighted Mean(加权平均数): 加权平均数是不同比重数据的平均数,加权平均数就是把原始数据按照合理的比例来计算。若在一组数中,x_1 出现 f_1 次,x_2 出现 f_2 次,$\cdots$,x_n 出现 f_n 次,那么 x_1、x_2、x_3……x_n 的加权平均数是:

$$\frac{x_1 f_1 + x_2 f_2 + x_3 f_3 + \cdots + x_n f_n}{f_1 + f_2 + f_3 + \cdots + f_n}$$

在上面的式子中,f_1,f_2,f_3,……f_n 分别是 x_1、x_2、x_3……x_n 的权。

3. Geometric Average(几何平均数): 几何平均数为 n 个数的乘积开 n 次方。

例如:a,b,c,d,f 五个数的几何平均数为 $\sqrt[5]{abcdf}$

注:算术平均数总是大于或等于几何平均数,对于两个数的情况则有如下式子成立:

$$\frac{a+b}{2} \geqslant \sqrt{ab},当 a=b 时此式的等号成立。$$

4. Median(中数): the middle measurement after the measurements are ordered by size (or the average of the two middle measurements if the number of measurements is even).

要得到 n 个数的中数,首先将这 n 个数按从大到小的顺序排列,如果 n 是奇数,中数被定义为中间的那个数;如果 n 是偶数,中数被定义为中间两个数的平均值。当 n 较大时,中数被定义为 50% 的线所通过的有序排列中的位置的那个数。也就是说如果 n 的具体数值不确定而为百分数,那么第 50% 的对象所对准的那一个数就是中数。中数的大小只受数的位置的制约,与一组数中最大数与最小数的值的大小无关。

5. Mode(众数): The mode of a list of numbers is the number that occurs most frequently in the list. 一组数中的众数是指出现频率最高的数。比如在 2,1,2,5,4,6 这组数的众数是 2。一组数的众数可能不止一个。例如:这组数——8,7,6,4,3,4,6,7,9,11 的众数就有 3 个,分别是:7,4 和 6。

二、位置的度量(measures of position)

在一组按从小到大的顺序排列的数列中,三个最基本的值或位置是开始,最后和中间。通常用 L 代表最小值,G 代表最大值,M 代表中数(median)。除此之外,最常用来度量位置的方法是 quartiles(四分位数)和 percentiles(百分位数)。

1. Quartiles(四分位数)

三个数值可以把一组按从小到大顺序排列的变量数列分成项数大致相等的四个部分,这三个数值就被定义为 quartiles(四分位数),分别称为第一四分位数、第二四分位数和第三四分位数,记作 Q_1、Q_2 和 Q_3。Q_2 通常是这组变量数列的 median(中数)。因为数列的项数很有可能不能被 4 整除,所以我们约定 $Q_2 = M$(中数)。中数把数列分成项数相等的两个部分——数值较小的一组数和数值较大的一组数。Q_1 等于较小的一组数的中数,Q_3 等于较大的一组数的中数。

例 3:求 9,4,2,4,5,7,9,7,7,8,7,7,7,8,9,9 的四分位数

解:先把这几个数按从小到大的顺序进行排列:2,4,4,5,7,7,7,7,7,7,8,8,9,9,9,9。一共 16 个数,中数是第 8 个数与第 9 个数的平均数,中数 M 等于 7,所以 $Q_2 = M = 7$;Q_1 等于前 8 个数的中数,$Q_1 = \dfrac{5+7}{2} = 6$;Q_3 等于后 8 个数的中数,$Q_3 = \dfrac{8+9}{2} = 8.5$。

在这道例题中,4 在这组数的前 25% 之内,借助四分数的概念我们可以用两种方式来表示这一结果:

- 4 is below the first quartile, that is, below Q_1(4 比第一四分位数小)
- 4 is in the first quartile(4 位于由 Q_1,Q_2 以及 Q_3 分成的四组数的第一组内)

2. Percentiles(百分位数)

用 99 个数值或 99 个点,将按大小顺序排列的观测值划分为 100 个等分,则这 99 个数值或 99 个点就称为百分位数,分别以 $P_1,P_2,P_3,\cdots,P_{99}$ 代表第 1 个,第 2 个,第 3 个…,第 99 个百分位数。百分位数通常用在项数比较多数组中。根据四分数和百分位数的概念,我们很容易得到:

$$Q_1 = P_{25}$$
$$M = Q_2 = P_{50}$$
$$Q_3 = P_{75}$$

以身高为例,身高分布的第五百分位表示有 5% 的人的身高小于此测量值,95% 的人的身高大于此测量值。

三、离散性的度量(measures of dispersion)

离散性的度量(measures of dispersion)用来表明数据的分布特点。在统计学中常用 range(值域)、interquartile range(四分位差)以及 standard deviation(标准差)来表示一组数据的离散性。

1. Range (值域)

The **range** of the numbers in a group of data is the difference between the greatest number G in the data and the least number L in the data; that is, $G - L$.

Range 是表明数的分布的量,其被定义为最大值与最小值的差。比如对 12,8,15,17,6,4 这组数的

Range＝17－4＝13。

当一组数中有异常大或异常小数(通常称为"outliers"——异常值),range(值域)不能很好地反映数据的离散性,因为 range(值域)直接受 outliers(异常值)的影响。

2. Interquartile range(四分位差)

Interquartile range(四分位差)被定义为第三四分位数与第一四分数的差,即 $Q_3－Q_1$。所以四分位差度量的是位于中间的这一半数值的分布区间。四分位差通常不受 outliers(异常值)的影响。

比如对 2,4,4,5,7,7,7,7,7,7,8,8,9,9,9,9 这一组数,它的值域 Range＝9－7＝2;它的四分位差 Interquartile range＝$Q_3－Q_1$＝8.5－6＝2.5

3. Boxplot(箱线图)

箱线图(Boxplot)也称箱须图(Box-whisker Plot),是利用数据中的五个统计量:最小值、第一四分位数、中位数、第三四分位数与最大值来描述数据的一种方法,它也可以粗略地看出数据是否具有对称性,分布的分散程度等信息,特别可以用于对几个样本的比较。

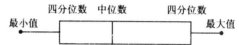

根据箱线图的定义,我们可以把 2,4,4,5,7,7,7,7,7,7,8,8,9,9,9,9 这一组数的箱线图来出来,如下所示:

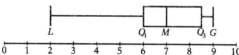

箱线图作为描述统计的工具之一,其功能有独特之处,比如可以直观明了地识别一批数据中的异常值,判断一批数据的偏态和尾重以及比较不同批次数据的形状等。箱线图美中不足之处在于它不能提供关于数据分布偏态和尾重程度的精确度量;对于批量较大的数据批,箱线图反映的形状信息更加模糊;用中位数代表总体平均水平有一定的局限性等等。所以,应用箱线图最好结合其他描述统计工具如均值、标准差、偏度、分布函数等来描述数据批的分布形状。

4. Standard deviation(标准差)

Standard deviation(标准差):a measure of dispersion among members of a set.

标准差是一组数据平均值分散程度的一种度量。一个较大的标准差,代表大部分数值和其平均值之间差异较大;一个较小的标准差,代表这些数值较接近平均值。

注:标准方差是用来表明数据的离散性的量,标准方差的求解步骤如下:

1) find the arithmetic mean(求算术平均值).

2) find the differences between the mean and each of the numbers(求每个数与算术平均值的差).

3) square each of the differences(把所得的差值分别平方).

4) find the average of the squared differences(求这些差值平方数的算术平均值).

5) take the nonnegative square root of this average(取这个算术平均值的非负平方根).

具体地说,有 n 个数分别为 $x_1,x_2\cdots x_n$,这 n 个数的算术平均值为 $\bar{x}$,那么这 n 个数的标准方差就可用下式表示:

$$\text{Standard deviation}=\sqrt{\frac{\sum_{i=1}^{n}(x_i-\bar{x})^2}{n}}$$

比如对 9,7,2,8,4 这五个数,求它们的标准差,我们要先求它们的算术平均值:

$$\overline{x} = \frac{9+7+2+8+4}{5} = 6$$

则它们的标准差是：

$$\text{Standard deviation} = \sqrt{\frac{(6-9)^2+(6+7)^2+(6-2)^2+(6-8)^2+(6-4)^2}{5}} = \sqrt{\frac{34}{5}} \approx 2.6$$

注意：当 n 的数值为确定的几个数时，上式中标准方差的分母一定是 n；但当题目告诉你这些数值为随机选取的样本时，那么计算随机选择的这 n 个数的 standard deviation 时，上式的分母应为 $n-1$。在 GRE 考试中，95% 的情况下分母为 n。

5. Standardization（标准化）

把每一个变量的值减去算术平均值后，再除以标准差的过程叫做标准化。

比如对 $9,7,2,8,4$ 这五个数，其算术平均数是 6，标准差是 2.6，则把这一组数标准化后，形式如下：

$$\frac{9-6}{2.6} = 1.15$$

$$\frac{7-6}{2.6} = 0.38$$

$$\frac{2-6}{2.6} = -1.54$$

$$\frac{8-6}{2.6} = 0.77$$

$$\frac{4-6}{2.6} = -0.77$$

从上面的数据可以看出，标准化值都在 -3 与 $+3$ 之间。实际上，在任何一组数据中，大多数的数据都是落在以平均值为中心，左右各 3 倍标准差的范围内。

6. Frequency distribution（频率分布）

频率分布用于展示不同数据出现的频率。

在某些集合中，如果用频率分布来描述集合中的数据会显得更会方便一些。下面这些数据表示居住在某个街区的 25 个家庭中每一个家庭所抚养的孩子数：

$1,2,0,4,1,3,3,1,2,0,4,5,2,3,2,3,2,4,1,2,3,0,2,3,1$

我们可以根据每个数据（x）出现的频率（f）把这些数据进行分类如下：

Frequency Distribution	
x	f
0	3
1	5
2	7
3	6
4	3
5	1
Total	25

从表中我们可以看出，用频率分布的方法对一个集合中的数据进行表示，不但快速概括了数据，而且大大简化了某些运算过程。比如我们要计算平均每一个家庭抚养的孩子数时，我们只要把每一个 x 值与其对应的频率 f 值相乘，然后再除以频率 f 值的和，即总的家庭数就可以了：

$$\frac{0\times3+1\times5+2\times7+3\times6+4\times3+5\times1}{25}=2.16$$

因为一共有 25 个家庭,所以这些数据的中数(median)是从小到大数的第十三个数。从上面表格中的 f 值我们可以看出第 13 个数一定是 2。该组数据的值域(range)是 $5-0$,即 5。标准方差(standard deviation)也可以根据频率分布很容易地算出来。

例 4: 根据下面的频率分布图,分别计算 mean,median,mode,range 和 standard deviation.

-2	-4	0	-1
-3	-1	-2	0
0	0	0	0
-4	-1	-1	-5
0	-1	-5	-2

Data Value x	Frequency f
0	7
-1	5
-2	3
-3	1
-4	2
-5	2
Total	20

解: Mean$=$

$$\frac{(0)(7)+(-1)(5)+(-2)(3)+(-3)(1)+(-4)(2)+(-5)(2)}{20}$$

$$=-1.6$$

Median$=\frac{(-1)+(-1)}{2}=-1$(第 10th 和 11th 的算术平均值)

Mode $=0$　　(0 出现的频率最高)

Range$=0-(-5)=5$

Standard deviation$=$

$$\sqrt{\frac{(-5+1.6)^2(2)+(-4+1.6)^2+\dots+(0+1.6)^2(7)}{20}}$$

$$\approx1.7$$

第三节　随机变量及其分布(**Random variable and Distributions**)

一、随机变量(Random variable)

在随机试验中,人们除对某些特定事件发生的概率感兴趣外,往往还关心某个与随机试验的结果相联系的变量。由于这一变量的取值依赖于随机试验结果,因而被称为随机变量。与普通的变量不同,对于随机变量,人们无法事先预知其确切取值,但可以研究其取值的统计规律性。比如一批灯炮的寿命,抽样检查产品时废品的个数,掷骰子出现的点数,一批零件的尺寸等这些都可称为随机变量。

为全面研究随机试验的结果,揭示随机现象的统计规律性,需将随机试验的结果数量化,即把随机试验的结果与实数对应起来。在有些随机试验中,试验的结果本身就由数量来表示;在另一些随机试验中,试验结果看起来与数量无关,但可以指定一个数量来表示。

随机变量能把数据分布与概念分布有机地联系起来。

随机变量按取值情况分为两类:

(1)离散型随机变量(Discrete random variable)

只可能取有限个或无限可列个值。

(2)连续型随机变量(Continuous random variable)

取值于一个连续区间全部数值的随机变量。比如所有位于 0 和 2 之间的数。

二、概率分布（Probability distribution）

如果随机变量 X 只取有限个或可列个可能值，而且以确定的概率取这些不同的值，则称 X 为离散型随机变量。

一般列成概率分布表：

X	x_1	x_2	x_3	x_4	……
P	p_1	p_2	p_3	p_4	……

也可写成 $P(X=x_k)=p_k \quad (k=1,2,\cdots)$

称之为概率函数。离散型随机变量的分布是指概率分布表或概率函数。

性质：

(1) $P_k \geqslant 0, k=1,2,\cdots$

(2) $\sum\limits_k P_k = 1$

上面的讲解比较抽象，下面我们通过举例来说明随机变量的频率分布。

比如，我们对 500 个 9 岁儿童的肺活量进行测定，每一个儿童都有一个确定的值。数据量很大，所以我们把他们肺活量的值分成 11 个区间，每一个区间的人数除 500 就是落在这个区间内的孩子的概率。

X 组段	$P(X)$ 频率
0.98—	4.17%
1.11—	4.17%
1.24—	5.83%
1.37—	11.67%
1.50—	15.83%
1.63—	24.17%
1.76—	12.50%
1.89—	10.00%
2.02—	5.00%
2.15—	3.33%
2.28—2.41	3.33%
合计	100%

根据此表，我们可以做出频率分布表，如下图所示：

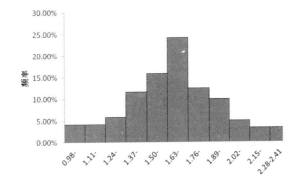

此图的纵坐标为频率,横坐标为肺活量,称此图为频率直方图。每一个直方条的面积＝频率,各组段的频率之和＝1,所以这个直方图的面积为1。如果样本量越大,每个组段的频率就越稳定,也就趋向概率。由此我们可得到:随机抽一个9岁男孩,其肺活量落在各个组段的概率。

假定各组段的概率如上图所示,则

$P(0.98L \leq 肺活量 < 1.11L) = 0.0417$

$P(肺活量 \geq 2.15L) = 0.0333 + 0.0333 = 0.0666$

$P(1.89L \leq 肺活量 < 2.15L) = 0.10 + 0.05 = 0.15$

由此可知:如果一个区间由若干组段构成,计算肺活量落在某个区间的概率等于计算这个区间中的各个直方条图的面积之和。根据上图,只能计算给定区间概率,不能计算任意区间概率。

随机变量 X(肺活量)的算术平均值也叫 X 的期望值(expected value),或叫做 X 的概述分布的平均值(the *mean of the probability distribution*)。

对于上述直方图,组距越小,组段越多,能够计算的概率区间就越多。当组距逐渐减小,直方图的顶端组成的曲线会越来越"光滑",最终会形成一条光滑的曲线,这条曲线叫分布曲线(distribution curve),也叫密度曲线(density curve)或频率曲线(frequency curve)

如下图所示:

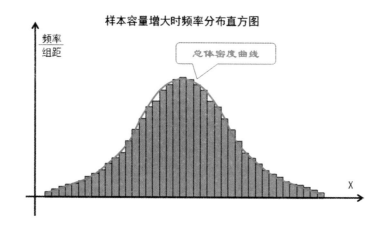

样本容量增大时频率分布直方图

三、正态分布(Normal distribution)

1.正态分布的概念

正态分布又称高斯(Gauss)分布,是最常见、最重要的一种连续型分布,人的许多指标的频数分布都呈正态分布,如身高、体重、脉搏、血红蛋白、血清总胆固醇等。

2.正态分布的图形

9岁男童肺活量的频数图如下:

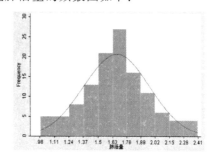 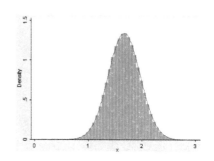

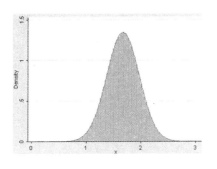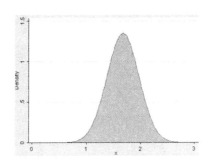

从上图可以看出,随人数逐渐增多,组段不断分细,则频数分布图中的直条逐渐变窄,就会逐渐形成一条高峰位于中央(均数所在处)、两侧逐渐降低且左右对称、不与横轴相交的光滑曲线,近似于数学上的正态分布曲线。

正态分布曲线呈对称的钟形,在平均数(mean)处最高,两侧逐渐低下,两端在无穷远处与横轴无限接近。

若变量 x 的频率曲线对应于数学上的正态分布曲线,则称该变量服从正态分布。

3. 正态分布的密度函数

正态分布曲线的密度函数为:

$$f(X) = \frac{1}{\sigma\sqrt{2\pi}}e^{\frac{-(X-\mu)^2}{2\sigma^2}},其中 -\infty < X < \infty$$

正态分布的参数:

μ 为总体均数(mean),σ 为总体标准差

固定常数:π 为圆周率,e 为自然对数的底

变量:$X(-\infty < X < \infty)$

正态分布概率密度曲线如下图所示,在图中阴影部分的面积表示随机变量的值落在 $a < X < b$ 区间内的概率。

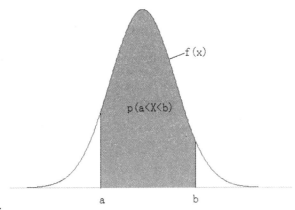

4. 正态分布的密度特征

1) 正态分布是单峰曲线,形状呈钟型,中间高,两端低,以平均值 μ 为对称轴,左右完全对称。

2) 在 $X = \mu$ 处,$f(x)$ 取得最大值。

3) 有两个参数:位置参数——平均数 μ;变异度参数——标准差 σ。前者反映了集中趋势,后者反映了离散趋势。平均数一定,标准差 σ 越大,数据越分散,曲线越平坦;标准差 σ 一定,平均数 μ 增大,曲线沿 X 轴向右平移。因此,不同的平均数 μ,不同的标准差 σ,对应不同的正态分布。

- σ^2 相等,μ 不等的正态分布图示

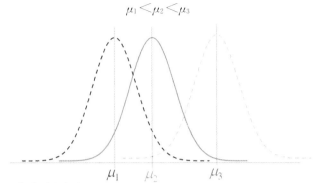

- μ 相等,σ^2 不等的正态分布图示

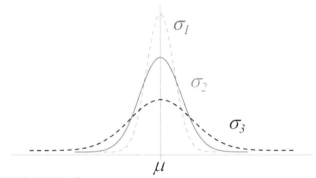

5. 正态密度函数曲线下的面积规律

1) 正态密度函数曲线与横轴间的面积恒等于 1 或 100%;

2) 正态分布是一种对称分布,其对称轴为直线 $X=\mu$,$X>\mu$ 与 $X<\mu$ 范围内曲线下的面积相等,各占 50%;

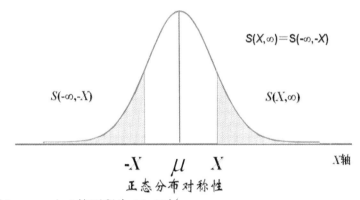

3) 曲线下在区间 $(\mu-\sigma,\mu+\sigma)$ 的面积为 68.27%,

曲线下在区间 $(\mu-1.64\sigma,\mu+1.64\sigma)$ 的面积为 89.90%,

曲线下在区间 $(\mu-1.96\sigma,\mu+1.96\sigma)$ 的面积为 95.00%,

曲线下在区间 $(\mu-2.58\sigma,\mu+2.58\sigma)$ 的面积为 99.00%。

标准正态分布	正态分布	面积或概率
$-1\sim1$	$\mu\pm\sigma$	68.27%
$-1.64\sim1.64$	$\mu\pm1.64\sigma$	89.90%
$-1.96\sim1.96$	$\mu\pm1.96\sigma$	95.00%
$-2.58\sim2.58$	$\mu\pm2.58\sigma$	99.00%

4）曲线在$(\mu-\sigma,\mu+\sigma)$、$(\mu-2\sigma,\mu+2\sigma)$、$(\mu-3\sigma,\mu+3\sigma)$内取值的概率。

区间	取值概率
$(\mu-\sigma,\mu+\sigma)$	68.26%
$(\mu-2\sigma,\mu+2\sigma)$	95.44%
$(\mu-3\sigma,\mu+3\sigma)$	99.74%

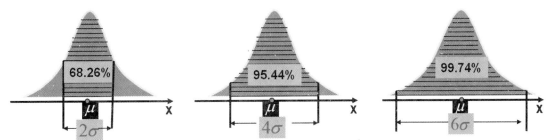

正态分布的值有99.74%落在$(\mu-3\sigma,\mu+3\sigma)$区间内，也就是说落在以平均值为中心的左右各 3 个 σ（共 6 个 σ）的范围内。

例 5： If X is a random variable that is normally distributed with a mean of 5 and a standard deviation of 2, what is $P(X>5)$? Approximately what is $P(3<X<7)$? Which of the four numbers 0.5, 0.1, 0.05, or 0.01 is the best estimate of $P(X<-1)$?

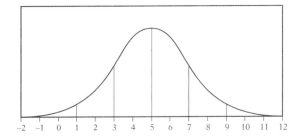

解： 因为随机变量的平均值是 5，所以随机变量的分布曲线关于平均数即 $X=5$ 对称，所以 $X>5$ 的概率等于正态分布曲线下面一半的面积。因而

$$P(X>5)=\frac{1}{2}$$

对于 $3<X<7$，因为标准差是 2，3 和 7 与平均值的差分别是 -2 和 $+2$。既然在离平均值一个方差范围内的分布曲线的面积是 $\frac{2}{3}$，所以 $P(3<X<7)=\frac{2}{3}$。

对于 $X<-1$，-1 在平均值的 3 倍标准差之下，而 $P(\mu-3\sigma,\mu+3\sigma)=99.74\%$，所以

$$P(X<\mu-3\sigma)=\frac{1-P(\mu-3\sigma,\mu+3\sigma)}{2}$$

$$=\frac{1-99.74\%}{2}=0.13\%$$

所以在题目中所给出的四个数中，与 $P(X<-1)$ 最接近的是 0.01。

例 6：

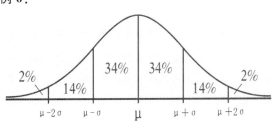

解：（1）$P(65<X<75)=P(\mu<X<\mu+2\sigma)$

$$=34\%+14\%$$

$$=48\%$$

所以身高在 65 到 75 厘米之间的成年企鹅数量 $=3000\times48\%=1440$

（2）$P(X<60)=P(X<\mu-\sigma)$

The figure shows a normal distribution with mean μ and standard deviation σ, including approximate percents of the distribution corresponding to the six regions shown.

Suppose the heights of a population of 3,000 adult penguins are approximately normally distributed with a mean of 65 centimeters and a standard deviation of 5 centimeters.

（1） Approximately how many of the adult penguins are between 65 centimeters and 75 centimeters tall?

（2） If an adult penguin is chosen at random from the population, approximately what is the probability that the penguin's height will be less than 60 centimeters? Give your answer to the nearest 0.05.

$$=14\%+2\%$$
$$=16\%$$

注意题目中要求精确到 0.05,所以最后取值 15%,也即随机选一只成年企鹅,其身高低于 60 厘米的概率是 0.15。

注:正态分布是理论上与实际应用中最重要的分布,是新 GRE 考试的重点。

第四节 级数与数列(Progressions and Sequence)

一、Progressions（级数）

设 a_1 , a_2 , a_3 , $\cdots\cdots$, a_n , $\cdots\cdots$ 是一个数列,则称 $a_1 + a_2 + a_3 + \cdots\cdots + a_n + \cdots\cdots$ 为"级数"或"无穷级数"。

You might encounter a GRE question involving a series of numbers (or other terms) in which the terms progress according to some pattern. Your task is to recognize the pattern and to identify unknown terms based on it.

1. Arithmetic Progression 或 Series(等差级数)

亦称算术级数。级数 $a+(a+d)+(a+2d)+\cdots\cdots+[a+(n-1)d]+\cdots\cdots$ 称为等差级数。

2. Geometric Progression 或 Series(等比级数)

亦称"几何级数"。级数 $a+ar+ar^2+ar^3+\cdots\cdots+ar^n+\cdots\cdots$ 称为"等比级数"。

例 7: In the series $\{N_1 , N_2 , N_3 \ldots\}$, where $N_x = x^2 - 2x$, what is the value of $(N_{50} - N_{49}) - (N_{48} - N_{47})$?

(A) -16   (B) 4   (C) 9

(D)22   (E) 49

解: 本题的正确答案是 (B),解答如下:

由 $N_x = x^2 - 2x$ 可得, $N_{50} = 50^2 - 2 \times 50$,

$$N_{49} = 49^2 - 2 \times 49$$
$$N_{48} = 48^2 - 2 \times 48,$$
$$N_{47} = 47^2 - 2 \times 47$$

$$\Rightarrow (N_{50}-N_{49})-(N_{48}-N_{47})$$
$$=(50^2-49^2-2\times50+2\times49)$$
$$\quad-(48^2-47^2-2\times48+2\times47)$$
$$=[(50+49)(50-49)-2(50-49)]$$
$$\quad-[(48+47)(48-47)-2(48-47)]$$
$$=(99-2)-(95-2)=4$$

注：在解答本题时一定不要急于去计算，要细心观察级数的特点，并综合利用多种解题技巧，如解答本题时利用两数平方差的计算公式"$a^2-b^2=(a+b)(a-b)$"就使解题过程大为简化。

二、Comparisons of Progression（级数的比较）

The test-makers might also ask you to compare two sets of numbers. Always look for a pattern among the numbers which provides a shortcut to determining their sum.

例 8： What is the difference between the sum of all positive even integers less than 102 and the sum of all positive odd integers less than 102?

(A) 0　　(B) 1　　(C) 50

(D) 51　　(E) 101

解： 本题的正确答案是(D)，解答本题的技巧是先比较两个序列数的前几项：

even integers：{2，4，6，8，…100}

odd integers：{1，3，5，7，…99，101}

通过对两个数列的对比，我们不难发现除 1 之外，偶数数列的每一项都比奇数数列小 1，两数列中这样的对应数一共有 50 个，再加上奇数数列多出的一项 1，可知小于 102 的正偶数比小于 102 的正奇数小 51。

三、Sequence（数列）

1. Arithmetic Sequence（等差数列）

如果数列从第二项开始，每一项与前一项的差为常数 d，则称该数列为"等差数列"，d 称为"**公差**"(**common difference**)。等差数列可写成 a，$a+d$，$a+2d$，…$a+(n-1)d$，…的形式。等差数列具有以下性质：

如果 a_1，a_2，a_3，…，a_n，…是一个以 a_1 为第一项，d 为公差和 a_n 为第 n 项的等差数列，则下式成立：

Ⅰ　$a_n=a_1+(n-1)d$

Ⅱ　S_n（前 n 项之和）$=\dfrac{n(a_1+a_n)}{2}=na_1+\dfrac{n(n-1)d}{2}$

Ⅲ　M（中项或中数）

- 当 n 为偶数时，M 为中间两项的算术平均 $M=\dfrac{a_{\frac{n}{2}}+a_{\frac{n}{2}+1}}{2}$

- 当 n 为奇数时，M 为中间项 $M=a_{\frac{n+1}{2}}$

2. Geometric Sequence（等比数列）

如果数列从第二项开始，每一项与前一项的比为常数 q，则称该数列为"等比数列"，q 称为"**公比**"(**common ratio**)。等比数列可以写成 a，aq，aq^2，…，aq^n，…的形式。等比数列具有如下性质：

如果 a_1，a_2，a_3，$\cdots$，a_n，$\cdots$ 是一个以 a_1 为第一项，q 为公比和 a_n 为第 n 项的等比数列，则下式成立：

Ⅰ $a_n = a_1 q^{n-1}$

Ⅱ S_n（前 n 项的和）$= \dfrac{a_1(1-q^n)}{1-q}(q \neq 1)$，或 $S_n = \dfrac{a_1 - a_n q}{1-q}(q \neq 1)$

Ⅲ M（中项或中数）

- 当 n 为偶数时，M 为中间两项的几何平均数：$M = \sqrt{a_{\frac{n}{2}} \times a_{\frac{n}{2}+1}}$
- 当 n 为奇数时，M 为中间项：$M = a_{\frac{n+1}{2}}$

例 9：有 10 个人参加一个联欢会，每个人都与其他各人仅握了一次手，问这次联欢会共有多少次握手？

解法一：将这 10 个人编为 1 至 10 号，则 1 号与 2 到 10 号这 9 人握 9 次手，2 号在前述计算中已计算了他与 1 号的握手，因而算 2 号时为计算 2 号与 3 到 10 号这 8 了 8 次手……由此可见这次联欢会总共握手的次数是 1 到 9 这一等差数列的和，其结果为 $\dfrac{(1+9) \times 9}{2} = 45$；

解法二：则题意可知，本题其实就是求 10 个人中取 2 个人有多少种组合的情况，也即 $C_{10}^2 = 45$；

解法三：共 10 个人，每人应握 9 次手，若 $9 \times 10 = 90$ 次，由于握手是由两个人参与的，也即重复了一倍，因而其结果为 $\dfrac{90}{2} = 45$。

第五节　排列、组合及概率
（Permutation，Combination and Probability）

一、有关概念

1. Factorial Notation（阶乘）：n 个自然数 $1,2,3,\cdots,n$ 的乘积称为 n 的"阶乘"，记作 $n!$。例如：$4! = 4 \times 3 \times 2 \times 1$。零的阶乘规定为 1，即 $0! = 1! = 1$。

2. Permutation（排列）：排列分为两种，非重复的排列问题和可重复的排列问题。前者简称排列问题。这个问题的一般提法是：从 n 个不同的元素 a_1，a_2，a_3，$\cdots$，a_n 中，无放回地任取 m（$1 \leqslant m \leqslant n$）个按照一定的顺序排成一列，问这样的排列共有多少种？这样的排列总数记为 P_n^m。

3. 可重复的排列：这个问题的一般提法是：从 n 个不相同的元素 $a_1,a_2,a_3,\cdots,a_n$ 中，有放回地任取 m 次，每次取一个，所得到不同的序列共有多少种？这种排列共有 n^m 种。

4. Recombination（组合）：从 n 个不同元素中，任取 m 个元素并成一组，叫做从 n 个不同的元素中取出 m 个元素的一个组合，用符号 C_n^m 表示。

5. Probability（概率）：亦称"或然率"、"几率"，某一类事件在相同的条件下可能发生也可能不发生，这类事件称为 **随机事件（random occurrence）**。概率就是用来表示随机事件发生的可能性大小的一个量。很自然地把必然发生的事件的概率定为 1，并把不可能发生的事件的概率定为 0，而一般随机事件的概率是介于 0 和 1 之间的一个数。

（1）等可能性事件的概率：如果一次试验中共有 n 种等可能出现的结果，其中事件 A 包含的结果有 m

种,那么事件 A 的概率 $P(A) = \dfrac{m}{n}$。

例 10: 有 7 个奇数,5 个偶数,从这 12 个数中任取一个是奇数的概率?

解: 这 12 个数任取 1 个有 12 种可能结果,取奇数的结果为 7 种,因此其概率为 $\dfrac{7}{12}$。

(2) 互斥事件发生的概率: 如果事件 A_1,A_2,$\cdots$,A_n 彼此互斥,那么事件 A_1,A_2,$\cdots$,A_n 中有一个发生的概率为这 n 个事件分别发生的概率的和,即 $P(A_1 + A_2 + \cdots + A_n) = P(A_1) + P(A_2) + \cdots + P(A_n)$,也即用"or,或"表达。(注:所谓互斥是指任两个之间都不可能同时发生)。

例 11: 在 12 个球中,8 个是一等品,3 个是二等品,1 个是三等品,求任取一个球是一等品或是二等品的概率?

解: 这 12 个球中,取一等品的概率为 $\dfrac{8}{12}$,取二等品的概率为 $\dfrac{3}{12}$,这两个事件是互斥的(因若取了一等品就不会是二等品,取了二等品就不会是一等品,因此根据上边公式可知本题的答案为 $\dfrac{8}{12} + \dfrac{3}{12} = \dfrac{11}{12}$。

(3) 相互独立事件同时发生的概率: 如果事件相互独立,那么 n 个事件同时发生的概率等于每个事件发生的概率的积,即 $P(A_1, A_2, \cdots, A_n) = P(A_1) P(A_2) \cdots P(A_n)$,也即用"且"或"and"来表达。

例 12: A 坛中有 7 个白球,有 3 个黑球,B 坛中有 4 个白球,5 个黑球,问从这两个坛中分别摸出一个都是白球的概率?

解: 从 A 坛中摸出一个白球的概率为 $\dfrac{7}{7+3}$,从 B 坛中摸出一个白球的概率为 $\dfrac{4}{4+5}$,这两个事件是相互独立的,互不影响,则根据上面所述其概率应为 $\dfrac{7}{10} \times \dfrac{4}{9} = \dfrac{14}{45}$。

(4) 独立重复试验发生的概率: 如果在一次试验中某事件发生的概率是 P,那么在 n 次独立重复试验中这个事件恰好发生 K 次的概率为 $P_n(K) = C_n^k \cdot P^k (1-P)^{n-k}$。

例 13: 某气象站天气预报准确率为 80%,求 5 次预报中有 4 次准确的概率?

解: 设 P 为预报一次,结果准确的概率,预报 5 次,相当于 5 次独立重复试验,根据上式则有:$P_5(4) = C_5^4 \times 0.8^4 \times (1-0.8)^{5-4} = 5 \times 0.8^4 \times 0.2 = 0.4096$。

6. 事件的包含与相等: 设有两个随机事件 A 和 B,如果 A 发生,那么 B 必发生,则称 B 包含 A,记作 $A \subset B$ 或 $B \supset A$,如果事件 A 包含 B,同时事件 B 也包含事件 A,则称事件 A 与 B 相等或等价,记作 $A = B$。

7. 事件的和与积: 事件"A 或 B"称为事件 A 与事件 B 的和,记作 $A+B$ 或 $A \bigcup B$;事件 A 且 B 称为事件 A 与 B 的积,记作 $A \cdot B$ 或 AB 或 $A \bigcap B$。事件的和与积可推广到多于两个事件的情形。

8. 对立事件与事件的差: 称事件"非 A"为 A 的对立事件,记作 $\overline{A}$。事件 A 同 B 的差表示 A 发生而 B 不发生的事件,记作 $A-B$ 或 $A\overline{B}$。

9. 事件的互不相等(Mutually exclusive events): 在一次试验中,如果事件 A 与事件 B 不能同时发生,即 $AB = V$(不可能事件),那么称 A 和 B 是互不相容的事件。

10. 条件概率: 若 A,B 是两个随机事件,$P(A) \neq 0$,则称在 A 发生的前提下 B 发生的概率为条件概率,记作 $P(B/A)$。

11. 事件的独立性(Independent events): 如果一个事件的发生并不影响另一个事件发生的概率,则称这两个事件是相互独立的。

二、有关性质

1. 排列与组合

① $P_n^m = \dfrac{n!}{(n-m)!}(1 \leqslant m \leqslant n)$

② $C_n^m = \dfrac{n!}{m!\,(n-m)!}(1 \leqslant m \leqslant n)$

③ $C_n^m = C_n^{n-m}(1 \leqslant m \leqslant n)$

④ $C_{n+1}^m = C_n^m + C_n^{m-1}$

⑤ $0! = 1, C_n^0 = P_n^0 = 1, C_n^1 = P_n^1 = n\ (n \geqslant 1)$

2. 任何随机事件 A 在相同的条件下发生的概率介于 0 和 1 之间,即 $0 \leqslant P(A) \leqslant 1$;必然事件 U 和不可能事件 V 发生的概率分别为 1 和 0,即 $P(U)=1, P(V)=0$。

3. 加法原则和乘法原则

加法原则:做一件事,完成它可以有 n 类办法,在第一类办法中有 m_1 种不同的方法,在第二类办法中有 m_2 种不同的方法……,在第 n 类办法中有 m_n 种不同的方法,那么完成这件事共有 $N = m_1 + m_2 + \cdots\cdots + m_n$ 种不同的方法(在表达中用"或,or"时即为加法原则)。

例 14:某天从 A 地到 B 地,可乘汽车,也可乘火车,还可乘飞机,一天中,汽车有 5 班,火车有 4 班,飞机有 2 班,问一天中 A 地到 B 地共有多少种走法?

解:根据加法原则可知共有 $5+4+2=11$ 种走法。

乘法原则:做一件事,完成它需分为 n 个步骤,做第一步有 m_1 种不同的方法,做第二步有 m_2 种不同的方法……,做第 n 步有 m_n 种不同的方法,则完成这件事共有 $N = m_1 \times m_2 \times \cdots\cdots \times m_n$ 种不同的方法。

例 15:由 A 到 B 有 3 条路,由 B 到 C 有 4 条路,问由 A 经 B 到 C 有多少种不同的走法?

解:根据乘法原则可知共有 $3 \times 4 = 12$ 种不同的走法。

4. 概率的加法公式

(1) $P(A) = 1 - P(\overline{A})$

(2) 若事件 A,B 互不相容,则 $P(A+B) = P(A) + P(B)$

(3) 对任意两事件 A,B,则 $P(A+B) = P(A) + P(B) - P(AB)$

5. 概率的乘法公式

(1) $P(B/A) = P(AB)\,/\,P(A), P(A) \neq 0$

(2) 若事件 A 和 B 是相互独立的,当 $P(A) \neq 0$ 时,$P(AB) = P(A)P(B)$

三、事件的运算规律

(1) $A+B = B+A$(加法交换律)

(2) $A+(B+C) = (A+B)+C$(加法结合律)

(3) $A+A = A$

(4) $A+\overline{A}=U$（"U"表示全集）

(5) $A+U=U$

(6) $A+V=A$（"V"表示空集）

(7) $A \cdot B=B \cdot A$（乘法交换律）

(8) $(AB)C=A(BC)$（乘法结合律）

(9) $A \cdot A=A$

(10) $A \cdot \overline{A}=V$

(11) $A \cdot U=A$

(12) $A \cdot V=V$

(13) $A(B+C)=AB+AC$（分配率）

(14) $AB+BC=B(A+C)$（结合率）

(15) $\overline{A+B}=\overline{A} \cdot \overline{B}$

(16) $\overline{A \cdot B}=\overline{A}+\overline{B}$

第六节　重点试题精练及解析

1. The average of three numbers, the greatest of which is 78.

The average of three numbers, the least of which is 3.

1. 解：本题的正确答案为（D）。比较的左项为最大数为 78 的三个数的平均值；比较的右项为最小数为 3 的三个数的平均值。该题具有一定的迷惑性，由于考试时常有思维定式，一不小心便得到想当然的结果。本题看似前者更大，但由于题中并未指明其余两数的大小，而平均值又依赖于三个数中每一个数的大小，所以该题为无法判断。

2. The average (arithmetic mean) of x, y, and 6 is 3.

$\dfrac{x+y}{2}$　　　　$\dfrac{3}{2}$

2. x，y，6 的算术平均值等于 3。

解：本题的正确答案为（C）。由题意可得：

$$\frac{x+y+6}{3}=3$$

$$\Rightarrow x+y=3 \Rightarrow \frac{x+y}{2}=\frac{3}{2}$$

3.

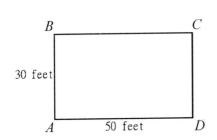

3. 左面图形表示一个长方形的娱乐区，有一个小孩站在 B 点，同时另一个小孩在 A 和 D 之间来回跑动。若跑步的小孩在 AD 边上的位置在任一时刻都是随机的，两个小孩最多相距 50 英尺的概率(probability)是多少？

解：本题的正确答案是（D）。根据题意可知，两

The figure above shows a rectangular play area in which one child stands at B while another child runs back and forth along the entire side AD. If the running child is in a position randomly located along side AD at a given time, what is the probability that the two children are at most 50 feet apart at that time?

(A) $\dfrac{1}{5}$　　(B) $\dfrac{2}{5}$　　(C) $\dfrac{3}{5}$

(D) $\dfrac{4}{5}$　　(E) 1

个孩子的位置及点 A 在任意时刻都可构成一个直角三角形,直角三角形的斜边长就是两个孩子之间的距离,两个孩子的距离不超过 50 英尺,即直角三角形的斜边不超过 50 英尺,$AB=30$ 英尺,根据勾股定理可知,跑步的小孩离 A 点的距离应不超过 40 英尺时,才能使他们之间的距离不超过 50 英尺。而跑步的小孩在 AD 上的位置是随机的,因此两个小孩最多相距 50 英尺的概率是 $\dfrac{40}{50}=\dfrac{4}{5}$

4. For each positive integer n,

$$a_n = \frac{1}{n} - \frac{1}{n+1}$$

$$a_1 + a_2 + a_3 + a_4 \qquad\qquad \frac{4}{5}$$

4. 对于每个正整数 n,$a_n = \dfrac{1}{n} - \dfrac{1}{n+1}$

解：本题的正确答案是(C)。诸如

$a_n = \dfrac{1}{n} - \dfrac{1}{n+1}$ 的求和公式如下得到：

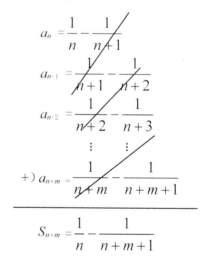

根据通用求和公式,把本题中的 $n=1,2,3,4$ 代入可得：

$$S_4 = 1 - \frac{1}{5} = \frac{4}{5}$$

5. COMPARISON OF TEST SCORES FOR TWO CLASSES

	Number of Scores	Mean Score	Median Score
Class A	15	80	84
Class B	30	74	72

5. 标题：两个班级考试分数的比较：

解：本题的正确答案是（D）。根据平均值（mean）与中数（median）的定义可知,它们两者之间不存在任何确定的关系。本题只可以算出左项,但无法得出右项,但右项必

The mean of the 45 scores	The median of the 45 scores

6. A linen shop has a certain tablecloth that is available in 8 sizes and 10 colors. What is the maximum possible number of different combinations of size and color available?

(A) 9　　(B) 18　　(C) 40

(D) 80　　(E) 90

6. 一亚麻布商店有某种桌布,这种桌布共有 8 种尺寸 10 种颜色,问最多可以有多少种尺寸与颜色的不同组合?

解:本题的正确答案为(D)。组合的实质是分别从 8 种尺寸和 10 种颜色中各选出一个,因此共计有 $C_8^1 \cdot C_{10}^1 = 80$ 种选法,即每一种尺寸都有 10 种颜色与之相配,所以共有 $8\times10 = 80$ 种不同的组合。

7. If one number is chosen at random from the first 1,000 positive integers, what is the probability that the number chosen is multiple of both 2 and 8?

(A) $\frac{1}{125}$　　(B) $\frac{1}{8}$　　(C) $\frac{1}{2}$

(D) $\frac{9}{16}$　　(E) $\frac{5}{8}$

7. 若从前1000个正整数中随机选出一个数,问该数是 2 和 8 的倍数的概率是多少?

解:本题的正确答案是(B)。在 1 至 1000 中,8 的倍数有 125 个,因为 2 和 8 的最小公倍数为 8,则该数是 2 和 8 的倍数的概率为:

$$\frac{125}{1000}=\frac{1}{8}$$

8. The probability that event R will occur is 0.38.

The probability that events R and W will both occur	0.40

8. 事件 R 发生的概率为 0.38。

解:本题的正确答案是(B)。比较的左项为事件 R 和 W 同时发生的概率的大小,因为事件 W 发生的概率最大为 1,则事件 R 和 W 同时发生的概率最大为 $1\times0.38 = 0.38$。

9. The geometric mean of any two positive numbers x and y is $\sqrt{xy}$.

The geometric mean of 4 and 8	The average (arithmetic mean) of 4 and 8

9. 任两个正整数 x 和 y 的几何平均值(geometric mean)是 $\sqrt{xy}$。

解:本题的正确答案是(B)。4 和 8 的几何平均值 $=\sqrt{4\times8}=4\sqrt{2}$

4 和 8 算术平均值为 $\frac{4+8}{2}=6$

$\sqrt{2}=1.414 < 1.5$,所以 $4\sqrt{2} < 6$。

10. The numbers 3，10，17，24，31，and 38 are the first six terms of an infinite sequence in which each term after the first is 7 greater than the preceding term. What is the 45th term of the sequence?

(A) 308　(B) 311　(C) 312
(D) 315　(E) 318

10. 数字 3，10，17，24，31 和 38 是一个无穷数列（infinite sequence）的前六项，该数列的每一项都比前一项大 7，问这个数列的第 45 项是多少？

解： 本题的正确答案是（B）。由题意可知，该数列是一个等差数列，其首项 $a_1 = 3$，其公差为 $d = 7$，根据等差数列的通项公式可得：

$$a_{45} = a_1 + (n-1)d = 3 + (45-1) \times 7 = 311$$

11.

k	a_k	p_k
1	100	0.10
2	200	0.25
3	300	0.20
4	400	0.25
5	500	0.20

If in an experiment the probabilities of obtaining the values a_1，a_2，a_3，a_4，and a_5 *are* p_1，p_2，p_3，p_4 and p_5，respectively，then the expected value is defined as $a_1 p_1 + a_2 p_2 + a_3 p_3 + a_4 p_4 + a_5 p_5$. For the values and their corresponding probabilities in the table above，what is the expected value?

(A) 350　(B) 320　(C) 300
(D) 270　(E) 250

11. 若在某个实验中，得到值 a_1，a_2，a_3，a_4 和 a_5 的概率分别为 p_1，p_2，p_3，p_4 和 p_5，那么期望值（expected value）被定义为 $a_1 p_1 + a_2 p_2 + a_3 p_3 + a_4 p_4 + a_5 p_5$，对于上面表格中的值及其相应的概率，问其期望值是多少？

解： 本题的正确答案是（B）。由题中所介绍的 expected value 的求法，考生可直接把表格中的数据代入公式计算：

$$100 \times 0.1 + 200 \times 0.25 + 300 \times 0.2 + 400 \times 0.25 + 500 \times 0.2 = 320$$

12.

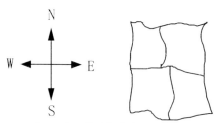

A precinct is divided into four wards as shown. The two northern wards have exactly 30 Democrats each and the two

12. 如图所示，某选区被分成四个行政区。两个北部行政区各有 30 名民主党员，两个东部行政区，平均（算术平均）每区有 35 名民主党员。

解： 本题的正确答案为（D）。比较的左项为两个南部选区民主党员的（算术）平均值。根据题中条件只能算出东南区有 $35 \times 2 - 30 = 40$ 个民主党员，但无法知道西南区民主党员的人数，所以无法判断南部选区民主党员的平均数。

eastern wards have an average (arithmetic mean) of 35 Democrats per ward.

The average (arithmetic mean) number of Democrats in the two southern wards   25

13. For which of the following sets of numbers is the product of the three numbers less than each member of the set?

I. $\frac{1}{4}, \frac{2}{3}, \frac{3}{4}$

II. $-\frac{1}{2}, -1, 4$

III. $-2, 3, 5$

(A) I only   (B) II only

(C) III only   (D) I and III

(E) II and III

14.

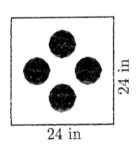

24 in

24 in

A square dart board has four dark circular regions of radius 3 inches, as shown in the design above. Each point on the dart board is equally likely to be hit by a dart that hits the board. What is the probability that a dart that hits the board will hit one of the circular regions?

(A) $\frac{\pi}{16}$ (B) $\frac{\pi}{48}$ (C) $\frac{\pi}{64}$

(D) $\frac{1}{3}$ (E) $\frac{1}{4}$

15. The average (arithmetic mean) of 50 measurements is 34.6, and the least and

13. 下面哪一个数集合中的三个数字的乘积比集合中的任一个元素都小?

I. $\frac{1}{4}, \frac{2}{3}, \frac{3}{4}$

II. $-\frac{1}{2}, -1, 4$

III. $-2, 3, 5$

解: 本题的正确答案为(D)。在解答此类题时, 考生要注意的是偶数个负数相乘,其积为正,奇数个负数相乘其积为负;正真分数相乘,其积越乘越小。

14. 如上面的图样所示,1 个正方形的标枪板上有 4 个半径为 3 英寸的圆形的黑色区域。标枪击中标枪板上的每个点的概率相同,击中标枪板的标枪击中 4 个圆形区域中的某一个的概率是多大?

解: 本题的正确答案是(A)。该题其实是问 4 个圆形区域的面积占标枪板的总面积的几分之几,这个分数就是击中标枪板的标枪击中 4 个圆形区域中的某一个的概率:

$$\frac{4\pi \times (3)^2}{24 \times 24} = \frac{\pi}{16}$$

15. 50 次测量的算术平均值是 34.6,测量的最大值和最小值分别为 18.3 和 50.9。

the greatest of the measurements are 18.3 and 50.9, respectively.

The median of the
50 measurements   34.6

解：本题的正确答案是(D)。考生在解答本题时，只要注意到 mean 和 median 之间没有任何确定的关系，就可推知本题为无法判断。

16. The standard deviation of the sample measurements 0,1,2,4, and 8

The standard deviation of the sample measurements 1,2,3,5 and 9

16. **解**：本题的正确答案为(C)。对于一个样本 $a_1, a_2 \cdots a_n$，设 a 是其算术的平均值，则样本的方差(deviation)为

$$b^2 = [(a_1-a)^2 + (a_2-a)^2 + \cdots + (a_n-a)^2]/n$$

$$= \sum_{i=1}^{n} (a_i-a)^2/n,$$

其标准方差(standard deviation)为 b。GRE 数学考试中一般不会考复杂的标准方差计算，大多数的题实际上只要求考生了解标准方差的含意即可。标准方差是度量数据之间离散程度的一个量，因此只要某数列中的最大值与最小值的差较大，或者该数列中有许多元素与该数列的算术平均值相差较大，则该数列的标准方差就大。对于本题，显然后一样本的每一值比前一样本对应值都小 1，故两者的平均值差 1，而 δ 没有变化。比较左项 5 个值的算术平均值为 3，比较右项 5 个值的算术平均值为 4，其标准方差分别为：

左项的标准方差＝

$$\sqrt{\frac{(0-3)^2+(1-3)^2+(2-3)^2+(4-3)^2+(8-3))^2}{5}}$$

$$= 2\sqrt{2}$$

右项的标准方差＝

$$\sqrt{\frac{(1-4)^2+(2-4)^2+(3-4)^2+(5-4)^2+(9-4))^2}{5}}$$

$$= 2\sqrt{2}$$

17. An experiment has three possible outcomes, I, J, and K. The probabilities of the outcomes are 0.25, 0.35, and 0.40, respectively. If the experiment is to be performed twice and the successive outcomes are independent, what is the probability that K will not be an outcome

17. 一个实验有 3 个可能的结果：I,J 和 K。这些结果出现的概率分别是 0.25，0.35 和 0.4，若连续进行该实验两次，并且两次的结果相互独立，问 K 不是任一次试验结果的概率有多大？

解：本题的正确答案是(A)。K 不是第一次试验结果的概率为：

either time?

(A) 0.36   (B) 0.40   (C) 0.60

(D) 0.64   (E) 0.80

$1-0.4=0.6$

同理 K 不是第二次试验结果的概率也为 0.6，两次试验的结果相互独立，所以 K 不是任一次试验结果的概率为 $0.6 \times 0.6 = 0.36$。

18. If a_1, a_2, a_3, ... a_n ... is a sequence such that $a_1 = -2$ and a_{n+1} is the reciprocal of the square of a_n for all $n \geq 1$, what is the value of a_4?

(A) 64   (B) 16   (C) $\dfrac{1}{16}$

(D) $\dfrac{1}{256}$ (E) -16

18. 若 $a_1, a_2, a_3 \ldots a_n \cdots$ 是一数列（sequence），且 $a_1 = -2$，对于所有的 $n \geq 1$，有 a_{n+1} 是 a_n 的平方的倒数，问 a_4 的值是多少？

解： 本题的正确答案为（D）。由题意可得：

$a_2 = \dfrac{1}{a_1^2}, a_3 = \dfrac{1}{a_2^2} = a_1^4, a_4 = \dfrac{1}{a_3^2} = \dfrac{1}{a_1^8} = \dfrac{1}{256}$

19. SURVEY OF PETS IN HOUSEHOLDS
IN AN APARTMENT COMPLEX

Kind of Pet	Number of Households
Dog	25
Cat	41
Other	19
No Pet	44

The total number of households with at least one pet   85

19. 标题：一个公寓区家庭拥有宠物的调查结果

解： 本题的正确答案为（D）。比较的左项为至少有一只宠物的家庭的总数，由上面三项数字可得它们的和为 $25+41+19=85$，但一个家庭可能拥有两只或两只以上的宠物，所以本题为无法判断。

20. The odds that a certain event will occur is the ratio of the probability that the event will occur to the probability that it will not occur. If the odds that Pat will win a prize are 4 to 3, what is the probability that Pat will not win the prize?

(A) $\dfrac{1}{4}$ (B) $\dfrac{1}{3}$ (C) $\dfrac{3}{7}$

(D) $\dfrac{4}{7}$ (E) $\dfrac{3}{7}$

20. 某事件发生的可能性（odds）为这件事将发生的概率与这件事不发生概率的比值。若 Pat 赢得一项奖的可能性为 4 比 3，Pat 赢不到该奖项的概率是多大？

解： 本题的正确答案是（C）。

$\text{odds} = \dfrac{\text{发生的概率}}{\text{不发生的概率}} = \dfrac{4}{3}$

$\Rightarrow$ Pat 赢不到该奖项的概率

$= \dfrac{\text{不发生的概率}}{\text{发生的概率}+\text{不发生的概率}} = \dfrac{3}{4+3} = \dfrac{3}{7}$

21. The median of $10, 15, x$ and y is 18.5, and $x < y$.

$$x \qquad\qquad 22$$

21. $10, 15, x$ 和 y 的中数（median）是 18.5，并且 $x < y$。

解： 本题的正确答案为（C）。由中数是 18.5，且 $x < y$，可以推出 $x > 15$，否则将无法得到四个数的中数等于 18.5 这个已知条件，所以有：

$$\frac{15+x}{2} = 18.5 \Rightarrow x = 22$$

22. An identification code read from left to right consists of 2 digits, a dash, 3 digits, a dash, and then 4 digits. Each digit can be any number from 0 through 9.

The number of different identification codes possible	10^9

22. 一个识别密码（identification code）从左至右包括 2 个数字，1 个连字符号，3 个数字，1 个连字符号，然后是 4 个数字，每个数字可以是 0 至 9 的任一个。

解： 本题的正确答案是（C）。题目中比较的左项是所有可能的密码数，dash 指连字符号，如 $123-456$ 中的"—"，它与密码数无关。密码中共有 9 个数字，每个数字都可能是 0 至 9 这 10 个数字中的一个，所以共有 10^9 种可能。

23. If the average (arithmetic mean) of x, y, z, 5 and 7 is 8, which of the following must be true?

I. The median of the five numbers cannot be 5.

II. At least one of x, y, and z is greater than 9.

III. The range of the five numbers is 2 or more

    (A) I only   (B) II only

    (C) III only   (D) I and III

    (E) II and III

23. 若 x, y, z, 5 和 7 的算术平均值是 8，下面哪一个一定正确？

I. 5 个数字的中数不能是 5。

II. x, y 和 z 中至少有一个大于 9。

III. 5 个数字的值域是 2 或更大。

解： 本题的正确答案是（E）。

I 不对，因为 5 个数的中数完全可以是 5。

II 一定正确，因为算术平均值为 8，则 x, y, z 中至少有一个大于 9。

III 一定正确，因为 x, y, z 中至少有 1 个大于 9，那么 range 至少大于 4，2 or more 必然满足大于 4。

24. A gardener wishes to plant 5 bushes in a straight row. Each bush has flowers of a different solid color (white, yellow, pink, red, and purple). How many ways can the bushes be arranged so that the middle bush

24. 一名园丁想将 5 种花丛种成一直排，每种花丛开不同颜色的花（白色、黄色、粉红、红色和紫色），有多少种种植方法可使中间的一种为开红色花的花丛？

解： 本题的正确答案为（A）。5 个元素中第 3 个

is the one with red flowers?

(A) 24　　(B) 30　　(C) 60

(D) 96　　(E) 120

25. The average （arithmetic mean） of 3 different positive integers is equal to the average of 5、7、8、9 and 11.

| The greatest possible value of the greatest of the 3 different integers | 21 |

26. One integer will be randomly selected from the integers 11 to 60, inclusive. What is the probability that the selected integer will be a perfect square or a perfect cube?

(A) 0.1　　(B) 0.125　　(C) 0.16

(D) 0.5　　(E) 0.9

27. The odds in favor of winning a game can be found by computing the ratio of the probability of winning to the probability of not winning. If the probability that Pat will win a game is $\frac{4}{9}$, what are the odds that Pat will win the game?

(A) 4 to 5　　(B) 4 to 9　　(C) 5 to 4

(D) 5 to 9　　(E) 9 to 5

28. What is the total number of different 5-digit numbers that contain all of the digits 2，3，4，7 and 9 and in which none of the odd digits occur next to each other?

为红色,另外 4 个为剩下的 4 种颜色,所以本题安排为:$P_4^4 = 24$。

25. 三个不同正整数的算术平均值等于 5、7、8、9 和 11 的平均值。

解：本题的正确答案为(C)。比较的左项为 3 个不同正整数中最大数的最大可能值。5、7、8、9 和 11 平均值是 8,故 3 个正整数的和为 $3 \times 8 = 24$，

因此当另外两数分别为 1 和 2 时,3 个不同正整数中最大数的最大可能值是 21。

26. 从 11 至 60,包括 11 和 60 的整数中随机挑出一个数,问其是完全平方数（perfect square）或完全立方数(perfect cube)的概率是多少？

解：本题的正确答案为（A）。11 至 60 间的完全平方数有 $4^2 = 16$,$5^2 = 25$,$6^2 = 36$,$7^2 = 49$；完全立方数有 $3^3 = 27$,共 5 个数,11 至 60 之间共有 50 个数,所以挑出的数为完全平方数或完全立方数的概率为 5/50＝0.1。

27. 赢得一场比赛的可能性可以通过计算获胜的概率与不获胜概率的比值得到,若 Pad 赢得比赛的概率为 $\frac{4}{9}$,那么 P 赢得比赛的可能性是多大？

解：本题的正确答案是（A）。Pad 赢得比赛的概率为 $\frac{4}{9}$,那么他不赢得比赛的概率为 $\frac{5}{9}$,由题意可得：Odds＝P（win）：P（not win）＝$\frac{4}{9} : \frac{5}{9} = 4 : 5$

28. 含有 2,3,4,7 和 9 这 5 个不同数字,且奇数不相邻的*5 位数*(5-digit numbers)的总数是多少？

解：本题的正确答案是（A）。这 5 个数中有三个

(A) 12　　(B) 10　　(C) 8

(D) 6　　(E) 1

29.

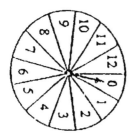

If for a given spin, the pointer shown in the figure above is equally likely to stop on any of the numbered sectors, what is the probability that the pointer will stop on an odd-numbered sector? (Assume that the pointer cannot stop on a dividing line between sectors.)

(A) $\dfrac{1}{2}$　　(B) $\dfrac{2}{3}$

(C) $\dfrac{7}{12}$　　(D) $\dfrac{6}{13}$

(E) $\dfrac{7}{13}$

30. In a series of races, 10 toy cars are raced, 2 cars at a time. If each car must race each of the other cars exactly twice, how many races must be held?

(A) 40　　　　(B) 90

(C) 100　　　(D) 180

(E) 200

31. RESULTS ON A HISTORY TEST

Class	Number of Students Taking Test	Average * Score
X	54	70
Y	41	73
Z	32	76

* Arithmetic mean

奇数,不相邻时它们应分别在个位、百位和万位,剩下 2,4 在十位和千位,由题意可得:

$$P_3^3 \cdot P_2^2 = 12$$

29. 若对于给定的转盘,左图所示的指针停于各个数字部分的概率都相等。问该指针将停在奇数部分的概率是多少?(假设该指针不会停在两个不同部分的分界线上。)

解: 本题的正确答案是(D)。图中的转盘被不同的数字分成了 13 个部分,其中奇数有 6 个:1,3,5,7,9,11,而指针停于各个部分的概率相等,所于指针停于奇数部分的概率为 $\dfrac{6}{13}$。

30. 在一系列比赛中,有 10 辆玩具汽车进行比赛,每场比赛有 2 辆汽车参加。若每辆汽车必须和其他的各辆汽车比赛两次,问一共要举行有多少场比赛?

解: 本题的正确答案为(B)。10 辆车中,每辆车与另一辆车比赛一次,共有 C_{10}^2 次,表示从 10 辆汽车中任选 2 辆车比赛,共 45 次;而比赛 2 次,则共有 $2 \times C_{10}^2 = 90$ 次。

31. 3 个班级所有学生的算术平均分是:

解: 本题的正确答案为(B)。本题若用式子(70+73+76)/3＝73 来计算平均值,将得到显然错误的结果;若采用计算公式(70×54＋73×41＋76×32)/(54＋41＋32)来求平均值,则显得比较麻烦;较为简便的方法是:先假设 y 的平均分 73 是三个班的平均分,

The average (arithmetic mean) score for all of the students in the 3 classes is

(A) less than 70

(B) between 70 and 73

(C) exactly 73

(D) between 73 and 76

(E) greater than 76

然后比较 x 和 z 班分别比平均分高多少或低多少：

x 班全班比平均分总计低 $54×3＝162$ 分。

z 班全班比平均分总计高 $32×3＝96$ 分＜162 分。

所以平均分应在 $70-73$ 之间。

---

32. The yearly rent for a rectangular office with dimensions 100 feet by 200 feet at the annual rate of $20 per square foot

$500,000

32. **解：**本题的正确答案是(B)。比较的左项是租费为每平方英尺 20 美元，面积为 100 英尺×200 英尺见方的长方形办公室的年租金，其值为

$$100×200×20＝\$400,000。$$

---

33. Three red marbles and 2 white marbles are placed in an empty box. One marble at a time is to be selected randomly and removed from the box until all 5 marbles have been removed. What is the probability that each of the first 3 marbles removed will be red?

(A) $\dfrac{1}{32}$　(B) $\dfrac{1}{20}$　(C) $\dfrac{1}{10}$

(D) $\dfrac{1}{2}$　(E) $\dfrac{3}{5}$

33. 一个空盒子中放有 3 个红色弹珠和 2 个白色弹珠，每次随机取出 1 个弹珠并且直到 5 个弹珠都被取出来。问取出的前 3 个弹珠全部是红色的概率有多大？

解：本题的正确答案是(C)。第一次取出红色弹珠的概率为 $\dfrac{3}{5}$；第一次取出后，盒子中剩 2 红 2 白，因此第二次取出红色弹珠的概率为 $\dfrac{2}{4}$；第二次取出后盒子中剩 2 白 1 红，因此第三次取出红色弹珠的概率为 $\dfrac{1}{3}$。前三次取出的球都是红球的概率是每次取出的球都是红球的概率的乘积，即

$$\dfrac{3}{5}·\dfrac{2}{4}·\dfrac{1}{3}＝\dfrac{1}{10}$$

---

34. What is the sum of the first 2,003 terms of the sequence 0, 2, 7, 1, 0, 2, 7, 1, 0, 2, 7, 1, ⋯ if the pattern 0, 2, 7, 1 is repeated throughout the sequence?

(A) 503　(B) 2,010　(C) 2,013

(D) 5,009　(E) 20,030

34. 若整个序列 0, 2, 7, 1, 0, 2, 7, 1, ⋯ 以 0, 2, 7, 1 循环，那么该数列前 2003 项的和是多少？

解：本题的正确答案为(D)。由于数列是以 0, 2, 7, 1 为周期循环，其周期长度为 4，所以

前 2003 项共有 2003/4＝500 个周期，并余 3 项：0，2，7。因此该数列前 2003 项的和为：

$$500 \times (0+2+7+1)+(0+2+7)=5009$$

35. A total of 40 tourists went on a trip. If 18 of the tourists visited site X，18 visited site Y，and 8 visited both site X and site Y，how many visited neither site X nor site Y?

(A) 4　　　(B) 10　　　(C) 12

(D) 22　　　(E) 28

35. 总计 40 个游客去旅行，若 18 人参观了景点 X，18 个人参观了景点 Y，8 个人既参观了景点 X 又参观了景点 Y，问有多少人既未参观景点 X，又未参观景点 Y？

解：本题的正确答案为(C)。显然可用图形来直观表示：

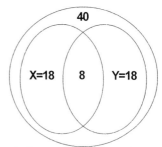

因此既未参观景点 X，又未参观景点 Y 的人数为：

$$40-(18+18-8)=12 人$$

36. Nine pieces of paper numbered consecutively from 1 to 9 are put into a hat. If one piece of paper is drawn at random from the hat, what is the probability that it will have an even number?

(A) $\frac{1}{9}$　(B) $\frac{2}{9}$　(C) $\frac{4}{9}$

(D) $\frac{1}{2}$　(E) $\frac{5}{9}$

36. 把标号为 1 至 9 的 9 片纸放入一个帽子中，若从帽子中随机地抽出 1 片纸，它是偶数的概率为多少？

解：本题的正确答案是(C)。1 至 9 中偶数有 2、4、6 和 8 共四个，那么随机抽出 1 张纸其标号为偶数的概率为 $\frac{4}{9}$。

37. The integers between 1 and 100，inclusive，are put in list A if they are divisible by 2 and in list B if they are divisible by 3. How many integers in list A are <u>not</u> in list B?

37. 在 1 至 100，且包括 1 和 100 的整数中，若能被 2 整除（divisible），就被放入 A 列中，若能被 3 整除就被放入 B 列中，有多少数在 A 列中而不在 B 列中？

(A) 11
(B) 16
(C) 25
(D) 33
(E) 34

解：本题的正确答案是(E)。1 至 100 中能被 2 整除的数显然是 50 个，那么如何算能够被 3 整除的数呢？在小于或等于 100 的正整数中能被 3 整除的最大的数是 3 的多少倍，就有多少个数能被 3 整除。在 1 至 100 中能被 3 整除的最大的数是 99,所以这 100 个数中能被 3 整除的数共有 33 个。在 A 列中而不在 B 列中的数等于在 A 列中的数减去即在 A 列中以在 B 列中数。A 和 B 的交集为能够被 6 整除的数。1 至 100 中被 6 整除的数的个数为：$\frac{100}{6}=16$ 余 4,即 16 个。所以在 A 中,而不在 B 中的数为 $50-16=34$。

38. What is the sum of the first 1,000 terms of the sequence 0, 0, 1, 2, 1, 0, 0, 1, 2, 1,... if the pattern 0, 0, 1, 2, 1 is repeated indefinitely?

(A) 200　　(B) 400　　(C) 800
(D) 1,000　　(E) 4,000

38. 一个数列 0, 0, 1, 2, 1, 0, 0, 1, 2, 1, … 的前 1000 项的和是多少,假设该数列以 0, 0, 1, 2, 1 无限重复？

解：本题的正确答案是(C)。该数列以 0, 0, 1, 2, 1 无限重复,也就是每 5 项重复一次,前 1000 项有 200 个循环,每个循环的和为 4,所以前 1000 项的和为 $200×4=800$。

39. A certain jar contains 100 jelly beans：50 white, 30 green, 10 yellow, 5 red, 4 purple, and 1 black. If a jelly bean is to be chosen at random, what is the probability that the jelly bean will be neither purple nor red?

(A) 0.09　　(B) 0.11　　(C) 0.55
(D) 0.91　　(E) 0.96

39. 一个罐子中装有 100 粒果冻豆：50 粒白的,30 粒绿的,10 粒黄的,5 粒红的,4 粒紫的,1 粒黑的。若从中随机挑出一粒果冻豆,问该粒果冻豆既不是紫色,又不是红色的概率是多大？

解：本题的正确答案是(D)。因为红色有 5 粒,紫色有 4 粒,且挑出任一粒的概率相同,所以随机挑出的果冻豆既不是红色又不是紫色的概率为：

$$\frac{100-9}{100}=0.91$$

40.　　　　LEAGUE RESULTS

Team	Number of Games Won
A	4
B	7

40. 根据左侧不完整的表格,若联盟中 6 支队伍中的每一支都与其他的各支队伍比赛 2 次,并且没有平局(tie),X 赢得了多少场比赛？(每个比赛只有 2 支队伍参加)

C	9
D	2
E	2
X	

According to the incomplete table above. If each of the 6 teams in the league played each of the other teams exactly twice and there were no ties. How many games did team X win? (Only 2 teams play in a game.)

(A) 4   (B) 5   (C) 6

(D) 7   (E) 10

解：本题的正确答案是(C)。由每支队伍都与另一队伍比赛了 2 次，且每次必有且仅有 1 支队伍获胜，可得总的获胜次数为：

$$2C_6^2 = 30$$

上表中前 5 项的和为：$4 + 7 + 9 + 2 + 2 = 24$

$30 - 24 = 6$，所以 X 胜了 6 场。

41. The 4 beads in a bag are identical except that 2 are red and 2 are blue. If 2 beads are to be simultaneously and randomly selected，what is the probability that they will both be blue?

(A) $\dfrac{1}{6}$ (B) $\dfrac{1}{4}$ (C) $\dfrac{1}{3}$

(D) $\dfrac{1}{2}$ (E) $\dfrac{5}{6}$

41. 一个袋子中有 4 个相同的珠子，其颜色为 2 红 2 蓝。若同时随机地取出 2 个珠子，问这两个珠子同为蓝色的概率是多少？

解：本题的正确答案为（A）。第一个珠子为蓝色的概率是 $\dfrac{2}{4}$，第二个仍为蓝色的概率是 $\dfrac{1}{3}$，所以两个同为蓝色的概率是：$P = \dfrac{2}{4} \times \dfrac{1}{3} = \dfrac{1}{6}$

42. The median of the positive integers l, m, n, r, and s is 10, where $l < m < n < r < s$.

$$\dfrac{l+s}{2} \qquad\qquad 10$$

42. 正整数 l，m，n，r 和 s 的中数是 10，且 $l < m < n < r < s$

解：本题的正确选项为（D）。中数定义如下：若一数列元素 $a_1, a_2, \cdots a_n$ 从小到大排列，当 $n = 2k + 1$ 时，数列的中数为 a_{k+1}，当 $n = 2k$ 时，数列的中数为 $\dfrac{1}{2}(a_k + a_{k+1})$。求数列中数时要注意，首先将数列中的元素从小到大的排列，其次要注意数列元素的个数是奇数还是偶数；第三是中数可能是数列中的元素，也可能不是。如果数列中元素的个数 $n = 2k + 1$，则中数（等于 a_{k+1}）自然是数列中元素；若 $n = 2k$，且 $a_k = a_{k+1}$，中数 $a_k = a_{k+1}$，若 $a_k \neq a_{k+1}$，则中数 $\dfrac{1}{2}(a_k + a_{k+1})$ 就不在数列里。由以上分析可知中数与数列的首项和末项之间无任何必然的联系。

43. The buyer of a certain mechanical toy must choose 2 of 4 optional motions and 4 of 5 optional accessories. How many different combinations of motions and accessories are available to the buyer?

(A) 8 (B)11 (C)15

(D) 20 (E) 30

44. A certain computer program generates a sequence of numbers P_1, P_2,......P_n by the rules $P_1=1$, $P_2=1$, and for $n \geqslant 3$, $P_n = P_{n-1} + 2P_{n-2}$, Which of the following equals P_5?

(A) 10 (B) 11 (C) 14

(D) 15 (E) 17

45. For which of the following lists of number is the median equal to the average (arithmetic mean)?

(A) 3,4,7 (B) 1,10,19 (C) 7,7,10,12

(D) 0,1,1,5 (E) 0,2,3,4

46. City Y has installed 30 parking meters at 15-foot intervals along a straight street. What is the number of feet between the first meter and the last meter?

(A) 200 (B) 420 (C) 435

(D) 450 (E) 465

47. In a soccer league, if there were 10 teams, and each team played each of the other teams 16 times, how many games did each team play?

(A) 144 (B) 140 (C) 134

(D) 125 (E) 106

43. 一购买机械玩具的顾客必须从 4 个可选择的机械装置中选择 2 个,且从 5 个附件中选择 4 个,问共有多少种不同机构装置和附件的组合可供这个顾客选择?

解:本题的正确答案为(E)。从 4 个机械装置中选出两个的组合数为 C_4^2,而从 5 个附件中选出 4 个的组合数为 C_5^4,所以总的组合数为 $C_5^4 \cdot C_4^2 = 30$

44. 某计算机程序根据规则 $P_1=1$,$P_2=1$,并且对于 $n \geqslant 3$,$P_n = P_{n-1} + 2P_{n-2}$ 产生一系列数字 P_1,P_2,……P_n,问下面哪一项等于 P_5?

解:本题的正确答案是(B)。解答本题时只要把数字代入规则即可:

$P_3 = P_2 + 2P_1 = 1 + 2 = 3$

$P_4 = P_3 + 2P_2 = 3 + 2 = 5$

$P_5 = P_4 + 2P_3 = 5 + 6 = 11$

45. 下面哪一列数的中数(median)等于其(算术)平均值?

解:本题的正确答案为(B)。五个选项中只有(B)的中数是 10,平均数也是 10。

46. 城市 Y 在某条直的街道上安装了 30 个停车计价器(每隔 15 英尺一个),问第一个计价器与最后一个计价器之间有多少英尺?

解:本题的正确答案为(C)。考生答对该题的关键在于明白只有 $(n+1)$ 个元素才能隔开 n 个距离。第一个计价器与最后一个计价器之间有 $(30-1)=29$ 个 15 英尺的距离,即:

$$29 \times 15 = 435$$

47. 某一足球协会有 10 支球队,若每支队与其他各队都踢 16 场球,问每支球队踢多少场比赛?

解:本题的正确答案是(A)。每个球队要与其他的 9 个球队中的每一个踢 16 场球,所以每个球队踢的球的总数是 $9 \times 16 = 144$ 场。

48. In a class of 120 students，60 percent can speak French and the rest can speak only English. If 25 percent of those in the class who can speak French can also speak English，how many of the students in the class can speak English?

(A) 54

(B) 60

(C) 66

(D) 84

(E) 90

48. 某个班级有120名学生，其中有60％的学生讲法语，其余的学生人只会讲英语。若讲法语的学生中有25％的学生也可以讲英语，问该班级中有多少人会讲英语？

解：本题的正确答案是(C)。班级里讲法语的学生中有25％的学生会讲英语，则会讲英语的学生总数为：

$$120 \times 60\% \times 25\% + 120 \times 40\% = 66$$

49.

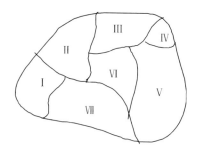

Regions sharing a common border are to be different colors.

| The minimum number of colors needed | | 3 |

49. 边界相同的地区的颜色不同。

解：本题的正确答案为(C)。图中的所有地区都两两相邻，边界的交点最多只为三块不同的地区所共有，所以3种颜色即可满足相邻不同色的要求。判断方法为在两两相邻的3个地区上用3种颜色，再看是否足够满足相邻不同色，如本题：在Ⅰ、Ⅱ、Ⅷ上分别用 a，b，c 三种颜色，Ⅵ用 a，Ⅶ用 c，Ⅴ用 a，Ⅳ用 b，可以满足相邻不同色。

50. S is a set of n consecutive integers.

The mean of S The median of S

50. S 是 n 个连续整数的集合

解：本题的正确答案为(C)。n 个连续整数的算术平均数 $= \dfrac{a_1 + a_n}{2}$（$a_1 a_2 \ldots a_n$，连续整数），

当 n 为奇数，即 $n = 2k + 1$，则 $\dfrac{a_1 + a_n}{2} = a_{k+1}$，

当 n 为偶数，即 $n = 2k$ 时，$\dfrac{a_1 + a_n}{2} = \dfrac{a_k + a_{k+1}}{2}$，显然 n 个连续整数的算术平均数与其中数是相等的。

51. Each person at a party shook hands exactly once with each of the other people at the party. There was a total of 21 handshakes exchanged at the party.

| The number of | 8 |
| people at the party | |

52. In a graduating class of 236 students, 142 took algebra and 121 took chemistry. What is the greatest number of students that could have taken both algebra and chemistry?

(A) 21   (B) 27   (C) 37
(D) 121   (E) 142

53. $M(r, s, t)$ denotes the average (arithmetic mean) of r, s, and t, and M (x, y) denotes the average of x and y.

M (70, 80, 90)   M $(x, 90)$ where
$$x = M (70, 80)$$

Question 54 － 55 ***refer to the following information.***

A sample of employees were tested on data－entry skills for one hour, and the number of errors (x) they made and the percent of employees (p) making x errors were recorded as follows.

51. 参加某次舞会中的每个人都与其他的所有与会者刚好握一次手。在这个舞会中共有21次握手。

解: 本题的正确答案为(B)。设出席舞会的人数为n,则握手的总次数为

$$C_n^2 = \frac{n!}{2!(n-1)!} = \frac{n(n-1)}{2} = 21$$
$$\Rightarrow n^2 - n - 42 = 0 \Rightarrow (n+6)(n-7) = 0$$

解二次方程可得,$n = -6$ 或 $n = 7$,舍去负根可得出席这次舞会的人数为7。

52. 一个236名学生的研究生班,有142人选修代数,121人选修化学,问最多有多少人既修代数又修化学?

解: 本题的正确答案为(D)。本题也即求两个集合交集的最大值,交集中的元素数小于或等于较小的集合中的元素数,所以最多有121个同时选了两门课。

53. $M(r, s, t)$表示 r, s 和 t 的算术平均值,$M(x, y)$表示 x 和 y 的算术平均值。

解: 本题的正确答案为(B)。左项的算术平均值等于80,右项的算术平均值等于

$$\left(\frac{70+80}{2}+90\right)/2 = 82.5$$

问题 54－55 参照下面的信息:

一个测试职员数据输入技巧的样本,在一小时中犯错误的次数(x)和犯该错误次数的职员的百分比(p)记录如左:

Number of Errors	Percent of Employees
x	p
0	2%
1	5%
2	10%
3	24%
4	17%
5	20%
6 or more	22%

54. If those employees who made 6 or more errors were removed from the sample and an employee were selected at random from those remaining，what is the probability that the employee selected made no errors?

(A) $\dfrac{1}{11}$ (B) $\dfrac{1}{22}$ (C) $\dfrac{1}{39}$

(D) $\dfrac{1}{50}$ (E) $\dfrac{1}{78}$

55. What was the median number of errors in the sample?

(A) 3

(B) 3.5

(C) 4

(D) 4.5

（E） It cannot be determined from the information given.

54. 若把犯 6 个或 6 个以上错误的职员移出样本，并且从剩余职员中随机挑出一名职员，问该职员未犯任何错误的概率是多少？

解：本题的正确答案为（C）。由表可知，有 6 个或 6 个以上错误的职员的百分比为 22%，移走这一部分后，剩余 78% 的职员中，不犯错误的职员占 2%，所以其概率为：

$$\frac{2\%}{78\%} = \frac{1}{39}$$

55. 样本中犯错误次数的中数是多少？

解：本题的正确答案是（C）。样本中犯错误次数的中数，指样本中中间一个人所犯的错误。考生可以设该样本中共有 100 人，因为 100 是偶数，所以样本中犯错误次数的中数为第 50 个人和第 51 个人犯错误次数的和除以 2。根据表格中的数据有：犯 0 个错误的人有 2 个，犯 1 个错误的人有 5 个，犯 2 个错误的人有 10 个，犯 3 个错误的人有 24 个，犯 4 个错误人的有 17 个，那么按错误数目排序的第 50 人和 51 人均有 4 个错误，所以中数为 4。

第 五 章

几何(Geometry)

GRE geometry problems involving interesting lines(相交线)，triangles(三角形)，quadrilaterals(四边形)，polygons(多边形) with five or more sides，circles(圆)，three-dimensional figures(立体图形)，and the coordinate plane(坐标平面)，the following is what you should know and learn：

- *Know the relationships among angles formed by interesting lines*
- *Know the characteristics of any triangle*
- *Learn the Pythagorean Theorem and apply it to any right triangle problems*
- *Recognize Pythagorean triplets in order to quickly solve right triangle problems*
- *Know the relationship between area and perimeter of an equilateral triangle*
- *Know the distinguishing characteristics of squares，rectangles，parallelograms，rhombuses，and trapezoids*
- *How to determine angle sizes of any polygon*
- *The characteristics of any circle，and relationship between a circle's radius，diameter，circumference，and area*
- *How to apply the area and circumference formulas to GRE circle questions*
- *How to handle hybrid problems，which combine circles with other geometric figures*
- *How to determine surface area and volume of rectangular solids，cubes，and right cylinders*
- *The relationship between the edges，faces，and volume of any rectangular solid*
- *How to solve coordinate geometry problems*

From the list above，we can see that the geometry section is limited primarily to measurement and intuitive geometry or spatial visualization. Extensive knowledge of theorems and the ability to construct proofs，skills that are unusually developed in a formal geometry course，are not tested.

第一节 平面几何(Plane Geometry)

一、Lines and Angles(直线和角)

1. Line(直线)：In geometry，"line" refers to straight line that extends without end in both directions.

2. Angle(角)：由一点发出的两条射线所夹的平面部分称为角。

3. Vertical Ange(对顶角)：两条直线相交(intersect)所形成的角称为对顶角，且对顶角相等。$180°$的角被称为平角(straight angle)，小于$90°$的角被称为锐角(acute angle)，大于$90°$而小于$180°$的角被称为钝角(obtuse angle)，等于$90°$的角被称为直角(right angle)。

4. Supplementary Angles(补角)：如果两个角的和是一个平角，这两个角互补(supplementary)，其中一

个角是另一个角的补角。

5. Complementary Angles(余角)：如果两角之和是一个直角,则称这两个角互为余角。**两条相交直线具有以下四个性质:**

> Opposite angles are equal in degree measure, or congruent (≌).

> If adjacent angles combine to form a straight line, their degree measures total 180°.

> If two lines are perpendicular[⊥]to each other, they intersect at right (90°) angles.

> The sum of all angles formed by intersecting lines is 360°.

6. Parallel(平行)：同一平面上的两条直线若在任何处都不相交,则两直线平行。

7. Transversal(两直线的截线)：如果一条直线与另外两直线分别相交,则该直线称为二直线的截线。二直线被截后形成八个角,二直线内部的四个角称为**内角(Interior Angles)**,二直线外部的四个角称为**外角(exterior angles)**。内、外角依在截线的同侧或异侧而分别有内错角(alternative interior angles)、外错角(alternate exterior angles)、同旁内角(interior angles on the same side of the transversal)和同旁外角(exterior angles on the same side of the transversal)之分。另外还有同位角(corresponding angles),即两直线相对于截线同位置的角。

如右图 1 所示:$L_1 /\!/ L_2$,L_3 与 L_1 和 L_2 都相交,形成了∠1,∠2,∠3,∠4,∠5,∠6,∠7,∠8 八个角。

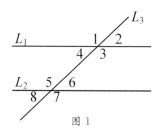

图 1

其中∠2 和∠6,∠3 和∠7,∠1 和∠5,∠4 和∠8 互为同位角,且相等;∠3 和∠6,∠4 和∠5 互为同旁内角,它们每两个的和为 180°,且互为补角;∠3 和∠5,∠4 和∠6 互为内错角,且相等;∠1 和∠7,∠2 和∠8 分别互为外错角,且相等;∠2 和∠7,∠1 和∠8 分别互为同旁外角,且互补。

总之:All the odd-numbered angles are congruent (equal in size) to one another. All the even-numbered angles are congruent (equal in size) to one another.

由上图的分析可知,两条直线在一个平面内的位置关系有两种:相交和平行。两条直线互相垂直只是相交的特例,当两条直线 L_1 和 L_2 互相垂直时,记作 $L_1 \perp L_2$。当一条直线和两条平行线相交时,有如下性质:

推论:① 同位角相等;

② 内错角、外错角相等;

③ 同旁内角、同旁外角互补。

① 同位角相等,两直线平行;

② 内错角、外错角相等,两直线平行;

③ 同旁内角、同旁外角互补,两直线平行。

④ 若一条直线垂直于两条平行直线中的一条,那么它也垂直于两条平行线中的另一条。

⑤ 若一条直线平行于两条平行直线中的一条,那么它也平行于两条平行线中的另一条。

二、Angles and Sides of Triangles(三角形的角和边)

1. 三角形的基本性质

① **Length of sides**：In any triangle, each side is shorter than the sum of the lengths of the other two sides(在三角形中,任一边的长度小于其他两边长度的和)。

推论:三角形中两边之差小于第三边。

② **Angle measures**:In any triangle,the sum of the three interior angles is 180°.

③ **Angles and opposite sides**:In any triangle,the relative angle sizes correspond to the relative lengths of the sides opposite those angles. In other words,the smaller the angle,the smaller the side opposite the angle (and vice-versa). Accordingly,if two angles are equal in size,the sides opposite those angles are of equal length (and vice-versa).

推论:Ⅰ. 三角形中若最小的两条边的平方和小于第三条边的平方和,则此三角形必为钝角三角形。

Ⅱ. 三角形中若最小的两条边的平方和大于第三条边的平方和,则此三角形必为锐角三角形。

④ **Area of a triangle**:The area of any triangle is equal to $\frac{1}{2}$ the product of its base and its height (height is also called the altitude):

$$\text{Area} = \frac{1}{2} \cdot base \cdot altitude(height) = \frac{1}{2}bh$$

在知道三角形的三边之长的情况下,可以用一特殊公式来求解三角形的面积。设三角形的三边边长分别为 a,b,c,$s = \frac{a+b+c}{2}$,则三角形面积为:

$$S_\triangle = \sqrt{s(s-a)(s-b)(s-c)}$$

⑤ 若两个三角形相似,则这两三角形的面积比等于相似比的平方。

⑥ 三角形的一个外角等于其不相邻的两个内角之和。

⑦ **Cautions**:

Ⅰ. *Do not equate altitude（height）with the length of any particular side. Instead，imagine the base on flat ground，and drop a plumb line straight down from the top peak of the triangle to define height of altitude. The only types of triangles in which the altitude equals the length of one side are right triangles.*

Ⅱ. *The ratio among angle sizes does not necessarily correspond precisely to the ratios among the lengths of the sides opposite those angles. For example，if a certain triangle has angle measures of* 30°, 60°, *and* 90°, *the ratio of the angles is* 1 : 2 : 3. *However，this does not mean that the ratio of the lengths of opposite sides is also* 1 : 2 : 3.

2. Right Triangles(直角三角形)

The only case where a triangle's altitude (height)equals the length of any of its sides is with a right triangle,in which one angle measures 90° and,of course,each of the other two angles measures less than 90°. The two sides forming the 90°angle are commonly referred to as the triangle's legs(勾或股,右边图中的 a 和 b),whereas the third (and longest side) is referred to as the hypotenuse(弦,右边图中的 c)。

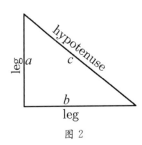

图 2

The Pythagorean Theorem expresses the relationship among the sides of any right triangles (*a* and *b* are the two legs,and *c* is the hypotenuse):

$$a^2 + b^2 = c^2$$

With any right triangle,if you know the length of two sides,you can determine the length of the third side with the Theorem.

3. Pythagorean Triplets(毕达哥拉斯三角形)

凡是三边的比例关系满足毕达哥拉斯定律的三角形都被称为毕达哥拉斯三角形。在下表的三角形中，前两个数代表两个直角边（legs）的相对长度,而第三个最大的数则代表斜边(hypotenuse)的相对长度。建议考生熟记下面表格中的毕达哥拉斯三角形的边的相对长度,为在考试中熟练地解决直角三角形方面的问题打下坚实的基础。

Ratio	Theorem
$1 : 1 : \sqrt{2}$	$1^2 + 1^2 = (\sqrt{2})^2$
$1 : \sqrt{3} : 2$	$1^2 + (\sqrt{3})^2 = (2)^2$
$3 : 4 : 5$	$3^2 + 4^2 = (5)^2$
$5 : 12 : 13$	$5^2 + 12^2 = (13)^2$
$8 : 15 : 17$	$8^2 + 15^2 = (17)^2$
$7 : 24 : 25$	$7^2 + 24^2 = (25)^2$

以上几个特殊值其实很好记,如 3,4,5,只要将 3 平方即 $3^2 = 9$,分为两个相邻的自然数的和 $9 = 5 + 4$,则较小的一个为直角边,较大的一个即为斜边,再如 5,12,13,$5^2 = 12 + 13$。这里必须是奇数的平方,再有上述所列数都乘以相同因子后所得数也满足勾股定理。如 3,4,5 分别乘以 2 后为 6,8,10。

4. Special Right Triangles(特殊的直角三角形)

In two（and only two）of the unique triangles we've identified as Pythagorean triplets, all degree measures are integers(在我们所定义的毕达哥拉斯三角形中,仅有两种所有的角的度数都是整数的三角形)。

① The corresponding angles opposite the sides of a $1 : 1 : \sqrt{2}$ triangle are $45°$, $45°$, and $90°$.

② The corresponding angles opposite the sides of a $1 : \sqrt{2} : 2$ triangle are $30°$, $60°$, and $90°$.

注：Two $45°-45°-90°$ triangles pieced together form a square, and two $30°-60°-90°$ triangles together form an equilateral triangle.

例 1：In the figure above, what is the length of AB?

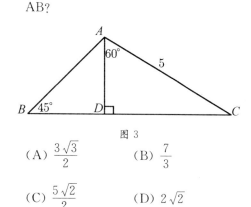

图 3

(A) $\dfrac{3\sqrt{3}}{2}$　　　　(B) $\dfrac{7}{3}$

(C) $\dfrac{5\sqrt{2}}{2}$　　　　(D) $2\sqrt{2}$

(E) $\dfrac{7}{2}$

解：The correct answer is (C). To find length of AB, you need to find AD and BD. The angles of $\triangle ADC$ are $30°$, $60°$, and $90°$. So you know that the ratio among its sides is $1 : \sqrt{3} : 2$. Given that $AC = 5$, $AD = \dfrac{5}{2}$. Next, you should recognize $\triangle ABD$ as a $45° - 45° - 90°$ triangle. The ratio among its sides is $1 : 1 : \sqrt{2}$. You know that $AD = \dfrac{5}{2}$. Accordingly, $AB = \dfrac{5\sqrt{2}}{2}$.

5. Isosceles Triangles(等腰三角形)

等腰三角形具有以下性质：

① Two of the sides are congruent (equal in length).

② The two angles opposite the two congruent sides are congruent (equal in size, or degree measure).

③ A line that bisects the angle formed by the equal sides bisects the opposite side.

6. Equilateral Triangles(等边三角形)

等边三角形具有以下性质：

① All three sides are congruent (equal in length)

② All three angles are 60°

③ The area $=\dfrac{s^2\sqrt{3}}{4}$ (s=the length of one side)

④ Any line bisecting one of the 60° angles divides an equilateral triangle into two right triangles with angle measures of 30°, 60°, and 90°; in other words, into two $1:\sqrt{3}:2$ triangles.

三、Quadrilaterals(四边形)

A quadrilateral is a four-sided figure. Here are the specific types of quadrilaterals you should know for the GRE : (1) square; (2) Rectangle; (3) Parallelogram; (4) Rhombus; (5) trapezoid. Each of these five figures has its own properties (characteristics) that should be second nature to by the time you take the GRE. The two most important properties are：

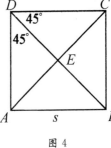

图 4

Ⅰ. Area (the surface covered by the figure on a plane)

Ⅱ. Perimeter (the total length of all sides)

All quadrilaterals share one important property： The sum of the four interior angles of any quadrilateral is 360°.

1. The Square(正方形)

所有的正方形都具有以下特点：

① 四条边的边长相等；

② 四个角都是 90°,四个内角的和是 360°；

③ 周长等于边长的 4 倍(Perimeter＝4a)；

④ 面积等于边长的平方(Area＝a^2)。

当把正方形的对角连接起来时,正方形又具有以下性质：

① 对角线互相垂直,且长度相等；

② 对角线平分正方形的每一个内角,即把每个内角都分成了两个 45°的角；

③ 每条对角线长度的平方的一半等于正方形的面积；

$$\text{Area of square}=\frac{(AC)^2}{2}=\frac{(BD)^2}{2}$$

④ 对角线生成的四个三角形,即△ABD,△ACD,△ABC 和△BCD 全等,每个三角形的面积都是正方形 ABCD 的面积的一半。这四个三角形三条边长的比例关系是 $1:1:\sqrt{2}$,三角形的三个角分别是 45°,45°和 90°。

⑤ 对角线还生成另外四个全等的三角形：即△ABE,△BCE,△CDE 和△ADE。每个三角形的面积都是正方形 ABCD 的面积的四分之一。这四个三角形三条边长的比例关系是 $1:1:\sqrt{2}$,三角形的三个角分别是 45°,45°和 90°。

2. Rectangles（矩形，又称长方形）

所有的矩形都有以下的性质：

① 对边相等，四个内角都等于 $90°$；

② 四个内角的和等于 $360°$；

③ 周长等于长与宽的和的两倍[Perimeter$=2(l+w)$]；

④ 面积等于长乘以宽（Area$=l×w$）；

⑤ 周长一定时，正方形的面积最大；

⑥ 面积一定时，正方形的周长最小。

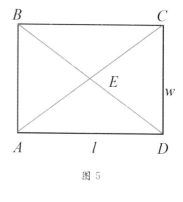

图 5

矩形的对角线具有以下性质：

① 对角线相等且互相平分（$AC=BD$，$AE=BE=CE=DE$）；

② 对角线把矩形分成了四个全等的三角形（即△ABD，△ACD，△ABC 和△BCD 全等），且每个三角形的面积是矩形面积的一半；

③ △ABE 和△CDE 全等，△BCE 和△ADE 全等，且他们都是等腰三角形，他们的面积是矩形面积的四分之一。

3. Parallelograms（平行四边形）

所有平行四边形都具有以下性质：

① 对边互相平行且相等；

② 对角相等，四个内角的和等于 $360°$；

③ 若平行四边形的一个内角等于 $90°$，那么它的所有内角都等于 $90°$；

④ 平行四边形的周长等于两相邻边长的和的 2 倍（Perimeter$=2l+2w$）；

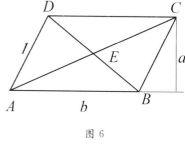

图 6

⑤ 平行四边形的面积等于底乘高[Area$=$base$(b)×$altitude(a)]；

平行四边形的对角线具有以下性质：

① 对角线相互平分（$BE=ED$，$CE=AE$）；

② 对角线把平行四边形分成四对全等的三角形：△ABD≌△CDB，△ACD≌△CAB，他们的面积都等于平行四边形面积的二分之一；△ABE≌△CDE，△BCE≌△DAE，它们的面积都等于平行四边形的面积的四分之一。

4. The Rhombus（菱形）

所有的菱形都具有以下性质：

① 所有的边都相等，且对边相互平行；

② 对角相等，四个内角的和等于 $360°$；

③ 周长等于边长的 4 倍（Perimeter$=4s$）；

④ 面积等于底乘高[Area$=$base$(b)×$altitude(a)]；

菱形对角线的性质：

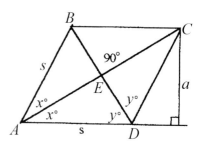

图 7

① 菱形的面积等于两条对角线乘积的一半（Area of the rhombus$=\dfrac{AC×BD}{2}$）；

② 对角线互相垂直且平分（$AC⊥BD$，$AE=CE$，$BE=DE$）；

③ 对角线平分菱形的四个内角；

④ 对角线把菱形分为两对全等的等腰三角形(即△ABD≌△CDB，△ACD≌△CAB)，且每个等腰三角形的面积都等于菱形面积的一半；

⑤ 对角线把菱形分为四个全等的直角三角形(即△ABE≌△CDE≌△BCE≌△ADE)，他们的面积等于菱形面积的四分之一。

5. Trapezoids(梯形)

所有的梯形都具有以下性质：

① Only one pair of opposite sides are parallel($BC /\!/ AD$)；

② The sum of all four interior angles is 360°；

③ Perimeter＝$AB+BC+CD+AD$；

④ Area＝$\dfrac{BC \times AD}{2} \times$ altitude(a)，即梯形的面积等于上底加下底的和乘以高再除以 2。

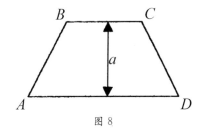

图 8

四、Polygons(多边形)

多边形的性质：

1. 多边形的内角和：Sum of interior angles＝($n-2$)×180°；

2. If all angles of a polygon are congruent (the same size)，then all sides are congruent (equal in length)；

3. If all sides of a polygon are congruent (the same length)，then all angles are congruent (equal in size).

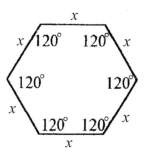

图 9

五、Circles(圆)

1. 有关圆的基本概念

① **Radius(半径)**：the distance from a circle's center to any point on the circle

② **Diameter(直径)**：the greatest distance from one point to another on the circle

③ **Chord(弦)**：a line segment connecting two points on the circle

④ **Circumference(周长)**：the distance around the circle (its "perimeter")

⑤ **Arc(弧)**：a segment of a circle's circumference (an arc can be defined either as a length or as a degree measure)

⑥ **Tangent to a circle (圆的切线)**：一条直线与圆只有一个交点称该直线与圆相切,交点叫做切点(point of tangency)；

⑦ **Secant to a circle(圆的割线)**：与圆有两个交点的直线称为圆的割线；

⑧ **Central angle(圆心角)**：顶点在圆心上并且两条边是圆的弦的角称为"圆心角"；

⑨ **Inscribed angle(圆周角)**：顶点位于圆周上并且两条边是圆的弦的角称为"圆周角"；

⑩ **Sector(扇形)**：圆弧和它对应的圆心角所围成的一部分平面区域称为"扇形"。

2. 圆的基本性质

① Every point on a circle's circumference is equidistant from the circle's center；

② The total number of degrees of all angles formed from the circle's center is $360°$;

③ Diameter is twice the radius;

④ Circumference$=2\pi r$, or πd;

⑤ Area$=\pi r^2$, or $\dfrac{\pi d^2}{4}$

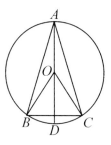
图 10

⑥ The longest possible chord of a circle passes through its center and is the circle's diameter(如右图中的 AD, $AD>AB$, $AD>AC$)；

⑦ 圆中同一段弧所对的圆心角是圆周角的两倍(如右图 10 中 $\angle BOC=2\angle BAC$)；

⑧ 垂直于弦的直径平分这条弦,也平分这条弦所对的圆心角和圆周角(如右图 10 中 $AD\perp BC$,则直径 AD 平分 $\angle BOC$ 和 $\angle BAC$)；

⑨ 连接圆心与切点的半径垂直于经过该切点的切线(如图 11 中的 $OC\perp AC$ 于 C,$OB\perp AB$ 于 B)。

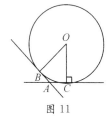
图 11

在圆中: $\dfrac{\text{弧长}}{\text{圆周长}}=\dfrac{\text{弧所对应的角度}}{360°}$

例 2: 某圆的半径为 3 米,求 $40°$ 角所对的弧的长度。

解: 由上面的公式有: $\dfrac{\text{弧长}}{2\pi\times 3}=\dfrac{40°}{360°}\Rightarrow \text{弧长}=\dfrac{2}{3}\pi$

3. Circles and Triangles(圆与三角形)

One common type of GRE circle problem is a "hybrid" involving a circle and a triangle. Generally speaking, there are three varieties on the GRE test：

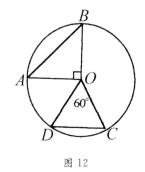
图 12

① 直角三角形的一个顶点在圆心,且这个顶点所对应的角是直角,则这个三角形一定是等腰直角三角形,这个三角形的三条边长之比为 $1:1:\sqrt{2}$,其面积为圆的半径的平方的一半。如图 12 中所示：在 $\triangle AOB$,$\angle AOB=90°$,$\angle OAB=\angle OBA=45°$,$OB=OA=r$,$AB=\sqrt{2}\,r$,$\triangle AOB$ 的面积等于 $\dfrac{r^2}{2}$。

② 三角形的一个顶点在圆心,另两个顶点在圆周上,如图 12 中的 $\triangle COD$ 所示。对于这种情况,只要知道 $\angle DOC=60°$,或知道 $DC=r$,那么就很容易推出 $\triangle COD$ 是等边三角形,即 $OC=OD=DC=r$,$\angle ODC=\angle OCD=\angle DOC=60°$。

③ 三角形内接于圆,即三个顶点都在圆周上时,若这个三角形的一条边长等于圆的直径,那么这个三角形一定是直角三角形;这个结论反过来也成立,即若这个三角形的一个角等于 $90°$,那么这个角所对的边一定等于圆的直径,如图 13 中的 $\triangle FGH$ 所示。

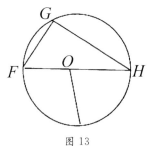
图 13

推论: 在图 13 的 $\triangle FGH$ 中,若 $FH=2r$,则当 G 点在圆周上时,$\angle FGH=90°$;当 G 点在圆周外时,$\angle FGH$ 必为锐角;当 G 点在圆周内时,$\angle FGH$ 必为钝角。

4. Circles and Squares (圆与多边形)

Inscribed Polygon in a Circle(圆的内接多边形): 如果一个多边形的所有顶点都在一个圆周上,那么该多边形称为圆的内接多边形；

Inscribed Circle in a Polygon(圆的外切多边形)：如果一个多边形的每条边都与圆相切,那么称该多边形为圆的外切多边形,称该圆为这个多边形的内切圆(the polygon is circumscribed about the circle and the circle is inscribed in the polygon)。

Another common type of GRE circle problem is a hybrid involving a circle and a square：

① A circle with an inscribed square(圆的内接正方形,图 14)

② A circle with a circumscribed square (圆的外切正方形,图 15)

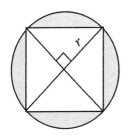

图 14

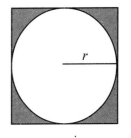

图 15

设圆的半径为 r，则圆的内接正方形的边长为 $\sqrt{2}r$,圆的外接正方形的边长为 $2r$,它们三者的比例为 $1：\sqrt{2}：2$，它们三者的面积之比 $\pi：2：4$；图 14 中的阴影部分的面积是 $(\pi-2)r^2$，图 15 中的阴影部分的面积是 $(4-\pi)r^2$，它们两者之比为 $\dfrac{\pi-2}{4-\pi}$；在两个图中每一小块分离阴影部分的面积都等于整个阴影部分的面积的四分之一,即在图 14 中，每一块月牙的面积 $=\dfrac{1}{4}(\pi-2)r^2$，在图 15 中每一小块分离的阴影面积 $=\dfrac{1}{4}(4-\pi)r^2$，它们两者之比也是 $\dfrac{\pi-2}{4-\pi}$。因为 $\pi-2>4-\pi$，所以图 14 中的阴影部分的面积大于图 15 中的阴影部分的面积。

例 3： If a circle whose radius is x has an area of 3, what is the area of a circle whose radius is $5x$?

解： 考生在做本题时一定要注意技巧。如若考生一上来就用圆的面积公式(Area$=\pi r^2$)去求 x，则显得极不明智,因为本题并没有问 x 的值是多少,而只是要你求半径为 $5x$ 的圆的面积。根据圆的面积公式(Area$=\pi r^2$)，略加分析你便可得出如下结论：

两个圆面积的比等于
这两个圆半径比的平方

由此很容易得到半径为 $5x$ 的圆的面积等于半径为 x 的圆的面积的 25 倍,即半径为 $5x$ 的圆的面积$=25\times 3=75$。

第二节　立体几何(Solids Geometry)

在 GRE 考试中,有关立体几何方面的问题主要是求长方体(rectangular solids or boxes),立方体(cube),圆柱(cylinders or tubes),圆锥(cone)及球(ball)的表面积和体积,其中前三种三维物体考到的可能性最大,下面将对这几种三维物体分别给以简单的介绍。

一、Rectangular Solids (长方体)

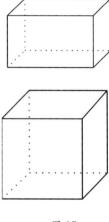

A rectangular solid is a three-dimensional(三维) figure formed by six rectangular surfaces, as shown on the right side. Each rectangular surface is a **face(面)**. Each solid or dotted line segment is an **edge(边)**, and each point at which the edges meet is a **vertex(顶点)**. A rectangular solid has six faces, twelve edges, and eight vertices. Opposite faces are parallel rectangles that have the same dimensions.

The volume (V) of any rectangular solid is the product of its three dimensions: length, width, and height.

Volume=length(长)×width(宽)×height(高)=$l \times w \times h$

Surface Area=$2lh+2lw+2hw=2(lh+lw+hw)$

图 17

二、Cube(立方体)

A cube is a special type of rectangular solid in which all six faces, or surfaces, are square. Because all six faces of a cube are identical in dimension and area, given a length "a" of one of a cube's sides—or edges—its surface area is six times the square of "a", and its volume is the cube of "a":

$$\text{Surface Area}=6a^2$$

$$\text{Volume}=a^3$$

立方体的体积和面积之间有如下关系:

$$\text{Volume}=(\sqrt{Area})^3$$

$$\text{Area}=(\sqrt[3]{Volume})^2$$

三、Cylinders(圆柱体)

右图是一个正圆柱体(right-circular cylinder, the tube is sliced at 90° angles)。在 GRE 考试中斜圆柱体(上下表面与圆柱体的轴线不垂直的圆柱体)是不做要求的。从右图中可以看出正圆柱体的表面积由三部分组成:

(1) the circular base(下底面)

(2) the circular top(上底面)

(3) the rectangular surface around the cylinder's vertical face（侧面,

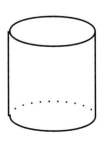

图 18

154

visualize a rectangular label wrapped around a soup can)

The area of the vertical face is the product of the circular base's circumference (i. e. , the rectangle's width) and the cylinder's height. Thus, given a radius "r" and height "h" of a cylinder:

$$\textbf{Surface Area} = 2\pi r^2 + 2\pi rh$$

圆柱体的体积等于底面积乘高

$$V = \pi r^2 h$$

四、Cones(圆锥)

如果圆锥的底面半径是 r,周长是 c,侧面母线长是 l,那么它的侧面积是

$$S_{侧面积} = \frac{1}{2}cl = \pi rl$$

它的总表面积是:

$$S_{总} = S_{侧面积} + S_{底面积} = \pi rl + \pi r^2 = \pi r(l+r)$$

如果一个圆锥的底面半径为 r,高为 h,那么它的体积是:

$$V_{圆锥} = \frac{1}{3}\pi r^3$$

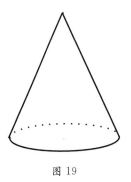

图 19

五、Balls(球)

球的表面面积等于它的大圆的面积的 4 倍: $S_{球} = 4\pi r^2$

如果球的半径是 r,那么它的体积是: $V_{球} = \frac{4}{3}\pi r^3$

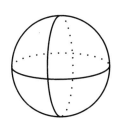

图 20

例 4: A certain cylindrical pail(桶) has a diameter of 14 inches and a height of 10 inches. If there are 231 cubic inches in a gallon, which of the following most closely approximates the number of gallons the pail will hold?

(A) 4.8　　(B) 5.1　　(C) 6.7

(D) 14.6　　(E) 44

注: 在近似计算中,一般都以 $\frac{22}{7}$ 代替 π。

解: 本题的正确答案是(C)。因为桶是圆柱形的,所以根据圆柱体的体积公式可得,桶的体积为:

$$V = \pi r^2 h = \frac{22}{7} \times \left(\frac{14}{2}\right)^2 \times 10$$

$$= \textbf{1540}(\textbf{cubic inches})$$

The gallon capacity of the pail $= \frac{1540}{231} \approx 6.7$

第三节　坐标几何(**Coordinate Geometry**)

On the GRE test, there always one or two coordinate geometry questions, which involve the rectangular coordinate plane (or xy-plane)(平面直角坐标系)defined by two axes—a horizontal x-axis and a vertical y-axis. A point's x-coordinate is its horizontal position on the plane, and its y-coordinate is its vertical position on the plane. You can denote the coordinates of a point with(x, y), where x is the point's x-coordinate and y is the point's y-coordinate.

一、The Rectangular Coordinate System(平面直角坐标系)

平面直角坐标系表示用有次序的实数对(order pair)确定平面各个点的位置。实数对称为"坐标"。这种坐标系由横轴或称 x 轴(x-axis)和纵轴或称 y 轴(y-axis)构成,两轴相互垂直,交点称为原点(origin),一般用 O 表示。一个点 A 在坐标平面内的坐标记作 $A(x,y)$,其中 x 表示点 A 的 x-坐标,y 表示点 A 的 y-坐标。

二、Coordinate Signs and the Four Quadrants(坐标平面和四个象限)

坐标平面的中心,即 x 轴和 y 轴的交点叫做原点,原点的坐标是$(0,0)$;任何一个在 x 轴上的点的 y 坐标都是 0,记作$(x,0)$;任何一个在 y 轴上的点的 x 坐标都是 0,记作$(0,y)$;x 和 y 两坐标轴把坐标平面分成四个象限(quadrants),四个象限的相对位置如图 21 所示。一个点的坐标若既不在 x 轴上和 y 轴上,也不是在原点上,那么它一定要落在四个象限中的某一个象限中,四个象限中,x 坐标和 y 坐标的符号如下所示:

Quadrant Ⅰ$(+,+)$

Quadrant Ⅱ$(-,+)$

Quadrant Ⅲ$(-,-)$

Quadrant Ⅳ$(+,-)$

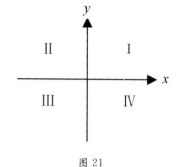

图 21

三、坐标平面内的点的对称性

坐标系中若某一点的坐标为(a,b),则此点:

关于直线 $\boldsymbol{y=x}$ 对称的点的坐标为$\boldsymbol{(b,a)}$;

关于直线 $\boldsymbol{y=-x}$ 对称的点的坐标为$\boldsymbol{(-b,-a)}$;

关于 $\boldsymbol{x}$ 轴对称的点的坐标为$\boldsymbol{(a,-b)}$;

关于 $\boldsymbol{y}$ 轴对称的点的坐标为$\boldsymbol{(-a,b)}$;

注:若两点关于某条直线对称,则这两点的连线被这条直线垂直平分。

例 5:若某一点 A 的坐标为 (a,b),另一点 B 与 A 的连线被 $y=x$ 这条直线垂直平分,C 点与 B 点的连线被 x 轴垂直平分,问 C 点的坐标?

解:由 A,B 两点的连线被 $y=x$ 垂直平分可知 A 和 B 两点一定关于 $y=x$ 这条直线对称,因此 B 点的坐标为(b,a),而 C 点与 B 点的连线又被 x 轴垂直平分,也即 C 点与 B 点关于 x 轴对称,所以 C 点的坐标为$(b,-a)$。

四、Distance Formula(两点间的距离公式)

设 $A(x_1,y_1)$ 和 $B(x_2,y_2)$ 为平面直角坐标系中的两点,则 A 和 B 两点间的距离为:

$$|AB|=\sqrt{(x_1-x_2)^2+(y_1-y_2)^2}$$

五、中点坐标公式

设 $A(x_1, y_1)$，$B(x_2, y_2)$ 和 $C(x, y)$ 为坐标系中的三点，并且 $C(x, y)$ 为线段 AB 的中点，则 $x = \dfrac{x_1 + x_2}{2}$，$y = \dfrac{y_1 + y_2}{2}$。

六、Slope and Intercepts of a Line（直线的斜率和截距）

1. Slope（斜率）： 表示一条直线对横坐标轴的倾斜程度。通常用直线和横坐标轴的交角的正切表示。

2. Intercept（截距）： 直线与 y 轴交点的纵坐标的绝对值。

七、直线方程（$y = ax + b$）

函数 $y = ax + b$ 在坐标系中表现为直线方程，a 称为直线的斜率，$|b|$ 为直线在 y 轴上的截距。当 $a = 0$ 时，$y = b$，这时，直线平行于 x 轴（当 b 也等于零时，直线就为 x 轴）；当 $a > 0$ 时，y 随 x 的增大而增大，函数为增函数；当 $a < 0$ 时，y 随 x 的增大而减小，函数为减函数。还要注意一个特殊的直线方程，那就是 $x = c$（c 为常数），它平行于 y 轴，在 x 轴上的截距为 $|c|$。

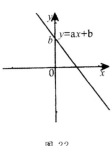

图 22

1. 由已知两点求直线方程（两点式）

如果直线上的两点坐标已知，分别为 $P_1(x_1, y_1)$ 和 $P_2(x_2, y_2)$，则直线的方程为：

$$\frac{y - y_1}{y_2 - y_1} = \frac{x - x_1}{x_2 - x_1}$$

直线的斜率（Slope）为 $a = \dfrac{y_2 - y_1}{x_2 - x_1}$，直线的截距（Intercept）为 $b = \dfrac{x_2 y_1 - x_1 y_2}{x_2 - x_1}$，由此直线方程，还可表示为：

$$y = \frac{y_2 - y_1}{x_2 - x_1}x + \frac{x_2 y_1 - x_1 y_2}{x_2 - x_1}$$

如果已知直线与横坐标正方向的夹角为 β，那么 $\mathrm{tg}\beta$ 就是直线的斜率；如果直线通过原点 $O(0, 0)$，即直线在 y 轴上的截距为零，可由直线上除原点以外的任意一点的坐标和直线的增减特点求得直线的斜率；平行于 x 轴的直线或 x 轴的斜率为零；平行于 y 轴的直线或 y 轴的斜率为无穷大。

2. 由直线的斜率和直线上某一点的坐标求直线方程（点斜式）

已知直线的斜率为 k，直线上点 P 的坐标为 (x_1, y_1)，则该直线的方程为：

$$y - y_1 = k(x - x_1)$$

例 6： Which of the following points lies on L_1 on the xy-plane pictured below?

(A) $\left(\dfrac{3}{8}, -\dfrac{3}{2}\right)$

(B) $\left(-1, -\dfrac{2}{3}\right)$

(C) $(2, 3)$

(D) $\left(-\dfrac{3}{2}, -2\right)$

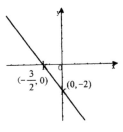

图 23

解： 本题的正确答案为（B）。在解答这类题目时，一般要根据已知的两点的坐标，求出直线的斜率，然后用点斜式求出直线的方程，最后把选项中各点的坐标逐一代入验证，从而找出题目的正确答案。

直线的斜率 $a = \dfrac{y_2 - y_1}{x_2 - x_1} = \dfrac{-2 - 0}{0 - \left(-\dfrac{3}{2}\right)} = -\dfrac{4}{3}$

(E) $\left(-\dfrac{8}{3},2\right)$

直线的方程为 $y-(-2)=-\dfrac{4}{3}(x-0)\Rightarrow y$

$=-\dfrac{4}{3}x-2$

经代入验证后发现(B)是正确答案。

八、抛物线方程（$y=ax^2+bx+c$，$a\neq0$）

函数 $y=ax^2+bx+c$ 在坐标系中表现为抛物线（parabola）方程，顶点坐标为 $\left(-\dfrac{b}{2a},\dfrac{4ac-b^2}{4a}\right)$。

当 $a>0$ 时，抛物线开口向上，并且 $x\geqslant-\dfrac{b}{2a}$ 时，函数为增函数，当 $x\leqslant-\dfrac{b}{2a}$ 时，函数为减函数；当 $x=-\dfrac{b}{2a}$ 时，y 取最小值 $\dfrac{4ac-b^2}{4a}$。当 $a<0$ 时，抛物线开口向下，并且 $x\geqslant-\dfrac{b}{2a}$ 时，函数为减函数，当 $x\leqslant-\dfrac{b}{2a}$ 时，函数为增函数；$x=-\dfrac{b}{2a}$ 时，y 取最大值 $\dfrac{4ac-b^2}{4a}$。$|c|$ 为抛物线在 y 轴上的截距，当 $c=0$ 时，抛物线经过原点；当 b 和 c 都为零时，抛物线以原点为顶点。

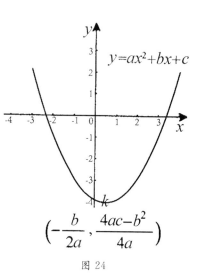

$\left(-\dfrac{b}{2a},\dfrac{4ac-b^2}{4a}\right)$

图 24

第四节 重点试题精练及解析

1.

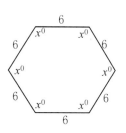

In square $PQRS$ above. T is the midpoint of side RS. If $PT=8\sqrt5$, What is the length of a side of the square?

(A) 16　　　(B) $6\sqrt5$　　　(C) $4\sqrt5$

(D) 8　　　(E) $2\sqrt6$

1. 在上面的正方形 $PQRS$ 中，T 是 RS 的中点（**midpoint**），若 $PT=8\sqrt5$，那么正方形的边长是多少？

解：本题的正确答案是(A)。设正方形边长是 $2a$，则 $|TS|=a$，$\triangle PST$ 是直角三角形，由勾股定理可知：

$$\sqrt{(2a)^2+a^2}=8\sqrt5\Rightarrow a=8$$

∴正方形的边长为 16。

2.

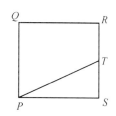

2. 左面图形中六边形（**hexagonal**）的面积是多少？

解：本题的正确答案是(A)。由图可知，此六边形是正六边形（边长相等，内角相等），连接正六边形的 3 条长对角线可构成 6 个全等

What is the area of the hexagonal region shown in the figure above?

(A) $54\sqrt{3}$ (B) 108

(C) $108\sqrt{3}$ (D) 216

（E）It cannot be determined from the information given.

的等边三角形,这些等边三角形的边长为 6,其面积可由勾股定理求出:$h=\sqrt{6^2-3^2}$ $=3\sqrt{3}$,则面积为:

$$6\times\frac{1}{2}(6\times3\sqrt{3})=54\sqrt{3}$$

3. A size S soup can is 10 centimeters high and a size T soup can is 12.5 centimeters high.

The height of a stack

of cans if each can

is size S except   62.5 centimeters

the can on the

bottom of the stack,

which is size T.

3. S 汤盒高 10 cm,T 汤盒高 12.5 cm。

解：本题的正确答案为(D)。比较的左项为一堆除最底部的一个汤盒的尺寸为 T,其余汤盒的尺寸均为 S 的盒子的总高度。"stack"意思是一堆,题目中没有给出这一堆汤盒的确切数量,因此无法确定这一堆盒子的高度。

4. If the areas of three of the faces of a rectangular solid are 6,10 and 15，what is the volume of the solid？

(A) 30

(B) 90

(C) 150

(D) 300

(E) 450

4. 若一个长方体 3 个面的面积为 6,10 和 15,该长方体(**rectangular solid**)的体积是多少？

解：本题的正确答案是(A)。设长方体的长,宽,高分别为 l,w,h,则有:

$$lw=6$$
$$wh=10$$
$$hl=15$$

长方体体积为 lwh,上面三项相乘得 $(lwh)^2=900,lwh=30$。

5. The area of square region S is 36.

The perimeter of S   24

5. 正方形区域 S 的面积是 36。

解：本题的正确答案为(C)。正方形面积为 36,边长显然为 $\sqrt{36}=6$,从而可得周长=$6\times4=24$。

6.

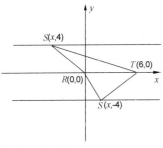

$\triangle RST$ lies in the XY-plane and points R and T have (x, y) coordinates $(0,0)$ and

6. $\triangle RST$ 位于 XY 坐标平面中,顶点 R 和 T 的坐标(**coordinate**)分别是 $(0,0)$ 和 $(6,0)$。$\triangle RST$ 的面积为 12。

解：本题的正确答案是(D)。由 $\triangle RST$ 的面积为 12,RT 长度为 6,可以推出 S 点的纵坐标±4,而横坐标则为直线 $y=+4$ 和 $y=-4$ 上的任一点,所以本题为无法判断。

$(6,0)$, respectively. The area of $\triangle RST$ is 12.

The x-coordinate of R	The y-coordinate of S

7.

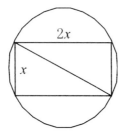

In the figure above, if the area of the inscribed rectangular region is 32, then the circumference of the circle is

(A) 20π (B) $4\pi\sqrt{5}$ (C) $4\pi\sqrt{3}$

(D) $2\pi\sqrt{5}$ (E) $2\pi\sqrt{3}$

8. What is the maximum number of nonoverlapping regions into which 3 lines can divide the interior of a circle?

(A) 4

(B) 6

(C) 7

(D) 8

(E) 9

9.

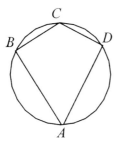

The diameter of the circle is 10.

The area of the

7. 在上面的图形中，若圆的内接长方形的面积等于32，那么圆的周长等于

解：本题的正确答案为（B）。由长方形的面积公式可得：

$$2x^2 = 32 \Rightarrow x = 4$$

应用勾股定理：

$$4R^2 = 4x^2 + x^2 \Rightarrow R = 2\sqrt{5}$$

∴ 圆的周长 $=2\pi R=4\pi\sqrt{5}$。

8. 3条直线最多可以把1个圆的内部分成多少个非重叠的区域？

解：本题的正确答案是（C）。其分法如下图所示：

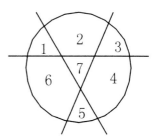

由图可知，最多可分成7个区。

9. 解：本题的正确答案为（D）。比较的左项为四边形（**quadrilateral**）$ABCD$ 的面积。四边形 $ABCD$ 是不规则四边形，在计算其面积时，可以把它分成两个三角形计算。对于该题，因为 A、B、C 和 D 四点的位置不确定，因此其面积也是不确定的。考生可以观察到当 B 和 D 点向 C 点靠近时，四边形面积 $ABCD$ 的面积将逐渐减小，且可以任意地小；而当

region enclosed by 40
quadrilateral *ABCD*

B、D 居中时，面积将逐渐增大，当 *ABCD* 为正方形时，*ABCD* 的面积达最大值 $= \frac{1}{2} \times 10 \times 5 \times 2 = 50$；综上所述，四边形 *ABCD* 的面积将在 0 至 50 之间波动，所以本题无法判断比较左项与右项的大小。

10.

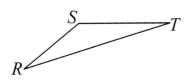

$(RS)^2 + (ST)^2$ $(RT)^2$

10. 解：本题的正确答案是（D）。从图中看，好像是 $\angle RST$ 是钝角，$(RS)^2 + (ST)^2 > (RT)^2$

但是该题的图中并没有表明 Figure drawn to scale，所以考生只能读图，不能度量，从而也就无法判断 $\angle RST$ 是否大于 $90°$，所以本题为无法判断。

注： $\angle RST = 90°$，则 $(RS)^2 + (ST)^2 = (RT)^2$
$\angle RST < 90°$，则 $(RS)^2 + (ST)^2 > (RT)^2$
$\angle RST > 90°$，则 $(RS)^2 + (ST)^2 < (RT)^2$

11.

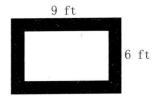

The rectangular rug shown in the figure above has a floral border 1 foot wide on all sides. What is the area, in square feet, of that portion of the rug that excludes the border?

(A) 28　　(B) 40　　(C) 45

(D) 48　　(E) 53

11. 左图所示的长方形地毯在各边均有 1 英尺宽的花边。以平方英尺为单位，地毯的非花边部分的面积是多少？

解： 本题的正确答案为（A）。由花边宽 1 英尺可知，这块地毯去除花边后，长和宽分别为 7 英尺和 4 英尺，所以其面积 $= 7 \times 4 = 28$ 平方英尺。

12.

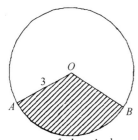

O is the center of the circle.

12. O 是圆心，阴影区的面积是 3π

解： 本题正确答案是（C）。该题主要考扇形的面积与圆的面积之间的关系：

$$\frac{扇形的面积}{圆的面积} = \frac{扇形所对的圆心角的度数}{360°}$$

根据上式可得 $\angle AOB = 360° \times \frac{3\pi}{9\pi} = 120°$

The area of the shaded region is 3 π.
The degree measure
of ∠AOB   120

注：有些考生认为∠AOB 既可以是外角可以可以
是内角，所以本题的正确答案应该为（D）。
在这一点上这类考生应当注意的：在数学
中，指某角时，若无特殊指明或加上某些符
号表示时，一般指内角。

13.

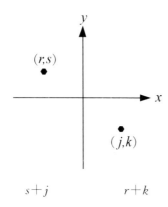

$s+j$ $r+k$

13. **解**：本题的正确答案为（A）。由图可知$(r,$ $s)$点在第二象限，而(j,k)点在第四象限。根据平面直角坐标系的四个象限中的点的坐标的正负规律：

$$I(+,+),II(-,+),$$
$$III(-,-),IV(+,-)$$

可知图中 $r<0$，$s>0$，$j>0$，$k<0\Rightarrow$ $s+j>r+k$

14.

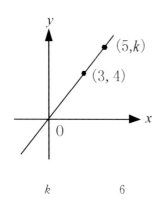

k 6

14. **解**：本题的正确答案为（A）。由图可知该直线过原点，因此其方程可写为：$y=ax$，再根据$(5,k)$，$(3,4)$两点在直线上可得：

$$4=3a，k=5a\quad\Rightarrow\quad k=\frac{20}{3}>6$$

15.

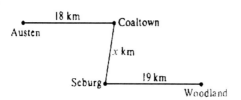

The map shows the only roads that connect the four towns and shows the distance along each road.

The road distance between Austen and Seburg	The road distance between Coaltown and Woodland

15. 左面的地图展示了连接 4 个城镇的仅有道路并且注明了每条道路的长度。

解：本题的正确答案是（B）。正确解答这道题的关键在于对"only"一词的把握，它表明了在这四个城镇之间除了图中表明的道路之外，别无它路可走。根据题中给出的图形，考生很容易得出：Austen 与 Seburg 之间的距离$(18+x)<$Coaltown 与 Woodland 之间的距离$(19+x)$。

16.

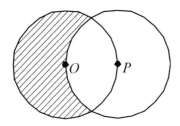

The circles above, with centers O and P, each have radius r.

| Twice the area of the shaded region. | The area of the circular region with center P. |

16. 上面图中以 O,P 为圆心的圆的半径均为 r

解：本题的正确答案为（A）。由图可知 P 点在圆 O 上，而 O 点在圆 P 上，过点 O 作圆 P 的切线，由该切线把阴影区分为两部分：半圆＋剩余部分。因为两圆面积相同，所以比较左项＝2×（半圆的面积＋剩余部分的面积）＝圆 P 的面积＋2×剩余部分的面积。由此可知比较左项显然大于比较右项。

17.

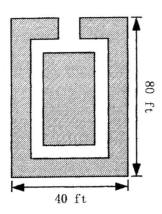

80 ft

40 ft

The diagram represents a rectangular garden. The shaded regions are planted in flowers, and the unshaded region is a walk 2 feet wide. All angles are right angles.

| The sum of the areas of the shaded regions | 2,800 square feet |

17. 左图是一个长方形花园的示意图，阴影区域中种植了花，非阴影区域是一条 2 英尺宽的路。所有的角度都是直角。

解：本题的正确答案为（D）。因为图中并没有指明 2 英尺宽的路在什么位置，所以路的面积和阴影部分的面积都是不定的。但是两者面积的和是一定的（40×80＝3200 平方英尺）。

路在中间位置时，路的面积最小，阴影部分的面积最大：

阴影部分的面积＝ 40×80－(2+2)(2+2)＝3184 当路在四周时，路的面积最大，阴影部分的面积最小：

阴影部分的面积＝(40－2－2)×(80－2－2)＝2736

所以阴影部分的面积在 2736 与 3184 之间。

18.

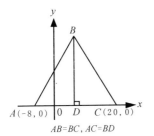

$AB=BC, AC=BD$

18. 在上面的 xy 平面中，B 点的坐标是多少？

解：本题的正确答案为（B）。由 $AB=BC$，可推知 $\triangle ABC$ 为一等腰三角形，$BD \perp AC$ 且平分 AC，则 D 点坐标为 $x=\dfrac{-8+20}{2}=6$，D 点在 x 轴上，所以其纵坐标等于 0。

B 点与 D 点在同一条与 y 轴平行的直线

What are the coordinates of point B in the xy-plane above?

(A) (6,12)　　(B) (6,28)　　(C) (8,20)

(D) (12,20)　　(E) (14,28)

19. The altitude of a certain triangular sail is 2 meters greater in length than its base. The area of the face of the sail is 24 square meters.

The length of the
base of the sail　　　　4 meters

20.

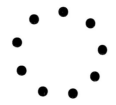

If 9 trees are originally planted in a circular pattern as shown above, what is the least number of trees that must be transplanted so that the 9 trees will be in 2 straight rows?

(A) 4　　(B) 5　　(C) 6　　(D) 7　　(E) 8

21. If the sum of the measures of two angles is 180°, each angle is a supplement of the other, whereas, if the sum of their measures is 90°, each is a complement of the other.

| The measure of an angle with a supplement that measures 130° | The measure of an angle with a complement that measures 40° |

上,所以 B 点的横坐标也为 6;A 和 C 两点都在 x 轴上,所以它们之间的距离等于两点的横坐标的差的绝对值,即 $AC=|-8-20|$ $=28$;又由 $BD=AC$ 可知,B 点纵坐标为28。综上所述 B 点的坐标(6,28)。

19. 一三角帆的高度比底边长 2 米,帆面的面积等于 24 平方米。

解:本题的正确答案为(A)。设底边边长为 x 米,则高为($x+2$)米,由题意可得:

$$S_{三角帆} = \frac{1}{2}x(x+2) = 24 \Rightarrow x = 6$$

20. 若 9 棵树最初以如左图所示的圆形种植,要使 9 棵树排在两条直线上,问最少需移植几棵树?

解:本题的正确答案为(B)。圆上的任意三点都不在同一条直线上,又根据在同一平面内的两点确定一条直线可知,要使这 9 棵树排在两条直线上,则至少得有 $9-2×2=5$ 棵树被移植。

21. 若两个角度数的和等于180°,则称一个角是另一个角的补角;若两角度数和等 90°,则称一个角是另一个角的余角。

解:本题的正确答案为(C)。比较的左项为补角等于130°的角的度数;比较的右项为余角等于 $40°$ 的角的度数。可能一些考生对 Supplement(补角)和 complement(余角)不认识,导致读题不清。其实在一时想不到是余角或补角时,只要弄清两者之间关系即可,根据题意可得:

$$180°-130°=90°-40°$$

22.

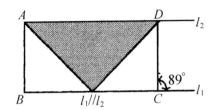

The area of the shaded region | The sum of the areas of the two unshaded triangular regions

22. 解：本题的正确答案为（A）。阴影区的面积 $= \frac{1}{2}|AD| \cdot h$，非阴影区面积和 $= \frac{1}{2}|BC| \cdot h$，因为 BC 与 h 夹角为 $89°$，所以 $|AD| > |BC|$，由此可得阴影区面积>两个非阴影三角形面积的和。

23. If a solid pyramid has 4 vertices and 4 faces, how many edges does the pyramid have?

(A) 2
(B) 3
(C) 4
(D) 6
(E) 8

23. 假如一个立体四角锥有 4 个顶点和 4 个面，该四角锥有多少条边？

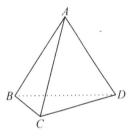

解：本题的正确的答案是（D）。解答这道题的关键是对 solid pyramid 的理解。根据题中对 solid pyramid 的描述可知，所谓 solid pyramid 就是立体几何中常见的四面体，如下图所示。四面体有四个面，四个顶点，六条边。

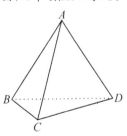

注：Solid *n*. 固体，立体（几何）；Pyramid *n*. 锥体（四角锥）；Vertices *n*. 顶点（*pl*.）

24.

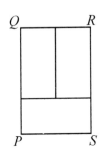

24. 解：本题的正确答案是（A）。上面的三个小长方形具有相同的尺寸（**dimension**）。具有相同的尺寸也即它们的长和宽都分别相同，由此可得三个小长方形的长都是宽的两倍，所以有：

$$\frac{PS}{RS} = \frac{2}{3}$$

The three small rectangles have the same dimensions.

$\dfrac{PS}{RS}$	$\dfrac{1}{2}$

25. A rectangular floor with an area of 12 square meters is drawn to scale with 2 centimeters representing l meter.

The area of the scale drawing of the floor	24 square centimeters

25. 按比例绘制面积为 12 平方米的长方形地板,以 2 厘米代表 l 米。

按比例尺绘制的地板面积	24 平方厘米 **(square centimeter)**

解: 本题的正确答案为(A)。设地板长为 l 米,宽为 w 米,绘成图后,图的长为 $2l$ 厘米,宽为 $2w$ 厘米。由题干给出条件可知,$lw=12$,绘制后的面积$=2l\cdot2w=4lw=48$ 平方厘米>24 平方厘米。

26. In the rectangular coordinate system, line k passes through the points $(0,0)$ and $(4,8)$; line m passes through the points $(0,1)$ and $(4,9)$.

The slope of line k	The slope of line m

26. 在一个平面直角坐标系中,直线 k 通过$(0,0)$和$(4,8)$两点,直线 m 通过$(0,1)$和$(4,9)$两点。

解: 本题的正确答案为(C)。

$$\text{Slope}=\frac{y_1-y_2}{x_1-x_2}\Rightarrow$$

$$\begin{cases}\text{Slope}_{(k)}=\dfrac{8-0}{4-0}=2\\[2mm]\text{Slope}_{(m)}=\dfrac{9-1}{4-0}=2\end{cases}$$

27.

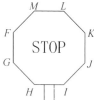

In the stop sign shown in the figure above, all sides have equal length and all angles have equal measure. If the figure could be rotated 225 degrees in a clockwise direction, point G would be in the position of point

(A) I (B) J (C) K (D) L (E) M

27. 在上面图形的 STOP 标志中,所有的边长都相等并且夹角也相等。如果该图形沿顺时针方向旋转 $225°$,问 G 点会在哪一个点的位置?

解: 本题的正确答案是(B)。由题意可知 $FGHIJKLM$ 是一个正八边形,正八边形每转过一边的角度等于正八边形的中心与两个相邻的顶点连线的夹角,即为 $360\div8=45°$,$225\div45=5$,所以 STOP 标志沿顺时针方向旋转 $225°$后,G 点在正八边形的边上沿顺时针方向移动了 5 条边长的距离,即 STOP 标志旋后 G 点在未旋转前 J 点的位置。

28. In the xy-coordinate system, the point $(x,$ $y)$ lies on the circle with equation
$$x^2 + y^2 = 1$$

$x+y$ 1.01

28. 在 xy 坐标系中,点 (x,y) 位于方程为 $x^2 +$ $y^2 = 1$ 的圆上。

解: 本题的正确答案为(D)。解答该题时考生要明白 $x^2 + y^2 = 1$ 指一个以原点为圆心,半径为 1 的圆。在该圆上,当点 (x,y) 都在第一象限,且 $x = y$ 时 $x + y$ 取最大值,由 $x^2 + y^2 = 1$ 可得此时 $x = y = \frac{\sqrt{2}}{2}$,$x + y = \sqrt{2}$;当点 (x,y) 都在第三象限,且 $x = y$ 时 $x + y$ 取最小值,此时 $x = y = -\frac{\sqrt{2}}{2}$,$x + y = -\sqrt{2}$;当点 (x,y) 在其他位置时其值在 $-\sqrt{2}$ 与 $\sqrt{2}$ 之间,也即 $-\sqrt{2} \leqslant x + y \leqslant \sqrt{2}$。

29.

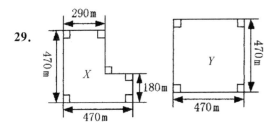

Fields X and Y are to be enclosed with fencing that costs $24 per meter.

| The cost of the fencing needed to enclose X | The cost of the fencing needed to enclose Y |

29. 准备用围墙把 X 和 Y 地围起来,围墙的成本为每米 $24。

解: 本题的正确答案为(C)。此题也就是求两场地的周长孰大孰小。但该题并不必要把两块场地的周长的值算出来。如下图所示把 X 场地补上虚线:

从图中可以看出 X 与 Y 周长相等,自然围墙所用的成本也相等。

30. What is the ratio of the perimeter of a pentagon with each side of length 6 to the perimeter of an octagon with each side of length 6?

(A) $\frac{5}{6}$ (B) $\frac{4}{5}$ (C) $\frac{3}{4}$

(D) $\frac{2}{3}$ (E) $\frac{5}{8}$

30. 每条边长都等于 6 的五边形(**pentagon**)的周长与每条边长都等于 6 的八边形(**octagon**)周长的比率是多少?

解: 本题的正确答案为(E)。能否解对本题的关键在于考生是否认得"pentagon"(五边形)和"octagon"(八边形)这两个词,由题意可得:
$$\frac{等边五边形的周长}{等边六边形的周长} = \frac{6 \times 5}{6 \times 8} = \frac{5}{8}$$

31. A, B, and C are points on a line. The distance between A and B is twice the distance between A and C. The distance between C and B is 10.

The distance between	
A and B	10

31. A、B 和 C 是同一条直线上的点。A 与 B 之间的距离等于 A 与 C 之间距离的2倍，C 和 B 之间的距离是10。

解： 本题的正确答案是（D）。解答本题的关键是对以下两种情况的把握：

(1) C 点在 A 和 B 的中间

$$\underset{A \qquad\quad C \qquad B}{\rule{4cm}{0.4pt}} \quad |AB|=20$$

(2) A 点在 B 和 C 的中间

$$\underset{B \qquad\quad A \qquad C}{\rule{4cm}{0.4pt}} \quad |AB|=\frac{20}{3}$$

32.

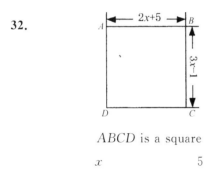

$ABCD$ is a square

x	5

32. 解： 本题的正确答案为（A）。因为 $ABCD$ 是正方形，所以其各边均相等，由此可以得到方程：$2x+5=3x-1 \Rightarrow x=6>5$。

33. A circular flower bed is inscribed in a flat, square garden plot that measures x meters on each side.

The fraction of the garden plot area that is <u>not</u> part of the flower bed if $x=50$ meters	The fraction of the garden plot area that is <u>not</u> part of the flower bed if $x=45$ meters

33. 一个圆形花圃内切（**inscribe**）于一个边长为 x 米的平面正方形花园中。

解： 本题的正确答案为（C）。左项为 $x=50$ 时花园中不是花圃的比例，右项是 $x=45$ 时花园中不是花圃的比例。该比例为：

$$\frac{x^2-\pi\left(\dfrac{x}{2}\right)^2}{x^2}=1-\frac{\pi}{4}$$

，由此可见 x^2 已消掉，也即半径的大小与该比例无关。

34.

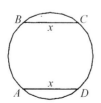

The length of arc ABC	The length of arc ADC

34. 解： 本题的正确答案为（D）。由 $BC=AD=x$，只能推出它们的对应弧长 BC，AD 相等，但是 AB 弧与 CD 弧的长度却不能确定，因此本题的为无法判断。只有当 $BC/\!/AD$ 时才能得到 ABC 弧的长度与 BCD 弧的长度相等。（$BC=AD$ 保证了与圆心等距）。

35.

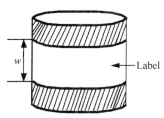

A rectangular label is attached to a right circular cylinder with radius r. The label, which encircles the cylinder without overlap, has width w and an area equal to the area of the base of the cylinder.

$$w \qquad r$$

36. The dimensions, in centimeters, of rectangular box R are 6 by 8 by 10. Which of the following CANNOT be the total surface area, in square centimeters, of two faces of R?

(A) 96

(B) 120

(C) 128

(D) 160

(E) 180

37.

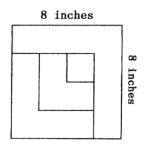

8 inches

8 inches

The figure above shows a large square formed by fitting three L-shaped tiles and one small square tile together. If a

35. 一个长方形的检签贴在半径为 r 的直圆柱上。该标签围绕圆柱体一周且不重叠,其宽度为 w,面积等于圆柱体底面的面积。

解: 本题的正确答案为(B)。由于该标签围绕圆柱体且不重叠,所以其长度等于圆柱体底面的周长 $=2\pi r$,则其面积 $=2\pi r \cdot w$(因为这是一个长方形标签),圆柱体底面积为 πr^2,由题意可得:

$$2\pi r \cdot w = \pi r^2 \quad \Rightarrow \quad w = \frac{r}{2}$$

36. 以厘米为单位,长方体盒子 R 的尺寸为 $6\times 8\times 10$,请问下列哪项不能是 R 的两个面的面积的和(以平方厘米为单位)?

解: 本题的正确答案为(E)。长方体盒子有六面,且对面两两相等,共有三个面积不同的面,分别是 $6\times 8=48$,$6\times 10=60$ 和 $8\times 10=80$,这些面两两相加,包括与自身相加,共有 6 个不同的取值:分别是:96,120,160,108,128,140。把这些值与题目的选项对照,发现(E)不等于长方体盒子两个面的面积的和。考生也可用另一种方法来解此题,在长方体中面积最大的一面为 $8\times 10=80$,所以两个最大面的面积和最大为 160,因此 180 显然不能是长方体两个面的面积的和。

37. 左面图形展示了由 3 个 L 形的瓦与 1 个小正方形的瓦所形成的大正方形。若给 1 个 12 英尺长,10 英尺宽的长方形地板贴上这种图样的大正方形,问需要多少块 L 形的瓦?

解: 本题的正确答案是(A)。1 foot=12 inches。长方形地板的长和宽换算成英寸为 144 inches 长 120 inches 宽,所以其面积为 $=120\times 144=17280$

$$17280 \div (8\times 8) = 270$$

rectangular floor 10 feet by 12 feet is to be tiled in large squares of this design, how many L-shaped tiles will be needed?

(A) 810　　(B) 405　　(C) 270

(D) 135　　(E) 45

因为一个正方形由 3 个 L 形构成,所以贴该地板需 L 形的瓦的数目为:$270 \times 3 = 810$

38. A certain rectangle has perimeter 54. If the ratio of the length of the rectangle to the width is 5 to 4, what is the length of the rectangle?

(A) 30　　(B) 27　　(C) 24

(D) 18　　(E) 15

38. 一长方形的周长等于 54,其长宽比为 5:4,问该长方形的长为多少?

解: 本题的正确答案为(E)。设该长方形的长和宽分别是 $5x, 4x$,由题意可得:
$$(5x + 4x) \times 2 = 54 \quad \Rightarrow \quad x = 3, \quad 5x = 15$$

39.

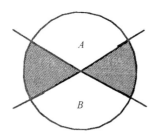

The areas of the two shaded regions of the circle are equal.

The area of	The area of
unshaded region	unshaded region
A of the circle	B of the circle

39. 上图中两个阴影区面积相同。

解: 本题的正确答案是(D)。若图中两条直线的交点在圆心上,则可推出 A 和 B 两区域的面积相等;但图中并未说明,所以两条直线完全可能不在圆心相交也可以导致两阴影面积相同,而在这种情况之下 A 和 B 两区域的面积孰大孰小是不能确定的。

40.

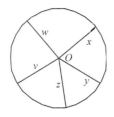

The area of the circular region with center O is 16π, and v, w, x, y and z represent the lengths of the line segments.

8π　　　　　　$v + w + x + y + z$

40. 以 O 为圆心的圆的面积为 16π,且 $v, w, x,$ y 和 z 代表线段长度。

解: 本题的正确答案为(A)。由圆 O 的面积等于 16π 可求出其半径 $r = 4$,而 $v, w, x, y,$ z 长度均等于半径,所以有:
$$v + w + x + y + z = 20 < 8\pi$$

41.

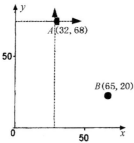

In the rectangular coordinate system above, the coordinates of points A and B are shown. If the dotted lines represent a second pair of coordinate axes with origin at A, and if the scale is the same on both pairs of axes, what are the coordinates of point B with respect to the second pair of axes?

(A) $(-33, 88)$ (B) $(33, 48)$

(C) $(33, -48)$ (D) $(97, 88)$

(E) $(97, -88)$

41. 在一个平面直角坐标系（**rectangular coordinate system**）中，已标出了 A 点和 B 点的坐标，如果虚线表示原点在 A 的另一坐标系，并且两坐标系的坐标轴的刻度的大小都相同，那么 B 点在第二个坐标系中所对应的坐标是多少？

解：本题的正确答案是(C)。由图可知，旧坐标系中的点 (x, y) 在新坐标系中的对应坐标为 $(x-32, y-68)$，由此可知 O 点在第二坐标系的坐标为 $(-32, -68)$，B 点在新坐标系中的坐标为 $(65-32, 20-68)$，也即 $(33, -48)$。

42.

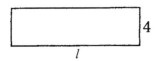

If the perimeter of the rectangle above is 36, then $l=$

(A) 9 (B) 14 (C) 16 (D) 28 (E) 32

42. 若上图中长方形的周长等于 36，则 $l=$

解：本题的正确答案为(B)。长方形周长 $(l+4) \times 2=36$，因而解出 $l=14$

43.

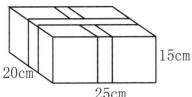

The rectangular box shown above has been wrapped with two tapes, each going once around the box without overlap and running parallel to the edges of the box. How many centimeters of tape were used on the box?

(A) 70   (B) 80   (C) 120

(D) 140   (E) 150

43. 上图所示长方体盒子被两条胶带捆住，每条胶带无重叠地缠绕长方体盒子一圈，且与长方体盒子的边缘相平行。问包盒子共用了多长的胶带？

解：本题的正确答案为(E)。该题实际上是让考生求长方体盒子的两个矩形周长的和，因此带长等于：

$2 \times (20+15) + 2 \times (25+15) = 150$ cm

44. A rectangular rug covers half of a rectangular floor that is 9 feet wide and 12 feet long. If the dimensions of the rug are in the same ratio as those of the floor, how many feet long is the rug?

(A) 6   (B) $\dfrac{21}{2}$ (C) $2\sqrt{7}$

(D) $6\sqrt{2}$ (E) $4\sqrt{6}$

45.

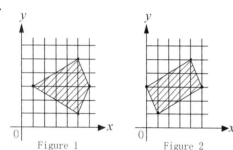

Figure 1   Figure 2

Note: Drawn to scale.

The area of the shaded region shown in Figure 1   The area of the shaded region shown in Figure 2

46.

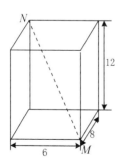

All faces of the solid above are rectangular.

The length of diagonal MN 15

---

44. 一个长方形地毯盖住 9 英尺长 12 英尺宽的地板的一半,若该地毯的长与宽的比例和地板的长与宽比例相同,问该地毯有多长?

解: 本题的正确答案为(D)。"dimension"指图形的维,在这里指长方形地毯的长和宽。由题意可得地毯的面积 $=\dfrac{1}{2}$ 地板面积 $=\dfrac{1}{2}\times 9\times 12=54$;而地毯长和宽比例也为 12:9。设地毯长为 n,则宽为 $\dfrac{9}{12}n$,那么 $\dfrac{9}{12}n\times n=54$ $\Rightarrow n=\sqrt{72}=6\sqrt{2}$

45. 解: 本题的正确答案为(C)。该题是让考生比较两个图中阴影区的面积。仔细观察后都会发现,两个阴影区都是由两个等底等高的三角形组成的,它们的面积自然是相等的。

46. 图中物体的所有的面都是矩形。

解: 本题的正确答案为(A)。由图中所给的条件可知,该物体是一个长方体,三条相交的边相互垂直。所以对角线(diagonal)MN 等于任意三条相交的边的平方和,即:
$MN^2=(6^2+8^2)+12^2=244>225=15^2$

47.

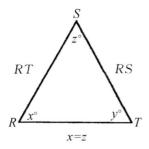

$x=z$

47. **解：** 本题的正确答案为(D)。根据 $x=z$，只能推出 $RT=ST$，而无法判断 RT 与 RS 的关系。

48.

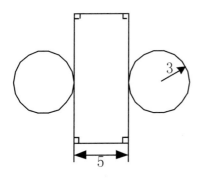

The figure above shows a cylindrical can that has been cut open and flattened.

The volume of
the can before
it was cut open　　　　45π

48. 左面的图形表示一个切开后并展开的圆柱体罐子。

解： 本题的正确答案为(C)。由图可知该圆柱体的高为 5，底面圆的半径为 3，根据圆柱体的体积公式可得该圆柱体的体积为：

$$\pi r^2 \cdot h = \pi \cdot 3^2 \cdot 5 = 45\pi$$

49. The sum of the lengths of two sides of isosceles triangle K is 7. K has a side of length 4.

　　　　The perimeter of K　　　　11

49. 等腰三角形（**isosceles triangle**）K 的两条边的和为 7，K 有一条边的长为 4。

解： 本题的正确答案为(D)。该题可分两种情况：
(1) 7 是两腰的和，则 4 是底边长，K 的周长等于 11；
(2) 若 7 是腰与底边和，则腰长可能为 3，也可能为 4。当腰长为 3 时，对应 K 周长等于 10；当腰长为 4 时，对应 K 的周长等于 11。

50. If B is the midpoint of line segment AD and C is the midpoint of line segment BD, what is the value of $\frac{AB}{AC}$?

(A) $\frac{3}{4}$

(B) $\frac{2}{3}$

50. 若 B 是线段 AD 中点，C 是线段 BD 中点，那么 $\frac{AB}{AC}$ 的值是多少？

解： 本题的正确答案为(B)。对于这种类型的几何题目，考生最好借助图形来解。A,B,C,D 四点的位置如下图所示：

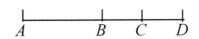

(C) $\dfrac{1}{2}$

(D) $\dfrac{1}{3}$

(E) $\dfrac{1}{4}$

由图很容易得出 $AB=\dfrac{1}{2}AD, AC=AB+BC$

$$=\dfrac{1}{2}AD+\dfrac{1}{4}AD=\dfrac{3}{4}AD$$

所以 $\dfrac{AB}{AC}=\dfrac{1}{2}AD\div\dfrac{3}{4}AD=\dfrac{2}{3}$

51.

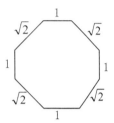

The figure above shows the lengths of the sides of an equiangular polygon. What is the area of the polygon?

(A) 7　(B) 8　(C) 9　(D) $14\sqrt{2}$

(E) It cannot be determined from the information given.

51. 上面图中标出了一个等角多边形（**equiangular polygon**）的各边边长,问该多边形的面积是多少?

解: 本题的正确答案为（A）。因为多边形是等角八边形,故每个内角为 $135°$,所以外角等于 $45°$,因而把四条边长等于 $\sqrt{2}$ 的边延长后将组成一个正方形。由此可知图中的八边形是由一个正方形切去四个大小相同的角构成的,该正方形的边长等于 $2\sqrt{2}$,切去的每个角都是一个等腰直角三角形,其直角边长为 $\dfrac{\sqrt{2}}{2}$。因此该等角八边形的面积等于正方形的面积减去四个小等腰直角三角形的面积： $(2\sqrt{2})^2-4\times\dfrac{1}{2}\times\dfrac{\sqrt{2}}{2}\times\dfrac{\sqrt{2}}{2}=7$

52.

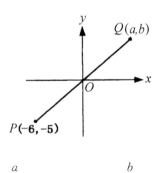

a　　　　b

52. **解:** 本题的正确答案为（A）。过 O、Q 点的直线为 $y=kx$, $k=\dfrac{y}{x}$

$$\dfrac{a}{b}=\dfrac{-6}{-5}=\dfrac{6}{5}$$

在第一象限内的点的坐标都是正值,所以由上式可以得到 $a>b$

53.

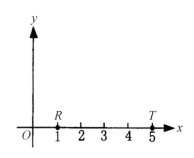

53. 点 S（未画）位于 x 轴的上方,$\triangle RST$ 面积等于 6。

点 S 的 x 坐标　　　　点 S 的 y 坐标

解: 本题的正确答案为（D）。该题是让考生比较 S 点的横坐标与纵坐标的大小。根据 $\triangle RST$ 面积等于 6 和底边 RT 长等于 4 可以求出 S 点的纵坐标数值（等于三角形的

Point S (not shown) lies above the x-axis such that $\triangle RST$ has area equal to 6.

| The x-coordinate of point S | The y-coordinate of point S |

54.

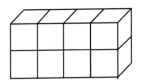

The rectangular solid above is made up of eight cubes of the same size, each of which has exactly one face painted blue. What is the greatest fraction of the total surface area of the solid that could be blue?

(A) $\dfrac{1}{6}$ (B) $\dfrac{3}{14}$ (C) $\dfrac{1}{4}$

(D) $\dfrac{2}{7}$ (E) $\dfrac{1}{3}$

55.

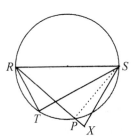

RS is a diameter of the circle

| The measure of $\angle RTS$ | The measure of $\angle RXS$ |

56.

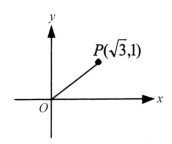

In the rectangular coordinate system,

高),而三角形底为 4,由三角形面积关系可以求出 $y=3$,而任意同底等高的三角形面积都相等,故 S 取 $y=3$ 直线上任一点均可满足条件,所以点 S 的 x 坐标是不确定的。

54. 上图所示的长方体由 8 块同样大小的立方体构成,每个立方体仅有一个面被涂成蓝色。问该长方体的表面是蓝色的部分占其总表面积的最大比例是多少?

解:本题的正确答案为(D)。蓝色部分占表面最大比例的情况是 8 个立方体的蓝色表面均露在外面,共有 8 个平方单位,而长方体的表面共有 28 个平方单位,因而蓝色部分占长方体表面积的最大比值为 $\dfrac{8}{28}=\dfrac{2}{7}$。

55. 解:本题的正确答案为(A)。如图所示,设 RX 与圆的交点为 P,把 S 点与 P 点用虚线连接起来。因为 RS 是圆的直径,所以有 $\angle RTS=\angle RPS=90°$。而 $\angle RPS$ 又是 $\triangle SPX$ 的一个外角,它等于 $\angle PXS$ 与 $\angle XSP$ 的和,因此 $\angle RTS>\angle RXS$。

56. 在直角坐标系中,线段 OP 逆时针旋转 $90°$ 到 OQ(未画出)

解:本题的正确答案为(C)。由图可知,点 P 在逆时针旋转之前,位于第一象限,根据 P 点的坐标可以推知 OP 与 x 轴的夹角等于 $30°$,逆时针旋转 $90°$ 后,得到的 Q 点的坐标在第二象限,OQ 与 x 轴的夹角等于 $30°$。而线段 OQ 又与线段 OP 等长,所以 Q 点的

segment OP is rotated counterclockwise through an angle of $90°$ to position OQ (not shown).

| The x-coordinate of point Q | -1 |

57.

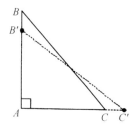

Triangular garden ABC is redesigned by increasing the length of AC by 20 percent to point C' and decreasing the length of AB by 20 percent to point B'.

| The area of the original garden ABC | The area of the redesigned garden $AB'C'$ |

58. If the perimeter of a triangle is 18, then the length of one of the sides CANNOT be

(A) 1　　　(B) 3　　　(C) 6

(D) 8　　　(E) 9

59.

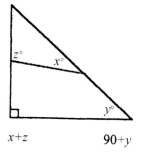

坐标为$(-1,\sqrt{3})$

57. 重新设计三角形花园 ABC,使其 AC 边长增加 20% 到 C' 点;AB 边长减少 20% 到 B' 点。

解:本题的正确答案为(A)。从表面上看,好像是变化前后花园的面积大小不变,但是若考生根据题意列出方程就可发现,变化后花园的面积是减小了:

$$S_{\triangle AB'C'} = \frac{1}{2}|AB'| \cdot |AC'|$$
$$= \frac{1}{2}(1-20\%)|AB| \cdot (1+20\%)|AC|$$
$$= 0.96 S_{\triangle ABC}$$

58. 若三角形的周长等于18,那么其边长不可能是:

解:本题的正确答案为(E)。三角形中任一边的长都小于其他两边的和,也即任意一边的长都小于三角形周长的一半。

59. 解:本题的正确答案为(C)。由三角形的内角和等于180°可得:

$$\angle A + 90 + y = \angle A + z + x = 180$$
$$\Rightarrow 90 + y = x + z$$

60.

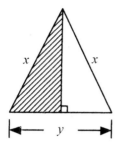

The area of the
shaded region $\qquad$ $\dfrac{xy}{4}$

61. △RST is isosceles and ∠RST = 40°

The sum of the
measures of the
two angles of $\qquad$ 120°
△RST that have
equal measure

62.

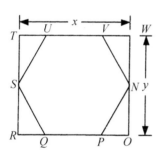

Polygon $SUVNPQ$ is equilateral and
equiangular and $TWOR$ is a rectangle.

$\dfrac{x}{y}$ $\qquad$ 1

63. Points P, R, and T lie on a straight line.
The distance from P to R is 21, and the
distance from P to T is 9.

The distance $\qquad$

---

60. 阴影区面积 $\qquad$ $\dfrac{xy}{4}$

解：本题的正确答案为（B）。设三角形的高为 h，很显然 $h < x$，则

阴影区面积 $= \dfrac{1}{2} \cdot \left(\dfrac{1}{2}y\right) \cdot h = \dfrac{1}{4}hy < \dfrac{1}{4}xy$

61. △RST 是等腰三角形，且∠RST = 40°

解：本题的正确答案为（D）。比较的左项为△RST 中两个底角的和，该题需分两种情况进行讨论：

① ∠RST 是顶角，则两个底角的和为：

180° − 40° = 140°

② ∠RST 是底角，则两个底角的和为：

2 × 40° = 80°

62. 多边形 SUVNPQ 是等边多边形，且其内角均相等，TWOR 是长方形。

解：本题的正确答案为（A）。由 n 边形内角和公式可得此等边六边形的内角和为：$(n-2) \cdot 180 = (6-2) \cdot 180 = 720°$，再由内角相等可得故每个内角为 $720/6 = 120°$，由此可以推出∠TUS = 60°，∠UST = 30°。设该多边形边长为 a，则根据三角形的边角关系（在直角三角形中 30°所对的直角边等于斜边的一半）和勾股定理，可以得到矩形的边长为：

$x = a + 2 \times \dfrac{a}{2} = 2a$，$y = 2 \times \dfrac{\sqrt{3}}{2}a = \sqrt{3}a$

$\dfrac{x}{y} = \dfrac{2}{\sqrt{3}} > 1$

63. 点 P、R 和 T 位于同一条直线上，P 到 R 的距离是 21，P 到 T 的距离是 9。

R 到 T 的距离 $\qquad$ 16

解：本题的正确答案为（D）。因为题目中并未给

出 P,R 和 T 的相对位置,所以 T 有两可能的位置:

① T 在 P 和 R 的中间,此时 $RT=12$;

② T 和 R 在 P 的两侧,此时 $RT=30$。

64.

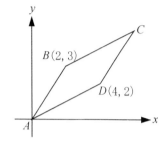

In the figure above, if *ABCD* is a parallelogram with *A* at the origin, what are the coordinates of *C*?

(A) (6,5)　　(B) (6,6)　　(C) (7,4)

(D) (8,5)　　(E) (8,6)

64. 如上图所示,$ABCD$ 是一个平行四边形,A 在原点,问 C 点坐标是多少?

解:本题的正确答案为(A)。因这平行四边形的对角线互相平分,也即 $\overline{AC}$,$\overline{BD}$ 具有相同的中点,所以位于直角坐标系中的平行四边形具有如下性质

$$\begin{cases} x_C + x_A = x_B + x_D \\ y_A + y_C = y_B + y_D \end{cases}$$
$$\Rightarrow x_c = 6, y_c = 5$$

65.

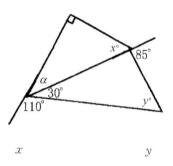

x　　　　　　　　y

65. 解:本题的正确答案为(B)。由三角形的内角之间关系可得:

$$x = 90° - a = 90° - (180° - 110° - 30°) = 50°$$

再根据三角形的外角等于三角形两不相邻的内角和可得:

$$y = 85° - 30° = 55°$$

66.

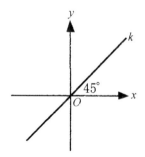

The point (not shown) with rectangular coordinates (*m*, *n*) is above line *k*.

　　　　m　　　　　　　　　n

66. 直角坐标为 (m,n) 的点(未标出)位于直线 k 的上方。

解:本题的正确答案为(B)。由直线 k 与 x 轴正方向的夹角等于 45°可得直线 k 的方程为 $y=x$。根据一般原则,若点在直线 $y=x$ 上方,则其纵坐标的值大于横坐标的值,即 $y>x$,若点在直线 $y=x$ 的下方,则其纵坐标的值小于其横坐标的值,即 $y<x$。

67.

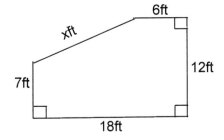

The figure shows the dimensions of a certain plot of land.

     x 12

67. 图中标出了某块地的尺寸。

解：本题的正确答案为（A）。考生在做几何题时，往往需要借助辅助线来完成，如下图中虚线所示做辅助线：

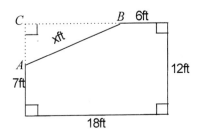

则直角三角形 ABC 的两直角边长分别为：

$BC = 18 - 6 = 12$ ft，$AC = 12 - 7 = 5$ ft

$\therefore AB = \sqrt{12^2 + 5^2} = 13$ ft

68.

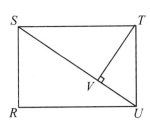

The area of rectangular $(TV)(SU)$ region $RSTU$

68. 解：本题的正确答案为（C）。从图中可以看出矩形 $RSTU$ 由 $\triangle SRU$ 和 $\triangle SUT$ 组成，这两三角形是全等的直角三角形，即 $\triangle SRU$ 的面积 $= \triangle STU$ 的面积 $= \dfrac{1}{2}(TV)(SU)$，因此矩形 $RSTU$ 的面积 $= (TV)(SU)$

69. Exactly four faces of a rectangular solid are painted.

     The fraction of the surface area that is painted $\dfrac{2}{3}$

69. 长方体的 4 个面被涂色

解：本题的正确答案为（D）。比较的左项为涂色的部分占表面的比例。长方体共有六个面，虽然有 4 个面涂色，但是由于不知道各面的面积大小，因而不能确定所求的比例。考生仔细考虑后就会发现，实际上，涂色的部分占表面的比例在 $\dfrac{1}{2}$ 与 1 之间，但不能等于 $\dfrac{1}{2}$ 和 1。

70.

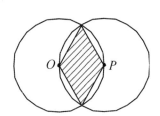

70. 在上面的图形中，O 和 P 是两个圆的圆心。若两个圆的半径都为 r，那么阴影部分的面积是多少？

解：本题的正确答案为（B）。阴影区所构成的四

In the figure above, O and P are the centers of two circles. If each circle has radius r, what is the area of the shaded region?

(A) $\frac{\sqrt{2}}{2}r^2$　　(B) $\frac{\sqrt{3}}{2}r^2$　　(C) $\sqrt{2r^2}$

(D) $\sqrt{3}r^2$　　(E) $2\sqrt{3}r^2$

边形的四条边都等于r,所以它可以分成两个边长为 r 的等边三角形,所以阴影区的面积

$$= 2 \cdot \frac{1}{2} \cdot r \cdot \frac{\sqrt{3}}{2}r = \frac{\sqrt{3}}{2}r^2$$

71. The boundaries of regions X and Y are parallelograms.

| The area of X if its sides have lengths 6 and 10 | The area of Y if its sides have lengths 5 and 12 |

71. X 和 Y 是平行四边形。

解: 本题的正确答案为(D)。比较的左项为边长分别是 6 和 10 的平行四边形 X 的面积;比较的右项为边长分别是 5 和 12 的平行四边形 Y 的面积。平行四边形公式为:$S = a \times b \sin\theta$,$\theta$ 为 a 和 b 的夹角,因而仅仅 $a \cdot b$ 乘积相等并不能表明他们的面积相等,面积的大小还受 a 和 b 的夹角大小的制约。

72.

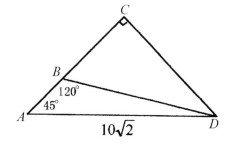

In the figure above, what is the length of AB?

(A) $\frac{10}{3}$　　(B) $\frac{10\sqrt{3}}{3}$　　(E) $\frac{20}{3}$

(C) $5 - \frac{5\sqrt{3}}{3}$　　(D) $10 - \frac{10\sqrt{3}}{3}$

72. 在上面图中,AB 的长度是多少?

解: 本题的正确答案为(D)。因为 $\angle CAD = 45°$,所以 $\triangle ADC$ 为等腰直角三角形,因而 $AC = CD = 10\sin45° = 10$;

而 $\angle CBD = 180° - 120° = 60°$

$\Rightarrow CB = CD \cdot \text{ctg}60° = \frac{10\sqrt{3}}{3}$

$\Rightarrow AB = AC - BC = 10 - \frac{10\sqrt{3}}{3}$。

73. What fraction of a cubic meter is the volume of a cubic block of stone with edge of length 10 centimeters? (1 meter $= 100$ centimeters)

(A) $\frac{3}{10}$　　(B) $\frac{1}{10}$　　(C) $\frac{1}{30}$

(D) $\frac{1}{100}$　　(E) $\frac{1}{1,000}$

73. 边长为 10 cm 的立方体(**cubic block**)石块的体积是 1 立方米(**cubic meter**)的几分之几?

解: 本题的正确答案为(E)。由 1 米 $=100$ 厘米可得 10 厘米等于 0.1 米,所以边长为 10 cm 的立方体石块的体积为:

$0.1 \times 0.1 \times 0.1 = 1 \times 10^{-3}$ 立方米

74.

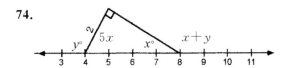

74. 解： 本题的正确答案为（C）。从图中可知，直角三角形的一条直角边等于2，其斜边等于4，因此可以推知 $x = 30$（30°所对的直角边等于斜边的一半），$y = 30 + 90 = 120$，所以 $5x = x + y$。

75.

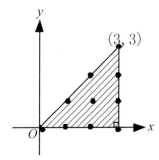

In the rectangular coordinate system above, for how many of the points that lie inside or on the boundary of the shaded region are both coordinates integers?

(A) Six   (B) Seven   (C) Eight

(D) Nine   (E) Ten

75. 在上图所示的直角坐标系中，位于阴影区内或边界上的点坐标是整数的点有多少个？

解： 本题的正确答案为（E）。由图可知，阴影区由 $y = x$，$y = 0$，$x = 3$ 这三条直线围成，其边界为这三条直线。因此阴影区内点的坐标范围为 $0 \leqslant x \leqslant 3$，$0 \leqslant y \leqslant 3$，$y \leqslant x$。当 x 和 y 只能取整数时，所求的点为：
$(0,0)$，$(0,1)$，$(0,2)$，$(0,3)$，$(1,1)$，$(1,2)$，$(1,3)$，$(2,2)$，$(2,3)$，$(3,3)$ 共计十点。

76. A rectangular tabletop consists of a piece of laminated wood bordered by a thin metal strip along its four edges. The surface area of the tabletop is x square feet, and the total length of the strip before it was attached was x feet. If the tabletop is 3 feet wide, what is its approximate length, in feet?

(A) 12   (B) 10   (C) 9

(D) 8   (E) 6

76. 一个长方形的桌面由一块四周镶有薄金属条的薄木板组成，桌面的面积为 x 平方英尺，金属条在镶上去之前的总长度为 x 英尺，若桌面的宽度为 3 英尺，问其长度大约是多少英尺？

解： 本题的正确答案为（E）。设桌面的长度为 y 英尺，

则
$$\begin{cases} 2(y+3) = x \\ 3y = x \end{cases}$$
$$\Rightarrow y = 6$$

77. In the coordinate plane, points A and B are endpoints of a diameter of a circle with center $(-2, 1)$. If the coordinates of A are $(-5, 5)$, what are the coordinates of B?

77. 在坐标平面上，A 和 B 两点是以 $(-2,1)$ 为圆心的直径的端点（endpoint）。若 A 点坐标为 $(-5,5)$，那么 B 点坐标是多少？

解： 本题的正确答案为（E）。设圆心坐标

(A) (0,0)　　(B) (3, −2)

(C) (3, −1)　　(D) (2, −2)

(E) (1, −3)

(x_0, y_0)，因为圆心是 A 和 B 中点，所以由平面内任两点中点的坐标公式可得：$x_A + x_B = 2x_0$，$y_A + y_B = 2y_0$。代入圆心与 B 点坐标，可求得 B 点坐标为$(1, −3)$。

78. Three solid cubes of lead, each with edges 10 centimeters long, are melted together in a level, rectangular shaped pan. The base of the pan has inside dimensions of 20 centimeters by 30 centimeters, and the pan is 15 centimeters deep. If the volume of the solid lead is approximately the same as the volume of the melted lead, approximately how many centimeters deep is the melted lead in the pan?

(A) 2.5　　(B) 3　　(C) 5

(D) 7.5　　(E) 9

78. 3 个实心的立方体铅块，每个的边长都是 10 厘米，融化在一个水平的长方体熔炉中。熔炉内表面的底部长 30 厘米，宽 20 厘米，且熔炉的深度为 15 厘米。若实心铅块的体积在融化前后大体相同，问熔炉中融化铅的深度大约是多少厘米？

解：本题的正确答案是(C)。3 个实心立方体铅块的总体积为：

$$3 \times 10^3 = 3000 \text{ cm}^3$$

则融化铅在熔炉中的深度为

$$3000 \div (20 \times 30) = 5 \text{ cm}$$

79.

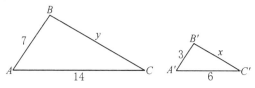

If corresponding sides of $\triangle ABC$ and $\triangle A'B'C'$ above are proportional, what is y in terms of x?

(A) $\dfrac{3x}{7}$　　(B) $\dfrac{6x}{7}$　　(C) $2x$

(D) $\dfrac{7x}{3}$　　(E) $\dfrac{14x}{3}$

79. 如果$\triangle ABC$ 与$\triangle A'B'C'$的对应边成比例，那么 y 用 x 来表示是多少？

解：本题的正确答案为（D）。因为$\triangle ABC$ 和$\triangle A'B'C'$的对应边成比例，所以有：

$$\frac{y}{x} = \frac{BC}{B'C'} = \frac{AB}{A'B'} = \frac{7}{3} \Rightarrow y = \frac{7x}{3}$$

80.

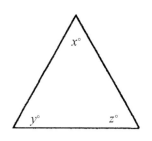

80. 在左侧的图形中，若 x，y 和 z 都是整数，且满足$x < y < z$，那么 $x + z$ 的最小值和最大值是多少？

解：本题的正确答案是(C)。由三角形的内角和等于$180°$可得：$x + z = 180° − y$，而$x < y < z$，且 x，y，z 为整数，则 y 最小值等于 2°，

In the figure above, if x, y, and z are integers such that $x<y<z$, then the least and the greatest possible values of $x+z$ are

(A) 59 and 91　　(B) 59 and 135

(C) 91 and 178　　(D) 120 and 135

(E) 120 and 178

最大值为89°，那么180°−y一定大于等于91°，而小于等于178°。

81.

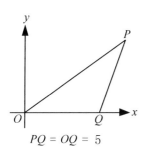

$PQ = OQ = 5$

The area of region OPQ　　10

81. 解：本题的正确答案为(D)。△OPQ面积=$\frac{1}{2}×OQ×PQ\sin\theta=12.5\sin\theta$，$\theta$是$QO$与$PQ$的夹角。因为△$OPQ$的面积随$\theta$的大小而变化，所以此题为无法判断。

82.

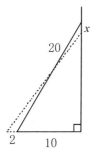

A 20-foot ladder leaning against a vertical wall with the base of the ladder 10 feet from the wall is pulled 2 feet farther out from the wall, causing the top of the ladder to drop x feet.

　　　　　x　　　　　　2

82. 一个20英尺的梯子，斜靠在一堵垂直的墙上且梯子的底部距墙根为10英尺，再把梯子的底部拉离墙根2英尺远，导致梯子的顶部向下移动x英尺。

解：本题的正确答案是(B)。在拉动梯子之前，其垂直高度为：$\sqrt{20^2−10^2}=10\sqrt{3}$，而拉动前后斜边长度不变，底边变为12，则梯子的垂直高度为：

$$\sqrt{20^2−12^2}=16,10\sqrt{3}−16≈1.32$$

83. The vertices of an equilateral triangle are on a circle.

The length of a side of the triangle	The diameter of the circle

83. 等边三角形（**equilateral triangle**）的顶点（**vertice**）在一个圆上。

解：本题的正确答案为(B)。设等边三角形的边长为a，根据三角形的边角关系可求出其外接圆的直径为$\frac{2\sqrt{3}}{3}a$，显然有$a<\frac{2\sqrt{3}}{3}a$。

84. The maximum possible number of lines determined by n points $(n>1)$ $\dfrac{n(n-1)}{2}$

85.

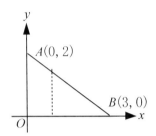

In the rectangular coordinate system above, if P, not shown, is a point on AB and if the x-coordinate of P is 1, what is the y-coordinate of P?

(A) $\dfrac{4}{3}$ (B) $\dfrac{3}{2}$ (C) $\dfrac{7}{3}$

(D) $\dfrac{5}{2}$ (E) $\dfrac{8}{3}$

86.

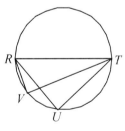

RT is a diameter of the circle above.

The measure of $\angle RUT$ The measure of $\angle RVT$

87.

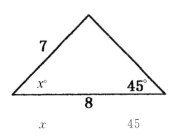

x 45

---

84. 解： 本题的正确答案为（C）。比较的左项为 n 个点所能确定的最大的直线数目，根据两点决定一条直线可知，若得最大直线的数目，任三点都不能在同一直线上，那么最大直线数目为

$$C_n^2=\dfrac{n(n-1)}{2}$$

85. 上图所示的直角坐标系中，若 P（未标出）是 AB 上一点，且 P 的横坐标为1，那么 P 的纵坐标为多少？

解： 本题的正确答案为（A）。先写出直线 AB 的方程，然后把 P 点的坐标代入即可：

$$\dfrac{y}{2}+\dfrac{x}{3}=1 \text{ 或 } y=-\dfrac{2}{3}x+2$$

由此方程可得当 $x=1$ 时，$y=\dfrac{4}{3}$

若考生对直线方程不太熟悉，则可以借助相似三角形的性质来解此题。显然由虚线切出的小三角形与 $\triangle ABO$ 相似，由此可推出

$$\dfrac{y}{2}=\dfrac{3-1}{3}\Rightarrow y=\dfrac{4}{3}$$

86. 解： 本题的正确答案为（C）。由图可知 $\angle RUT$ 和 $\angle RVT$ 都是直径 RT 所对应的圆周角，而同一段弧所相对的圆周角相等。

87. 解： 本题的正确答案是（D）。该题看似简单，但由于 x 有两个不同的取值，所以是无法判断的。如下图所示：

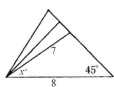

由 x 角的顶点向对边引一条垂线得到一个直角三角形,由其一个角等于 $45°$ 可得这个等腰直角三角形的直角边长度为 $4\sqrt{2}<7$,由此可见可以得出两个位置不同,但长度都为 7 的边,一个与长度为 8 的底边所成角度大于 $45°$,另一小于 $45°$。

88.

There are six marked points on the circle above. How many different lines can be drawn that contain two of the marked points?

(A) 5   (B) 6   (C) 12

(D) 15   (E) 30

88. 在上面的圆周上有 6 个标出的点。问能画出多少条含两个标识点的不同直线?

解: 本题的正确答案为(D)。由图可知由这六个点中的任意三点都不在同一条直线上,由两个点确定一条直线可和这 6 个点能确定的不同直线数是其任 2 个点的组合数:$C_6^2 = \dfrac{6\times5}{2} = 15$ 条。

89. The circumference of a rectangle is 40

The greatest area of the rectangle   100

89. 某长方形的周长等于 40

解: 本题的正确答案是(C)。比较的左项为该长方形的最大面积,如前所述,对长方形来说,当其周长一定时,正方形的面积最大。也就是说当该长方形的边长为 $a=10$ 的正方形时,该长方形的面积最大,等于 100。考生也可用另一种方法来求解:设该长方形的长和宽分别为 a,b,则 $2(a+b)=40$,关于算术平均值和几何平均值之间有如下的性质:

$$\frac{a+b}{2} \geqslant \sqrt{ab} \quad (a,b>0)$$

$$10 \geqslant \sqrt{ab} \quad ab \leqslant 100$$

90.

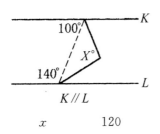

$K /\!/ L$

x 120

90. 解: 本题的正确答案为(C)。此题不好直接找出所给出的三个角的相互关系,因此要借助辅助线。如图所示做辅助线,根据同旁内角互补及三角形的内角和等于 $180°$ 可得:$x+100°+140°=360° \Rightarrow x=120°$

91.

| The area of a table cloth that overhangs a square tabletop by 3 inches on all sides | The area of a table cloth that overhangs a rectangular tabletop by 2 inches on all sides |

91. 解：本题的正确答案为(D)。比较的左项为在一个正方形桌面上各边都垂下 3 英寸的桌布面积，比较右项为一个长方形桌面上各边垂下两英寸的桌布的面积，因为题目中并未给出长方形以及正方形的边长，所以无法判断左项与右项的大小。

92.

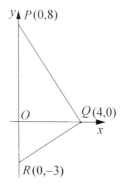

Points P, Q, and R have rectangular coordinates $(0, 8)$, $(4, 0)$, and $(0, -3)$, respectively.

The perimeter of $\triangle PQR$　　25

92. 点 P、Q 和 R 的直角坐标分别为 $(0, 8)$，$(4, 0)$和$(0, -3)$。

解：本题的正确答案为(B)。在直角坐标系中画出 $\triangle PQR$，由图可知 $|PQ| = \sqrt{4^2 + 8^2} = 4\sqrt{5}$，$|QR| = \sqrt{4^4 + 3^2} = 5$，$|PR| = 11$，$\triangle PQR$ 的周长 $= 16 + 4\sqrt{5} = 16 + \sqrt{80} < 16 + \sqrt{81} = 25$。

93.

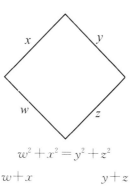

$w^2 + x^2 = y^2 + z^2$

$w + x$　　　$y + z$

93. 解：本题的正确答案是(D)。由题中所给的条件可知，x 与 w 所夹的角是直角，y 与 z 所夹的角是直角，而 x 与 y 及 w 与 z 所夹的角的大小，却是无法确定的。因此图中所给的已知条件只是说明了两个直角三角形的斜边相等，斜边相等的直角三角形有无穷多个，其直角边的和也有无穷多个，所以本题为无法判断。

94. $2AF = AB = BD = DE = AE$

| The sum of the area of triangular region ABF and the area | The area of rectangular region $BCEF$ |

94. 解：本题的正确答案为(D)。考生在做该题时要借助图形来解。根据题中所给出的已知条件，可知 A，B，D，E 四点可构成一个菱形，而 B，C，F，E 四点则构成一个长方形。左项为 $\triangle ABF$ 与 $\triangle CDE$ 面积之和，右项为长方形 $BCEF$ 的面积。则存在两个三

of triangular

region *CDE*

角形和一个长方形,且两三角形的一边为长方形的一边,由此考生可以通过以上已知条件画出下面两个图形,它们都完全满足$2AF=AB=BD=DE=AE$。

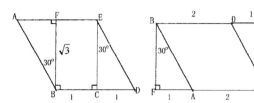

在上面的左边的图形中,△*ABF* 与 △*CDE* 面积之和等于长方形 *BCEF* 面积;而在右边的图形中 △*ABF* 与 △*CDE* 的面积之和很显然不等于长方形 *BCEF* 的面积,中间多了一个四边形 *AEDB*,所以本题为无法判断。

95.

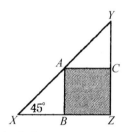

The shaded region is rectangular

The perimeter of

the shaded region $XZ+YZ$

95. 本题的正确答案为(C)。由∠$YXZ=45°$,阴影区是长方形可知△XZY 是等腰直角三角形,因此 $XB=AB$,$AC=YC$,所以阴影区周长$=XZ+YZ$。

96. In a rectangular coordinate system, line k has x-intercept 4 and slope-2.

The y-intercept of k 2

96. 在一个平面直角坐标系中,直线 k 在 x 轴上的截距为4,其斜率为2。

解: 本题的正确答案是(A)。根据点斜式可以写出该直线的方程如下:

$$y=-2(x-4)=-2x+8$$

当 $x=0$ 时,$y=8$,也即直线 k 在 y 轴上的截距为8。

97.

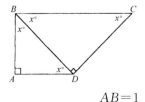

$AB=1$

The perimeter of   6

quadrilateral *ABCD*

97. 解: 本题的正确答案为(B)。由图可知 $AB=AD=1$,由勾股定理可知 $BD=\sqrt{2}$;由 $BD=CD=\sqrt{2}$ 可得 $BC=2$,所以四边形的边长$=AD+DC+CB+BA=4+\sqrt{2}$。

98.

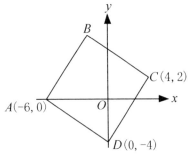

In the figure above, *ABCD* is a square. What are the coordinates of point *B*?

(A) $(-4,2)$ (B) $(-2,4)$

(C) $(-2,6)$ (D) $(4,-6)$

(E) $(6,-2)$

99.

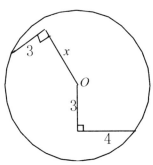

O is the center of the circle

x 5

100. Board *A* measures between 2.15 feet and 2.25 feet in length; board *B* measures between 2.20 feet and 2.30 feet in length.

The length of board *A*	The length of board *B*

98. 左上面的图形中,*ABCD* 是一个正方形,*B* 点的坐标是多少?

解:本题的正确答案为(C)。设 *B* 点的坐标为 (x,y),由 *ABCD* 是一个正方形,可知其对角线互相垂直平分,设 *A* 点与 *C* 点连线的中点坐标为 (x',y'),则

$$x' = \frac{-6+4}{2} = -1, \quad y' = \frac{0+2}{2} = 1$$

即中点为 $(-1,1)$,也即 *B* 与 *D* 的中点的坐标为 $(-1,1)$,从而可以得出:

$$-1 = \frac{0+x}{2}, \quad 1 = \frac{-4+y}{2} \Rightarrow x=-2, \quad y=6,$$

即 *B* 点的坐标为 $(-2,6)$。

99. 解:本题的正确答案为(B)。由图可知,圆的半径等于 $\sqrt{3^2+4^2} = 5$,而 x 的长度明显小于圆的半径长。

100. A 板的长度测量值在 2.15 到 2.25 英尺之间,B 板的长度测量值在 2.10 到 2.30 英尺之间。

解:本题的正确答案为(D)。由题可知,两块板的长度测量值并不固定,且有重叠部分,因此不能判断两块板孰长孰短。

第 六 章

数据解释(Data Interpretation)

在 GRE 的笔试中,数学部分的每个 Section 的最后都有一组(一般为五道题)数据解释题;GRE 改为机考以后,每个 Section 有两组(一般为每组两个题)数据解释题,它们一般出现在每个 Section 的中间部分。在我国的小学和中学的课本中,这类题目出现得较少,因此大多数中国考生都对这部分题感到头痛。众所周知,要想获得 GRE 高分,数学部分的每一个题都是不能放弃的。实际上这部分并不难,只不过是因为我们见得少而感到生疏罢了。考生只要能掌握住这类题的套路,并稍加训练,这部分的所谓难题就可迎刃而解。

第一节 数据解释题的类型及解题策略

一、数据解释题的要求

Data Interpretation questions require you to analyze information presented graphically in statistical charts, graphs, and tables.

二、数据解释中的图表类型

1. Tables(表格)
2. Pie charts(圆形图)
3. Bar graphs(条带图)
4. Line graphs(线型图)
5. Cumulative graphs(累积图)

三、图表的含义

1. 表格:分类排列记录事项的文件。如:统计表、收支对照表等;

2. 圆形图:表示部分与整体的关系,通常以百分比表示图中的每个部分。图中整个圆代表100%,占总数一定百分比的一个量以相同的比例用一个"扇面(Sector)"表示,扇面越大,所占的比率越高;

3. 线形图:主要用来描述某一量的连续变化过程,通常以时间作为变化参数。如果曲线向上延伸,则表示数量增加;如果曲线向下延伸,则表示数量减少;如果曲线向水平方向延伸,则表示数量没有变化。有些图中可能不止一条曲线,这些曲线在变化时可能会交叉或重叠,且交叉重叠部分又往往是 ETS 的考点,因此考生在做题时对曲线中交叉重叠的部分要倍加注意;

4. 条带图:主要利用条带的长度或高度来进行比较,每个条带可能表示一个量,也可能将其分割成几段以表示不同的量。这些图的条带有些是水平方向的,有些是垂直方向的。不同的量用密度不同的斜线或黑色的深浅来区分;

5. 累积图: 以累积带图的形式,将累积条带的高度按比例分成不同的数量,用以比较几个项目。

四、数据解释题的形式

1. Data Interpretation questions always appear in the Problem Solving format;

2. Each question in a set pertains to the same graphical data;

3. On the paper-based exam, a set may involve anywhere from one to four distinct displays (tables, charts, graphs). On the computer-based exam, each set involves either one or two distinct displays (the size of the computer screen does not allow for more than two displays).

五、数据解释题的特点

1. 数据解释题一般都以 Problem Solving 的形式出现。

2. 数据解释题一般都比较长且繁琐。

3. 在机考中,图表一般出现在问题的上面,因此为了看到整个题目,有时需要不断地上下翻屏,以浏览到所有的与解题有关的信息。

4. 较难的题往往需要综合两个或多个图表的信息才能正确解答。

5. 并非所有的图表都是按比例画出的。如果一个图是按比例画出的,那么你就会在图的下面看到"Note,Drawn to scale"。一般说来,图形是否按比例画出,具有以下规律:

① Bar graphs will be drawn to scale

② Line charts will be drawn to scale

③ Pie charts will not drawn to scale

④ Visual scale is irrelevant with tables

6. 题目中一般会在图表的上面或下面给出解释图表所必要的额外信息。

7. 大多数的问题只要求近似解。

六、数据解释题的解题策略

数据解释题不同于数值计算题和数量比较题,考生必须具有敏锐的洞察力,透过图表以抓住解题的关键数据和信息。解答数据解释题时要注意以下几点:

1. 首先对整个图表做一大致了解,但不要深入到图表中。一开始就希望对其全面了解,会浪费大量的时间,且获得的许多信息又是无用的。一个图形或表格所包括的信息量是很大的,而题目一般只有两个,根本不可能涉及所有的内容,因此我们只要做到"按需索取"即可。题目要求回答什么问题,就到图表中寻找相关的信息。对图表的大致了解不能只集中在"big picture",还要注意"big picture"的周围,即:

① 图表的标题,一般位于上方;

② 横坐标的意义,位于其下方;

③ 纵坐标的意义,位于图表的左边或右边或左右两边都有;

④ 线轴所表示的量或扇形区所表示的量;

⑤ 条式或线式图表中线轴所表示的量的范围;

⑥ 圆式图表的总值;

⑦ 日期,测量单位;

⑧ 阴影部分或其他符号所代表的关键内容；

⑨ 脚注，有的用"＊"号在标题中引出，有的直接给出，由于它位于图表的底端，有时字体较小，最易遗漏，应引起考生的重视。

2. 在图表中如有读数困难，可用草纸或铅笔帮助量取；

3. 对较复杂的问题，不要知难而退，可将其分解为几部分，再各个击破。对多个图表同时出现的问题，经常需将在某一个图表中读取的信息带到另一个图表中方能得到最后的结论；

4. 问题中所使用的单位有时与图表中的不一致，考生务必用正确的单位回答问题；

5. 许多问题只要求近似答案，所以有时可以取近似值以节省时间和脑力；

6. 不要不合理地取舍数据，以造成计算结果错误；

7. 勿搞混小数与百分数，例如 0.3％实际上等于 0.003；

8. 勿搞混百分数与原始数，例如把 70％当作 70 处理；

9. 对任何问题的回答必须依据图表所提供的信息，不能凭自己所了解的背景知识进行主观臆断。

第二节　重点试题精练及解析

AVERAGE GASOLINE PRICES AND TAXES
JUNE 1, 1989

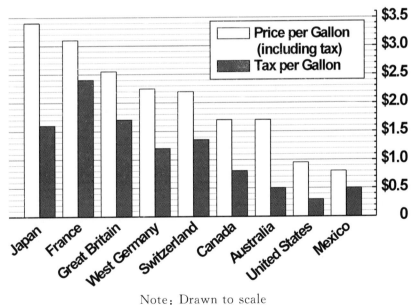

Note：Drawn to scale

1. This question refers to the graph above. In the question all references to gasoline prices and taxes refer to average prices, including tax, and average taxes, in United States dollars, On June 1, 1989.

If the tax per gallon of gasoline in Canada were doubled and the increase in tax added to the price per gallon of gasoline, what percent of the resulting price per gallon would the tax then be?

(A) 36%   (B) 50%   (C) 64%

(D) 75%   (E) 90%

1. 若加拿大每加仑汽油的税款加倍,那么税款的增长与每加仑汽油价格相加以后,税款将会是每加仑汽油的最终价格的百分之多少?

解:本题的正确答案为(C)。由图可知,加拿大每加仑汽油的含税价格是 $1.7,而税款为每加仑 $0.8,税款加倍后为每加仑 $1.6,因此每加仑的税款将是每加仑汽油最终价格的 1.6/(1.7+0.8) = 0.64。

NUMBER OF FARMS IN THE UNITED STATES, 1850—1990 (in millions)

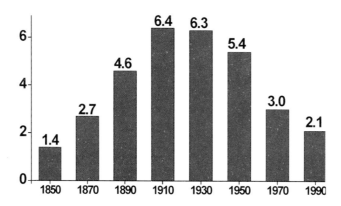

2. The average acreage per farm was approximately 140 in 1910 and 220 in 1950. The ration of the total farmland acreage in 1910 to the total in 1950 was most nearly

(A) $\frac{3}{4}$ (B) $\frac{2}{3}$ (C) $\frac{3}{5}$

(D) $\frac{1}{2}$ (E) $\frac{2}{5}$

2. 标题:1850 ～ 1990 年美国农场数量(in millions)

在 1910 年每个农场的面积大约是 140 英亩,在 1950 年每个农场的面积大约是 220 英亩。1910 年农场的总面积与 1950 年农场的总面积之比最接近于下面哪一项?

解:本题的正确答案为(A)。由图可知 1910 年农场总数为 6.4 million,1950 年农场总数为 5.4 million,因此两者面积之比等于 (6.4×140)/(5.4×220)=0.752。

Question 3—4 refer to the following data.

AVERAGE COSTS TO OPERATE THREE TYPES OF CARS OVER

A FOUR-YEAR PERIOD

(based on 15,000 miles per year)

	Standard Car	Compact Car	Subcompact Car
Purchase Price	$8,000	$5,600	$4,800
Interest	2,112	1,479	1,267
Insurance	2,000	2,000	2,000
Maintenance/Tires	1,120	1,080	920
Fuel*/Oil	6,429	4,500	3,000
Subtotal	19,661	14,659	11,987
Resale Value	−2,000	−1,400	−1,200
Total Cost to Operate the Car	$17,661	$13,259	$10,787

AVERAGE ANNUAL SAVINGS* THROUGH CAR-POOLING TO WORK RATHER THAN DRIVING ALONE

Type of Car	Annual Cost Driving to Work Alone	Annual Savings Per Person			
		2-person Car Pool	3-person Car Pool	4-person Car Pool	5-person Car Pool
Standard	$2,491	$1,146	$1,544	$1,719	$1,843
Compact	1,870	860	1,159	1,290	1,384
Subcompact	1,521	700	943	1,050	1,126

AVERAGE DAILY COST* OF VAN-POOLING TO WORK

Round-Trip Miles	Van Pool Cost per Passenger
20	$1.45
25	1.54
30	1.63
40	1.81
50	1.99
60	2.17

* Based on $1.50 per gallon for fuel.

3. If the cost of oil is negligible, what is the mileage (average miles per gallon of fuel) of a compact car?

(A) 13

(B) 18

(C) 20

(D) 25

(E) 28

3. 若 Oil 的成本可以忽略不计,问每加仑的汽油能使小型汽车运行多少英里?

解: 本题的正确答案为(C)。要算出每加仑的汽油能使小型汽车运行多少英里,就要知道小型汽车每年运行的总英里数及其所消耗的汽油加仑数。题目标题的括号中的"based on 15,000 miles per year"以及题目的尾注中的"Based on $1.50 per gallon for fuel"都是考生应当注意的内容,但考生一定要注意到限制性语言"per year",因为第一个表格中的花费为"four-year",找到图表中的第五栏中 Fuel/Oil 一行,根据 Oil 可以忽略不计,可得一辆小型汽车 4 年的 Fuel 花费用

为 $4500，由此可得每年的 Fuel 花费为 $4500/4 = $1125，而汽油价格为 $1.5/gallon，所以每年一辆小型汽车所需的 Fuel 为 $1125/ $1.5 = 750 gallons，每年的总英里数为 15,000 英里。总英里数除以总加仑数即可得本题的答案：15,000/750 = 20miles/gallon。

4. If 2 people, who would otherwise be driving alone in subcompact cars, drive in a 2-person car pool using subcompact cars, what is the total of their average annual costs of transportation to work?

(A) $821

(B) $1,400

(C) $1,521

(D) $1,642

(E) $2,342

4. 若本来可以单独驾驶微型汽车的两个人，现在共同驾驶 1 辆双座的微型汽车，他们平均每年的总交通费用是多少？

解： 本题的正确答案为(D)。题目的表格 2 中给出了单独驾车的费用和驾驶二、三、四、五座的汽车，平均每人可以节省的开支。根据表格中的数据可知，若两个人都各驾驶一辆微型汽车，则每年的总费用为：$1521×2 = $3042；但若两人共同驾驶一辆双座微型汽车，则每人可节省 $700，也即共节省：$700×2 = $1400，因此两人每年的平均总费用为 $3042 - $1400 = $1642。

Questions 5—6 refer to the following graphs.

SALES AND EARNINGS OF COMPANY X

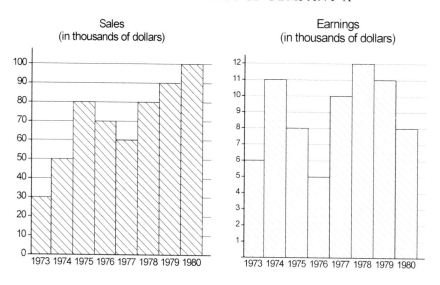

Note: Drawn to scale.

5. If at the end of 1973 Company X sold 30,000 shares of common stock for 35 times Company X's earnings for the year, what

5. 假如 X 公司在 1973 年底以该公司一年赢利的 35 倍价钱售出 30,000 份普通股。在当时普通股的价钱是多少？

194

was the price of a share of common stock at that time?

(A) $7.00   (B) $10.00

(C) $17.50   (D) $35.00

(E) $70.00

解： 本题的正确答案为（A）。考生解答该题的关键是对"sell... for..."短语的理解，for后面接的词语多表示买进或卖出的价钱，如果能建立这种观念，本题就迎刃而解。根据Earnings图，可以找到X公司在1973年的赢利是$6,000,所以每股普通股的价钱 $= \dfrac{35 \times \$6,000}{30,000} = \$7.00$

6. If Company X considered a good year to be any year in which earnings were at least 20 percent of sales, how many of the years shown were good years?

(A) None   (B) One   (C) Two

(D) Three   (E) Four

6. 若X公司认为只要一年中它的赢利至少占销售额的20%,那么该年就是好年头。根据图中显示,有多少个好年头?

解： 本题的正确答案为（C）。该题是要找出对应的年份赢利（Earnings）与销售（Sales）的比值,经过简单计算,发现只有1973和1974两个年头满足要求。

Questions 7—9 refer to the following graph.

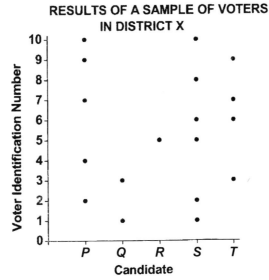

The graph above shows how a sample of 10 different voters (vertical axis) voted for 5 different candidates (horizontal axis). Each voter voted for either one or two of the five candidates (No voter voted twice for the same candidate). The two candidates receiving the most votes were the winners. The sample constituted 5 percent of those in the district who voted, and the number of votes in the district for each candidate was in the same proportion as the number of votes in the sample for each candidate.

问题7—9参照下面的图表信息：

标题：X地区一个选民样本的选举结果

上面图表表明了10个不同的投票者(纵轴),对5个不同的候选人的投票(横轴)选举样本。每个选民投票支持5个候选人中的某一个或某两个(没有投票者对同一候选人投2次票)。两个获得选票最多的候选人为获胜者。该样本占这个地区投票总人数的5%,并且这个地区每个候选人得到的选票的比例与该样本中的比例相同。

7. What fraction of the total number of votes cast did the two winners receive?

(A) $\dfrac{11}{18}$ (B) $\dfrac{11}{22}$ (C) $\dfrac{1}{2}$

(D) $\dfrac{1}{3}$ (E) $\dfrac{3}{10}$

7. 两个获胜者获得的选票占投票总数的比例是多少?

解: 本题的正确答案是(A)。从图中可以看出两个获胜者是 P 和 S,分别获得了 5 张和 6 张选票,而该样本中共有 18 张选票,所以获胜者获得的选票比例为 $\dfrac{11}{18}$。

8. What percent of the sample voted for at least one of the two winners?

(A) 11%   (B) 20%   (C) 55%

(D) 61%   (E) 90%

8. 样本中至少投票赞成两名获胜者中的某一个的百分比是多少?

解: 本题的正确答案是(E)。该题也即问有几个人没有投两名获胜者的票。由图可知,只有 3 号选民没有投两名获胜者的票,所以 10 人中至少投两名获胜者中的某一个的有 9 人,其百分比为 90%。

9. How many votes were cast in district X?

(A) 18   (B) 90   (C) 200

(D) 360   (E) 400

9. X 地区的选民共投了多少张选票?

解: 本题的正确答案是(D)。根据样本的 18 张选票占总选票量的 5% 可以推出 X 地区共有 18÷5%=360 张选票。

Questions 10—11 refer to the following graphs.

COLLEGE R: ENROLLMENT AND CONTRIBUTIONS

1976—1980

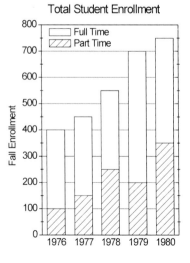

Note: Drawn to scale

10. In the 1978—1979 school year, if 12 percent of the amount of contributions allocated to scholarships and operational expenses was allocated to heating costs, approximately how much was NOT allocated to heating costs?

(A) $2,000   (B) $25,000

(C) $176,000   (D) $205,000

(E) $250,000

10. 在 1978—1979 学年,若分配给奖学金和实验费用的捐资的 12% 用于取暖,大约有多少费用没有分配给取暖?

解: 本题的正确答案为(D)。从捐资分配图(Allocation of All Contributions)中可以观察到 1978—1979 学年学院 R 所获得的捐资共约 $233,000,从而没有分配给取暖的费用约为 $233,000 × (1 − 12%) = $205,040,与选项(D)的结果相一致。

11. Approximately what was the total amount of contributions to College R from the 1978—1979 school year through the 1980—1981 school year, inclusive?

(A) $967,000   (B) $1,000,000

(C) $9,000,000   (D) $9,667,000

(E) $10,000,000

11. 学院 R 从 1978—1979 学年到 1980—1981 学年(包括二者)获得的捐资总额约为多少?

解: 本题的正确答案为(B)。从捐资分配图(Allocation of All Contributions)可以发现学院三个学年获得的捐资额分别为 $233,000, $300,000, $467,000,因此其总额为三者之和,等于 $1,000,000。

Questions 12—13 refer to the following data.

EXPENDITURES ON FOOD AND SELECTED NONFOOD ITEMS. 1973

Percent of Average Annual Income (before taxes) Spent by Families on

Food and Selected Nonfood Items

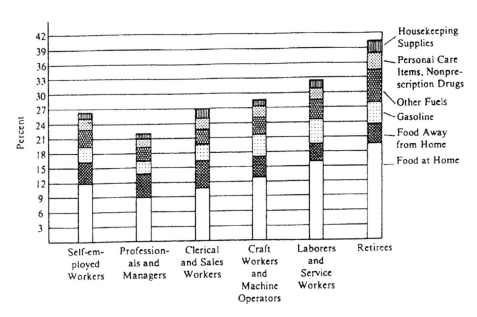

Occupational Category of Family Head

| | Percent of Food and Household Expenditures | | | | | | |
| Occupational Category of Family Head | Food at Home | | | Food Away from Home | Personal Care Items, Nonprescription Drugs | Housekeeping Supplies | Average Weekly Food and Household Expenditures |
	Meats, Poultry, Seafood	Cereals, Bakery and Dairy Products, Fruits and Vegetables Other	Food at Home				
Self-employed Workers	22	25	14	22	10	7	$35.88
Professionals and Managers	19	23	11	29	11	7	$38.77
Clerical and Sales Workers	21	22	11	28	11	7	$32.07
Craft Workers and Machine Operators	23	25	15	21	9	7	$35.44
Laborers and Service Workers	24	27	14	19	9	7	$28.86
Retirees	23	29	14	16	11	7	$19.83

Average Weekly Food and Household Expenditures

12. For which of the following categories was the percent of the average annual income（before taxes）spent on food at home the least?

(A) Self-employed workers

(B) Professionals and managers

(C) Clerical and sales workers

(D) Craft workers and machine operators

(E) Laborers and service workers

13. Approximately what percent of the total average annual income（before taxes）of retirees was spent on meats，poultry，and seafood（consumed at home）?

(A) 7%

(B) 10%

(C) 20%

(D) 23%

(E) 31%

12. 12—13 参照下列信息：

标题：食物和非食物选项的花费：1973 年家庭在食物和非食物选项上的花费占平均年收入（税前）的百分比

下面哪一类人在家用食物上所花的费用占平均年收入（税前）的百分比最小？

解：本题的正确答案为（B）。该题需认真阅读第一图——食物和非食物选项的花费（Expenditures on Food and Selected Nonfood Items）。图中不同的阴影区表示不同的项目，其长度表示百分比。图中白色区表示家用食物所占各年收入的百分比，我们找出最短的即可，由图可知 Professionals and Managers 的白色区最短。

13. 退休职员花在肉、禽和海味（家用消费）上的费用约占他们总平均年收入（税前）的百分之几？

解：本题的正确答案为（A）。解答此题时需先参照表格，再参照图表。由表格中的数据可知，肉、禽和海味占退休职员的家用消费的比例为：

$$\frac{23}{23+29+14}=\frac{23}{66}$$

由图表可知,家用消费占年收入(税前)的比例为 21%,所以肉、禽和海味占年收入(税前)的比例为:

$$\frac{23}{66} \times 21\% \approx 7\%$$

Question 14 refers to the following table.

CONSUMER COMPLAINTS RECEIVED BY THE CIVIL AERONAUTICS BOARD

Category	1980 (percent)	1981 (percent)
Flight problems	20.0%	22.1%
Baggage	18.3	21.8
Customer service	13.1	11.3
Oversales of seats	10.5	11.8
Refund problems	10.1	8.1
Fares	6.4	6.0
Reservations and ticketing	5.8	5.6
Tours	3.3	2.3
Smoking	3.2	2.9
Advertising	1.2	1.1
Credit	1.0	0.8
Special passengers	0.9	0.9
Other	6.2	5.3
Total Number of Complaints	100.0% 22,988	100.0% 13,278

14. If the circle graphs below (drawn to scale) represent total consumer complaints for 1980, which graph shows a shaded sector that corresponds to Flight problems and Refund problems combined?

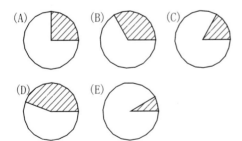

14. 标题:民用航空委员会收到的消费者投诉

若下面的饼图(按比例)代表 1980 年的消费者投诉,哪一图的阴影区所显示比例对应 Flight 问题和 Refund 问题之和?

解: 本题的正确答案为(B)。从题干的表格中,很容易找出 1980 年 Flight 问题占总问题的 20.0%,Refund 问题占总问题的 10.1%,总计占 30.1%。若用饼图来表示该数据,则扇形区域的圆心角应为 120°左右,显然只有(B)图正确。

Questions 15 refers to the following graphs.

DOMESTIC AIR CARRIERS: OPERATING REVENUES.
MILES FLOWN, AND NUMBER OF PASSENGERS CARRIED.
1960 TO 1975

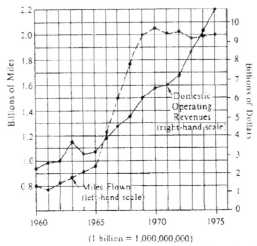
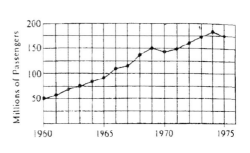

(1 billion = 1,000,000,000)

Note: Graphs drawn to scale

15. In 1969 what was the ratio of dollars of domestic operating revenues to miles flown?

   (A) $\frac{4}{1}$ (B) $\frac{3}{1}$ (C) $\frac{3}{2}$

   (D) $\frac{2}{3}$ (E) $\frac{1}{4}$

15. 标题：1960 年到 1975 年国内航班的营业收入，飞行里程和载客人数

1969 年国内航班的营业收入（以美元计）与飞行里程（以英里计）的比是多少？

解：本题的正确答案为(B)。从第一张图中查得 1969 年 Billions of Dollars = 6，Billions of Miles = 2.0，所以有 $\frac{6}{2}$ = 3。

Question 16 refers to the following graphs.

FEDERAL BUDGET OUTLAYS OF THE UNITED STATES
FOR MILITARY EXPENDITURES, 1966—1979

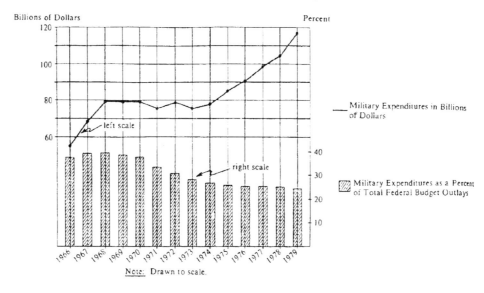

Note: Drawn to scale.

WORLDWIDE MILITARY EXPENDITURES: 1968 TO 1977

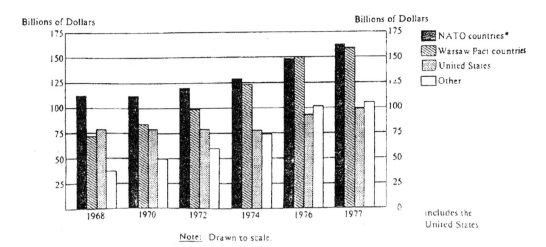

Note: Drawn to scale.

16. In 1977, federal budget outlays for the United States totaled approximately how many billion dollars?

(A) 200
(B) 300
(C) 400
(D) 500
(E) 600

16. 此题参照上图信息：

标题：1966—1979 年美国联邦预算军需开支

1977 年，美联邦预算经费总计是多少亿美元？

解： 本题的正确答案为（C）。题干给出的第一幅图中靠下面的的柱状图采用右侧标度，表示军需开销占总预算的百分比，靠上面的曲线，采用左侧的标度，表示实际的军需费用是多少亿。1977 年军费约为 $100 billions，约占总预算的 25％，所以总预算约为 100÷25％＝400 billions。

Question 17 refers to the following graphs.

PERCENT CONTRIBUTED TO PROFITS BY EACH OF THE
6 DIVISIONS P THRU U OF COMPANY Y FOR 1979 AND 1980

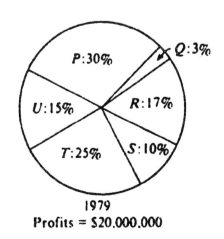

1979
Profits = $20,000,000

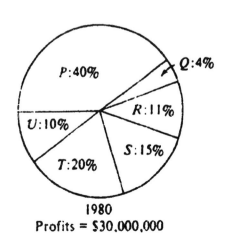

1980
Profits = $30,000,000

17. In 1980 what was the average of the amounts contributed to profits by Division U and Division T?

(A) $1,000,000   (B) $1,500,000
(C) $3,000,000   (D) $4,500,000
(E) $6,500,000

17. 标题：1979 年和 1980 年 Y 国的 6 个区（从 P 区到 U 区）上缴利润的百分比

1980 年 U 区和 T 区上缴利润的平均额是多少？

解：本题的正确答案为（D）。由第二个图可知，1980 年 U 和 T 上缴利润的百分比分别为：10% 和 20%，因此两者的平均值为（10% + 20%）× $30,000,000/2 = $4,500,000。

Questions 18—20 refer to the following chart and information.

LAST WEEK'S TOTAL HOURS WORKED AND HOURLY WAGES FOR THE CASHIERS AT MARKET X

Cashier	Hourly Wage	Total Hours Worked
P	$4.25	40
Q	4.75	32
R	5.00	26
S	5.50	25
T	5.50	22

Note: Last week no more than two cashiers worked at any one time, no cashier worked more than 12 hours on the same day, and on each day each cashier worked continuously.

问题 18—20 参照上述信息：

表头题目：上周市场 X 中的出纳员的总工作小时数及其每小时的工资。

注：上周任何时候工作的出纳员的人数都不会超过 2 人，每个出纳员同一天工作都不超过 12 小时，且每天出纳员的工作都是持续不断的。

18. On Saturday of last week, Market X was open for 15 hours and exactly four cashiers worked. What was the greatest possible amount that the market could have paid in cashiers' wages for that day?

(A) $132.00   (B) $157.50
(C) $161.25   (D) $163.00
(E) $165.00

18. 在上周六，市场 X 开业 15 小时，并且仅有 4 名出纳员工作，问那一天市场付给出纳员最大的工资量是多少？

解：本题的正确答案是（C）。问最大可能的工资量，则使工资高的出纳员工作的时间尽可能地长，且任何时候都是 2 人同时工作，因此应使 S 和 T 各工作 12 小时，R 和 Q 各工作 3 小时，工资量为：

(5.5 + 5.5) × 12 + (5 + 4.75) × 3 = 161.25

19. If Market X is open 96 hours per week, for how many hours last week were two cashiers working at the same time?

(A) 49   (B) 48   (C) 36

19. 若市场 X 每周开业 96 小时，问上一周两个出纳员同时工作的小时数是多少？

解：本题的正确答案是（A）。出纳员工作总小时数为：

(D) 24   (E) 12

20. If Cashier S's hourly wage were to increase by 10 percent and S's weekly hours were to decrease by 10 percent from last week's total hours, what would be the change, if any, in S's total weekly wage?

(A) An increase of $1.3

(B) An increase of $0.55

(C) No change

(D) A decrease of $0.55

(E) A decrease of $1.37

$$40+32+26+25+22=145$$

出纳员同时工作的小时数为：

$$145-96=49 \text{ 小时}$$

20. 若出纳员 S 的每小时工资增长 10%,并且 S 每周的工作小时数比上一周的总数下降 10%,若 S 的每周总工资有所变化的话,问其变化是多少?

解：本题的正确答案为(E)。S 上周的每小时工资为 $5.5/小时,则增长后的工资为

$$5.5\times(1+10\%)=6.05$$

而 S 工作小时数比上周下降 10%则 S 共工作了：

$$25\times(1-10\%)=22.5$$

则 S 总工资为：

$$22.5\times6.05=136.125$$

所以工资的变化为：

$$5.5\times25-136.125=1.375$$

Questions 21—22 refer to the following graphs.

RETAIL SALES OF NEW CARS IN THE UNITED STATES, 1970—1983

(in millions)

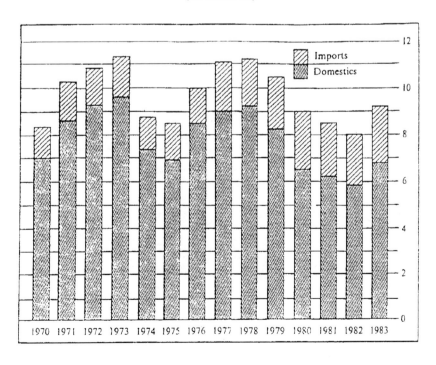

HOW THE 1983 RETAIL SALES OF NEW CARS IN THE UNITED STATES WERE DIVIDED

(100％＝9.16 million)

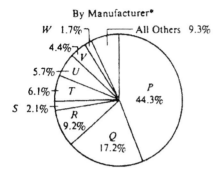

By Manufacturer*

W 1.7%
4.4% V
5.7% U
6.1% T
S 2.1%
R 9.2%
Q 17.2%
P 44.3%
All Others 9.3%

*Domestic: P, Q, R, and S
Japanese: T, U, and V
West German: W

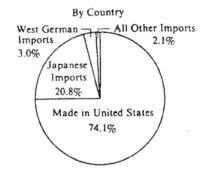

By Country

West German Imports 3.0%
All Other Imports 2.1%
Japanese Imports 20.8%
Made in United States 74.1%

Note: Drawn to scale.

21. For the year shown in which the total number of new cars sold was less than the number of new domestic cars sold the previous year，approximately how many fewer new domestic cars were sold than in the previous year?

(A) 500,000

(B) 1,000,000

(C) 1,600,000

(D) 2,200,000

(E) 3,000,000

22. Approximately what percent of the new domestic cars sold retail in the United States in 1983 were manufactured by Company Q?

(A) 10％   (B) 12％   (C) 15％

(D)17％   (E) 23％

21. 21—22 题参照上图信息：

标题：1970—1983 美国新汽车的零售情况（单位为百万）

在图中销售的新车总数比前一年销售的新国产车数少的那一年,大约比前一年少销售多少辆新国产车?

解: 本题的正确答案为（D）。题目中的"total number of new cars"指包括新进口车和新国产车在内的所有车。从题干中的矩形图中不难发现 1974 年满足题设条件,从此图中可以读出,1973 年新国产车的零售量约为 9.6 million 辆,1974 年新国产车的零售量约为 7.4 million 辆,两者差值约为 2.2 million。

22. 1983 年在美国零售的新国产车大约有百分之几是 Q 公司生产的?

解: 本题的正确答案为(E)。解答此题的信息依赖于第一个饼图。由此图可以看出,在美国零售的新车中,新国产车主要由 P、Q、R 和 S 四家公司制造,由图可得:

Q 公司的车占新国产车的比例

＝17.2％/（17.2％＋44.3％＋9.2％＋2.1％）＝23.6％。

Question 23—25 refer to the following distribution.

TEST SCORES FOR A CLASS OF

8 JUNIORS AND 12 SENIORS

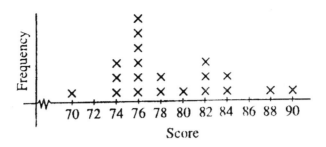

23. The median score for the class is

(A) 76

(B) 77

(C) 78

(D) 79

(E) 80

24. If 5 points were added to each score，which of the following would NOT be affected?

(A) The highest score

(B) The mean for all scores

(C) The median for the seniors' scores

(D) The mode for the juniors' scores

(E) The standard deviation for all scores

25. If the mean score for the juniors were known，which of the following could be calculated from the information given?

I　The range of the scores for the seniors

II　The median score for the juniors

III　The mean score for the seniors

(A) None

(B) I only

23. 23—25 题参照上述分布：

标题：一个由 8 名大学三年级学生和 12 名大学四年级学生组成的班级的考试分数

该班级考试分数的中数是多少？

解：本题的正确答案是（B）。该班级共有 20 名学生，考试分数的中数是指第 10 名和第 11 名学生分数的算术平均数。本题分布为从小到大，则第 10 人的分数为 76，第 11 人分数为 78，他们的算术平均数 $=\dfrac{76+78}{2}=77$。

24. 若每个分数加 5 分，下面哪一个数将不受加分的影响？

解：本题的正确答案是（E）。每个分数加 5 分后，最高分显然加了 5 分，平均分相应也高了 5 分，同理大学四年级学生分数的中数也增加 5 分。"mode"是指出现频率最高的数，本题为 76，加了 5 分之后，mode 将变为 81 分，根据标准方差的计算公式可知，"Standard deviation"在加分前后是不变的。

25. 若大学三年级学生的平均分数已知，那么根据给出的信息可以计算出下面哪一项？

I　大学四年级学生分数的值域

II　大学三年级学生分数的中数

III　大学四年级学生分数的平均值

解：本题的正确答案是（C）。I 无法判断，因为无法判断出四年级学生分数的最大值和最

(C) III only

(D) I and II

(E) II and III

Questions 26—27 refer to the following graphs.

小值;II 无法判断,因为无法知道每个大学三年级学生的分数;III 可以判断,已知大学三年级学生的平均数,然后用所有学生分数的和减去大学三年级学生的平均数与 8 的积,最后再除以 12 即可得到大学四年级学生分数的平均值。

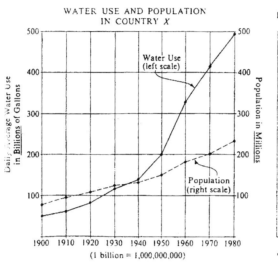

WATER USE AND POPULATION IN COUNTRY X

(1 billion = 1,000,000,000)

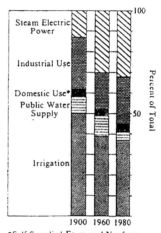

DISTRIBUTION OF WATER USES

*Self-Supplied Farm and Nonfarm

Note: Drawn to scale.

26. In 1970, if 5 percent of the water use was for domestic purposes, approximately what was the daily average number of gallons of water used per capita for domestic purposes?

(A) 105

(B) 50

(C) 20

(D) 10

(E) 5

26. 26—27 参照上述信息:

标题:X 国的水的利用和人口

在 1970 年,若 5% 的水用于家用,那么平均每人每天用大约多少加仑的水?

解: 本题的正确答案为(A)。求平均就要找出用水总量与用水人数。从本题题干的第一个图中可以找出这两个量,图中用实线表示每日水消费量,用虚线表示人口数;1970 年每日使用水的总量约为 420 Billion 加仑,人口为 220 Million,因而平均每人日用水量为:

$$420,000 \times 5\% / 200 = 105 \text{ 加仑}$$

27. If in 1900 the water use in Country K was the same as that in Country X, but increased at the constant rate of 3 billion gallons every year, then the two countries would again have had the same water use in approximately what year?

27. 若 1900 年 K 国的用水量与 X 国的相同,但 K 国以每年 3 billion 加仑的速度匀速增长,大约在哪年这两个国家的用水量会再次相同?

解: 本题的正确答案为(E)。结合本题第一图,1900 年 X 国和 K 国均消耗约 50 billion 加

(A) 1910　　(B) 1920　　(C) 1930

(D) 1940　　(E) 1950

仓的水;对于 K 国,每十年的用水量增加 30 billion 加仑,大约到 1950 年两国消耗水的量会再次相同,约为 200 billion 加仑的水。

Questions 28—29 refer to the following data.

STATE AND LOCAL GOVERNMENT EMPLOYMENT AND SALARY,
BY OCCUPATION AND SEX, 1977

By Occupation

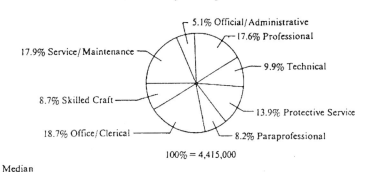

100% = 4,415,000

Median Annual Salary				Females As a Percent of the Total, By Occupation
Male	Female			
$12,390	$ 9,093	All Occupations		38.0
18,723	14,066	Official/Administrative		20.7
15,740	12,650	Professional		41.7
12,885	9,445	Technical		34.2
13,622	9,827	Protective Service		6.6
9,054	7,761	Paraprofessional		67.7
9,723	8,456	Office/Clerical		86.2
11,657	8,892	Skilled Craft		6.1
9,547	7,307	Service/Maintenance		17.4

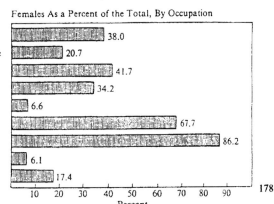

178

Percent

28. For state and local government employees, approximately what was the difference between the number of females employed as professionals and the number of females employed in service/maintenance occupations?

(A) 75,000

(B) 185,000

(C) 765,000

(D) 1,070,000

(E) 1,840,000

28. 28—29 参照下列信息:

标题:1977 年国家和地方政府的就业和薪水(按职业和性别分)

在国家和地方政府雇员中,作为专业人员被雇用的女性人数与作为服务人员被雇用的女性人数差大约为多少?

解: 本题的正确答案为(B)。根据题干的饼图,从事"professionals"和"service/maintenance"工作的职员比例分别为17.6%和17.9%,雇员总人数为4,415,000;而根据题干中的矩形图可知,在这两方面工作的妇女占女性雇员总人数的比例分别为 41.7%和17.4%,所以两者的差为(17.6%×41.7%—17.9%×17.4%)×4,415,000=186,516。

29. Which of the following statements about state and local government employees can be inferred from the data?

I Fewer than $\frac{1}{3}$ of those in paraprofessional occupations were males.

II There were more than 5 times the number of females in the technical occupations as in the skilled craft occupations.

III There were more than 6 times the number of females in the professional occupations as in the official/administrative occupations.

(A) I only　　　(B) II only

(C) I and II only (D) II and III only

(E) I，II and III

29. 下面哪些关于国家和地方政府雇员的叙述能从所给的数据中推出？

I 专业助理职位中的男性人数不到 $\frac{1}{3}$。

II 技术职位上的女性人数是熟练手艺职位上的女性人数的 5 倍多。

III 技术职位上的女性人数是女官员和女管理人员的 6 倍多。

解： 本题的正确答案为（E）。根据题干中的条形图可以判断，专业助理中女性占 67.7%，因而男性不足 1/3，所以 I 正确；根据题干中的饼图可知，技术职员约占 9.9%，熟练手艺职员约占 8.7%，而这两个职位的女性分别占 34.2% 和 6.1%，所以有 9.9% × 34.2%/(8.7% × 6.1%) ＝ 6.37，所以 II 正确；专业人员和行政管理人员分别占总体人数的 17.6% 和 5.1%，而女性在这两个职业中的比例分别为 41.7% 和 20.7%，因而 (17.6% × 41.7%)/(5.1 × 20.7%) ＝ 6.95，所以 III 正确。

Question 30 refer to the following graph.

AVERAGE * DAILY TOTAL AMOUNT OF SALES AND NUMBER OF SALES FOR STORE X

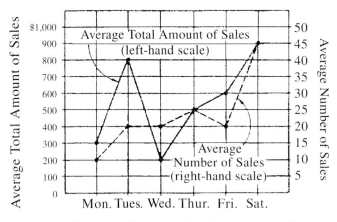

"Average" means "arithmetic mean."

Note: Drawn to scale.

30. During the first week of a certain month, how many more sales were made in Store X on Saturday than on Monday?

(A) 15

30. 标题：商店 X 的日平均销售额与日平均销售量在某月的第一个星期，X 商店在周六比周一多卖多少货？

(B) 25

(C) 30

(D) 35

(E) It cannot be determined from the

information given.

解：本题的正确答案为(E)。图中的虚线表示商品销售数量(Number of sales)在一周内的变化,单位在右侧标出。从图中可以看到,周六比周一多卖货的数量为 45-10=35。由此许多考生就认为(D)是正确答案。但是选(D)的考生疏忽了一点,那就是图中所给出的销售量的变化,只是取平均后的情况,并不能说明每个星期的销售量都如图中所示变化。因此本题无法根据图中的信息进行判断。

Question 31 refer to the following graph.

FAMILY X'S EXPENDITURES AS A PERCENT OF ITS GROSS ANNUAL INCOME *

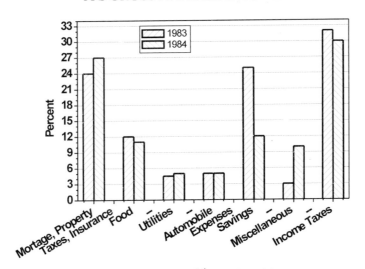

* In 1983, 100% = $50,000

In 1984, 100% = $45,000

Note: Drawn to scale.

31. Family X's gross income is the sum of Mr. X's income and Mrs. X's income. In 1983 Mr. and Mrs. X each had an income of $25,000. If Mr. X's income increased by 10 percent from 1983 to 1984, by what percent did Mrs. X's income decrease for the same period?

(A) 10% (B) 15% (C) 20%

(D) 25% (E) 30%

31. 标题：X 家庭的开支占其总收入的百分比

X 家庭的总收入是 Mr. X 和 Mrs. X 的收入之和。1983 年,Mr. X 和 Mrs. X 的收入均为 $25,000。若 Mr. X 在 1983 年至 1984 年收入增加 10%,那么 Mrs. X 的同期收入减少了百分之几?

解：本题的正确答案为(E)。根据图中下部小字可知 1984 年 Mr. X 和 Mrs. X 的收入之和为 $45,000,设 Mrs. X 的收入减少了 x%,由题意可得：

$$\$ 25,000 \times (1+10\%)+\$ 25,000\,(1-x\%)$$
$$= \$ 45,000 \Rightarrow x = 30$$

Question 32—34 refer to the following graph.

1977—1978 TEXTBOOK INVENTORY FOR SCHOOLS X AND Y
BY YEAR OF PURCHASE

（as a percent of the 1977—1978 inventory）

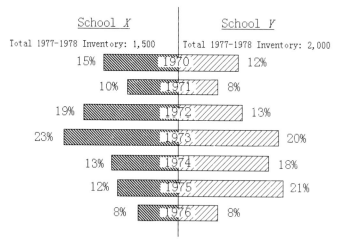

Note：All books were purchased new on July 1 of each year.

32. How many of the inventoried textbooks were purchased by the two schools combined during the years 1974，1975 and 1976?

(A) 495

(B) 940

(C) 1,020

(D) 1,435

(E) 2,800

32. 32—34 题参照上图：

标题：1977 至 1978 年度学校 X 和学校 Y 教科书的库存，按购买时间分类。（作为 1977—1978 年度库存的百分比）

注：所有书都在每年的 7 月 1 日购买

1974,1975,1976 年两个学校购买的库存教科书的总数是多少?

解：本题的正确答案是（D）。学校 X 在 1974, 1975,1976 年购买的图书总数为：

$$1500 \times (13\% + 12\% + 8\%) = 495$$

学校 Y 在 1974,1975,1976 年购买的图书总数为：

$$2000 \times (18\% + 21\% + 8\%) = 940$$

两个学校购买图书的总数 $= 495 + 940 = 1435$，所以（D）is correct。

33. If School X purchased 300 textbooks in 1971 and all of these textbooks either were counted in the inventory or had been discarded before the inventory, what percent of these textbooks had been discarded?

(A) 10%   (B) 20%   (C) 50%

(D) 80%   (E) 100%

34. Which of the following statements can be inferred from the graph?

I   School X has a smaller enrollment than School Y.

II   If the age of a book is the number of years since purchase, then the average (arithmetic mean) age of a book in the School Y inventory is less than that of a book in the School X inventory.

III   According to the inventory, School X and School Y purchased the same number of textbooks in 1976.

(A) None

(B) I only

(C) II only

(D) I and II

(E) II and III

33. 若学校 X 在 1971 年购买了 300 本教科书，且所有的这些教科书或者进入库存或者在进入库存前被废弃，那么被废弃的教科书占这些书的百分之几？

解： 本题的正确答案是(C)。1971 年学校 X 库存图书数目为：

$$1500 \times 10\% = 150$$

所以被废弃图书所占的百分比为：

$$(300 - 150) \div 300 = 50\%$$

34. 下面哪一句话可以从题目的图表中推断出来？

I   学校 X 的在册学生比学校 Y 的在册学生少；

II   若书的年龄为图书购买后的年数，那么学校 Y 库存图书的平均年龄比学校 X 库存图书的平均年龄小；

III   根据库存，学校 X 和学校 Y 在 1976 年购买的教科书的数目相同。

解： 本题的正确答案是(C)。由图表中图书的库存信息无法得到学校 X 与学校 Y 的学生的多少，所以 I 肯定不对；II 中涉及库存图书的平均年龄，学校 X 库存图书的平均年龄为：$8 \times 15\% + 7 \times 10\% + 6 \times 19\% + 5 \times 23\% + 4 \times 13\% + 3 \times 12\% + 2 \times 8\% = 5.23$，学校 Y 库存图书的平均书龄为：$8 \times 0.12\% + 7 \times 0.08\% + 6 \times 0.13\% + 5 \times 0.2\% + 4 \times 0.18\% + 3 \times 0.21\% + 2 \times 0.08\% = 3.91$，所以 II 一定正确，其实由图表也可观察到学校 X 的年龄比较大的图书所占的比例均大于学校 Y 的也可判断 II 是正确的；由两学校的库存总量不同，可推知 III 肯定不对。

Questions 35 refer to the following graphs.

HEALTH EXPENDITURES IN THE UNITED STATES,
1950 AND 1979

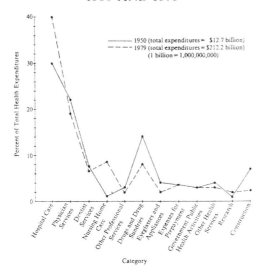

35. In 1979 for how many of the categories was the amount of health expenditures less than $21 billion?

(A) Two
(B) Three
(C) Nine
(D) Ten
(E) Twelve

35. 标题：1950 年和 1979 年美国的保健支出

在 1979 年有多少项的保健费用不到 $21 billion?

解：本题的正确答案为(D)。图中的虚线表示 1979 年的各项保健支出,由于 1979 年的总保健费用是 $212.2 billion,因此少于 $21 billion 项的支出,一定是那些与总支出的比不到 10% 的项,从图中可以发现,只有两项,即 Hospital Care 和 Physician Services 超出了总支出的 10%。所以共有 12−2 = 10 项的支出不到 $21 billion。

Questions 36 refer to the following graphs.

DISTRIBUTION OF EARNINGS AND REVENUES FOR COMPANY X, 1978−1983
ELECTRONIC AND NONELECTRONIC OPERATIONS
(1 billion＝1,000,000,000)

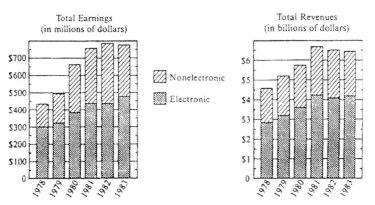

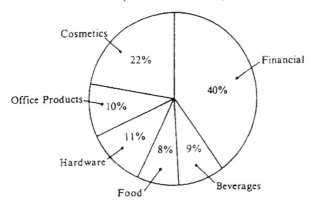

Distribution of Earnings from Nonelectronic Operations, 1983
(in millions of dollars)

Cosmetics 22%

Financial 40%

Office Products 10%

11%

Hardware

8% 9%

Food

Beverages

Note: Drawn to scale.

36. For the two years in which earnings from electronic operations were most nearly equal, the combined earnings from nonelectronic operations were most nearly

(A) $340 million   (B) $520 million
(C) $670 million   (D) $780 million
(E) $1,520 million

36. 标题：1978—1983 年 X 公司的电子经营和非电子经营的盈利与收入的分布

在电子经营的盈利非常相近的那两年,其非电子经营的盈利额的总和接近于

解：本题的正确答案为(C)。图中不同方向和不同密度的阴影柱图表示电子或非电子经营的盈利和收入。根据"Total Earnings"图,可以发现 1981 和 1982 两年的电子利润近似相等,由此可得这二年的非电子经营盈利约为：

$(760+780)-(440+440)=\$660$ million

Question 37 refer to the following data.

UNION MEMBERSHIP IN THE LABOR FORCE，1968—1980

Labor Force

Year	Workers (in millions)
1968	75.9
1970	78.6
1972	81.7
1974	85.9
1976	87.5
1978	94.4
1980	96.5

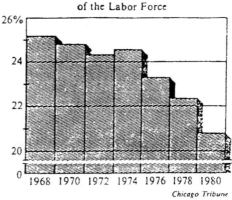

Union Membership as a Percent of the Labor Force

Chicago Tribune

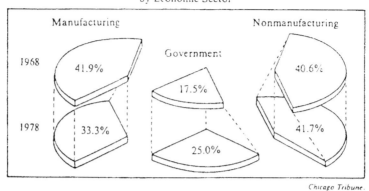

Distribution of Union Membership
by Economic Sector

Manufacturing
Government
Nonmanufacturing

1968 41.9%
1978 33.3%

17.5%
25.0%

40.6%
41.7%

Chicago Tribune.

Note: Drawn to scale.

37. From 1968 to 1980，the size of the labor force increased by approximately what percent?

(A) 20%

(B) 21%

(C) 27%

(D) 73%

(E) 80%

Question 38 refer to the following graph.

37. 标题：1968—1980 年劳动力中的工会成员

从 1968 至 1980 年,劳动力中工人的数量增长大约多少?

解：本题的正确答案为（C）。由题干中的有关 Labor Force 的表格可知,1968 年工人的数量为 75.9 million,1980 年工人的数量为 96.5 million,因而增长的比率为：

(96.5－75.9)/ 75.9＝27%

MEDIAN INCOME OF
COLLEGE GRADUATES VS. NONGRADUATES IN
REGIONS X AND Y

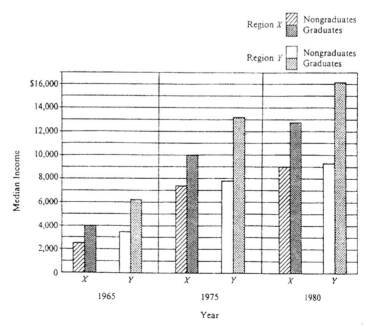

38. Of the following 1980 median-income ratios, the greatest was the ratio of the median incomes of

   (A) graduates in Region Y to graduates in Region X

   (B) nongraduates in Region Y to nongraduates in Region X

   (C) graduates in Region Y to nongraduates in Region Y

   (D) graduates in Region X to nongraduates in Region X

   (E) graduates in Region X to nongraduates in Region Y

38. 标题：X 地区和 Y 地区的中等收入的大学毕业生与非大学毕业生的对比

在 1980 年中等收入的比率中，下面哪些中等收入的比率最大？

解： 本题的正确答案为（C）。在 1980 年有四种不同的中等收入，若想让某两个的比值最大，自然需用收入最高的与收入最低的相比。由图可知，1980 年收入最高的是 Region Y 的 graduates，收入最低的是 Region X 的 Nongraduates。

Questions 39 refer to the following table.

UNITED STATES POPULATION

(official census 1890—1980)

Year	Population (in millions)	10-year Increase (in millions)	Year	Population (in millions)	10-year Increase (in millions)
1890	62.9		1940	131.7	8.9
1900	76.0	13.1	1950	150.7	19.0
1910	92.0	16.0	1960	179.3	28.6
1920	105.7	13.7	1970	103.2	23.9
1930	122.8	17.1	1980	223.9	20.7

39. If the percent increase in population from 1910 to 1920 had been approximately the same as the percent increase from 1900 to 1910, the 10-year increase, in millions, from 1910 to 1920, would have been approximately

   (A) 3

   (B) 6

   (C) 16

   (D) 19

   (E) 29

39. 标题：美国的人口（1890—1980 年官方的统计结果）

若 1910 年至 1920 年人口增长的百分数与 1900 至 1910 年人口增长的百分数相同，那么以百万为单位，从 1910 至 1920 年的十年期间人口大约会增长多少？

解： 本题的正确答案为（D）。从人口数据表中可知，1900 至 1910 年人口增长的百分比为：$\dfrac{16.0}{76.0} \times 100\%$，若按照这个比率计算，1910 至 1920 年人口的增长量为：

$$92.0 \times \frac{16.0}{76.0} = 19.37$$

Questions 40—41 refer to the following graph.

FOREIGN TRADE OF COUNTRY X, 1964—1980

(in United States dollars)

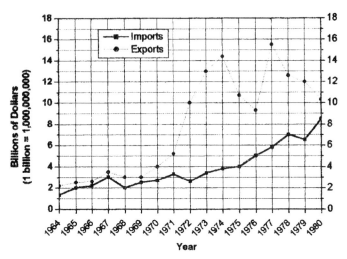

Note: Drawn to scale.

40. In 1974 the dollar value of imports was approximately what percent of the dollar value of exports?

(A) 4%

(B) 17%

(C) 27%

(D) 79%

(E) 367%

40. 40—41参照上图信息

标题：1964—1980 年 X 国的外贸（以美元计）

1974 年美元进口额大约是美元出口额的百分之几？

解：本题的正确答案为(C)。图中有一实一虚两条曲线，其中虚线代表出口额随年份的变化，实线代表进口额随年份的变化。由两条曲线可以看出，1974 年进口额约为 $3.8 billion，出口额约为 14.2 billion，因而进口额与出口额的百分比为：

$$3.8/14.2 \approx 27\%$$

41. If it were discovered that the import dollar amount shown for 1978 was incorrect and should have been $5.3 billion instead, then the average（arithmetic mean）import dollar amount per year for the 17 years would be how much less?

(A) $100 million   (B) $53 million

(C) $47 million   (D) $17 million

(E) $7 million

41. 若发现图中所示的 1978 年的进口额有误，正确值应为 53 亿美元，那么这 17 年进口额的（算术）平均值将会减少多少？

解：本题的正确答案为（A）。1978 年的进口额的正确值为 $5.3 billion，与图中所示的 $7 billion 相比，少了 1.7 billion，因此这将使 17 年的进口额的算术平均值减少量为：

$$1.7/17 = \$0.1 \text{ billion} = \$100 \text{ million}$$

Question 42 refer to the following graph.

INCOME AND EXPENDITURES OF AN INTERNATIONAL SERVICE AGENCY-YEAR X

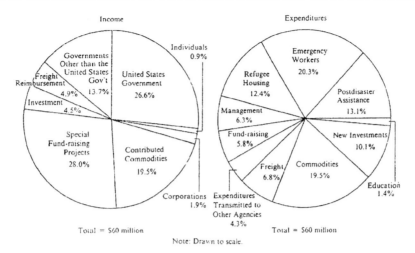

42. Of the following, the category that had expenditures most nearly equal to the average (arithmetic mean) expenditures per category was

(A) refugee housing

(B) emergency workers

(C) postdisaster assistance

(D) new investments

(E) commodities

42. 标题：X 年某国际服务机构的收入和支出

下列选项中，支出最接近各类支出的（算术）平均值的项目是

解：本题的正确答案为（D）。根据支出分布饼图可知该机构的支出项目共计有十种，因而每个项目的平均花费应占总体花费的 10%，由此可以得出新投资（New Investment）一项的 10.1% 的支出与平均支出最为接近。

Questions 43—44 refer to the following graphs. All references to "dollars" in these questions are the 1985 dollars referred to in the graphs.

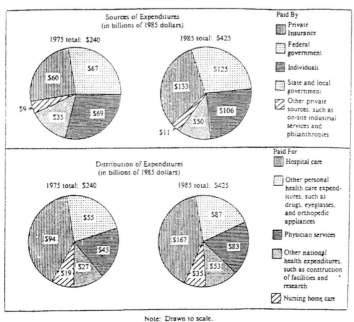

43. In 1985 approximately what percent of all medical expenditures was paid for physician services?

(A) 20%

(B) 25%

(C) 30%

(D) 35%

(E) 40%

43. 标题：1975 和 1985 年美国的医疗保健总支出。在 1985 年医生的劳务费大约占总医疗费用的百分之多少？

解：本题的正确答案为（A）。根据 1985 年的支出分布图（Distribution of Expenditures）可知，1985 年各项费用的总支出为 $425 billion，医生的劳务费（physician services）为 $83billion，因而占总支出的百分比为 $83/$425≈20%。

44. What was the approximate percent increase in total medical expenditures from 1975 to 1985?

(A) 44%　　(B) 77%　　(C) 85%

(D) 88%　　(E) 135%

44. 从 1975 年到 1985 年，总的医疗费用增长了大约百分之几？

解：本题的正确答案为（B）。由医疗费用来源图上的说明文字可知，1970 年总的医疗支出是 $240，1985 年总的医疗支出是 $425，所以增长的百分比为（425 － 240）/ 240 = 77.08%。

Questions 45—46 refer to the following graph.

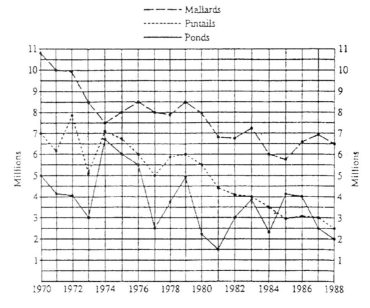

THE NUMBER OF PONDS AND THE POPULATIONS OF TWO SPECIES OF DUCKS (MALLARDS AND PINTAILS) IN A REGION OF NORTH AMERICA: 1970 – 1988

45. By approximately how many million did the mallard population decrease from 1970 to 1988

45. 标题：1970－1988 年北美某地区的两种鸭子(野鸭和长尾凫)数量和池塘数量

1970 至 1988 年野生鸭的数量大约减了几

(A) 0.6　　(B) 2.8　　(C) 3.6

(D) 4.3　　(E) 7.0

46. In 1984 the population of pintails was approximately what fraction of the mallard population?

(A) $\dfrac{5}{7}$　　(B) $\dfrac{7}{12}$　　(C) $\dfrac{1}{3}$

(D) $\dfrac{1}{4}$　　(E) $\dfrac{3}{20}$

百万?

解：本题的正确答案为(D)。野鸭(mallard)的数量随时间的变化在图中用长虚线表示。根据此曲线可知 1970 年野鸭数量约 10.8million,1988 年为 6.5 million,因而其数量约减少了 4.3 million。

46. 在 1984 年长尾凫的数量大约是野鸭数量的几分之几?

解：本题的正确答案为(B)。由图可知,在 1984 年,长尾凫的数量是 3.5 million 只,而野鸭的数量为 6 million 只,所以长尾凫的数量与野鸭的数量的比为：$3.5/6 = \dfrac{7}{12}$。

Questions 47—49 refer to the following graph.

EXISTING AND NEW ONE-FAMILY HOMES* SOLD IN THE UNITED STATES FROM 1970 TO 1982 AND THE MEDIAN SALE PRICE FOR SELECTED YEARS

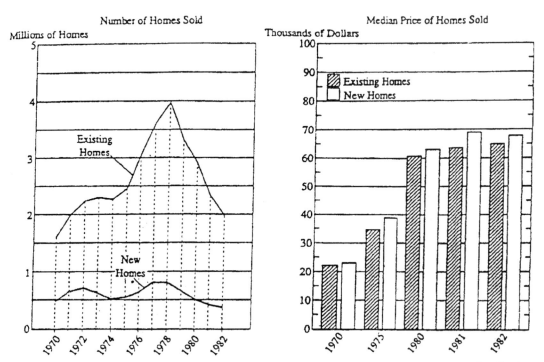

* All references to homes in the data and test questions should be interpreted as one-family homes.

Note：Graphs drawn to scale.

47. For which of the following years was there an increase over the previous year in the number of existing homes sold, but a decrease in the number of new homes sold?

    (A) 1972   (B) 1973   (C) 1974

    (D) 1977   (E) 1979

47. 标题：1970－1982 年美国新旧独户房的销售以及这些房子在选定年份的中等价格

下列哪一年的旧房销售数量比前一年有所增长,而新房销售数量却比前一年有所减少?

解：本题的正确答案为(B)。根据房子的销售量与年份的关系图(Number of Homes Sold),可知 1972－1973 年,旧房(Existing Homes)的销售曲线上升,而新房(New Homes)的销售曲线下降,因此 1973 年满足题目的条件。

48. In the year shown in which the median price of existing homes sold was closest to the median price of new homes sold, approximately how many million existing homes were sold?

    (A) 1.2   (B) 1.6   (C) 2.0

    (D) 2.4   (E) 2.8

48. 在图中,旧房销售价格的中数与新房最接近的那一年,大约销售了几百万座旧房?

解：本题的正确答案为(B)。根据房子的中等售价图(Median Price of Homes Sold)可以发现,旧房与新房的中等销售价格在 1970 年近似相等,该年份销售的旧房数量需根据房子的销售量与年份的关系图(Number of Homes Sold)来确定,由此图可知 1970 年旧房的销售量约为 1.6 million。

49. In 1977 the number of existing homes sold was approximately how many times the number of new homes sold?

    (A) 3

    (B) 3.5

    (C) 4.5

    (D) 5.5

    (E) 6

49. 1977 年,旧房销售量是新房销售量的多少倍?

解：本题的正确答案为(C)。根据"Median Price of Homes Sold"图可知,1977 年旧房的销售量约为 3.5 million,新房的约为 0.75 million,因而旧房的销售量是新房的约 3.5/0.78≈4.5 倍。

Question 50 refer to the following graph and table.

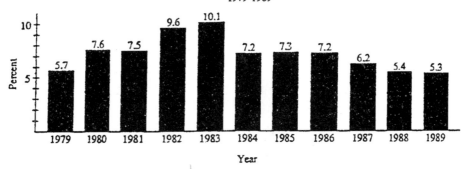

UNITED STATES JUNE UNEMPLOYMENT RATES AS A PERCENT OF WORK FORCE
1979-1989

UNEMPLOYMENT DATA FOR THE ELEVEN STATES WITH THE LARGEST POPULATIONS IN 1989

State	Unemployment Rate May (as a percent of state work force)	Unemployment Rate June (as a percent of state work force)	Number of Unemployed June (in thousands)
California	5.5	5.6	797
New York	5.3	5.0	439
Texas	5.9	6.1	502
Illinois	5.7	5.5	325
Pennsylvania	4.6	4.0	239
Florida	6.4	6.1	384
Ohio	5.4	5.6	307
Michigan	6.7	7.3	339
New Jersey	3.0	4.2	165
North Carolina	3.7	3.6	124
Massachusetts	3.6	4.0	125

50. The change in the unemployment rate in the United States from June 1986 to June 1987 was how many times the change in the unemployment rate from June 1988 to June 1989?

(A) 0.01　　(B) 0.1　　(C) 1.0

(D) 10.0　　(E) 100.0

50. 标题：1979—1989 年美国 6 月份劳动力中的失业百分比

美国 1986 年 6 月至 1987 年 6 月失业率的变化是 1988 年 6 月至 1989 年 6 月失业率变化的多少倍？

解： 本题的正确答案为（D）。题干中的柱状图显示了各年 6 月份的失业率,从图中可以看出 1986、1987、1988 和 1989 四年 6 月份的失业率分别为 7.2％、6.2％、5.4％和 5.3％,由此 1986 至 1987 年失业率的变化为 1％, 1988 至 1989 年失业率的变化 0.1％,因而前者的变化率是后者的 1％/0.1％＝10 倍。

Questions 51—52 refer to the following graph.

PERCENT RETURN ON SHAREHOLDERS' EQUITY
MANUFACTURER X VERSUS ALL UNITED STATES MANUFACTURERS

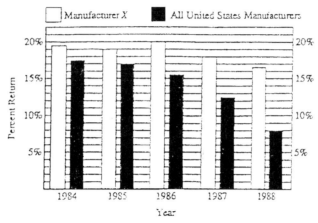

Note: Graph drawn to scale.

51. For the year shown, other than 1987, in which the percent return on shareholders' equity for Manufacturer X was most nearly equal to that for 1987, what was the percent return for all United States manufacturers?

(A) 8%   (B) $12\frac{1}{2}\%$ (C) $15\frac{1}{2}\%$

(D) 17%   (E) $17\frac{1}{2}\%$

52. Which of the following statements can be supported by the data in the graph?

I   The percent return on shareholders equity for all United States manufacturers decreased from 1984 to 1988 by less than 10 percentage points.

II   A return on shareholder' equity of more than 7 percent was achieved by each United States manufacturer in 1988.

III   The shareholders' equity for Manufacturer X was greater in 1987 than in 1988.

51. 标题：制造商 X 的股东的普通股盈利百分比与美国所有其他制造商的对比

除 1987 年的其他年份中，制造商 X 的股东的普通股盈利百分比最接近 1987 年的那一年，所有美国厂商普通股盈利的百分比是多少？

解： 本题的正确答案为（D）。图中 X 厂商的普通股盈利百分比是用白色柱状图来表示的，从图中可以看出与 1987 年的盈利最为接近的年份是 1985 年，该年份全美厂商普通股盈利的百分比为 17%。

52. 图中的数据支持下面哪些陈述？

I   1984 至 1988 年全美厂商股东的普通股盈利率的下降不到 10 个百分点。

II   1988 年每个美国制造商的股东的普通股的盈利都超过了 7 个百分点。

III   X 厂商的股东在 1987 年所拥有的普通股数多于 1988 年的。

解： 本题的正确答案为（A）。对于此类题目，考生只能根据图表逐条进行判断。由图可知 1984 年全美厂商的盈利率约为 17.5，而 1988 年的盈利率约为 8%，所以其盈利率的下降不超过 10%；因为柱状图只给出全美厂商整体股票的盈利率，没有给出单个厂商

(A) I only (B) II only

(C) I and III only (D) II and III only

(E) I, II, and III

的具体信息,所以无法判断每个厂商的股票盈利率,同样也无法确定每年股票持有者的股票数量,因此 II 和 III 无法从图中推出。

Questions 53—55 refer to the following chart.

ENROLLMENT FACULTY SIZE, FACULTY SALARY,
AND TUITION AT COLLEGE R FOR SELECTED YEARS

	1960	1970	1980
Number of Students Enrolled	1,490	1,600	1,790
Number of Faculty members	166	160	—
Ratio of students to Faculty	—	$\frac{10}{1}$	$\frac{11}{1}$
Average* Faculty Salary	—	$14,360	$28,400
Tuition per Student	$1,400	$2,000	$3,700
Total Faculty Salaries	$1,245,000	—	$4,629,200
Income from Tuition	$2,086,000	$3,200,000	—

* Arithmetic mean

53. If the increase in the number of students enrolled from 1950 to 1960 was half the increase from 1960 to 1970, what was the student enrollment in 1950?

(A) 745

(B) 1,340

(C) 1,380

(D) 1,435

(E) 1,545

53. 标题:学院 R 在选定年份的在册职工人数、职工的工资以及学生的学费

若 1950 至 1960 年注册学生人数的增长量是 1960 至 1970 年增长量的一半,则 1950 年注册学生人数是多少?

解:本题的正确答案为(D)。从表格中可以看出,1970 年的注册学生人数比 1960 年的增长了 1600－1490＝110 人,因此 1960 年比 1950 年多注册了 110/2＝55 人,所以 1950 年注册学生人数为 1,490－55＝1,435 人。

54. The increase in tuition per student from 1970 to 1980 was approximately how many times as great as the increase from 1960 to 1970?

(A) 2 (B) $2\frac{1}{2}$ (C) 3

(D) 3 (E) 4

54. 1970 至 1980 年每个学生的学费增长额大约是 1960 至 1970 年的多少倍?

解:本题的正确答案为(C)。由表可知,1960、1970 和 1980 三年每个学生的学费分别为 $1400,$2000 和 $3700,因此增长倍数为($3700－$2000)/($2000－$1400)≈3。

55. If the total amount of faculty salaries in 1980 was paid from tuition income, approximately how much of each student's

55. 若 1980 年教职工的所有工资都由学费收入支付,大约每个学生的学费的多少被用于支付教职工的工资?

tuition was used to pay faculty salaries?

(A) \$160　　(B) \$1,100

(C) \$1,250　(D) \$2,600

(E) \$3,700

解：本题的正确答案为(D)。教职工的工资总额为 \$4,629,200，平均分到每个学生身上约为：

$$4,629,200 \div 1790 \approx \$2,586 \approx \$2,600。$$

Questions 56—57 refer to the following map.

A MAP OF FUNNY BROOK FARM SHOWING ELEVATIONS (in feet), AND LAND-USE BOUNDARIES (fences)

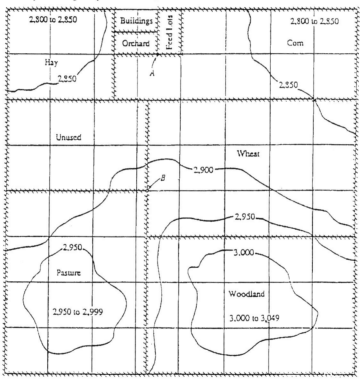

Note: Map drawn to scale.

56. The land at the farm's highest elevation is used for which of the following

(A) Hay and corn　　(B) Orchard

(C) Pasture　　　　(D) Woodland

(E) Wheat

56. 标题：乐趣小溪农场的海拔图及土地使用分界线(用栅栏表示)

农场上海拔最高的土地用于下面哪个项目？

解：本题的正确答案为(D)。图中的曲线表示等高线，等高线上的数值表示海拔高度，从图中可以看出海拔最高是 3000—3049 米的 Woodland。

57. Approximately how many acres are used to grow hay?

(A) 40   (B) 45   (C) 50

(D) 60   (E) 75

57. 草地的面积大约有多少英亩?

解：本题的正确答案为(C)。由图中的说明文字可知,每一个篱笆线分开的区域都具有不同的用途,从图中可以看出草种在图中的左上角,一共占用了 5 个网格的面积,每一小网格代表 10 英亩,因此草地的面积约为 50 亩。

Questions 58—59 refer to the following data.

HOUSEHOLD DISCRETIONARY INCOME BY HEAD OF HOUSEHOLDS AGE-GROUP

Head of Household's Age-Group (in years)	Number of Households (in thousands) with Discretionary Income	Percent of Households with discretionary Income	Average * Household Income	Average * Discretionary Income per Household
15 to 24	972	18.7%	$30,124	$7,790
25 to 29	2,646	27.4	36,618	9.130
30 to 34	3,419	31.5	40,067	10.919
35 to 39	3,319	33.0	43,585	12.405
40 to 44	2,605	30.5	47,891	13.999
45 to 49	2,299	33.4	49,968	14.448
50 to 54	2,008	31.8	49,079	13.550
55 to 59	2,252	35.0	44,906	14.584
60 to 64	1,848	28.8	44,262	14.356
65 to 69	1,523	25.0	38,968	12.921
70 and older	2,946	22.8	32,344	11.015
All age Groups	25,869	28.9%	$41,940	$12,332

* Based on households with discretionary income.

58. For which age-group was the percent of households with discretionary income most nearly equal to $\frac{2}{9}$?

(A) 15 to 24   (B) 25 to 29

(C) 40 to 44   (D) 60 to 64

(E) 70 and older

58. 标题：家主位于不同年龄组的家庭的自由收入哪一年龄组拥有自由收入的家庭的比例最接近$\frac{2}{9}$?

解：本题的正确答案为(E)。表中第三列是拥有自由收入的家庭所占的百分比,因为$\frac{2}{9} \approx$ 22.2%,所以很显然 70 岁以上年龄组的家庭最接近于$\frac{2}{9}$。

59. Which of the following statements can be inferred from the data?

I   Each household in the age-group 15 to 24 had at least $7,500 in discretionary income.

59. 从表中数据能推出下列哪项陈述?

I   每一个位于 15 至 24 岁年龄组的家庭至少都有 $7,500 的自由收入。

II   在列出的年龄组中,55 至 59 岁年龄组有自由收入的家庭比例最大。

II   Of the age groups listed, the age-group 55 to 59 had the greatest percent of households with discretionary income.

III   For the age-group 50 to 54, average discretionary income per household was less than one-fourth of the average household income.

(A) II only

(B) III only

(C) I and II only

(D) II and III only

(E) I, II, and III

III   对 50 至 54 岁年龄组,每户平均的自由收入少于每户平均收入的 1/4。

解:本题的正确答案为(A)。由表中的数据可知,15 至 24 年龄组的家庭平均自由收入为 $7,790,但这不能表明任一家庭的平均自由收入都超过 $7,790;对于 II,从表中可以查到比例 35% 是最高的,这一值对应于 55 至 59 岁年龄组;而对于 50 至 54 年龄组,每户平均收入为 $49,079,平均自由收入为 $13,550,大于每人收入的 $\frac{1}{4}$,因此 III 不正确。

Question 60 refer to the following graphs.

TYPE OF WORK SCHEDULING IN 300 SURVEYED COMPANIES

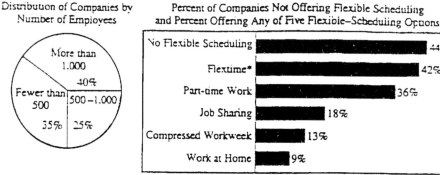

60. How many companies offered the compressed-workweek option?

(A) 39   (B) 30   (C) 27

(D) 13   (E) 9

60. 标题:300 家被调查公司的工作计划的类型
多少公司提供压缩工作周选择?

解:本题的正确答案为(A)。根据图表中的条形图可知,提供压缩工作周选择的公司所占的百分比为 13%,而公司总数为 300,因而提供这种选择的公司为 300×13% = 39 家。

DISTRIBUTION OF THE UNITED STATES POPULATION
BY AGE AND SEX, 1980 AND 1986

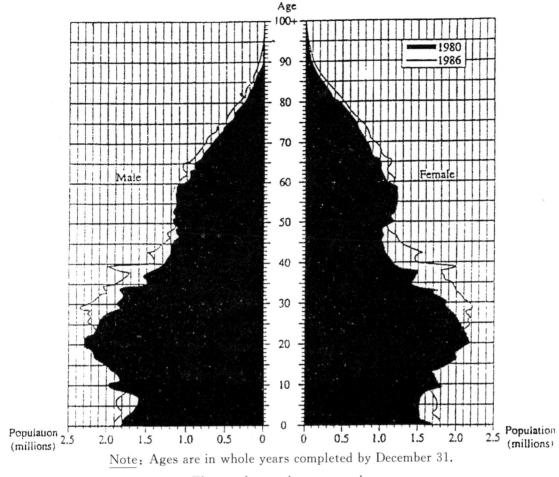

Note: Ages are in whole years completed by December 31.

The graphs are drawn to scale.

61. In 1980 the total population of females from 50 to 59 years old, inclusive, was closest to

(A) 1,200,000

(B) 1,400,000

(C) 12,000,000

(D) 14,000,000

(E) 20,000,000

61. 标题：1980 年和 1986 年美国人中按年龄和性别的分布

在 1980 年 50 至 59 岁（包括 50 和 59 岁）的女性总人口接近于

解： 本题的正确答案为（C）。图中的右侧为妇女的人口随年龄的分布，其中粗线表示 1980 年妇女的人口分布曲线，从此曲线上可以看出 50 至 59 岁的每一年龄妇女人口数目大约均在 1.2 million，因此这一年龄段的妇女人口总计约为 12 million。

62. The "combined age" of a group of people is the sum of the ages of all of the people in

62. 一群人的总年龄是这群人中所有人的年龄和。在 1986 年，下面哪群人的总年龄最大？

the group. Which of the following groups had the greatest combined age in 1986?

(A) 20-year-old males

(B) 20-year-old females

(C) 60-year-old males

(D) 60-year-old females

(E) 80-year-old females

解：本题的正确答案为(D)。从图中找出每群人的人数，然后再乘以他们的人数，最后再比较大小。由图可知：20 岁的男性和女性人数均约为 2.2 million，因而这两群人的总年龄约为 44 million 岁；60 岁男性约为1.1 million，因而总年龄为 66 million 岁；60 岁女性约为 1.2 million，因而总年龄为 72 million岁；而 80 岁女性约为 0.5 million，总年龄为 40million 岁。综上所述 60 岁女性的总年龄最大。

Question 63 refer to the following graphs.

INCOME OF ORGANIZATION X IN 1990, BY SOURCE

(total income = $43,000,000)

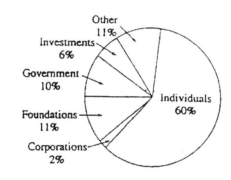

63. From 1989 to 1990, if annual membership dues increased from $12 to $15, what was the approximate percent increase in the total dollar amount generated from membership dues?

(A) 50%　　(B) 40%　　(C) 25%

63. 标题：1990 年协会 X 的收入(按来源分,总收入等于 $43,000,000)

从 1989 年至 1990 年,若年会员费从 $12 增至 $15,那么会费的总数约增长百分之几？

解：本题的正确答案为(A)。从柱状图中可以看出,1989 年约有会员 1,000,000 人,1990

(D) 20%   (E) 5%

年约有会员 1,200,000 人,因此 1990 年会

费增长的百分比约为:

$(1,200,000 \times 15 - 1,000,000 \times 12)/$

$(1,000,000 \times 12) = 50\%$

Question 64 refer to the following graph.

PER CAPITA HEALTH EXPENDITURES OF SEVEN COUNTRIES, 1989

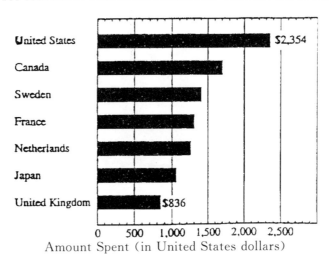

Amount Spent (in United States dollars)

Note: Drawn to scale.

64. If the population of the United States was approximately 2.5×10^8 in 1989, what was the approximate total health expenditure, in dollars, for the United States that year?

(A) 3×10^8 (B) 6×10^8

(C) 5×10^{10} (D) 4×10^{11}

(E) 6×10^{11}

64. 标题:1989 年,七个国家的人均保健支出

若 1989 年美国人口约为 2.5×10^8,以美元为单位,美国该年的保健总支出约是多少?

解: 本题的正确答案为(E)。条形图中条的长短表示各国人均保健支出的多少,从图中可以得知,美国 1989 年的人均保健支出为 $2,354,所以其总支出为:

$$\$2,354 \times 2.5 \times 10^8 \approx \$5.89 \times 10^{11}.$$

Question 65 refer to the following graph.

JULY ELECTRICITY USAGE FOR THE SMYTHE HOUSEHOLD

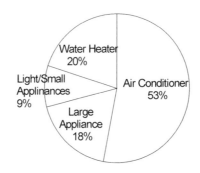

Electricity used: 800 kilowatt-hours

65. The electricity used by the water heater was measured separately and its cost per kilowatt-hour was one-half the cost per kilowatt-hour of the rest of the electricity used. The cost of the electricity used by the water heater was most nearly what fraction of the total cost of all the electricity used?

(A) $\dfrac{1}{11}$ (B) $\dfrac{1}{9}$

(C) $\dfrac{1}{8}$ (D) $\dfrac{1}{5}$

（E）It cannot be determined from the information given.

65. 标题：Smythe 家庭 7 月份的用电分布

热水器用的电是分开计算的，它消耗的电的每千瓦/时的价格是其他用电设备的一半。热水器的电费占总电费的比例最接近于下面哪一项？

解： 本题的正确答案为（B）。由题干中的饼图可知热水器的用电量占总用电量的 20%，而其他各项占总用电量的 80%，设热水器的电费为 $\$X$ 千瓦/小时，则其他各项的电费为 $\$2X$ 千瓦/小时，由此可知热水器的电费占总电费的比例为：

$$\frac{20\% X}{20\% X + 80\% \times 2X} = \frac{1}{9}$$

Questions 66—67 refer to the following graphs.

DISTRIBUTION OF FUNDS BY CHARITY X

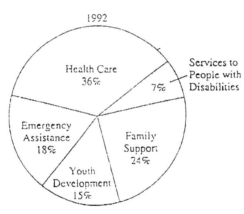

Total Funds Distributed: $2.54 million

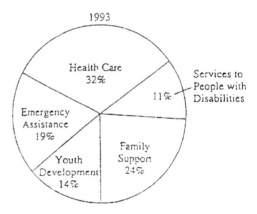

Total Funds Distributed: $2.93 million

66. The funds distributed in 1992 for youth developments were approximately

(A) $38,000 (B) $170,000

(C) $380,000 (D) $450,000

(E) $1,700,000

66. 标题：慈善团体 X 的资金分配

在 1992 年所分发的青年发展基金是多少？

解： 本题的正确答案为（C）。由 1982 年的资金分配图可知，青年发展基金占总资金的 15%，所以金额为：$\$2.54 \times 15\% = \$0.381$ million $= \$380,0000$。

67. The increase in the amount of money distributed for family support from 1992 to 1993 was closest to which of the following?

67. 从 1992 至 1993 年，分配给家庭资助部分的金额的增加量最接近于下列哪一项？

解： 本题的正确答案为（E）。从 1992 年和 1993 年的资金分配饼图可知，这两年分给家庭资

(A) $0
(B) $24,000
(C) $40,000
(D) $60,000
(E) $94,000

助部分的比例未变,但1993年的总的资金($2,930,000)比1992年的($2,540,000)有所增加,所以家庭资助部分的金额增加量为:

$(2,930,000-2,540,000)×24\%=93,600$

Question 68 refer to the following graph.

CAR REGISTRATIONS IN COUNTRY X

（Note：Each car is registered to one owner only.）

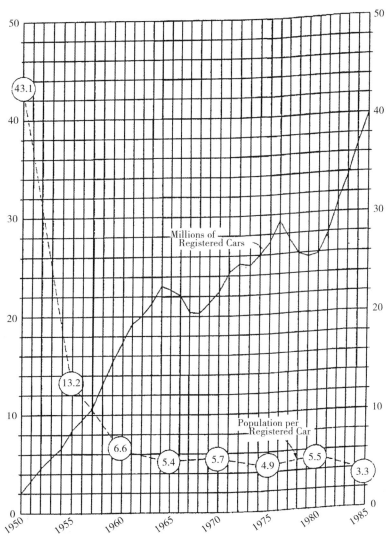

Note：Drawn to scale.

68. From 1950 to 1985，the population of Country X increased by approximately how many million people?

(A) 45

68. 标题：X国的注册汽车(注：每辆汽车仅注册给一个人)

从1950年到1985年,X国的人口大约增长了几百万?

(B) 80

(C) 165

(D) 200

(E) It cannot be determined from the information given.

解：本题的正确答案为（A）。图中的实线是在册的汽车数随年份的变化，虚线是每辆汽车所载的人数随年份的变化，所以美国的汽车数乘以每辆车所载的人数：

1950 年时，X 国的人口为：$2 \times 43.1 = 86.2$

1985 年时，X 国的人口为：$3.3 \times 40 = 132$

∴增加的人口为：$132 - 86.2 = 45.8$

Question 69—70 refer to the following table.

POPULATION DATA FOR TEN SELECTED STATES IN 1980 AND 1987

State	Population (in thousands)		Percent Change in Population, 1980—1987	Population Per Square Mile in 1987
	1980	1987		
A	23,668	27,663	16.9	177
B	17,558	17,825	1.5	372
C	14,229	16,789	18.0	64
D	9,746	12,023	23.4	222
E	11,864	11,936	0.6	266
F	11,427	11,582	1.4	208
G	10,798	10,784	−0.1	263
H	9,262	9,200	−0.7	162
I	7,365	7,672	4.2	1,027
J	5,882	6,413	9.0	131

69. In 1987 the average (arithmetic mean) population of the three most populous of the ten selected states was most nearly equal to

(A) 18 million

(B) 19 million

(C) 20 million

(D) 21 million

(E) 22 million

69. 标题：1980 年和 1987 年美国 10 个特定州的人口数据

在 1987 年，十个选定的州中人口最多的三个州的人口算术平均值最接近于：

解：本题的正确答案为（D）。"populous"是人口众多的意思。根据表格中的数据可知，排在前面的 A，B，C 三个州的人口最多，分别为 27,663,000，17,825,000 和 16,789,000，因此他们的算术平均值为：

$$\frac{27,663,000 + 17,825,000 + 16,789,000}{3}$$

$$= 20,749,000$$

计算结果与 21 million 最为接近。

70. Of the following expressions, which represents the population per square mile of the region consisting of states B and E

70. 下列各表达式中，哪个最能代表由 B 州和 E 州组成的地区在 1987 年每平方英里的人口数？

in 1987?

(A) $\dfrac{372+266}{2}$ (B) $\dfrac{17,825+11,936}{372+266}$

(C) $\dfrac{17,825}{372}+\dfrac{11,936}{266}$

(D) $\dfrac{372}{17,825}+\dfrac{266}{11,936}$

(E) $\dfrac{17,825+11,936}{\dfrac{17,825}{372}+\dfrac{11,936}{266}}$

解：本题的正确答案为(E)。用总人口除以总面积即可得人口密度。由表可知 B 州在 1987 年的总人口为 17,825 千人，每平方英里住 372 人；E 州在 1987 年的总人口为 11,936 千人，每平方英里住 266 人，所以 B 州和 E 州的人口密度为(E)选项的内容。

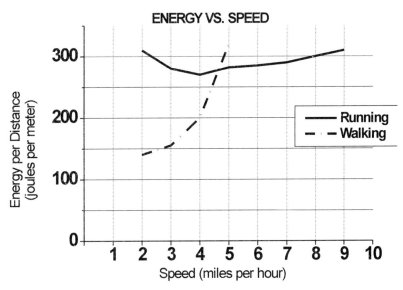

Note: Drawn to scale.

71. According to the graph above, at approximately what speed, in miles per hour (mph), is the energy per distance used in running approximately twice the energy per distance used in walking?

(A) Between 6.5 and 7 mph

(B) Between 5.5 and 6 mph

(C) Between 4.5 and 5 mph

(D) Between 3.5 and 4 mph

(E) Between 2.5 and 3 mph

71. 标题：能量与速度

根据上图，大约在多大速度（以 mph 为单位）时，跑每单位距离消耗的能量约是走单位距离所消耗能量的 2 倍？

解：本题的正确答案为(E)。题目中图形的横轴代表速度(mph)，纵轴代表单位距离所消耗的能量（焦耳/米）；图中的实线是跑步时速度与能量之间的关系，虚线代表走路时速度与能量之间的关系。根据以上分析再结合图形可知，在速度为 2.5～3 mph 时，跑每单位距离的路程所消耗的能量约是走单位距离的路程所消耗能量的 2 倍。

72.

Month	Temperatures
January	32,14,24,28
April	45,50,58,47
June	76,80,74,79
August	84,95,100,89
November	48,43,39,42

In a set of measurements, the range is defined as the greatest measurement minus the least measurement. According to the table above, during the first four days of which month was the range of temperatures at noon the greatest?

(A) January   (B) April

(C) June   (D) August

(E) November

72. 在某一组测量集中,测量的值域被定义为测量的最大值与测量的最小值的差。根据上表,哪个月前 4 天中午的温度变化范围最大?

解：本题的正确答案为（A）。由表可知各月份的温度变化范围分别为：

January：$32-14=18$

April：$58-45=13$

June：$80-74=6$

August：$100-84=16$

November：$48-39=9$

第 三 篇

GRE 数学考前冲刺过关训练 120 题

1. If x is an even integer and y is an odd integer, then which of the following is an even integer?

(A) $x^2 + y$

(B) $x^2 - y$

(C) $(x^2)(y)$

(D) $x + y$

(E) $x - y$

2. A square region, P, and a rectangular region, Q, both have areas of 64.

Length of a side of P	Length of Q if its width is 4

3. If the ratio of men to women on a committee of 20 members is 3 to 2, how many members of the committee are women?

4. If a certain chemical costs $50 for 30 gallons, then how many gallons of the chemical can be purchased for $625?

(A) 12.5

(B) 24

(C) 325

(D) 375

(E) 425

5. A particular stock is valued at $40 per share. If the value increases 20 percent and then decreases 25 percent, what is the value of the stock per share after the decrease?

6. Tickets to a concert cost $25 and $13. An agent sells 11 tickets for a total price of $227

The number of $25 tickets sold	The number of $13 tickets sold

7. A salesperson works 50 weeks each year and makes an average (arithmetic mean) of 100 sales per week. If each sale is worth an average (arithmetic mean) of $1,000, then what is the total value of sales made by the salesperson in a year?

(A) $50,000

(B) $100,000

(C) $500,000

(D) $1,000,000

(E) $5,000,000

8. A laborer is paid $8 per hour for an 8-hour day and $1\frac{1}{2}$ times that rate for each hour in excess of 8 hours in a singe day. If the laborer received $80 for a single day's work, how long did he work on that day?

(A) 6 hr. 40 min.

(B) 9 hr. 20 min.

(C) 9 hr. 30 min.

(D) 9hr. 40min.

(E) 10hr.

9. When n is divided by 49, the remainder is 0.

| The remainder when n is divided by 7 | 7 |

10. If the ratio of women to men in a meeting is 4 to 1, what percent of the persons in the meeting are men?

(A) 20%

(B) 25%

(C) $33\frac{1}{3}\%$

(D) 80%

(E) 100%

11. Kathleen's weekly salary was increased 8 percent to $237.60. What was her weekly salary before the increase?

12. A rhombus has a base of 10 and a height of 4

| The area of the rhombus | The perimeter of the rhombus |

13.

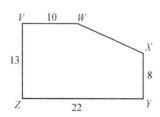

What is the perimeter of pentagon $VWXYZ$ shown above?

(A) 53

(B) 58

(C) 60

(D) 66

(E) 70

14. The population of City X decreased by 5 percent while the population of City Y decreased by 7.5 percent

| The loss of population by City X | The loss of population by City Y |

15. Which of the following can be expressed as the sum of three consecutive integers?

(A) 17

(B) 23

(C) 25

(D) 30

(E) 40

Questions 16—19 are based on the graphs below

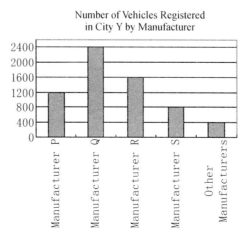

Number of Vehicles Registered in City Y by Manufacturer

SELECTED MOTOR VEHICLE REGISTRATION DATA
FOR TWO CITIES (BY MANUFACTURER)

Distribution of Motor Vehicles Registered in
City X According to Manufacturer
(100%=8400)

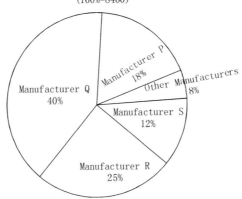

Number of Vehicles Registered in City X Manufactured by Other Manufacturers

Manufacturer T	212
Manufacturer U	210
Manufacturer V	250

16. In City X, how many of the registered motor vehicles were manufactured by Manufacturer Q?

(A) 1,512

(B) 1,600

(C) 2,400

(D) 3,360

(E) 6,000

17. How many more of the motor vehicles registered in City Y were manufactured by Manufacturer R than were manufactured by Manufacturer P?

(A) 400

(B) 688

(C) 800

(D) 1,200

(E) 1,688

18. Of the following, which is the closest approximation to the percentage of motor vehicles registered in City X that were manufactured by Manufacturer V?

(A) 45%

(B) 37%

(C) 8%

(D) 3%

(E) 1%

19. In City Y, the number of motor vehicles registered that were manufactured by Manufacturer R accounted for what percentage of all motor vehicles registered in City Y?

(A) 4%

(B) 8%

(C) 12.5%

(D) 16%

(E) 25%

20. What is the maximum number of cubes with sides of a length that could fit inside a cube with sides of length 2s?

(A) 8

(B) 16

(C) 32

(D) 64

(E) 128

21. The perimeter of square $PQRS$ is $12\sqrt{3}$.

length of side $\overline{PQ}$ $3\sqrt{3}$

22. Two cars started from the same point and traveled on a straight course in opposite directions for exactly 2 hours, at which time they were 208 miles apart. If one car traveled, on average, 8 miles per hour faster than the other car, what was the average speed for each car for the 2-hour trip?

23. If the areas of the three different sized faces of a rectangular solid are 6, 8, and 12,

then what is the volume of the solid?

(A) 576

(B) 288

(C) 144

(D) 48

(E) 24

24. In a certain population, 40 percent of all people have biological characteristic X; the others do not. If 8,000 people have characteristic X, how many people do not have X?

(A) 3200

(B) 4800

(C) 12,000

(D) 16,000

(E) 20,000

25.

FAMILY X'S EXPENDITURES AS A PERCENT OF
ITS GROSS ANNUAL INCOME*

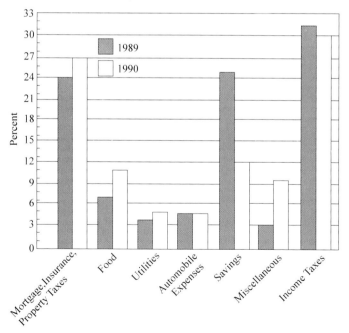

*1989 Gross annual income: $50,000
1990 Gross annual income: $45,000

(1) In 1989 Family X used a total of 49 percent of its gross annual income for two of the categories listed. What was the total amount of Family X's income used for

238

those same categories in 1990 ?

(2) Family $X's$ gross income is the sum of Mr. $X's$ income and Mrs. $X's$ income. In 1989 Mr. and Mrs. X each had an income of $25,000. If Mr. $X's$ income increased by 10 percent from 1989 to 1990, by what percent did Mrs. $X's$ income decrease for the same period?

26. A car dealer who gives a customer a 20 percent discount on the list price of a car still realizes a net profit of 25 percent of cost. If the dealer's cost is $4800, what is the usual list price of the car?

(A) $6000
(B) $6180
(C) $7200
(D) $7500
(E) $8001

27. Joe works two part-time jobs. One week Joe worked 8 hours at one job, earning $150, and 4.5 hours at other job, earning $90. What were his average hourly earnings for the week?

(A) $8.00
(B) $9.60
(C) $16.00
(D) $19.20
(E) $32.00

28.

If the spaces between the lettered points in the figure above are all equal, then $\dfrac{PT}{2} - \dfrac{QS}{2}$ is equal to which of the following?

(A) $PS-QR$
(B) $QR-QS$
(C) PR
(D) QT
(E) ST

29. The length of side of   The length of the
    any equilateral polygon   diameter of circle O
    inscribed in circle O

30. During a sale at an office supply store, for every box of paper clips purchased for 15 cents, a second box can be purchased for 4 cents. How many boxes of paper clips did Paul buy if he spent 91 cents on boxes of paper clips?

(A) 6
(B) 7
(C) 8
(D) 9
(E) 10

31. If n is an integer between 0 and 100, then any of the following could be $3n + 3$ EXCEPT

(A) 300
(B) 297
(C) 208
(D) 63
(E) 6

Question 32－35 are based on the following graphs

INVESTMENT PORTFOLIO

Total Investment Profile
$1,080,192=100%

Government Bonds
and Securities

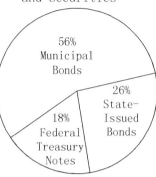

Municipal Bonds

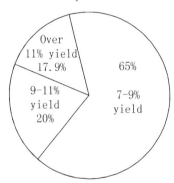

32. According to the graphs, approximately how much money belonging to the investment portfolio was invested in high-risk stocks?
    (A) $95,000
    (B) $89,000
    (C) $50,000
    (D) $42,000
    (E) $36,000

33. Approximately how much money belonging to the investment portfolio was invested in state-issued bonds?
    (A) $260,000
    (B) $125,000
    (C) $34,000
    (D) $26,000

(E) $500

34. Which of the following was the greatest?
    (A) The amount of money invested in municipal bonds that yielded between 7% and 9%
    (B) The amount of money invested in municipal bonds that yielded over 9%
    (C) The amount of money invested in federal treasury notes
    (D) The amount of money invested in state-issued stocks
    (E) The amount of money invested in high-risk stocks

35. Which of the following earned the least amount of money for the investment

portfolio?

(A) Municipal bonds

(B) State-issued bonds

(C) Government bonds and securities

(D) Mutual funds

(E) Cannot be determined from the information given.

36. $2000 is deposited into a savings account that earns interest at the rate of 10 percent per year, compounded semiannually. How much money will there be in the account at the end of one year?

(A) $2105

(B) $2200

(C) $2205

(D) $2400

(E) $2600

37. The average (arithmetic mean) of five number is 26. After one of the numbers is removed, the average (arithmetic mean) of the remaining numbers is 25. What number has been removed?

(A) 20

(B) 25

(C) 26

(D) 30

(E) 32

38. A theater sells children's tickets for half the adult ticket price. If 5 adult tickets and 8 children's tickets cost a total of $27, what is the cost of an adult ticket?

39.

AVERAGE AND HIGH WIND SPEED FOR SELECTED STATIONS OVER A 10-YEAR PERIOD (1971-80) (miles per hour)		
Station	Average	High
Atlanta, GA	9.1	71
Boston, MA	12.6	65
Buffalo, NY	12.3	91
Chicago, IL	10.4	60
Cincinnati, OH	7.1	49
Denver, CO	9.0	56
Miami, FL	9.2	132
Montgomery, AL	6.7	72
New York, NY	9.4	70
Omaha, NE	10.8	109
Pittsburgh, PA	9.3	58
San Diego, CA	6.7	51
Washington, DC	9.3	78

SPEED AND OFFICIAL DESIGNATIONS OF WINDS	
Designation	Miles per Hour
Calm	Less than 1
Light air	1 to 3
Light breeze	4 to 7
Gentle breeze	8 to 12
Moderate breeze	13 to 18
Fresh breeze	19 to 24
Strong breeze	25 to 31
Near gale	32 to 38
Gale	39 to 46
Strong gale	47 to 54
Storm	55 to 63
Violent storm	64 to 73
Hurricane . . . . 74 and above	

(1) Which station has a high wind speed that is the median of the high wind speeds for all the stations listed?

(2) For those stations that have recorded hurricane winds at least once during the 10-year period, what is the

arithmetic mean of their average wind speeds?

(3) For how many of the stations is the ratio of high wind speed to average wind speed greater than 10 to 1?

40. In a certain company, the ratio of the number of women employees to the number of men employees is 3 to 2. If the total number of employees is 240, then how many of the employees are men?

(A) 40

(B) 48

(C) 96

(D) 144

(E) 160

41. In 1960, the number of students enrolled at a college was 500. In 1980, the number of students enrolled at the college was $2\frac{1}{2}$ times as great as that in 1960. What was the number of students enrolled at the college in 1980?

(A) 1,750

(B) 1,250

(C) 1,000

(D) 500

(E) 250

42.

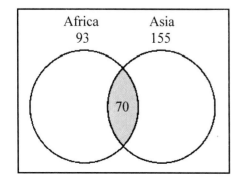

In a survey of 250 European travelers, 93 have traveled to Africa, 155 have traveled to Asia, and 70 have traveled to both of these continents, as illustrated in the *Venn diagram* above.

(1) How many of the travelers surveyed have traveled to Africa but not to Asia?

(2) How many of the travelers surveyed have traveled to at least one of the two continents Africa and Asia?

(3) How many of the travelers surveyed have traveled neither to Africa nor to Asia?

43. A person is standing on a staircase. He walks down 4 steps, up 3 steps, down 6 steps, up 2 steps, up 9 steps, and down 2 steps. Where is he standing in relation to the step on which he started?

(A) 2 steps above

(B) 1 step above

(C) the same place

(D) 1 step below

(E) 2 steps below

44. The product of three consecutive integers must be

I. Divisible by 3

II. Divisible by 5

III. Divisible by 6

(A) I only

(B) II only

(C) I and II only

(D) I and III only

(E) I, II, and III

45. Point P has coordinates $(-2,2)$; Point Q has coordinates $(2,0)$.

  4   The distance from P to Q

46.

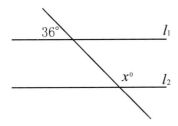

In the preceding figure, if $l_1 /\!/ l_2$, what is

the value of x?

(A) 36

(B) 54

(C) 90

(D) 144

(E) 154

47. If one side of a square decreases by 10% and the adjacent side increases by 30%, by what percent does its area increase?

(A) 15%

(B) 17%

(C) 20%

(D) 22%

(E) 25%

Question 48—51 refer to the graph below.

PUBLIC TRANSPORTATION IN METROPOLITAN AREA P

□ Subways ▨ Commuter Rail ■ Buses

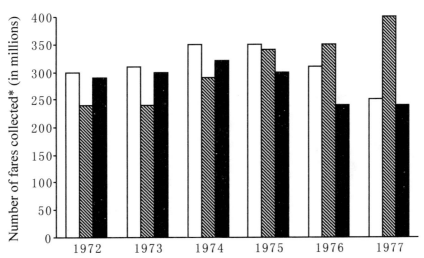

* One passenger paying one fare for one trip

48. From 1972 to 1977, inclusive, the total number of fares collected for subways was approximately how many million?

(A) 1,900

(B) 1,700

(C) 1,500

(D) 1,300

(E) 1,100

49. From 1975 to 1977, the number of fares collected for subways dropped by approximately what percent?

(A) 90

(B) 35

(C) 25

(D) 15

(E) 9

50. If in 1974 the average subway fare collected was 50 ¢ and the average bus fare collected was 30 ¢, then the ratio of the total dollar amount of subway fares collected to the total dollar amount of bus fares was approximately

(A) $\dfrac{1}{4}$

(B) $\dfrac{1}{3}$

(C) $\dfrac{3}{5}$

(D) 1

(E) $\dfrac{7}{4}$

51. The number of commuter rail fares collected in 1977 accounted for approximately what percent of all fares collected on subways, buses, and commuter rail in that year?

(A) 200%

(B) 100%

(C) 50%

(D) 28%

(E) 12%

52. For all real numbers P and Q, $P * Q = P + Q - PQ$.

$$4 * 1 \qquad 4 * 2$$

53. Two students spent a total of 35 hours on a school project. One of the students spent

25% fewer hours on the project than the other.

| The difference in the number of hours spent by each | 6 |

54. A bookshelf contains 16 books written in French and 8 books written in Italian and no other books. 75% of the books written in French and 50% of the books written in Italian are removed from the bookshelf.

| The proportion of the original number of books remaining on the shelf | $\dfrac{2}{3}$ |

55. Which of the following fractions expressed in the form $\dfrac{P}{Q}$ is most nearly approximated by the decimal. PQ, where P is the tenths' digit and Q is the hundredths' digit?

(A) $\dfrac{1}{8}$

(B) $\dfrac{2}{9}$

(C) $\dfrac{3}{4}$

(D) $\dfrac{4}{5}$

(E) $\dfrac{8}{9}$

56. Point P has coordinates (x, y); point Q has coordinates $(x-1, y-1)$.

| The distance from P to the origin | The distance from Q to the origin |

57. A figure that can be folded over along a straight line so that the result is two equal halves which are then lying on top of one another with no overlap is said to have a line of symmetry. Which of the following figures has only one line of symmetry?

(A) Square

(B) Circle

(C) Equilateral triangle

(D) Isosceles triangle

(E) Rectangle

58.

The number of primes of which 11 is an integer multiple	The number of primes of which 13 is an integer multiple

59. A painter has painted one-third of a rectangular wall which is ten feet high. When she has painted another 75 square feet of wall, she will be three-quarters finished with the job. What is the length (the horizontal dimension) of the wall?

(A) 18 feet

(B) 12 feet

(C) 10 feet

(D) 9 feet

(E) 6 feet

60. Martha invited 4 friends to go with her to the movies. There are 120 different ways in which they can sit together in a row. In how many of those ways is Martha sitting in the middle?

61. The sum of a group of numbers is 4,550. The average of the group of numbers is 325.

The number of numbers in the group	15

62. Exactly three years before the year in which Anna was born, the year was $1980-x$. In terms of x, on Anna's twentieth birthday, the year will be

(A) $1977+x$

(B) $1997+x$

(C) $2003-x$

(D) $2003+x$

(E) $2006+x$

63.

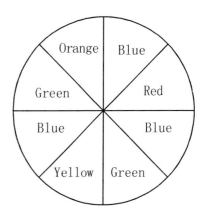

The figure above shows a wheel of fortune divided into sections of equal size and painted with the colors indicated. If the wheel has a diameter of 64 centimeters, what is the total area of the wheel that is painted blue (expressed in square centimeters)?

(A) 3π (B) 24π (C) 40π

(D) 128π (E) 384π

64. The diagonal of the floor of a rectangular closet is $7\frac{1}{2}$ feet. The shorter side of the closet is $4\frac{1}{4}$ feet. What is the area of the closet in square feet?

(A) 37   (B) 27   (C) $\frac{54}{4}$

(D) $\frac{21}{4}$ (E) 5

65.

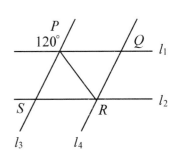

In the figure above, $l_1 /\!/ l_2$, and $l_3 /\!/ l_4$. If $PQ=3$ and $QR=3$, then what is the length of PR?

(A) 6　　(B) $3\dfrac{\sqrt{3}}{2}$　　(C) 3

(D) $9\sqrt{5}$　　(E) $\dfrac{\sqrt{3}}{2}$

66. How many 3-digit positive integers are odd and do not contain the digit "5"?

67. In a certain group of people, $\dfrac{3}{8}$ of the people are men, and $\dfrac{2}{3}$ of the men have brown eyes. If $\dfrac{3}{4}$ of the people have brown eyes, then what fraction of the group are women who do not have brown eyes?

(A) $\dfrac{1}{8}$　　(B) $\dfrac{3}{16}$　　(C) $\dfrac{1}{4}$

(D) $\dfrac{5}{16}$　　(E) $\dfrac{3}{8}$

68. From a box of 10 light bulbs, 4 are to be removed. How many different sets of 4 bulbs could be removed?

69. A truck departed from Newton at 11:53 a.m. and arrived in Far City, 240 miles away, at 4:41 p.m. on the same day. What was the approximate average speed of the truck on this trip?

(A) $\dfrac{16}{1,200}$MPH　　(B) $\dfrac{240}{288}$MPH

(C) $\dfrac{1,494}{240}$MPH　　(D) 50MPH

(E) $\dfrac{5,640}{5}$MPH

70. A student conducts an experiment in biology lab and discovers that the ratio of the number of insects in a given population having characteristic X to the number of insects in the population not having characteristic X is $5:3$, and that $\dfrac{3}{8}$ of the insects having characteristic X are male insects. What proportion of the total insect population are male insects having the characteristic X?

(A) 1　　(B) $\dfrac{5}{8}$　　(C) $\dfrac{6}{13}$

(D) $\dfrac{15}{64}$　　(E) $\dfrac{1}{5}$.

71. A prize of $\$240$ is divided between two persons. If one person receives $\$180$, then what is the difference between the amounts received by the persons?

(A) $\$30$　　(B) $\$60$　　(C) $\$120$

(D) $\$210$　　(E) $\$420$

72. In the frequency distribution below, y represents age on last birthday for 40 people. Find the mean, median, mode, and range for y.

y	f
17	2
18	7
19	19
20	9
21	2
22	0
23	1

73. When $x+5$ is divided by 3, the remainder is 2.

The remainder when x is divided by 2　　　　1

74. The people eating in a certain cafeteria are either faculty members or students, and the number of faculty members is 15

percent of the total number of people in the cafeteria. After some of the students leave, the total number of persons remaining in the cafeteria is 50 percent of the original total. The number of students who left is what fractional part of the original number of students?

(A) $\frac{17}{20}$ (B) $\frac{10}{17}$ (C) $\frac{1}{2}$

(D) $\frac{1}{4}$ (E) $\frac{7}{20}$

75. A talent contest has 8 contestants. Judges must award prizes for first, second, and third places. If there are no ties, (1) in how many different ways can the 3 prizes be awarded, and (2) how many different groups of 3 people can get prizes?

76. If $pq \neq 0$ and $p = \frac{1}{3}q$, then the ratio of p to $3q$ is

(A) 9 : 1   (B) 3 : 1   (C) 1 : 1

(D) 1 : 3   (E) 1 : 9

77.

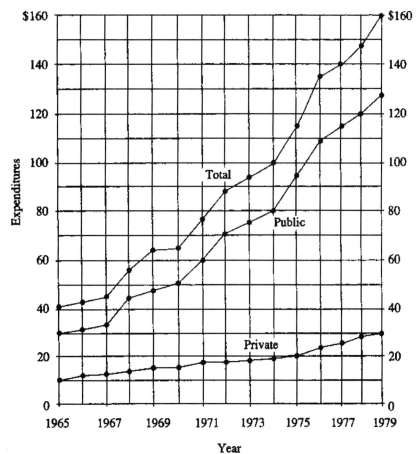

PUBLIC AND PRIVATE SCHOOL EXPENDITURES
1965 – 1979
(in billions of dollars)

(1) In which year did total expenditures increase the most from the year before?

(2) In 1979 private school expenditures were approximately what percent of total expenditures?

78. The enrollments at College X and College Y both grew by 8 percent from 1980 to 1985. If the enrollment at College X grew by 800 and the enrollment at College Y grew by 840, the enrollment at College Y was how much greater than the enrollment at College X in 1985?

(A) 400

(B) 460

(C) 500

(D) 540

(E) 580

79. Mr. Norwalk borrowed $1,000 for one year. Mr. Palisano borrowed $500 for two years.

The amount of interest Mr. Norwalk owes on his loan	The amount of interest Mr. Palisano owes on his loan

80.

The least number greater than 12 that is divisible by 12 but not by 8	48

81. Mary has $5 less than Sam, and Mark has half as much money as Sam.

Amount of money that Mary has	Amount of money that Mark has

82. From the time 6:15 p.m. to the time 7:45 p.m. of the same day, the minute hand of a standard clock describes an arc of

(A) 30°

(B) 90°

(C) 180°

(D) 540°

(E) 910°

83.

The number of pears in a cubical box with a side of 24 inches	The number of potatoes in a cubical box with a side of 36 inches

84. A child withdraws from his piggy bank 10% of the original sum in the bank. If he must add 90 ¢ to bring the amount in the bank back up to the original sum, what was the original sum in the bank?

(A) $1.00

(B) $1.90

(C) $8.10

(D) $9.00

(E) $9.90

85. Lin and Mark each attempt independently to decode a message. If the probability that Lin will decode the message is 0.80, and the probability that Mark will decode the message is 0.70, find the probability that

(1) both will decode the message

(2) at least one of them will decode the message

(3) neither of them will decode the message

86.

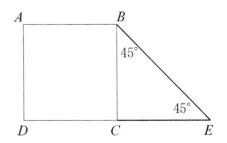

If the area of the triangle BCE is 8, what is the area of the square ABCD?

(A) 4

(B) 8

(C) 16

(D) 22

(E) 82

87. The greatest prime factor of 243 | The greatest prime factor of 180

88. How many minutes will it take to completely fill a water tank with a capacity of 3,750 cubic feet if the water is being pumped into the tank at the rate of 800 cubic feet per minute and is being drained out of the tank at the rate of 300 cubic feet per minute?

(A) 3 min. 36 sec.

(B) 6 minutes

(C) 7 min. 30 sec.

(D) 8 minutes

(E) 1,875 minutes

89.

Column A	Column B
The product of three number between 3 and 4	The product of four numbers between 2 and 3

90. If x^5 is odd and $(x + y)^5$ is even, then which of the following must be odd?

I. $x + y$

II. xy

III. $x^2 y^2$

(A) I only

(B) II only

(C) I and II only

(D) II and III only

(E) I, II and III

91.

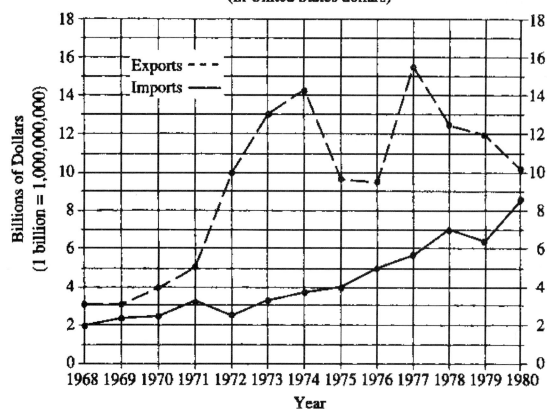

FOREIGN TRADE OF COUNTRY X, 1968-1980
(in United States dollars)

(1) For which year shown on the graph did exports exceed the previous year's exports by the greatest dollar amount?

(2) In 1973 the dollar value of imports was approximately what percent of the dollar value of exports?

(3) If it were discovered that the import dollar amount shown for 1978 was incorrect and should have been $3.1 billion instead, then the average (arithmetic mean) import dollar amount per year for the 13 years would be how much less?

92. Paul is standing 180 yards due north of point P, Franny is standing 240 yards due west of point P. What is the shortest distance between Franny and Paul?

(A) 60 yards

(B) 300 yards

(C) 420 yards

(D) 900 yards

(E) 9,000 yards

93. An apartment building has 5 floors, one of which has only 2 apartments. Each of the other floors has 4 apartments.

3 times the number of floors in the building	The number of apartments in the building

94. If the following were arranged in order of magnitude, which term would be the middle number in the series?

(A) $\dfrac{3^8}{3^6}$

(B) $3^3 - 1$

(C) 3^0

(D) 3^{27}

(E) $3(3^2)$

95. A family-size box of cereal contains 10 ounces more and costs 80 ¢ more than the regular size box of cereal.

Cost per ounce of the cereal in the family-size box	8 ¢

96.

The time it takes Jimmy to drive 300 miles at a rate of 52 miles per hour	The time it takes Bobby to drive 240 miles at a rate of 40 miles per hour

97.

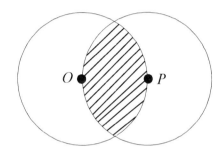

In the figure above, if the radius of the circles is 1, then what is the perimeter of the shaded part of the figure?

(A) $\dfrac{1}{6}\pi$ (B) $\dfrac{2}{3}\pi$

(C) $\dfrac{4}{3}\pi$ (D) $\dfrac{3}{2}\pi$

(E) Cannot be determined from the information given.

98.

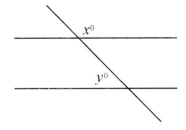

x	y

99.

PLAYER	AGE
Juanita	35
Brooke	28
Glenda	40
Marcia	22
Dwight	24
Tom	30

Tom's age	Average(arithmetic mean) age of the six players

100.

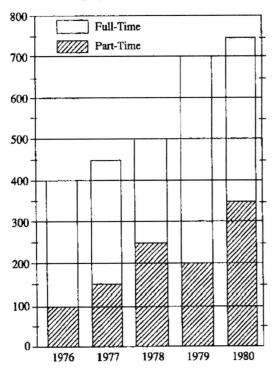

TOTAL STUDENT ENROLLMENT (PART-TIME + FULL-TIME) IN COLLEGE *R* : 1976-1980

(1) For which year was the ratio of part-time enrollment to total enrollment the greatest?

(2) What was the full-time enrollment in 1977?

(3) What was the percent increase in total enrollment from 1976 to 1980?

101.

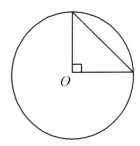

O is the center of the circle. The area of the triangle is 4.

Radius of the circle	4

102. A business firm reduces the number of hours its employees work from 40 hours per week to 36 hours per week while continuing to pay the same amount of money. If an employee earned x dollars per hour before the reduction in hours, how much does he earn per hour under the new system?

(A) $\dfrac{1}{10}$

(B) $\dfrac{x}{9}$

(C) $\dfrac{9x}{10}$

(D) $\dfrac{10x}{9}$

(E) $9x$

103.

The number of different duos that can be formed from a group of 5 people	The number of different trios that can be formed from a group of 5 people

104. If the value of a piece of property decreases by 10 percent while the tax rate on the property increases by 10 percent, what is the effect on the taxes?

(A) Taxes increase by 10 percent.

(B) Taxes increase by 1 percent.

(C) There is no change in taxes.

(D) Taxes decrease by 1 percent.

(E) Taxes decrease by 10 percent.

105. The lengths of two sides of an isosceles triangle are 15 and 22, respectively. What are the possible values of the perimeter?

106.

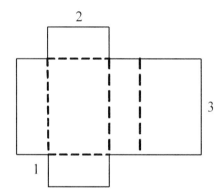

A rectangular box with a top is created by folding the figures above along the dotted lines. What is the volume of the box in cubic feet?

(A) 6

(B) 9

(C) 12

(D) 18

(E) 24

107. A man buys 16 shirts. Some of them cost $13 each, while the remainder cost $10 each. The cost of all 16 shirts is $187.

| The number of $13 shirts purchased | The number of $10 shirts purchased |

108. The sum of four consecutive odd positive integers is always

(A) an odd number

(B) divisible by 4

(C) a prime number

(D) a multiple of 3

(E) greater than 24

109. A group can charter a particular aircraft at a fixed total cost. If 36 people charter the aircraft rather than 40 people, then the cost per person is greater by $12. What is the cost per person if 40 people charter the aircraft?

110. x, y and z are consecutive positive integers, not necessarily in that order, and x and z are odd

$$xy \qquad\qquad yz$$

111. If n is a positive integer and 95 and 135 are divided by n, and the remainders are 5 and 3 respectively, then $n=$

(A) 6

(B) 8

(C) 10

(D) 15

(E) 21

112. If $3x-4y=5$ and $\dfrac{y}{x}=\dfrac{1}{3}$, then what is x?

(A) $-5y$

(B) $-5x$

(C) 1

(D) 3

(E) 4

113. If 3 times Jane's age, in years, is equal to 8 times Beth's age, in years, and the difference between their ages is 15 years, how old are Jane and Beth?

114. A survey of 100 persons revealed that 72

of them had eaten at restaurant P and that 52 of them had eaten at restaurant Q. Which of the following could not be the number of persons in the surveyed group who had eaten at both P and Q?

(A) 20

(B) 24

(C) 30

(D) 50

(E) 52

115. The weight of package x is more than twice the weights of packages y and z combined.

The weight of package z	$\dfrac{1}{3}$ the weight of package x

116. Pat invested a total of $3,000. Part of the money yields 10 percent interest per year, and the rest yields 8 percent interest per year. If the total yearly interest from this investment is $256, how much did Pat invest at 10 percent and how much at 8 percent?

117. If cylinder P has a height twice that of cylinder Q and a radius half that of cylinder Q, what is the ratio between the volume of cylinder P and the volume of cylinder Q?

(A) 1:8

(B) 1:4

(C) 1:2

(D) 1:1

(E) 2:1

118. If the width of a rectangle is increased by 25% while the length remains constant, the resulting area is what percent of the original area?

(A) 25%

(B) 75%

(C) 125%

(D) 225%

(E) Cannot be determined from the information given.

119. For a given two-digit positive integer, the tens digit is 5 greater than the units digit. The sum of the digits is 11. Find the integer.

120. The table shows the distribution of a group of 40 college students by gender and class.

	Sophomores	Juniors	Seniors
Males	6	10	2
Females	10	9	3

If one student is randomly selected from this group, find the probability that the student chosen is

(1) not a junior

(2) a female or a sophomore

(3) a male sophomore or a female senior

GRE 数学考前冲刺过关训练 120 题参考答案

1. C	2. B	3. 8	4. D	5. $36
6. A	7. E	8. B	9. B	10. A
11. $220	12. C	13. D	14. D	15. D
16. D	17. A	18. D	19. E	20. D

21. C   22. 48 mph and 56 mph   23. E   24. C

25. (1) $17,550 (2) 30%   26. D   27. D   28. E

29. B   30. D   31. C   32. A   33. B

34. A   35. E   36. C   37. D   38. $3

39. (1) New York (2) 10.4 (3) Three   40. C   41. B

42. (1) 23 (2) 178 (3) 72   43. A   44. D   45. B

46. D   47. B   48. A   49. C   50. E

51. C   52. A   53. B   54. B   55. E

56. D   57. D   58. C   59. A   60. 24

61. B   62. C   63. E   64. B   65. C

66. 288   67. A   68. 210   69. D   70. D

71. C   72. mean＝19.15, median＝19, mode＝19, range＝6

73. D   74. B   75. (1) 336 (2) 56   76. E

77. (1) 1976 (2) 19%   78. D   79. D   80. B

81. D   82. D   83. D   84. D

85. (1) 0.56 (2) 0.94 (3) 0.06   86. C   87. B

88. C   89. D   90. D   91. (1) 1977 (2) 25% (3) $300 million

92. B   93. B   94. B   95. D   96. B

97. C   98. D   99. A   100. (1) 1978 (2) 300 (3) 87.5

101. B   102. D   103. C   104. D   105. 52 or 59

106. A   107. A   108. B   109. $108   110. D

111. A   112. D   113. Beth is 9; Jane is 24   114. A

115. D   116. $800 at 10%; $2,200 at 8%   117. C

118. C   119. 83   120. (1) $\frac{21}{40}$ (2) $\frac{7}{10}$ (3) $\frac{9}{40}$

第 四 篇

最新 GRE 数学预测模拟试题

一、最新 GRE 数学预测模拟试题（一）*

1.

Quantity A	Quantity B
the ratio 3:13	the ratio 13:51

2.

Quantity A	Quantity B
$\frac{4}{5}$ of $\frac{6}{7}$	$\frac{7}{8}$ of $\frac{9}{10}$

3. 63% of a is 72

Quantity A	Quantity B
2a	250

4.

Quantity A	Quantity B
Remainder when 1,003 is divided by 4	Remainder when 1,004 is divided by 3

5. $u \otimes v = (v-u)^u (u-v)^v$

Quantity A	Quantity B
$9 \otimes 11$	$11 \otimes 9$

6. For the line with equation y＝ax＋b, ab≠0, the x-intercept is twice the y-intercept.

Quantity A	Quantity B
The slope of the line	$\frac{1}{2}$

7. A cylinder of gas has height 48 inches, and the base has radius 2 feet

Quantity A	Quantity B
Volume of the cylinder	Surface area of the cylinder

8. A jar contains two red and two green marbles

Quantity A	Quantity B
Probability of choosing two red	Probability of choosing two green

9.

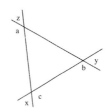

Quantity A	Quantity B
$a+b+c$	$x+y+z$

＊ 本篇的五套数学预测试题每套 25 题,建议时间为 40 分钟。需要提醒读者注意的是：GRE 机考时每个 Section 为 20 题,时间为 35 分钟。

For the following question, enter your answer in the box.

10. In a graduating class of 236 students, 142 took algebra and 121 took chemistry. What is the greatest possible number of students that could have taken both algebra and chemistry?

    [   ] students

11. The fabric needed to make 3 curtains sells for $8.00 per yard and can be purchased only by the full yard. If the length of fabric required for each curtain is 1.6 yards and all of the fabric is purchased as a single length, what is the total cost of the fabric that needs to be purchased for the 3 curtains?

    (A) $40.00   (B) $38.40   (C) $24.00
    (D) $16.00   (E) $12.80

12. All three circles shown have radius 1 and are tangent to each other. Find the perimeter of the shaded region.

    (A) 3   (B) π (C) $\dfrac{2}{3}\pi$
    (D) 2π (E) 3π

13. The USS Mathematica sailed 6 knots north, then 5 knots east, then 2 knots south. How far, in knots, was the ship from her starting point?

    (A) 3   (B) $\sqrt{41}$ (C) $\sqrt{61}$
    (D) 41   (E) 61

Questions 14 and 15 are concerned with the tables below. ∗

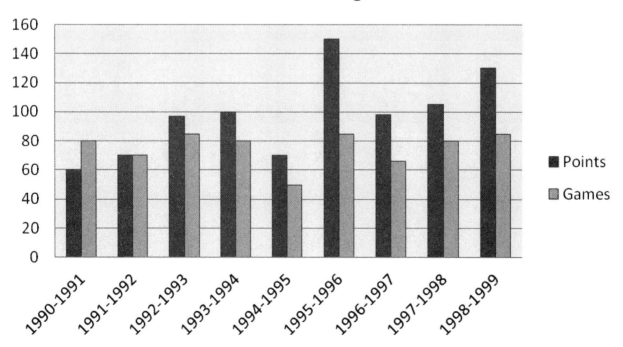

Jaromir Jagr

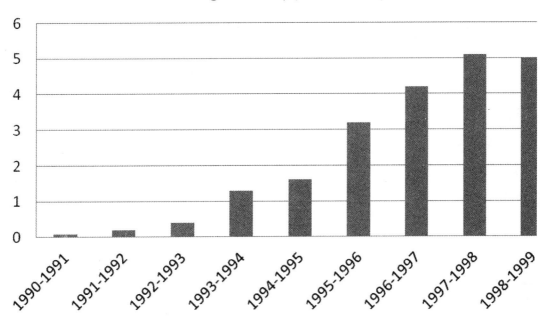

Jagr's Salary (In millions)

* **Data from the Internet Hockey database; salaries from Hockey Zone Plus.**

14. In which season did Jagr earn the most money per game?
    (A) 1994-1995   (B) 1995-1996
    (C) 1996-1997   (D) 1997-1998
    (E) 1998-1999

15. In which season did Jagr average the most points per game?
    (A) 1990-1991   (B) 1995-1996
    (C) 1996-1997   (D) 1997-1998
    (E) 1998-1999

16. Draw all diagonals in a regular eight-sided polygon. What is the largest number of diagonals that meet in a single point?
    (A) 2   (B) 3   (C) 4
    (D) 5   (E) 6

17. In the xy-plane, line k is a line that does not pass through the origin. Which of the following statements individually provide(s) sufficient additional information to determine whether the slope of line k is negative? Indicate all such statements.
    (A) The x-intercept of line k is twice the y-intercept of line k.
    (B) The product of the x-intercept and the y-intercept of line k is positive.
    (C) Line k passes through the points (a, b) and (r, s), where $(a-r)(b-s)<0$.

18. Which of the following values is closest to $\sqrt{201}$?
    (A) 13.3   (B) 13.9   (C) 14.2
    (D) 14.8   (E) 15.3

AVERAGE VEHICLE OCCUPANCY RATE FOR COMMUTERS TO CITY P AND ITS SIX SUBURBAN COUNTIES

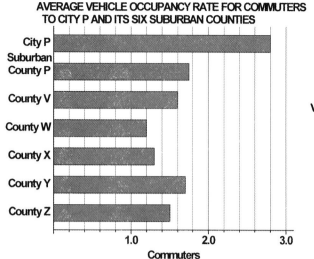

MEANS OF TRAVEL FOR COMMUTERS TO CITY P

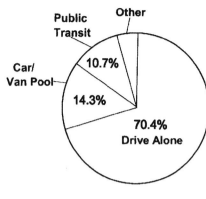

Note: Drawn to scale.

19. If the average vehicle occupancy rate for commuters to County X were to increase to 2.8, what would be the approximate percent increase in the occupancy rate?

    (A) 46%　　(B) 54%　　(C) 87%

    (D) 115%　　(E) 215%

20. If the total number of commuters to County W is twice the number to County Z, and if the average number of vehicles that transport commuters daily to County W is 30,000, what is the approximate average number of vehicles that transport commuters daily to County Z?

    (A) 12,000　(B) 15,000　(C) 18,000

    (D) 27,000　(E) 36,000

21. The advertised rate for roaming charges is 0.002 cents per second. What is that in dollars per hour?

    (A) 7.2　　(B) 2　　　(C) 0.72

    (D) 0.2　　(E) 0.072

22. In 2000 Paul was twice as old as his brother Biko. In 2008 Paul was only four years older than his brother. In what year was Biko born?

    (A) 1990　　(B) 1992　　(C) 1996

    (D) 1998　　(E) 2000

23. In the xy-plane, the point with coordinates $(-6, -7)$ is the center of circle C. The point with coordinates $(-6, 5)$ lies inside C, and the point with coordinates $(8, -7)$ lies outside C. If m is the radius of C and m is an integer, what is the value of m?

    [　　　　　]

24. What is the average of four consecutive odd numbers starting with 2n+1?

    (A) 4　　　(B) 2n+3　　(C) 2n+4

    (D) 2n+5　(E) n+4

25. The company at which Mark is employed has 80 employees, each of whom has a different salary. Mark's salary of $43,700 is the second-highest salary in the first quartile of the 80 salaries. If the company were to hire 8 new employees at salaries that are less than the lowest of the 80 salaries, what would Mark's salary be with respect to the quartiles of the 88 salaries at

the company, assuming no other changes in the salaries?

(A) The fourth-highest salary in the first quartile

(B) The highest salary in the first quartile

(C) The second-lowest salary in the second quartile

(D) The third-lowest salary in the second quartile

(E) The fifth-lowest salary in the second quartile

二、最新 GRE 数学预测模拟试题（二）

1. A jar contains n red and n green marbles where $n \geq 2$. You pick two marbles from the jar.

Quantity A	Quantity B
Number of ways to pick one of each color	n^2

2. Maria's average after three tests was 86. She scored 94 on her fourth test and has only one test remaining.

Quantity A	Quantity B
Score Maria need to score on herfifth test to have a 90 average	95

3. In a certain store, each record costs X dollars and each tape costs Y dollars. The total cost of 3 records and 2 tapes is $39.

Quantity A	Quantity B
The cost of 1 record	The cost of 1 tape

4.

Quantity A	Quantity B
Price of a $30,000 car after a 10% discount and 10% sales tax	Price of a $30,000 car after a 7% discount and 7% sales tax

5. The operation ◆ is defined for all positive numbers r and t by $r \blacklozenge t = \dfrac{(r-t)^2 + rt}{t}$

Quantity A	Quantity B
71 ◆ 37	37 ◆ 71

6. A school group charters three identical buses and occupies $\dfrac{4}{5}$ of the seats. After $\dfrac{1}{4}$ of the passengers leave, the remaining passengers use only two of the buses.

Quantity A	Quantity B
The fraction of the seats on the two buses that are now occupied	$\dfrac{9}{10}$

7. A case of soda costs $16.75. The cost of p individual cans of soda is $1.20 per can.

Quantity A	Quantity B
The lowest possible value of p if the cost of p cans of soda is greater than the cost of a case of soda.	15

8.

Quantity A	Quantity B
The distance on the xy-plane from the point defined by the (x,y) coordinates $(-2, -1)$ to the point defined by the (x,y) coordinates $(1, -3)$	The distance on the xy-plane from the point defined by the (x,y) coordinates $(3,2)$ to the point defined by the (x,y) coordinates $(1, -3)$

9.

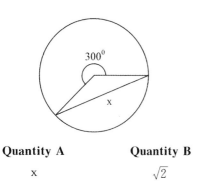

| **Quantity A** | **Quantity B** |
| x | $\sqrt{2}$ |

10. In a singles tennis tournament that has 125 entrants, a player is eliminated whenever he loses a match. How many matches are played in the entire tournament?

☐

11. Because her test turned out to be more difficult than she intended it to be, a teacher decided to adjust the grades by deducting only half the number of points a student missed. For example, if a student missed 10 points, she received a 95 instead of a 90. Before the grades were adjusted the class average was A. What was the average after the adjustment?

(A) $50 + \dfrac{A}{2}$ (B) $\dfrac{1}{2}(100 - A)$

(C) $100 - \dfrac{1}{2}A$ (D) $\dfrac{50 + A}{2}$

(E) $A + 25$

For the following question, select all the answer choices that apply.

12. In triangle ABC, $AB = AC = 2$. Which of the following could be the area of triangle ABC? Indicate all possible areas.

(A) 0.5   (B) 1.0   (C) 1.5

(D) 2.0   (E) 2.5   (F) 3.0

13. Each integer from 1 to 50 whose units digit is a 3 is written on a slip of paper and placed in a box. If two slips of paper are drawn at random, what is the probability that both the numbers picked are prime?

☐
☐

14. A jar contains 20 marbles: 4 red, 6 white, and 10 blue. If you remove marbles one at a time, randomly, what is the minimum number that must be removed to be certain that you have at least 2 marbles of each color?

(A) 6   (B) 10   (C) 12

(D) 16   (E) 18

Questions 15 and 16 are based on the following data. *

Average U.S. apple prices by consumption	2001	2002	2003	2004
All sales (cents per pound)	15.80	18.90	20.90	15.80
Fresh consumption (cents per pound)	22.90	25.80	29.40	21.70
All processing (dollars per ton)	108.00	130.00	131.00	107.00
Canned (dollars per ton)	139.00	161.00	154.00	149.00
Juice and cider (dollars per ton)	83.40	104.00	103.00	73.00
Frozen (dollars per ton)	139.00	175.00	173.00	172.00
Dried (dollars per ton)	84.70	108.00	107.00	77.30

* Data from U.S. Apple Association www. usapple. org.

Apple Production

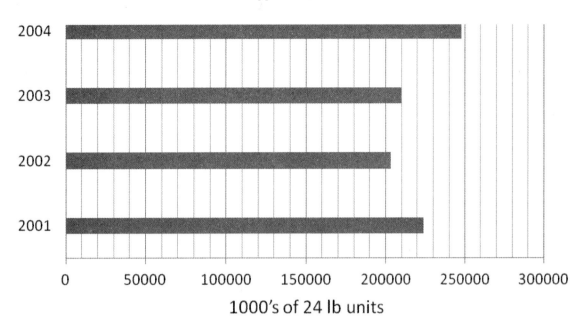

1000's of 24 lb units

15. Comparing 2001 to 2003 what is the approximate percentage change in value of the apple crop?

(A) increase of 25% (B) decrease of 25%

(C) increase of 6% (D) decrease of 6%

(E) increase of 12%

16. Which is worth the most?

(A) 25% of the 2001 crop sold for juice

(B) 10% of the 2002 crop sold for canning

(C) 5% of the 2003 crop sold for freezing

(D) 15% of the 2004 crop sold dried

(E) 1% of the 2001 crop sold fresh

17. Martina needs 35 gallons of fuel in each winter month to heat her home. Each spring and fall month she uses 15 gallons of fuel. She uses no fuel during the summer. What part of her annual heating bill is spent during the winter?

Give your answer as a fraction:

18. George earned 80, 85 and 90 on the first three tests in his geography class. Because he didn't have time to study, he decides to guess randomly on the final test. That test has ten true-false questions, each worth 10 points. What is the probability his final average is more than 85?

(A) $\dfrac{12}{2^8}$　　　(B) $\dfrac{11}{2^8}$　　　(C) $\dfrac{12}{1024}$

(D) $\dfrac{11}{1024}$　　　(E) 0.5

19. If a and b are the lengths of the legs of a right triangle whose hypotenuse is 10 and whose area is 20, what is the value of $(a + b)^2$?

(A) 100　　(B) 120　　(C) 140

(D) 180　　(E) 200

For the following question, select all the answer choices that apply.

20. Every year between 70% and 85% of the students at Central High School attend the homecoming rally. If one year 1435 students attended the rally, which of the

following could have been the number of students at Central High School that year? Indicate all possible numbers of students.

(A)1675   (B)1775   (C)1875
(D)1975   (E)2075

21. Jordan has taken 5 math tests so far this semester. If he gets a 70 on his next test, it will lower the average (arithmetic mean) of his test scores by 4 points. What is his average now?

[   ]

22. An investor wants to sell some of the stock that he owns in Micro Tron and Dynaco Corporations. He can sell Micro Tron stock for $36 per share, and he can sell Dynaco stock for $52 per share. If he sells 300 shares altogether at an average price per share of $40, how many shares of Dynaco stock has he sold?

(A) 52   (B) 75   (C) 92
(D) 136   (E) 184

23. Two buses are 515 miles apart. At 9:30 a. m., they start traveling toward each other at rates of 48 and 55 miles per hour. At what time will they pass each other?

(A) 1:30 p. m.   (B) 2:00 p. m.
(C) 2:30 p. m.   (D) 3:00 p. m.
(E) 3:30 p. m.

24. A developer has land that has x feet of lake frontage. The land is to be subdivided into lots, each of which is to have either 80 feet or 100 feet of lake frontage. If $\frac{1}{9}$ of the lots are to have 80 feet of frontage each and the remaining 40 lots are to have 100 feet of frontage each, what is the value of x?

(A) 400   (B) 3,200   (C) 3,700
(D) 4,400   (E) 4,760

25. In a normal distribution, 68% of the scores lie within one standard deviation of the mean. If the SAT scores of all the high school juniors in Center City followed a normal distribution with a mean of 500 and a standard deviation of 100, and if 10,200 students scored between 400 and 500, approximately how many students scored above 600?

(A) 2,400   (B) 4,800   (C)5,100
(D) 7,200   (E) 9,600

三、最新 GRE 数学预测模拟试题（三）

1. A number is a *palindrome* if it reads exactly the same from right to left as it does from left to right. For example, 959 and 24742 are palindromes.

Quantity A	**Quantity B**
The probability that a three-digit number chosen at random is a palindrome	$\frac{1}{10}$

2.

If (7,3) is the center of the circle above, then the radius of the circle could be equal to which of the following?

(A) 2   (B) 3   (C) 5
(D) 7   (E) 9

3. If revenues of $196,000 from division A of Company X represent 28 percent of the total revenues of Company X for the year, what were the total revenues of Company X for the year?

(A) $141,100   (B) $272,000

(C) $413,300   (D) $596,100

(E) $700,000

4. The perimeter of rectangle RSTU is 750, and RS = 350

Quantity A	Quantity B
ST	50

5. $S = 1 - \frac{1}{2} + \frac{1}{3} + \frac{1}{4} + \frac{1}{5} + \frac{1}{6} + \frac{1}{7} + \frac{1}{8} + \frac{1}{9} - \frac{1}{10}$

Quantity A	Quantity B
S	$\frac{1}{2}$

6. A certain doctor suggests that an individual's daily water intake be $\frac{1}{2}$ ounce per pound of body weight plus 8 ounces for every 25 pounds by which the individual exceeds his or her ideal weight. If this doctor suggests a daily water intake of 136 ounces for a particular 240-pound individual, how many pounds above his or her ideal weight is that individual?

(A) $12\frac{1}{2}$ (B) 16   (C) 30

(D) 50   (E) 120

7.

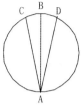

AB is a diameter of the circle.

Quantity A	Quantity B
The length of AB	The average (arithmetic mean) of the lengths of AC and AD

8. A political poll showed that 80 percent of those polled said they would vote for proposition P. Of those who said they would vote for proposition P, 70 percent actually voted for P, and of those who did not say they would vote for P, 20 percent actually voted for P. What percent of those polled voted for P?

(A) 56%   (B) 60%   (C) 64%

(D) 76%   (E) 90%

Questions 9-11 refer to the following graph.

AVERAGE ANNUAL NATIONAL SAVINGS RATE AND
REAL GROSS NATIONAL PRODUCT (GNP) GROWTH
RATE FOR SELECTED COUNTRIES (1971 – 1985)

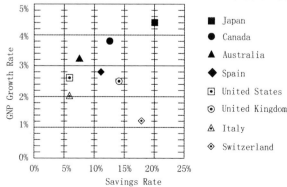

9. For which country was the ratio of its savings rate to its real GNP growth rate greatest?

(A) Japan　(B) Canada　(C) Australia

(D) Italy　(E) Switzerland

10. For how many of the countries shown was the savings rate more than 5 times the real GNP growth rate?

(A) Five　(B) Four　(C) Three

(D) Two　(E) One

11. Which of the following statement can be inferred from the graph?

I On the average, people in the United States saved about the same amount as people in the United Kingdom.

II The median of the savings rates for the eight countries was greater than 11 percent.

III Only two of the countries had a higher savings rate than Italy.

(A) I only　(B) II only　(C) III only

(D) I and II　(E) II and III

12. $y = x + \dfrac{1}{x}$, $0 < x < 10$

Quantity A　　**Quantity B**

The value of y　　　100

13. In a group of 80 students, 24 are enrolled in geometry, 40 in biology, and 20 in both. If a student were randomly selected from the 80 students, what is the probability that the student selected would not be enrolled in either course?

(A) 0.20　(B) 0.25　(C) 0.45

(D) 0.55　(E) 0.60

14. At a sale, the cost of each tie was reduced by 20 percent and the cost of each belt was reduced by 30 percent.

Quantity A　　**Quantity B**

The percent reduction
on the total cost　　25%
of 1 tie and 2 belts

15. The average (arithmetic mean) number of trees per acre in a 40-acre plot is 140. If a 10-acre section of the plot contains 90 trees per acre, how many trees are there in the remaining 30 acres?

(A) 5,700　(B) 4,700　(C) 4,200

(D) 3,600　(E) 2,700

16. There are 100 people on a line. Aviva is the 37th person and Naomi is the 67th person. If a person on line is chosen at random, what is the probability that the person is standing between Aviva and Naomi?

17. S is the sum of the first n negative integer powers of 2, i.e., $S = 2^{-1} + 2^{-2} + \cdots + 2^{-n}$.

Quantity A　　**Quantity B**

S　　　　　1

18. If the vertices of a triangle have rectangular coordinates (0,0), (8,0), and (8,6) respectively, then the perimeter of the triangle is

(A) 10　(B) 14　(C) 24

(D) 36　(E) 48

19.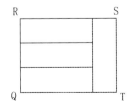

Rectangular region QRST is divided into four smaller rectangular regions, each with length l and width w.

Quantity A	**Quantity B**
$\dfrac{QR}{RS}$	$\dfrac{3}{4}$

20. In a crate of fruit that contained strawberries, blueberries, and raspberries, the ratio of the number of pints of strawberries to the number of pints of blueberries to the number of pints of raspberries was 6 to 4 to 5, respectively. If the crate contained a total of 45 pints of these fruits, how many more pints of strawberries than blueberries were there in the crate?

(A) 2   (B) 3   (C) 4

(D) 5   (E) 6

21.

Quantity A	**Quantity B**
$\dfrac{0.205}{0.305}$	$\dfrac{2}{3}$

22. For a project, a square piece of cloth is folded in half and sewed together to form a rectangle that has a perimeter of 36 centimeters. What was the area in square centimeters of the piece of cloth before it was folded?

(A) 16   (B) 36   (C) 81

(D) 108   (E) 144

23. How many positive 4-digit integers begin (on the left) with an odd digit and end with an even digit?

(A) 250   (B) 500   (C) 2,000

(D) 2,500   (E) 5,000

24. The 20 people at party are divided into n mutually exclusive groups in such a way that the number of people in any group does not exceed the number in any other group by more than 1.

Quantity A	**Quantity B**
The value of nif at least one of the groups consists of 3 people	6

25. In a group of 100 students, more students are on the fencing team than are members of the French club. If 70 are in the club and 20 are neither on the team nor in the club, what, is the minimum number of students who could, be both on the team and in the club?

(A) 10   (B) 49   (C) 50

(D) 60   (E) 61

四、最新 GRE 数学预测模拟试题(四)

1.

Quantity A	**Quantity B**
The average (arithmetic mean) of all the positive multiples of 5 less than 26	The average (arithmetic mean) of all the positive multiples of 7 less than 26

2. The water level in a tank is lowered by 6 inches, then raised by $8\frac{1}{2}$ inches, and then lowered by 4 inches. If the water level was x inches before the changes in level, which of the following represents the water level, in inches, after the changes?

(A) $x - 1\frac{1}{2}$ (B) $x + 1\frac{1}{2}$

(C) $x - 6\frac{1}{2}$ (D) $x + 6\frac{1}{2}$

(E) $x - 18\frac{1}{2}$

3.

Quantity A	Quantity B
The number of prime numbers between 70 and 76	The number of prime numbers between 30 and 36

4.

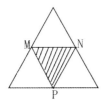

In the figure above, M, N and P are midpoints of the sides of an equilateral triangle whose perimeter is 18. What is the perimeter of the shaded region?

(A) 2   (B) 3   (C) $4\frac{1}{2}$

(D) 6   (E) 9

5. Which of the following sets of numbers has the greatest standard deviation?

(A) 2, 3, 4   (B) 2.5, 3, 3.5

(C) 1, 1.25, 1.5   (D) -2, 0, 2

(E) -20, 21, 21.5

6.

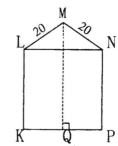

KLNP is a square with perimeter 128

Quantity A	Quantity B
MQ	42

7. When 9 students took a zoology quiz with a possible score of 0 to 10 inclusive, their average (arithmetic mean) score was 7.5. If a tenth student takes the same quiz, what will be the least possible average score on the quiz for all 10 students?

(A) 6.5   (B) 6.75   (C) 7.0

(D) 7.25   (E) 7.5

Questions 8-10 refer to the following graph.

CORPORATE SUPPORT FOR THE ARTS BY SECTOR IN 1988 AND 1991

Total for 1988: $630 million

Total for 1991: $529 million

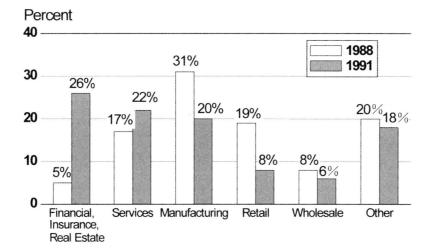

266

8. Approximately how many million dollars more did the wholesale sector contribute to the arts in 1988 than in 1991?

   (A) 10.4   (B) 12.6   (C) 14.0
   (D) 16.5   (E) 19.2

9. From 1988 to 1991 which corporate sector decreased its support for the arts by the greatest dollar amount?

   (A) Services   (B) Manufacturing
   (C) Retail   (D) Wholesale
   (E) Other

10. Of the retail sector's 1991 contribution to the arts, $\frac{1}{4}$ went to symphony orchestras and $\frac{1}{2}$ of the remainder went to public television. Approximately how many million dollars more did the retail sector contribute to public television that year than to symphony orchestras?

    (A) 5.2   (B) 6.3   (C) 10.4
    (D) 13.0   (E) 19.5

11. If x is 1, 2, or 3 and y is either 2 or 4, then the product xy can have how many different possible values?

    (A) Three   (B) Four   (C) Five
    (D) Six   (E) Seven

12. The median salary for professional group A is $40,610. The median salary for professsional group B is $40,810.

    | The median salary for groups A and B combined | $40,710 |

13. If the radius of a circular region were decreased by 20 percent, the area of the circular region would decrease by what percent?

    (A) 16%   (B) 20%   (C) 36%
    (D) 40%   (E) 44%

14. Workers at Companies X and Y are paid the same base hourly rate. Workers at Company X are paid 1.5 times the base hourly rate for each hour worked per week in excess of the first 37, while workers at Company Y are paid 1.5 times the base hourly rate for each hour worked per week in excess of the first 40. In a given week, how many hours must a Company X worker work in order to receive the same pay as a Company Y worker who works 46 hours?

    (A) 46   (B) 45   (C) 44
    (D) 43   (E) 42

15. The probability that events E and F will both occur is 0.42

Quantity A	Quantity B
The probability that event E will occur	0.58

16. If the cube of n is 180 greater than the square of n, then n =

    (A) 10   (B) 9   (C) 8
    (D) 7   (E) 6

17. Carol's age, in years, can be expressed by reversing the digits in her father's age, in years. The sum of the digits in each age is 10.

Quantity A	Quantity B
The positive difference between Carol's age, in years, and her father's age, in years	36

Questions 18-19 refer to the following information about student enrollment in a certain small college.

267

DISTRIBUTION OF ENROLLMENT
BY CLASS AND SEX
(Total enrollment: 1,400)

	Males	Females
Freshmen	303	259
Sophomores	215	109
Juniors	182	88
Seniors	160	84
Total	860	540

PERCENT OF TOTAL ENROLLMENT
MAJORING IN EACH OF THE
FOLLOWING ACADEMIC AREAS

(No student is majoring in more than one area.)

Area	Percent
Humanities	33%
Social Sciences	30%
Physical Sciences	24%

18. The ratio of the number of male freshmen to the number of female sophomores is approximately

(A) 2 to 1　　(B) 3 to 1　　(C) 3 to 2

(D) 4 to 1　　(E) 5 to 3

19. Which of the following can be inferred from the tables?

I The number of males majoring in physical sciences is greater than the number of females majoring in that area.

II Students majoring in either social sciences or physical sciences constitute more than 50 percent of the total enrollment.

III The ratio of the number of males to the number of females in the senior class is less than 2 to 1.

(A) I only　　(B) II only　　(C) I and II

(D) I and III　　(E) II and III

20. How many students are either juniors or males or both?

(A) 678　　　(B) 766　　　(C) 948

(D) 1,130　　(E) 1,312

21. $0 < p < 1$

Quantity A	**Quantity B**
$p^4 - p^6$	$p^3 - p^5$

22. If a is increased by 25% and b is decreased by 25%, the resulting numbers will be equal. What is the ratio of a to b?

23. a and b are positive integers

Quantity A	**Quantity B**
$\dfrac{a}{b}$	$\dfrac{a+3}{b+3}$

24. Josh works on the second floor of a building. There are 10 doors to the building and 8 staircases from the first to the second floor. Josh decided that each day he would enter by one door and leave by a different one, and go up one staircase and down another. How many days could Josh do this before he had to repeat a path he had previously taken?

(A) 80　　　(B) 640　　　(C) 800

(D) 5040　　(E) 6400

For the following question, select all the answer choices that apply.

25. Which of the following is an equation of a line that is perpendicular to the line whose equation is $2x + 3y = 4$?

Indicate all such equations.

(A) $3x + 2y = 4$　　　(B) $3x - 2y = 4$

(C) $2x - 3y = 4$　　　(D) $4 - 3x = -2y$

(D) $4 + 2x = 3y$

五、最新 GRE 数学预测模拟试题（五）

1. For how many positive integers $m \leq 100$ is $(m-5)(m-45)$ positive?

   (A)45 (B)50 (C)58

   (D)59 (E)60

2. $a \blacksquare b = (a+b)(a-b)$

Quantity A	Quantity B
$2 \blacksquare 2$	$-2 \blacksquare -2$

3. On the xy-coordinate plane appear four points—A, B, C and D —which have (x, y) coordinates of $(-2, -1)$, $(4, -1)$, $(-2, 3)$, and $(3, 4)$ respectively.

Quantity A	Quantity B
The distance from A to B	The distance from C to D

4.

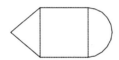

Three carpet pieces in the shapes of a square, a triangle, and a semicircle are attached to one another, as shown in the figure above, to cover the floor of a room. If the area of the square is 144 feet and the perimeter of the triangle is 28 feet, what is the perimeter of the room's floor, in feet?

   (A) $32 + 12\pi$ (B) $40 + 6\pi$ (C) $34 + 12\pi$

   (D) $52 + 6\pi$ (E) $52 + 12\pi$

5. In the series $\{N_1, N_2, N_3, \dots\}$, $N_1 = -1$, and $N_{(x+1)} = -|N_x + x|$.

Quantity A	Quantity B
$N_2 - N_3$	$N_4 - N_5$

6. Two competitors battle each other in each match of a tournament with nine participants. What is the minimum number of matches that must occur for every competitor to battle every other competitor?

   (A) 27 (B) 36 (C) 45

   (D) 64 (E) 81

7. p is a positive integer.

Quantity A	Quantity B
The remainder when $3p+5$ is divided by 3	The remainder when $7p+8$ is divided by 7

8. If q workers can paint a house in d days, how many days will it take $q+2$ workers to paint the same house, assuming all workers paint at the same rate?

   (A) $d+2$ (B) $d-2$ (C) $\frac{q+2}{qd}$

   (D) $\frac{qd+2b}{q}$ (E) $\frac{qd}{q+2}$

9. $s > 1$

Quantity A	Quantity B
The volume of a cube with a side of s	The volume of a rectangular solid with sides of s, $s+1$, and $s-1$

10.

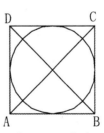

If the circumference of the circle above is 16π, and if the length of AC equals the length of BD, what is the length of AC?

   (A) $4\sqrt{2}$ (B)16 (C) $16\sqrt{2}$

   (D) 32 (E) 16π

11. As two wheels—A and B—roll across the ground, they both rotate at a rate of 60 revolutions per second. The radius of wheel A is 3. The radius of wheel B is 1.5.

Quantity A	Quantity B
The distance wheel A travels per minute	The distance wheel B travels per second

12. Dan drove home from college at an average rate of 60 miles per hour. On his trip back to college, his rate was 10 miles per hour slower and the trip took him one hour longer than the drive home. How far is Dan's home from the college?

(A) 65 miles   (B) 100 miles

(C) 200 miles   (D) 280 miles

(E) 300 miles

13. A certain five-member committee must be assembled from a pool of five women — A, B, C, D and E, and three men — X, Y, and Z, what is the probability that the committee will include B, C, E, Y and Z?

(A) $\frac{1}{30}$ (B) $\frac{1}{25}$ (C) $\frac{2}{35}$

(D) $\frac{1}{15}$ (E) $\frac{3}{32}$

14. Of 40 pairs of socks in a drawer, x pairs are solid white, y pairs are solid gray, and more than 19 of the pairs are striped.

Quantity A	Quantity B
x − y	The number of striped pairs of socks in the drawer

Question 15 and 16 refer to the following chart.

PRICE OF COMMON STOCK OF XYZ
CORP. AND ABC CORP (YEAR X)

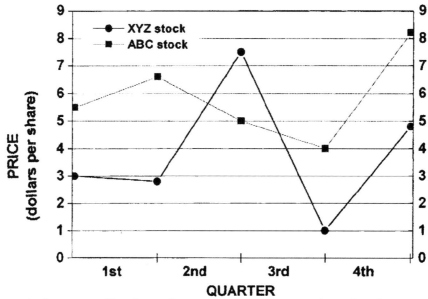

15. At the time during year X when the difference between the price of ABC common stock and the price of XYZ common stock was at its greatest, the price of XYZ common stock was approximately what percent of the price of XYZ common stock and ABC common stock combined?

(A) 16%   (B) 30%   (C) 36%

(D) 42%   (E) 103%

16. At the time during year X when the aggregate price of ABC and XYZ stock was the greatest, the price of ABC stock was approximately what percent of the price of XYZ stock?

(A) 25　　　(B) 60　　　(C) 70

(D) 140　　(E) 170

17.

Quantity A	Quantity B
The volume of a solid cube whose total surface area is 24	The volume of a 3-dimensional rectangular solid whose total surface area is 25

18. If $x + y = 16$, and if $x^2 - y^2 = 48$, then $x - y =$

(A) 3　　　(B) 4　　　(C) 6

(D) 32　　(E) 36

19. A buyer pays a $1.00 tax on an item that costs $10.00 after the tax is added.

Quantity A	Quantity B
The percentage rate of the tax	11%

20.

Quantity A	Quantity B
The ninth number in the following sequence: $\{3,3,4,6,9,13...\}$	31

21.

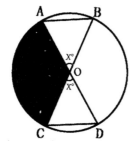

Point O lies at the circle's center, $x = 60$

Quantity A	Quantity B
The area of the shaded region	The combined area of the two triangles

22. John bought a $100 DVD player on sale at 8% off. How much did he pay including 8% sales tax?

(A) $84.64　(B) $92.00　(C) $96.48

(D) $99.36　(E) $100.00

23. Mary read from the top of page 10 to the bottom of page 24 in 30 minutes. At this rate, how long, in minutes, will it take her to read from the top of page 25 to the bottom of page 50?

 minutes

24. A number x is chosen at random from the set of positive integers less than 10. What is the probability that $\frac{9}{x} > x$?

For the following question, select all the answer choices that apply.

25. At Florence Pizza, the only slices of pizza available are plain and pepperoni, which cost $1.50 and $2.00 respectively. Small, medium, and large cups of soda cost $1.00, $1.50, and $1.75 respectively. Which of the following could be the total cost of two slices of pizza and two sodas? Indicate all such costs.

(A) $5.00　　　(B) $5.25

(C) $6.00　　　(D) $6.25

(E) $7.00　　　(F) $7.25

四、最新 GRE 数学预测模拟试题参考答案

(一)最新 GRE 数学预测模拟试题(一)

1. B	6. B	11. A	16. C	21. E
2. B	7. B	12. B	17. ABC	22. C
3. B	8. C	13. B	18. C	23. 13
4. A	9. A	14. D	19. D	24. C
5. C	10. 121	15. B	20. A	25. E

(二)最新 GRE 数学预测模拟试题(二)

1. C	6. C	11. A	16. A	21. 94
2. A	7. B	12. ABCD	17. $\frac{7}{13}$	22. B
3. D	8. B	13. $\frac{3}{5}$	18. D	23. C
4. B	9. B	14. E	19. D	24. D
5. A	10. 124	15. A	20. BCD	25. B

(三)最新 GRE 数学预测模拟试题(三)

1. C	6. D	11. B	16. $\frac{29}{100}$	21. A
2. C	8. B	12. D	17. B	22. E
3. E	7. A	13. C	18. C	23. D
4. B	9. E	14. D	19. C	24. D
5. A	10. D	15. B	20. E	25. E

(四)最新 GRE 数学预测模拟试题(四)

1. A	6. A	11. C	16. E	21. B
2. A	7. B	12. D	17. D	22. $\frac{3}{5}$
3. A	8. E	13. C	18. B	23. D
4. E	9. B	14. B	19. E	24. D
5. D	10. A	15. D	20. C	25. B,D

(五)最新 GRE 数学预测模拟试题(五)

1. D	6. B	11. A	16. E	21. D
2. C	7. A	12. E	17. D	22. D
3. A	8. E	13. A	18. A	23. 52
4. B	9. A	14. B	19. A	24. $\frac{2}{9}$
5. C	10. C	15. B	20. C	25. A、C、D、E、F

The Revised GRE Quantitative Reasoning 考试样题

1.

p is a prime

Quantity A	**Quantity B**
The number of factors of $p+1$	The number of factors of p

A. Quantity A is greater

B. Quantity B is greater.

C. The two quantities are equal.

D. The relationship cannot be determined from the information given.

2.

$$(x-2y)(x+2y)=4$$

Quantity A	**Quantity B**
x^2-4y^2	8

A. Quantity A is greater.

B. Quantity B is greater.

C. The two quantities are equal.

D. The relationship cannot be determined from the information given.

3. A certain recipe requires $\dfrac{3}{2}$ cups of sugar and makes 2 dozen cookies. (1 dozen＝12)

Quantity A	**Quantity B**
The amount of sugar required for the same recipe to make 30 cookies	2 cups

A. Quantity A is greater.

B. Quantity B is greater.

C. The two quantities are equal.

D. The relationship cannot be determined from the information given.

4. A power station is located on the boundary of a square region that measures 10 miles on each side. Three substations are located inside the square region.

Quantity A	**Quantity B**
The sum of the distances from the power station to each of the substations	30 miles

A. Quantity A is greater.

B. Quantity B is greater.

C. The two quantities are equal.

D. The relationship cannot be determined from the information given.

5.

$$6 < x < 7$$
$$y = 8$$

Quantity A	**Quantity B**
$\dfrac{x}{y}$	0.85

A. Quantity A is greater.

B. Quantity B is greater.

C. The two quantities are equal.

D. The relationship cannot be determined from the information given.

6.

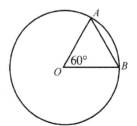

O is the center of the circle and the perimeter of △AOB is 6.

Quantity A	Quantity B
The circumference of the circle	12

A. Quantity A is greater.

B. Quantity B is greater.

C. The two quantities are equal.

D. The relationship cannot be determined from the information given.

7.

Quantity A	Quantity B
The standard deviation of a set of 5 different integers each of which is between 0 and 10	The standard deviation of a set of 5 different integers each of which is between 10 and 20

A. Quantity A is greater.

B. Quantity B is greater.

C. The two quantities are equal.

D. The relationship cannot be determined from the information given.

8.

$$x > 1$$

Quantity A	Quantity B
$x(x^2)^4$	$(x^3)^3$

A. Quantity A is greater.

B. Quantity B is greater.

C. The two quantities are equal.

D. The relationship cannot be determined from the information given.

9.

$$x \neq 0$$

Quantity A	Quantity B
$|x| + |-2|$	$|x-2|$

A. Quantity A is greater.

B. Quantity B is greater.

C. The two quantities are equal.

D. The relationship cannot be determined from the information given.

10. A reading list for a humanities course consists of 10 books, of which 4 are biographies and the rest are novels. Each student is required to read a selection of 4 books from the list, including 2 or more biographies. How many selections of 4 books satisfy the requirements?

A. 90   B. 115   C. 130

D. 144   E. 195

11. In triangle ABC, the measure of angle A is $25°$ and the measure of angle B is greater than $90°$. Which of the following could be the measure of angle C?

Indicate **all** possible values.

A. $12°$ B. $15°$

C. $45°$ D. $50°$

E. $70°$

Click on your choice(s).

12.

House Prices	Number of Houses
$100,000 — $133,000	12
$134,000 — $166,000	25
$167,000 — $199,000	8

The table shows the distribution of prices of 45 houses for sale in a certain region.

Select two of the following choices and place them in the blanks below so that the resulting statement is true.

$175,000 $185,000 $190,000

at most $42,000   at least $57,000

If the highest price of the 45 houses is _____, then the range of the prices of the 45 houses is _____.

Click on a choice, then click on a blank.

13. In the sunshine, an upright pole 12 feet tall is casting a shadow 8 feet long. At the same time, a nearby upright pole is casting a shad-

ow 10 feet long. If the lengths of the shadows are proportional to the heights of the poles, what is the height, in feet, of the taller pole?

A. 10   B. 12   C. 14

D. 15   E. 18

14. If a is the smallest prime number greater than 21 and b is the largest prime number less than 16, then $ab=$

A. 299   B. 323   C. 330

D. 345   E. 351

15. The total amount of Judy's water bill for the last quarter of the year was $40.50. The bill consisted of a fixed charge of $13.50 plus a charge of $0.0075 per gallon for the water used in the quarter. For how many gallons of water was Judy charged for the quarter?

[   ] gallons

Click on the answer box, then type in a number. Backspace to erase.

16.

    Data set S: 28, 23, 30, 25, 27
    Data set R: 22, 19, 15, 17, 20

The median of data set S is how much greater than the median of data set R?

A. 8   B. 10   C. 12

D. 13   E. 15

Questions 17-21 refer to the following graph.

Corporate Support for the Arts by Sector in 1988 and 1991

Total for 1988: $630 million
Total for 1991: $520 million

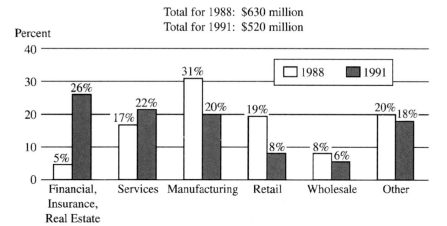

17. The two corporate sectors that increased their support for the arts from 1988 to 1991 made a total contribution in 1991 of approximately how many million dollars?

A. 112   B. 125   C. 200

D. 250   E. 315

18. How many of the six corporate sectors listed each contributed more than $60 million to the arts in both 1988 and 1991?

A. One   B. Two   C. Three

D. Four   E. Five

19. Approximately how many million dollars more did the wholesale sector contribute to the arts in 1988 than in 1991?

A. 10.4

B. 12.6

C. 14.0

D. 16.5

E. 19.2

20. From 1988 to 1991, which corporate sector decreased its support for the arts by the greatest dollar amount?

A. Services

B. Manufacturing

C. Retail

D. Wholesale

E. Other

21. Of the retail sector's 1991 contribution to the arts, $\frac{1}{4}$ went to symphony orchestras and $\frac{1}{2}$ of the remainder went to public television. Approximately how many million dollars more did the retail sector contribute to public television that year than to symphony orchestras?

A. 5.2

B. 6.3

C. 10.4

D. 13.0

E. 19.5

22. The symbol $\triangle$ represents one of the four operations of addition, subtraction, multiplication, and division, and $3 \triangle 1 = 3$.

For each of the following equations, indicate whether the equation must be true, must be false, or could be either true or false.

Equation	Must Be True	Must Be False	Could Be True or False
$6 \triangle 2 = 3$			
$6 \triangle 2 = 4$			
$6 \triangle 2 = 12$			

Click on your choices.

23. Of the 20 lightbulbs in a box, 2 are defective. An inspector will select 2 lightbulbs simultaneously and at random from the box. What is the probability that neither of the lightbulbs selected will be defective?

Give your answer as a fraction.

24. Of the 750 participants in a professional meeting, 450 are females and $\frac{1}{2}$ of the female and $\frac{1}{4}$ of the male participants are less than thirty years old. If one of the participants will be randomly selected to receive a book prize, what is the probability that the person selected will be less than thirty years old?

A. $\frac{1}{8}$ B. $\frac{1}{3}$

C. $\frac{3}{8}$ D. $\frac{2}{5}$

E. $\frac{3}{4}$

For the following question, select all the answer choices that apply.

25. The total amount that Mary paid for a book was equal to the price of the book plus a sales tax that was 4 percent of the price of the book. Mary paid for the book with a $10 bill and received the correct change, which was less than $3.00. Which of the following statements must be true?

Indicate all such statements.

A. The price of the book was less than $9.50.

B. The price of the book was greater than $6.90.

C. The sales tax was less than $0.45.

The Revised GRE Quantitative Reasoning 考试样题参考答案

1. D   2. B   3. B   4. D   5. D

6. A   7. D   8. C   9. D   10. B

11. A, B, C, D   12. $190,000   at least $57,000   13. D

14. A   15. 3600   16. A   17. D   18. C

19. E   20. B   21. A

22. (1) Could Be True or False   (2) Must be False   (3) Could Be True or False

23. $\dfrac{153}{190}$ 24. D   25. C

正确迅速解题"小窍门"小结

1. 0 和 1 有独特的性质。如 $3^0 = 1, 1^4 = 1$。

2. 变量可能是正数,也可能是负数。

   变量可能是整数,也可能是分数或小数。

   变量可能等于 0。

3. 比较分数的大小一般采用交叉相乘法。

   但有时在运算前,可以找出一些规律和简化的方法,迅速找到答案。

4. 熟记直角三角形的边长关系,最常考到的边长比为 $3:4:5$ 或 $5:12:13$。还可能出现与它们成倍数的边长,如 $6:8:10$。

5. 二次方程有两个解。漏算一个会出错。

6. 比较型试题 A 栏与 B 栏如果含有相同项目时,可从 A 栏及 B 栏减去相同项目,然后比较。

7. 比较型 A 栏 B 栏含有平方根时,开平方比较费时,可以将 A 栏及 B 栏自乘后比较,容易解题。

8. 比较型试题与不等式有类似的性质:

   如果 A 栏 B 栏加上或减去等量,其相对大小关系保持不变。

   如果 A 栏 B 栏乘以或除以等量正数,其相对大小关系保持不变。

   如果 A 栏 B 栏乘以或除以等量负数,其相对大小关系就逆转。稍微粗心就会出错。

   因此 A 栏 B 栏不可乘以或除以变量,变量可能是负数或等于 0。

9. 比较型试题,如果是数值运算,(不含变量或几何图形),其答案不可能是 D。

10. 比较型试题,如有几何图形,按已知条件图形变化不定,答案很可能是 D。如果含有变量,代以数值,而变化不定,答案很可能是 D。当本人犹豫困惑时,可以猜题。

11. 遇有变量,有时可用不同的简单的数值代入,看它的变化,然后比较或选择。

12. 大于 1 的正数,开方后数值减小。小于 1 的正数开方后数值增大(如 $\sqrt{1.44} = 1.2$;$\sqrt{0.25} = 0.5$)。

13. 复习明确 prime number, factor（又称 divisor）, prime factor, multiple 等词的定义。考题中常出现。忽视"小节"易出错。

14. $percent\ change = \dfrac{new\ amount - original\ amount}{original\ amount\,(基数)}$

   如果题目按时间而言,则

   $percent\ change = \dfrac{后期数 - 前期数}{前期数}$

   如果题目问 A is what percent greater (or less) than B?

   $percentage = \dfrac{A\ 数 - B\ 数}{B\ 数}$

   即以 than 之后的数作为基数。

15. 几何图形只有少数题目标明 drawn to scale。大多数题目的图形不是按比例绘制,不可凭视觉或测量判断,要根据几何知识解题。有些几何图形需添加辅助线。

16. 阅读题目后,先看下面五个选择的形式和单位,例如分数、小数、根号或百分比,演算时进行配合。

17. 在数轴上表示不等式的解集时,实心黑点表示包括该点,空心圆圈表示不包括该点。

18. 统计题内,注意各组数字中是否含有重复的内容。

19. 图表题要注意:其单位是数量还是百分比? 是 million 还是 billion?

    只有图表中列出的项目和数据可以运用,不要张冠李戴。

    同一图表内可能有几条曲线,几个不同标度(scale)和单位,不要搞错。

20. 注意 could be(可能是)和 must be(必定是)的区别。这区别不仅数学试题要注意,在
    逻辑分析试题中也十分重要。

GRE 常用数学术语汇编

abscissa	横坐标	absolute value	绝对值,例如 $\|a\|=\|-a\|$,其中 a 为任意实数
acute angle	锐角	acute triangle	锐角三角形
add (addition)	加（加法）	adjacent angle	邻角
adjacent vertices	相邻顶点	algebra	代数
algebraic expression	代数式	algebraic fraction	分式,如 $\dfrac{2m}{m+n}$
algebraic term	代数项	aliquant	除不尽的
aliquot	除得尽的	alternant	替代物,交替函数,交替行列式
alternate angle	内错角	altitude	高
amount to	合计	angle	角
angle bisector	角平分线	apiece	每个,每件,每人
approximate	近似	arc	弧
arithmetic mean	算术平均值	arithmetic progression (sequence)	等差数列
arm	直角三角形的股	average value	平均值（即 arithmetic mean）
bar graph	柱状图	base	底边,乘幂的底数,例如 6^4 中的 6
be equivalent to another equation	与另一方程同等	billion	10 亿
binomial	二项式	bisect	平分
blot out	涂掉	brace	一双,如：a brace of cats 两只猫
calculate to three decimal places	计算结果保留三位小数	cancellation	相消,相约
car pool	汽车的合伙使用	cardinal	基数
cent	美分	center of a circle	圆心
centigrade	摄氏	central angle	圆心角
chord	弦	circle	圆
circle graph	饼图,扇面图,圆形图	circular cylinder	圆柱体
circumference	周长	circumscribe	外接,外切
clear an equation of fractions	将分式方程整式化	clockwise	顺时针方向
coefficient	系数	combination	组合：$C_n^m=\dfrac{n!}{m!\,(n-m)!}$
common base triangles	同底三角形	common denominator	公分母
common divisor	公约数	common factor	公因子
common fraction	普通分数,简分数	common logarithm	常用对数
common multiple	公倍数	common ratio	公比
common year	平年,指 365 天的一年	complementary angle	余角
complementary function	余函数	complete quadratic equation	完全二次方程,如 $x^2+4x+4=0$
complex fraction	繁分数	complex number	复数,如 T+i

composite number	合数,除 1 及本身外还有其他因子的数	compound annual interest	年复利
compounded interest	复利	concave polygon	凹多边形
concentric circles	同心圆	cone	圆锥(体积$=\frac{1}{3}\pi r^2 \cdot h$)
congruent	全等的	consecutive even integer	连续偶数
consecutive number	连续整数	consecutive odd integer	连续奇数
constant	常数	convex polygon	凸多边形
coordinate	坐标	coordinate system	坐标系
corresponding angle	同位角	cross multiply	交叉相乘
cross section	横截面	cube	立方体,立方数
cube root	立方根	cubic metre	立方米
cumulative graph	累积图	decagon	十边形
decimal	小数	decimal arithmetic	十进制运算
decimal fraction	纯小数	decimal point	小数点
decimal system, decimal scale	十进制	decrease	减少
decrease by	减少了	decrease to	减少到
define	定义,化简	denominator	分母
denote	代表,表示	depreciation	折旧
depth	深度	diagonal	对角线
diameter	直径	difference	差
differential	微分	digit	数字
dime	一角,一角硬币	dimension	大小,度量(指长、宽、高等)
direct proportion	正比	discount	折扣
distinct	不同的	divide	除
divided evenly	被整除	dividend	被除数,红利
divisible	可被整除的,如 10 is divisible by 5	division	除法
division sign	除号÷,斜线分数号(/)	divisor	因子,除数
down payment	直接付款,首付	dozen	一打,十二个
edge	棱	endpoint	端点
equal	相等	equation	方程
equation of the first degree	一次方程	equilateral	等边形,相等的边
equilateral triangle	等边三角形	equivalence relation	等价关系
equivalent equation	同解方程式,等价方程式	equivalent fractions	等值分数
estimation	近似	even integer, even number	偶数
evenly even integer	能再平分的数	evenly spaced	等间隔的
exponent	指数,幂	extent	维数(A plane figure is 2-extent)
exterior angle	外角	exterior angles on the same side of the transversal	同旁外角
factor	因子	factorable quadratic equation	可因式分解的二次方程
factorial	阶乘		
face of a solid	立体的面	factorization	因式分解
Fahrenheit	华氏	finish line	终点线
foot	英尺	fraction	分数

gallon	加仑(1 gallon＝4 quart)	geometric mean	几何平均数,如 $\sqrt[4]{abcd}$
geometric progression (sequence)	等比数列	geometry	几何
graph	图	graph theory	图论
gross	十二打;总额	heptagon	七边形
hexagon	六边形	hyperbola	双曲线
hypotenuse	斜边	improper fraction	假分数
inch	英寸	included angle	夹角
included side	夹边	incomplete quadratic equation	不完全二次方程,如: $2x^2+5$
increase	增加	increase by	增加了
increase to	增加到	inequality	不等式
inference	推理,推论	infinite decimal	无穷小数
infinitesimal	无穷小	infinity	无穷大
inscribe	内切	inscribed triangle	内接三角形
integer	整数	intercalary year (leap year)	闰年(366 天)
intercept	截距	interest	利息
interior angle	内角	intersect	相交
inverse	倒数	inverse function	反函数
inverse proportion	反比	irrational	无理数
irrational number	无理数	isosceles triangle	等腰三角形
least common denominator	最小公分母	least common multiple	最小公倍数
least possible value	最小可能值	leg	三角形的直角边,梯形的两条不平行的边
length	长	less than	小于
like terms	同类项	line	直线
line graph	线图	line segment	线段
linear	一次的,线性的	linear algebra	线性代数
linear equation	线性方程,一次方程	linear function	线性函数,一次函数
linear transformation	线性变损,一次变换	list price	标价
literal coefficient	字母系数	logarithm	对数
margin	利润,赚头	markup (markdown)	涨价(降价)
maximum	极大值	mean	平均数
median	中数	median of a triangle	三角形的中线
meter	米	micron	微米
midpoint	中点	minimum	最小值
minuend	被减数	minus (take away)	减,负,负数
minute	分(角的度量单位,60 分＝1 degree)	mixed decimal	混合小数
mixed number	带分数	mode	众数
monomial	单项式	multilateral	多边的
multinomial	多项式	multiple	倍数
multiplicand	被乘数	multiplication	乘法
multiplier	乘数	multiply (times)	乘
natural logarithm	自然对数	natural number	自然数
negative number	负数	negative whole number	负整数

nickel	五美分硬币	nonagon	九边形
nonnegative	非负的	normal matrix	正规矩阵
null set (empty set)	空集	number line	数轴
number theory	数论	numerator	分子
numerical coefficient	数字系数		
oblateness (ellipse)	椭圆形	oblique	斜三角形
obtuse angle	钝角	octagon	八角形
odd integer, odd number	奇数	opposite	(直角三角形中的)对边
ordinal	序数	ordinary scale	十进制
ordinate	纵坐标	origin	原点
original equation	原方程	overlap	重叠
parallel lines	平行线	parallelogram	平行四边形
parentheses	括号	penny	一美分硬币
pentagon	五边形	per capita	人均
percentage	百分比	perimeter	周长
permutation	排列$(P_n^m = \dfrac{n!}{(n-m)!})$	perpendicular	垂直的,垂直
pie chart	饼图	pint	品脱
plane	平面	plane geometry	平面几何
polygon	多边形	polynomial	多项式
positive number	正数	power	幂,乘方
prime factor	质因子	prime number	质数
product	积	profit	利润
progression	数列	proper fraction	真分数
proper subset	真子集	proportion	比例
pyramid	角锥体	Pythagorean theorem	毕达哥拉斯定理,勾股定理
quadrant	象限	quadratic equation	二次方程
quadrihedron	三角锥	quadrilateral	四边形
quantic	齐次多项式,多元齐次多项式	quart	夸脱(1 quart $= \dfrac{1}{4}$ gallon $=$ 2pint)
quarter	四分之一		
quartic equation	四次方程	quotient	商
radian	弧度	radical sign	根号
radius	半径	range	值域
ratio	比率	rational number	有理数
real number	实数	reciprocal	倒数,倒数的
rectangle	长方形	rectangular coordinate	直角坐标系
rectangular hyperbola	等轴双曲线	rectangular solid	长方体
recurring decimal	循环小数	regular polygon	正多边形
regular prism	正棱柱	regular pyramid	正棱锥
regular solid (regular polyhedron)	正多面体	remainder	余数
remote interior angle	不相邻内角	retail price	零售价
rhombus	菱形	right angle	直角
right circular cone	直圆锥	right circular cylinder	直圆柱体
right triangle	直角三角形	root	根
root sign	根号	round angle	周角
round off	四舍五入	round to/ round off	四舍五入
scalene	斜的,不等边的	scalene cylinder	斜柱体
scalene triangle	不等边三角形	score	二十(指 20)

segment of a circle	弧形	semicircle	半圆
sequence	序列,数列	set	集合
side	边长	sign	符号
similar terms	同类项	simple（common）fraction	简分数
simple interest	单利	simultaneous equations	联立方程组
slope	斜率	solid	立体
solid geometry	立体几何	solution	解,答案
solution set	解集	sphere	球体（表面积 $4\pi r^2$,体积 $\frac{4}{3}\pi r^3$)
square	正方形,平方	square measure	平方制单位
square root	平方根	straight angle	平角,即 $180°$ 角
straight line	直线	subtract	减
subtrahend	减数	sum	和
supplementary angles	补角	surface area	表面积
table	表格	tangent	切线
tens	十位	tenths	十分位
the extremes of a proportion	比例外项	the means of a proportion	比例内项
tie	并列,打平	to the nearest	四舍五入,精确到
transversal	截线	trapezoid	梯形
triangle	三角形	triangle inequality	三角不等式
trigonometric function	三角函数	trigonometry	三角学
trinomial	三项式	union	并集
unit	单位	units	个位
variable	变量	vertex（vertices）	顶点
vertical angle	对顶角	volume	体积
vulgar fraction	普通分数（与 decimal fraction 相对）	weighted average	加权平均值
whole number	整数	width	宽
yard	码	zero	零

GRE 常用数学符号及其英文表达

$+$	plus，positive
$-$	minus，negative
$\times$	multiplied by，times
$\div$ (/)	divided by
$=$	is equal to，equals
$\neq$	not equal to
$\approx$	is approximately equal to，approximately equals
$>$	greater than
$<$	less than
$\geqslant$	equal to or greater than
$\leqslant$	equal to or less than
$\gg$	much greater than
$\ll$	much less than
$\in$	is a member of the set
$\subset$	is a subset of
( )	round brackets，parentheses
[ ]	square brackets
{ }	braces
$\backsim$	similar to
$\cong$	congruent to
$\perp$	perpendicular to，at right angles with
$/\!/$	parallel to
$\angle$	angle
$\odot$	circle
$\overline{AB}$	length of line from A to B
e	the base of natural logarithms，approx. 2.71828
π	pi；the ratio of the circumference of a circle to its diameter，approx. 3.14159
$n!$	factorial n，n $(n-1)$ $(n-2)$ $(n-3)\cdots 1$
$|x|$	the absolute value of x
x^2	x square；x squared；the square of x；the second power of x；x to the second power；x raised to the second power
x^3	x cube；x cubed；the cube of x；x to the third power；the third power of x；x raised to the third power
x^{-10}	x to the minus tenth (tenth power)
$\sqrt{x}$	the square root of x，root x
$\sqrt[3]{x}$	the cube root of x

x^n	the nth power of x, x to the power n, x raised to the nth power, x to the nth power
$\dfrac{1}{x^n}$	one over x to the n
$\dfrac{\alpha^5}{\beta^2}$	α to the five over β squared
$x^{\frac{1}{n}}\ (\sqrt[n]{x}\,)$	the nth root of x, x to the power one over n
$y=f(x)$	y is a function of x
$a+b$	a plus b; the sum of a and b; the total of a and b; a added to b; a increased by b; a more than b; a greater than b
$a-b$	a minus b; a less b; the difference of a and b; from a subtract b; a takes away b; d decreased by b; a diminished by b; b is subtracted from a; b less than a
$a\times b$	(a) (b); $a\cdot b$; a multiplied by b; the product of a and b; a times b
$a\div b$	a divided by b; the quotient of a and b
$a:b$	the ratio of a to b
$a:b::c:d$	$a:b=c:d$; a is to b as c is to d; the ratio of a to b equals the ratio of c to d
$xX+yY=1$	little x times big X plus little y times big Y equals one
$\dfrac{x}{X}+\dfrac{y}{Y}=\dfrac{z}{Z}$	little x over big X plus little y over big Y equals little z over big Z
%	per cent
‰	per mille
$\dfrac{1}{2}$	a half; one half
$\dfrac{3}{4}$	three fourths; three quarters
$3\dfrac{1}{2}$	plus three and a half
0.035	decimal (point) naught three five
5.32	five point three two
4.03$\overset{\cdot\cdot}{25}$	four point naught three two five, two five recurring
100℃	100 hundred degrees Centigrade
50°F	fifty degrees Fahrenheit
$a\in A$	a is a member of set A
$a\notin A$	a is not a member in set A
$A\subset B, A\subseteq B$	set A is contained in set B
$A\not\subset B$	set A is not contained in set B
$A\cap B, A\cdot B$	intersection of sets A and B
$A\cup B, A+B$	union of sets A and B

Measurements

Length：1 mile (mi) = 1,760 yards =5280 feet

　　　　1 yard (d) = 3 feet

　　　　1 foot (ft) = 12 inches (in)

Area：　1 square yard (sq yd) = 9 square feet (sq ft)

　　　　1 square foot (sq ft) = 144 square inches (sq in)

Time：　1 decade = 10 years

　　　　1 year = 52 weeks

　　　　1 year = 365 days

　　　　1 week = 7 days

　　　　1 day = 24 hours

　　　　1 hour = 60 minutes

　　　　1 minute = 60 seconds

Volume：1 quart (qt) (夸脱)= 2 pints (pt) (品脱)

　　　　1 gallon (gal 加仑) =4 quarts (qt)

　　　　1 bushel (bu) (蒲式耳) = 4 pecks (pk) (配克)

　　　　1 pint = 2 cups

Weight：1 ton (T) = 2,000 pounds

　　　　1 pound (1 b) = 16 ounces (oz)

　　　　1 ounce = 16 drams (打兰)

GRE 常用数学公式

1. Permutation: $P_n^m = \dfrac{n!}{(n-m)!} = n(n-1)(n-2)\cdots(n-m+1)$

2. Combination: $C_n^m = \dfrac{n!}{m!\,(n-m)!} = \dfrac{n(n-1)(n-2)\cdots(n-m+1)}{1\times2\times3\cdots m}$

3. Discount＝Cost×rate of Discount

4. The number of factors of $Z = x^a \cdot y^b \cdot z^c$ (x,y,z is prime number), $n=(a+1)(b+1)(c+1)$

5. Quadratic formula $x = \dfrac{1}{2a}(-b \pm \sqrt{b^2-4ac})$

6. Arithmetic progression $a_n = a_1 + (n-1)d, S_n = \dfrac{n(a_1+a_n)}{2} = na_1 + \dfrac{n(n-1)}{2}d$

7. Geometric progression $a_n = a_1 q^{(n-1)}, S_n = \dfrac{a_1(1-q^n)}{1-q}$

8. Distance between points (x,y) and (a,b) is $\sqrt{(x-a)^2(y-b)^2}$

9. Area of triangle $= \dfrac{1}{2}bh$

10. Special formula of area of triangle $= \sqrt{s(s-a)(a-b)(s-c)}$, $s = \dfrac{1}{2}(a+b+c)$

11. Area of rectangular $= lw$

12. Area of parallelogram $= bh$

13. Area of a rhombus $= \dfrac{Product\ of\ two\ diagonals}{2}$

14. Area of a trapezoid $= \dfrac{(b_1+b_2)}{2}h$

15. Volume of cubic solid $= a^3$

16. Volume of rectangular solid $= l \times w \times h$

17. Volume of right circular cylinder $= \pi r^2 \cdot h$

18. Volume of right circular cone $= \dfrac{1}{3}\pi r^2 \cdot h$

19. Volume of ball $= \dfrac{4}{3}\pi r^3$

读者反馈表

尊敬的读者：

您好！非常感谢您对**新东方大愚图书**的信赖与支持，希望您抽出宝贵的时间填写这份反馈表，以便帮助我们改进工作，今后能为您提供更优秀的图书。谢谢！

为了答谢您对我们的支持，我们将对反馈的信息进行随机抽奖活动，当月将有 20 位幸运读者可获赠**《新东方英语》**期刊一份。我们将定期在新东方大愚图书网站 www.dogwood.com.cn 公布获奖者名单并及时寄出奖品，敬请关注。

来信请寄： 北京市海淀区海淀东三街 2 号新东方南楼 19 层　北京新东方大愚文化传播有限公司
图书部收

邮编：100080　　　　　　　　　　　　　　　　E-mail：bj62605588@163.com

姓名：_____　年龄：_____　职业：_____　教育背景：_____　邮编：_____

通讯地址：_____　联系电话：_____

E-mail：_____　您所购买的书籍的名称是：_____

1. 您是通过何种渠道得知本书的（可多选）：
   □书店　□新东方网站　□大愚网站　□朋友推荐　□老师推荐　□@新东方大愚图书（http://weibo.com/dogwood）
   □其他_____

2. 您是从何处购买到此书的？　□书店　□新东方大愚淘宝网　□其他网上书店　□其他_____

3. 您购买此书的原因（可多选）：
   □封面设计　□书评广告　□正文内容　□图书价格　□新东方品牌　□新东方名师　□其他_____

4. 您对本书的封面设计满意程度：　□很满意　□比较满意　□一般　□不满意　□改进建议_____

5. 您认为本书的内文在哪些方面还需改进？　□结构编排　□难易程度　□内容丰富性　□内文版式　□其他_____

6. 本书最令您满意的地方：□内文　□封面　□价格　□纸张

7. 您对本书的推荐率：□没有　□1 人　□1—3 人　□3—5 人　□5 人以上

8. 您更希望我们为您提供哪些方面的英语类图书？
   □少儿英语类　□初高中英语类　□四六级类　□考研类　□IELTS 类　□TOEFL 类　□GRE、GMAT 类　□SAT、SSAT 类
   □留学申请类　□BEC、TOEIC 类　□实用英语类　□商务英语类　□休闲欣赏类　□英语读物类　□其他_____
   您目前最希望我们为您出版的图书是：_____

9. 您在学习英语过程中最需要哪些方面的帮助？（可多选）
   □词汇　□听力　□口语　□阅读　□写作　□翻译　□语法　□其他_____

10. 您最喜欢的英语图书品牌：_____
    理由是（可多选）：□版式漂亮　□内容实用　□难度适宜　□价格适中　□对考试有帮助　□其他_____

11. 您对新东方图书品牌的评价：_____

12. 您对本书（或其他新东方图书）的意见和建议：_____

_____

_____

13. 填表时间：_____ 年 _____ 月 ____ 日